TREASURES OF
Minnesota

Minnesota Capitol Building in St. Paul

by William Faubion and Stacy Corrington

a part of the Morgan & Chase Treasure Series
www.treasuresof.com

MORGAN & CHASE PUBLISHING INC.

THE
TREASURE
SERIES

Morgan & Chase Publishing, Inc.
531 Parsons Drive, Medford, Oregon 97501
(888) 557-9328
www.treasuresof.com

Printed and bound by Taylor Specialty Books—Dallas TX
First edition 2007
ISBN: 978-1-933989-12-9

*I gratefully acknowledge the contributions
of the many people involved in the writing and production of this book.
Their tireless dedication to this endeavour has been inspirational.*
—Damon Neal, *Publisher*

The Morgan & Chase Publishing Home Team

Operations Department:
 V.P. of Operations—Cindy Tilley Faubion
 Travel Writer Liaison—Anne Boydston
 Shipping & Receiving—Virginia Arias
 Human Resources Coordinator—Heather Allen
 Customer Service Relations—Casey Faubion, Terrie West, Sue Buda, Marie Manson
 IT Engineer—Ray Ackerman
 Receptionist—Samara Sharp

Production Department:
 Proof Editors—Avery Brown, Clarice Rodriguez, Tiffany Myers
 Editor/Writers—Gregory Scott, Robyn Sutherland
 House Writer—Megan Glomb
 Photo Coordinator—Wendy L. Gay
 Photo Assistant—Donna Lindley
 Photo Editor—Mary Murdock
 Graphic Design Team—C.S. Rowan, Jesse Gifford, Tamara Cornett, Jacob Kristof

Administrative Department:
 CFO—Emily Wilke
 Accounting Assistants—Danielle Barkley, David Grundvig, Cari Qualls
 Website Designer—Molly Bermea
 Website Software Developer—Ben Ford

Contributing Writers:
 Mary Beth Lee, Lynda Kusick, Mark Allen Deruiter, Stacy Corrington,
 Caddy Rowland, Don Patton, Dusty Alexander, Paul Hadella, Mary Knepp,
 Chris McCrellis-Mitchell, Laura Young, Todd Wels, Jennifer Buckner, Carol Bevis,
 Amber Dusk, Alexis McKenna, Maggie McClellen, Nancy McClain

Special Recognition to:
 Pam Hamilton, Gene Mitts

I dedicate this book to my husband,
David Anthony Rowland, a life-long Minnesotan
who absolutely loves this state. In addition,
he exemplifies all that is Minnesotan—loyalty,
kindness to others, dedication to hard work
and hard play, and most of all a respect
and love for our natural resources.

—*Caddy Rowland*
Minnesota Travel Writer

This book is also dedicated to the emergency
first responders of Minnesota who risked their lives
in the wake of the I-35W bridge collapse.
We thank you for your service,
your courage and your compassion.

—*Morgan & Chase Publishing*

Manitoba

Ontario

L. of the Woods

Roseau

RAINY RIVER

Rainy L.   Seine River

International Falls

Kabetogama L.   Namakan L.

Agassiz Pool   Voyageurs NP   Lac la Croix   Saganaga L.

Warren   Crooked L.   Basswood L.

Thief River Falls   Upper Red L.   Pelican L.   Grand Portage NM

Little Fork R.   Trout L.

Clearwater R.   Lower Red L.   **MINNESOTA**   Ely

Crookston   Vermilion L.   Birch L.   Babbitt

Big Fork R.   Seven Beaver L.   Lake

Bemidji   Bowstring L.   Mountain Iron   Virginia   Superior

L. Winnibigoshish   Eveleth

Cass L.   Mississippi R.   Hibbing   Whiteface Res.

Wild Rice River   Leech L.   Grand Rapids   Silver Bay

Fish L. Res.   Island L. Res.   Two Harbors

Park Rapids   Big Sandy L.   Duluth

Detroit Lakes   Cloquet   Superior   Apostle Islands NL

Moorhead   Washburn   **Michiga**

Fargo   Barnesville   Perham   Big Pine L.   Ashland

L. Lizzie   Hurley   Bessemer

North   L. Lida   Rush L.   Pelican L.   Crosby   Turtle Flambeau Flowage

Dakota   Otter Tail L.   Wadena   Gull L.   Brainerd   Saint Croix NSR

Wahpeton   Otter Tail R.   Staples   Round L.   Park Falls

Fergus Falls   Mille Lacs L.   Lac Curte Oreilles   Chippewa R.

Spooner   L. Chippewa

Little Falls   Mora   **Wisconsin**   Willow Res.

Alexandria   Long Prairie   Pine City   Rice Lake   Ladysmith

L. Osakis   Barron   Flambeau R.

South Dakota   Glenwood   Sauk Centre   Milaca   Princeton   Wapogasset L.   Bloomer

L. Traverse   Morris   L. Minnewaska   St. Cloud   Amery   Medford

Big Stone L.   Cold Spring   Big Lake   East Bethel   Chippewa Falls

Ortonville   Benson   Paynesville   Monticello   Ramsey   Mississippi NRA   Bald Eagle L.

Milbank   Litchfield   Buffalo   Fridley   North Oaks   Lower Saint Croix NSR   **Eau Claire**   Big Eau Pleine Res.

L. Kampeska   Madison   Willmar   Cokato   Plymouth   Maplewood   Ellsworth   Durand   Mondovi

Watertown   Montevideo   Hutchinson   **Minneapolis**   **St. Paul**   Lake City   Chippewa R.   Arcadia

Granite Falls   Olivia   Glencoe   **Bloomington**   Jordan   Red Wing   L. Pepin   Wabasha

Canby   Minnesota River   Lakeville   Northfield   Zumbrota   Peterwell L.

Marshall   Redwood Falls   Le Sueur   Faribault   Winona   Mississippi R.

Brookings   Tracy   New Ulm   Springfield   Swan L.   Mankato   Waseca   Owatonna   **Rochester**   Winona   Holmen   Sparta   Tomah

Pipestone   Slayton   Windom   Wells   Stewartville   Spring Valley   La Crescent   Castle Rock Flowage

Dell Rapids   Luverne   Worthington   Fairmont   Albert Lea   Austin   Caledonia   Viroqua

Sioux Falls   Spirit Lake   Estherville   Cresco   Decorah   L. Wisconsin

Canton   Milford   **Iowa**   Osage   WISCONSIN RIVER

How to use this book

Treasures of Minnesota is divided by region and by category. Categories range from accommodations to wineries, with headings such as attractions, bakeries, galleries, recreation, restaurants and shopping in between.

In the index, all of these Treasures are listed alphabetically by name as well as by the city where you can visit them.

We have provided contact information for every Treasure in the book. These are places and businesses that we encourage you to visit on your travels through Minnesota.

We sincerely hope you find this book to be both beautiful and useful.

Minnehaha Falls in Minneapolis

MINNESOTA FACTS:

Admitted to the Union: 1858, the 32nd state
Population (2006): 5,167,101
Largest City: Minneapolis, 372,811
Largest Metro Area: Minneapolis-Saint Paul, 3,500,000
Highest Elevation: Eagle Mountain, 2,301 feet

Bird: Common Loon
Fish: Walleye
Flower: Pink and White Lady Slipper
Gemstone: Lake Superior Agate
Insect: Monarch Butterfly (*Danaus plexippus*)
Motto: *L'Étoile du Nord* (Star of the North)
Nicknames: Land of 10,000 Lakes, North Star State, Gopher State
Trees: Norway Pine (*Pinus resinosa*)

STATE OF MINNESOTA

Office of Governor Tim Pawlenty

130 State Capitol • 75 Rev. Dr. Martin Luther King Jr. Boulevard • St. Paul, MN 55155

I'm pleased to welcome you to *Treasures of Minnesota*, a look at our wonderful state.

Sometimes non-Minnesotans think of us as just another small population, fly-over state with some "weather challenges." That is, until they learn more and discover what an amazing place Minnesota is.

It's no accident that national groups have named Minnesota the healthiest, smartest, and most livable state in America. Minnesota leads the nation in workforce participation, voter turn-out, and educational test scores. We lead the nation because our citizens are engaged in making this great place even better.

We work hard and we play hard. We enjoy the outdoors all four seasons. We have festivals throughout the year that celebrate our cultures and heritage. Our system of parks and trails is second to none. Our museums and theaters continue to win national awards. We are small enough to have a "hometown feel" but large enough to have four major professional sports teams and attract top concert tours.

We're such a modest people (someone once described Minnesota as "a dog that is too shy to wag its own tail"). But we gave the world Judy Garland, Bob Dylan, Garrison Keillor, and Charles Lindbergh, as well as Scotch tape, water skiing, and SPAM, so we're worth checking out. We have lots of new and interesting things to offer and hope you'll explore them for yourself.

Sincerely,

Tim Pawlenty
Governor

Overlooking the Mississippi

Mississippi River

Mississippi River and Great River Road

Experience the Mississippi River on Minnesota's Great River Road. The Great River Road runs for 575 miles alongside the legendary Mississippi River and passes through a variety of scenic landscapes. The Federal Highway Administration has designated the road a National Scenic Byway for its cultural, historical, scenic and recreational qualities. From the pristine northern headwaters to the central lakes region, through ribbons of lush forest and farmland, past big cities and rolling bluffs, the Great River Road is a weeklong vacation unto itself. Nature lovers find ample opportunity to view wildlife and unique geological features in the 11 Great River Road State Parks that border the route. If you have less than a week to travel or want a more focused Mississippi River experience, use the six regional descriptions that follow as a guide. Each region offers its own character and attractions and is anchored by cities that offer a host of lodging, dining and entertainment options. Follow the green and white Great River Road pilot's wheel signs to explore what lies around the next river bend. Read on to discover the treasures of Minnesota's Great River Road Regions: Mississippi Headwaters, Mississippi Northwoods, Mississippi Crossings, Scenic Mississippi, Metro Mississippi and the Mississippi Bluffs. Enjoy the ride.

To plan your Mississippi River experience, be sure to visit the website. The Minnesota Great River Road National Scenic Byway is promoted, preserved and enhanced through the work of the Mississippi River Parkway Commission. This section is provided by the Commission with funds from Explore Minnesota Tourism.

www.MnMississippiRiver.com

Photo courtesy of MN-MRPC photo library

All photos courtesy of Explore Minnesota Tourism, except where noted

Mississippi Headwaters
Lake Itasca to Bemidji

The Mississippi Headwaters region of the Great River Road is about 30 miles long. It begins at the headwaters in Itasca State Park, Minnesota's oldest state park. Walk through the forests, along lakes and past historic Indian sites. In your car or by bicycle, explore Wilderness Drive, which includes a 2,000-acre Wilderness Sanctuary, one of seven National Natural Landmarks in the state. Itasca's Mary Gibbs Mississippi Headwaters Center is a National Great River Road Interpretive Center, one of several throughout the state that tell compelling stories about the river. The Great River Road heads north from the park, tracing the path of the Mississippi through forests and wetlands until it reaches Bemidji, the first city on the river. This thriving university town is built on the shores of Lake Bemidji. The lake takes its name from an Ojibwe word meaning *lake with cross waters*, describing the river's course in and out of the lake. Enjoy quality shopping, dining and cultural attractions in Bemidji. Create lasting memories with a photograph by the giant statues of legendary Paul Bunyan and his sidekick, Babe the Blue Ox. With so much to see and do, plan your historic trek to the Mississippi Headwaters region of the Great River Road today.

Mississippi Northwoods
Bemidji to Grand Rapids

The Mississippi Northwoods region of the Great River Road extends about 95 miles and runs from Bemidji to Grand Rapids through 1,000-plus square miles of the Chippewa National Forest. This journey takes you by two of Minnesota's larger lakes, Cass and Winnibigoshish, in an area rich with Native American lore. The Cass Lake chain of lakes was once a branch of the Red Lake-Leech Lake Trail, a series of interconnected waterways used as a highway by Indian traders. The Cass Lake Museum displays many Native American artifacts and mementos from the 19th century. Chippewa National Forest also boasts the largest nesting population of bald eagles in the United States, and the birds often grace travelers with sightings. At Grand Rapids, once a famous logging community, visitors can relive history at the Forest History Center, one of the National Great River Road Interpretive Centers. Grand Rapids offers many amenities and attractions. During the first weekend in June, an annual festival of the arts occupies several downtown blocks. Discover the wild beauty of the Great River Road's Mississippi Northwoods region.

www.MnMississippiRiver.com

Mississippi Crossings
Grand Rapids to Little Falls

From Grand Rapids to Little Falls, the Mississippi Crossings region of the Great River Road extends about 145 miles. It has a layered history of crossings by river, rail and road. The Mississippi River was originally the main highway of the native peoples of Minnesota and later for the booming fur trade of the 18th and 19th centuries. Today, many of the 25 steamboat landings once located between Grand Rapids and Aitkin, the midpoint of the journey, are water access and camping sites, where travelers can access the river for an afternoon of fun. Aitkin was established as a Northern Pacific Railroad site in the 1870s, supporting the trade in wood and iron ore. In Crosby, you can visit the 17-acre Croft Mine Historical Park and see an original 630-foot-deep mine shaft, take a guided tour simulating underground mining and browse the museum of mining artifacts. Biking and hiking enthusiasts will enjoy the beautiful scenery and amenities of the area's Cuyuna Lakes and Paul Bunyan State Trails. Birdwatchers will love the abundance of this migratory flyway. Just north of Little Falls is Camp Ripley, home of the Minnesota Military Museum. This unusual history museum features indoor and outdoor exhibits that depict the experiences of military men and women from the early years of Minnesota to the present day. Explore Minnesota history throughout the Mississippi Crossings region of the Great River Road.

Scenic Mississippi
Little Falls to Elk River

The Scenic Mississippi region of the Great River Road is about 90 miles long and offers travelers an unspoiled river experience. Parks and gardens, ornamented with footbridges and fountains, dot the riverbanks from Little Falls to Elk River. In Little Falls, natural waterfalls were developed for power as early as 1849. Visitors can wander the beautifully landscaped Maple Island Park and Gardens at the falls site and watch the river bubble through man-made chutes. The Visitors Bureau offers walking and driving tour brochures to guide you to attractions, including the dam and historic Main Street. Both Little Falls and St. Cloud, the midpoint of the journey, boast historic downtowns with handsome architecture, history museums and great antique shopping. Don't miss the magnificent riverside Munsinger Gardens and the adjacent Clemens Rose Gardens in St. Cloud. Traveling onward to Elk River, the road winds through lush farmland and open prairie. A brief detour takes you onto Wildlife Drive through the Sherburne National Wildlife Refuge, a patchwork of tall grasslands, oak savanna and wetland habitats where bald eagles, sand hill cranes, geese and songbirds nest. Elk River, which sits on the northwestern fringe of the Twin Cities metropolitan area, offers amenities and entertainment in a suburban atmosphere. Enjoy the beauty of Minnesota on the Great River Road's Scenic Mississippi journey.

www.MnMississippiRiver.com

Metro Mississippi
Elk River to Hastings

Past Elk River, the Mississippi meanders into the buzzing metropolitan area of the Twin Cities. The Metro Mississippi journey extends about 75 miles and offers big city attractions interspersed with historical and natural landmarks. In Minneapolis, the Riverfront District is the center of both culture and history. Tour the riverfront up close and personal by riverboat, trolley, horse and carriage, on foot, bike or even Segway. The St. Anthony Falls Heritage Trail guides your riverfront experience, telling the tale of the two cities and of the role the Mississippi River played in their creation on signs, kiosks and at the Mill City Museum, a National Great River Road Interpretive Center. Today, the historic buildings along the Trail house inviting shops, cafes and galleries. Both Minneapolis and St. Paul offer fine dining, world-class shopping and a thriving theater scene. Visit St. Paul's Science Museum of Minnesota, the State Capitol, the History Center and the Cathedral of St. Paul. The road continues to historic Hastings, nationally known for its Victorian architecture. Hastings boasts more than 60 buildings on the National Register. The city's charming downtown features gift shops, natural food stores and galleries in buildings dating back to the 1800s. Explore Minnesota's largest river cities on the Metro Mississippi journey of the Great River Road.

Mississippi Bluffs
Hastings to Iowa Bluffs

Heading south from Hastings, the Mississippi Bluffs leg of the Great River Road runs about 140 miles and rambles to the Iowa border through the surprising southeast corner of Minnesota. Ancient glaciers flattened most of central Minnesota, but this region avoided the advancing ice wall, preserving a dramatic landscape of soaring bluffs and deep, cool valleys. Here the Mississippi River travels below towering ridges of limestone as it makes its way from the metropolitan region back to green forests and farmlands. Just below Red Wing you pass through Frontenac State Park, a birdwatcher's paradise. Birders have observed more than 260 species in the diverse habitats around Lake Pepin, which include bluff land, prairie, floodplain and hardwood forests. Learn about America's national bird at Wabasha's National Eagle Center, also a National Great River Road Interpretive Center. Further along is Great River Bluffs State Park, where you can spot ruffed grouse, wild turkey and coyote. The Mississippi Bluffs is dotted with quaint river towns, where steamboats dock near 19th century hotels, antique shops and specialty stores. The rugged landscapes of the bluffs have helped keep these historic towns relatively untouched through the years, preserving a character distinct from the rest of Minnesota. Discover the majestic vistas and historical charm of the Mississippi Bluffs on the Great River Road.

www.MnMississippiRiver.com

The Mississippi River reflecting the lights of Minneapolis

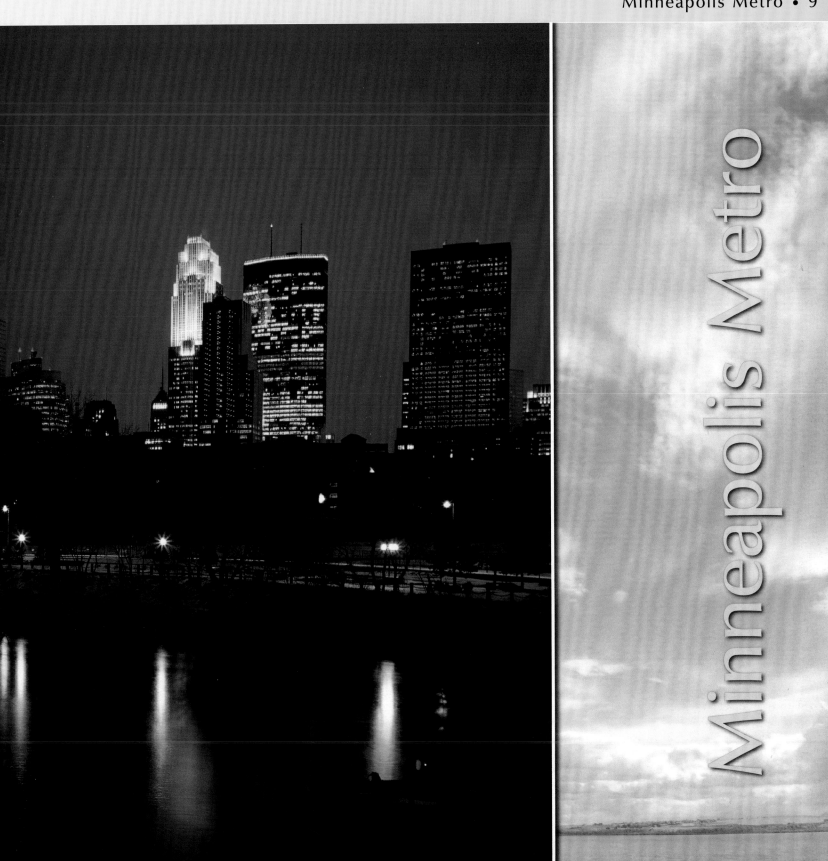

Minneapolis Metro

The Northland Inn & Executive Conference Center

The Northland Inn & Executive Conference Center is located just 10 minutes north of downtown Minneapolis, 30 minutes from St. Paul/Minneapolis International Airport, and 20 minutes from downtown St. Paul. This central location and easy freeway access to all the Twin Cities have to offer has made The Northland a favorite gathering place for all types of events, from corporate meetings and national conventions to fundraising galas and family celebrations. At The Northland, technology and design come together in a learning environment that is second to none. With more than 33,000 square feet of function space, the 25 conference rooms are designed for maximum comfort and productivity. The culinary team at The Northland creates regional American cuisine for America's Harvest Restaurant, all of the conference dining and banquets for up to 600 people. The Northland is managed by Benchmark Hospitality International, a recognized leader in conference center, resort, conference hotel and golf club management. Benchmark's approach to conference center management is to provide a setting that facilitates idea exchange, problem solving and retention of learning in a professional business environment, free from distractions and interruptions of daily business life. For great hospitality, visit The Northland Inn & Executive Conference Center today.

7025 Northland Drive, Minneapolis MN
(763) 536-8300
www.northlandinn.com

Love On The Wing

If one or more parrots own you, then you owe it to yourself to check out Love On The Wing, which is often called the Parrot Lover's Paradise. Don and Kathy Kurta's bird business started accidentally when their admiration of these splendid creatures incited them to purchase a pair of breeding parrots that needed a good home. (These parrots are now over 40 years old.) After breeding a few baby parrots, they could not locate the appropriate high-quality cages, toys, food and supplies they needed. This led them on a quest across the U.S. and overseas to find the best parrot-related products available. They even began manufacturing some products themselves. Love On The Wing, which they started in 1993, has become the largest bird supply store in the Midwest. The shop has tons, literally, of healthy parrot food, sure to please even the fussiest beak. Bird health and safety are number one at Love On The Wing, so expect to find more than 1,000 safe cages for all sizes of birds from tiny finches to larger-than-life macaws. The huge selection of parrot paraphernalia includes thousands of toys, from small hand-toys and acrylics to huge six-foot long destructibles made of safe woods, leathers, ropes and so on. Don served six years as president of the Minnesota Companion Bird Association, a club of more than 200 avid parrot owners that has been in existence for 30 years. Don, Kathy and their expert staff really know birds, tirelessly promote bird health and safety, and love to talk about birds with their many customers. While you're visiting, be sure to browse the gift shop, which overflows with an incredible variety of beautiful and unique bird-themed items. When you come to Love On The Wing, your life and your parrot's life will be all the better for it.

26101 Newton Circle, Elko MN
(952) 461-1975 or (888) 821-5440
www.loveonthewing.com

LuLu & Luigi

LuLu & Luigi is a store for felines with flair and pooches with panache, and of course, the people who love them. LuLu and Luigi was founded in 2003, and is named after two rescued pets, LuLu (a Maltese) and Luigi (a Tuxedo Rag-a-Muffin cat). Here, you'll discover the latest in pet fashion trends, unique pet accessories, stylish pet apparel, the tastiest treats, wholesome bakery goods, breathtaking gifts and home accents for all pet lovers. The shop carries a variety of hip hound and kitty-cat merchandise, including cozy bedding, chic water and food bowls, stylish pet carriers and accessories. (How about a rhinestone collar?) Outfits range from baby's first outfit to trendy T-shirts, and to top it off, bridal attire including top hats. Bring along your pet because they will be sure to get a tasty treat. The staff at LuLu & Luigi specializes in personal service and is knowledgeable about the many products. As pet enthusiasts, they understand that pet owners desire the very best for their furry companions and they offer nothing less. At LuLu & Luigi Grooming Pawlour, they satisfy both their furry clients and their owners by delivering superior products and services that help create and maintain healthy pets, from nose to tail. The Pawlour menu has more than 20 different services that are sure to make all tails wag with pleasure. The LuLu & Luigi flagship store is located in the Excelsior & Grand retail community, which combines greenways, pedestrian traffic, parking and close proximity to the city lakes. The LuLu & Luigi Wayzata store and Grooming Pawlour is located in the Wayzata Village Shoppes, which feature dozens of high-quality specialty shops along the lakefront. LuLu & Luigi is also just a click away. Visit their online store or join their mailing list to hear of exclusive products and special offers. As the trademarked slogan has it, this is a shop For Discriminating Pets and the People Who Love Them.

3844 Grand Way, St. Louis Park MN
(Excelsior & Grand)
(952) 929-1200
812 E Lake Street, Wayzata MN
(Wayzata Village Shoppes)
(952) 249-0330
www.luluandluigi.com

Gray's Leather

Fans of fine leather will delight in the variety at Gray's Leather. Owners Dave and Noelle Gray opened the Minneapolis store in 2006, catering to leather crafting customers looking to make everything from bridles to clothing. You will also find pre-made clothing here. Among the hundreds of hides you'll see everything from cow, deer and elk to the rarer kangaroo and bison hides. The store carries many dyes and leather care products along with high quality hardware, such as eyelets, buttons and punches, for making such items as purses and wallets. The sewing supplies, stamps and decorative hardware give crafters everything they need for creative leatherwork. Dave and Noelle are always on hand to help customers with their projects by offering instructions and even performing small repairs as needed. Men will appreciate the clothing made just for them, from shirts, vests and pants to chaps and hats. Women's apparel includes skirts and dresses. When you need leather and leather accessories for your projects, come to Gray's Leather.

3401 Nicollet Avenue, Minneapolis MN
(612) 823-3183
www.graysleather.com

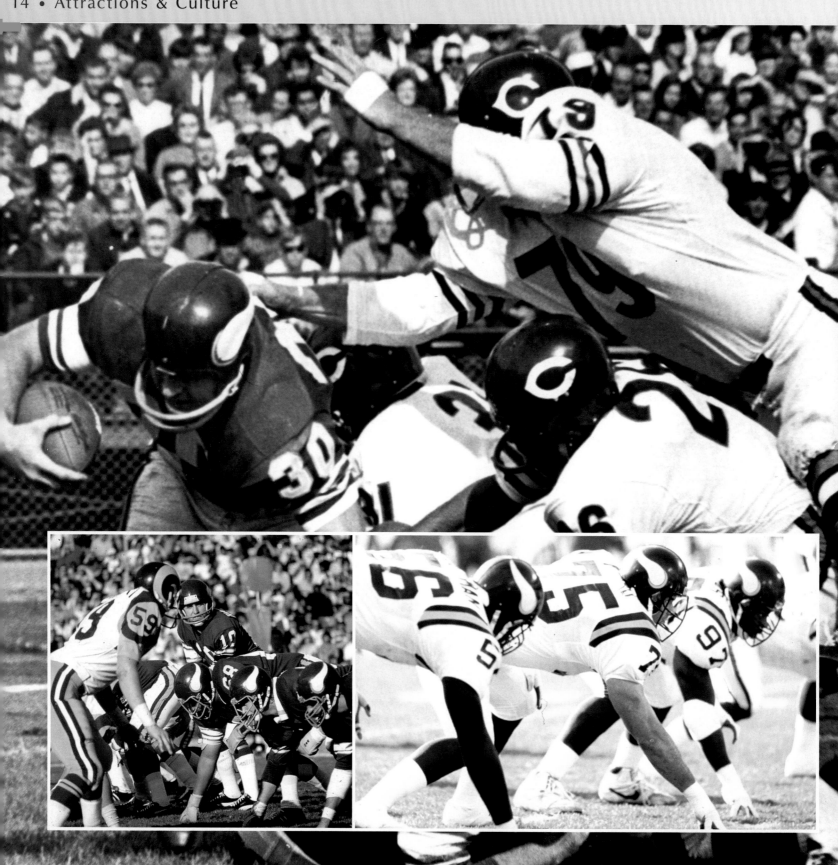

The Minnesota Vikings

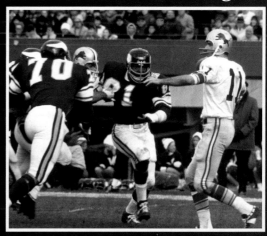

Real football fans wear purple. At least in Minnesota they do, because that's the team color of the Minnesota Vikings, one of pro football's most storied franchises. During a stretch of 11 seasons beginning in 1968, the team won 10 divisional titles. It has played in four Super Bowls, led by Hall of Fame coach Bud Grant each time. What student of football history hasn't heard of Alan Page and Carl Eller, the duo at the heart of the ferocious defensive corps dubbed the Purple People Eaters? These two terrorized running backs and quarterbacks during the championship years, while scrambling quarterback Fran Tarkenton guided the offense. Heroes from the more recent past include wide receiver Cris Carter, whose jersey number was retired in 2003, and Pro Bowl guard Randall McDaniel. Both were instrumental in taking the team to the playoffs several times in the 1990s. In his first year as a starting quarterback, Daunte Culpepper led the Vikings to the top of the NFC Central in 2000, the same year that Robert Smith ran for a team record 1,521 yards and seven touchdowns. It's always a sea of purple at the Hubert H. Humphrey Metrodome when 64,000 fans pack the stands for a home game. The most rabid get decked out in full viking regalia, including horned headgear. Clashes with divisional rivals the Chicago Bears, Detroit Lions or Green Bay Packers are particularly exciting. See if you can get tickets while you're in town, or catch all the action on television. Soon, purple will be your favorite color, too.

9520 Viking Drive, Eden Prairie MN
(612) 338-4537
www.vikings.com

Photo by Scott Knutson

Photo by John Gregor

Minnesota Landscape Arboretum

There's beauty to behold in each flower and leaf at the Minnesota Landscape Arboretum, a spectacular collection of public gardens. The 1,047 acres of the arboretum contain trails that, depending on the season, encourage leisurely strolling and vigorous walking or cross-country skiing and snowshoeing. These pathways wind through northern woodlands, native prairie and natural marshes. Ponds and falls dot their course. *USA Today* named the arboretum one of the 10 great places in America to smell the flowers, but behind all the serene natural beauty, serious scientific work is taking place. In fact, researchers have evaluated and developed cold-climate plants at the arboretum for more than 100 years. The Minnesota Landscape Arboretum is part of the College of Food, Agricultural and Natural Resource Sciences at the University of Minnesota. Scientists at the Hardiness Laboratory may have developed the frost-resistant tree that you buy for your yard this year. An army of 800 volunteers helps groom the gardens and welcomes about 250,000 visitors annually. Come to the Minnesota Landscape Arboretum and be dazzled by 32 display and specialty gardens, 48 general plant collections and more than 5,000 plant species and varieties.

3675 Arboretum Drive, Chaska MN
(952) 443-1400
www.arboretum.umn.edu

Riverview Theater

What's a night at the movies without popcorn? At the Riverview Theater, you can still get popcorn flavored with real butter as you enjoy a selection of mainstream, independent and even locally produced films. The Riverview has outlived many newer theaters, partly because of its progressive entertainment strategy that focuses on fun. Film festivals such as the *Lord of the Rings Trilogy* and the 48-Hour Film Project are special treats. Twice a month on Saturdays at midnight, the theater runs *The Rocky Horror Picture Show* for its fanatical clientele. The Riverview is also the place to go to view occasional significant sporting events, such as the Tour de France, the World Cup and local teams progressing through the playoffs. Surrounded by hundreds of fans, the enthusiasm is contagious. The friendly admission and concession prices combined with the congenial neighborhood atmosphere all support the multi-faceted magic of the cinema. Moviegoers sometimes come early to view the pop/modern retro furnishings in the lobby and admire the original marble tables, imported from Italy. This is the same décor that impressed visitors on opening day in 1948. The theater seats 700 people in comfortable, updated seating surrounded by a first-class sound system. Join the cognoscenti to experience the Riverview Theater, 50 years old and still going strong. Oh, and the popcorn—the *St. Paul Pioneer Press* says it's the best in the Twin Cities. Munch some and you'll agree.

3800 42ⁿᵈ Avenue S, Minneapolis MN
(612) 729-7369
www.riverviewtheater.com

Segway Magical History Tour

The Segway Magical History Tour uses new-fangled scooters to bring you to some of Minneapolis' most famous landmarks. Tour participants ride individual Segway Human Transporter scooters. They are "like an extension of your body," says owner Bill Neuenschwander of these ingenious machines. Segways feature an internal system of gyroscopes that mimic the human body's balancing ability, reacting to a rider's every move. They are easy to operate and steer and, most importantly, they save riders from having to walk the full distance of the tour. People of all ages, ranging from teenagers to 90-year-olds, find the Segways easy and enjoyable to operate. You'll roll your way to the Stone Arch Bridge, Mill Ruins Park and even into the Mill City Museum, covering more than five miles with magical ease. The guides stop along the way and use a PA system give a narrative interpretation on each exciting location. The company also offers Segways for corporate and team-building events. Segway Magical History Tour is the first Segway tour company in the world and the number-one Segway operator in the United States. For a one-of-a-kind approach to the wonders of Minneapolis, scoot your way across town on a Segway Magical History Tour.

125 Main Street SE, Minneapolis MN
(952) 888-9200 or (800) 749-5584
www.magicalhistorytour.com

Photo by Act One, Too LTD

Chanhassen Dinner Theatres

When Chanhassen Dinner Theatre opened in 1968 with one 600-seat theater, few people in the Twin Cities knew what dinner theater was or where Chanhassen was located. Today, the Chanhassen Dinner Theatres entertain up to 250,000 guests in a year-round, multiple theater facility. Chanhassen is the nation's largest professional dinner theater and the largest privately owned restaurant in Minnesota, typically serving up to 1,000 dinners in the two-hour period before a play. The entertainment varies enough to please many tastes. Full-scale musicals are the specialty in the Main Dinner Theatre, where hits like *Cats*, *Westside Story* and *Beauty and the Beast* have delighted sellout crowds. The Fireside Theatre specializes in comedies and small-cast musicals, while the Club and Playhouse feature musical revues and comedy acts. The artistic staff can really stretch its creative muscles, thanks to on-site facilities for building costumes, props and sets. With tableside service and a full menu featuring varied entrées, specialty appetizers, cocktails and desserts, it's easy to understand why *AAA Magazine* says "Any Twin Cities trip should include an evening at Chanhassen." The *Los Angeles Times* agrees and calls Chanhassen "one of the best dinner theaters in the country." Chanhassen is extremely popular with business groups and tour parties. Private rooms are available for meetings, pre-theater gatherings, weddings and banquets. For a memorable evening of dining and theater, join the eight million guests who have been served at the elegant Chanhassen Dinner Theatres.

501 W 78th Street, Chanhassen MN
(952) 934-1525 or (800) 362-3515
Groups: (952) 934-1547 or (800) 355-6273
www.chanhassentheatres.com

Historic Murphy's Landing

Historic Murphy's Landing offers visitors of all ages a chance to re-live the 1800s from 1840 to 1890. This one-of-a-kind living history museum is nestled along the Minnesota River Valley near Shakopee. Visitors can wander among dozens of historic buildings, ranging from Oliver Faribault's 1840s fur-trade log cabin to an elegant 1890s Victorian home. Visitors can tour the site on foot or, for a genuine 19th century perspective, take a ride on a horse-drawn trolley. Costumed interpreters will guide you as they portray the daily lives of immigrant settlers through demonstrations and activities that visitors can take part in. A Pioneer Kids' Play Area keeps young ones busy with a washtub for laundry, pots and pans, building blocks, and costumes to try on. The Landing also schedules seasonal special events featuring military life during the Civil War, woodworking, and ethnic holidays and traditions. Browse the gift shop's extensive array of 19th century toys and gadgets, and purchase an intriguing keepsake or fascinating book. Come to Historic Murphy's Landing for a hands-on experience of life in the 1800s.

2187 E Highway 101, Shakopee MN
(763) 694-7784
www.murphyslanding.org

Illusion Theater

The perception of theater as something more than entertainment goes all the way back to the ancient Greeks, who had a word for the powerful effect that a performance can have upon an audience. This welling of emotions, which the Greeks called *catharsis*, is a common experience for audiences of the nonprofit Illusion Theater in Minneapolis. Envisioning itself as a catalyst for personal and social change, Illusion was established in 1974 with the mission to illuminate the illusions, myths and realities of our times. Its willingness to tackle controversial topics is a longstanding tradition. In 1978, Illusion created and staged *Touch*, a play about the prevention of the sexual abuse of children that never fails to prompt dialogue wherever it is staged around the world. In 1990, Illusion produced David Feldshuh's play about the Tuskegee syphilis experiments called *Miss Evers' Boys*. At the symposium held in conjunction with the production, the head of the Department of Health and Human Services denounced the government for

betraying the trust of the men involved in the experiments. After the play was made into a popular movie, President Clinton invited survivors of the study and their heirs to Washington for a formal apology. For theater that is an active force for raising consciousness and provoking change, check out the latest production from Illusion Theater.

528 Hennepin Avenue, Suite 704, Minneapolis MN
(612) 339-4944
www.illusiontheater.org

Tysaun Harris, Anton Lewis, Tim Schirm, Adnan al Shati and Sahro Lilja Vedder
Six Lives by Ping Chong and Sara Zatz in collaboration with Michael Robins and Bonnie Morris
Photo by Aaron Fenster

Minnesota Dance Theatre

Exploring the infinite world of movement is the mission of Minnesota Dance Theatre (MDT). Whether this company of talented performers is *Puttin' on the Ritz*, dancing a blues ballet or presenting a dizzying, innovative production of *Carmina Burana*, you are in for quite a show. With a history spanning almost half a century, MDT is one of the state's most acclaimed arts organizations. Even as it approaches middle age, it shows no sign of wanting to play things safe. New, cutting-edge works appear on each season's calendar, and even the historic masterpieces are given new life. "There's so much to look at," said one theater critic of a recent performance, "that the broad strokes and tiny details set off little explosions in your head." No doubt you'll be on your feet cheering at the end of the evening, while feeling a bit exhausted after witnessing all of those energized bodies in motion. Teaching young dancers the tricky choreography and

graceful movements seen on stage is the goal of MDT's dance education program, called the Dance Institute. Here, students are trained with a dance syllabus rooted in the classical tradition while being encouraged to explore such other dance forms as modern, jazz and even hip-hop. Be moved this season by the Minnesota Dance Theatre.

528 Hennepin Avenue, 6th Floor, Minneapolis MN
(612) 338-0627
www.mndance.org

Melanie Verna, Minnesota Dance Theatre 2006
Photo by Eric Saulitis

Great Harvest Bread Co.

Bread is best when you keep it simple. This is the philosophy of Tom Amundson and Sally Weissman, owners of the neighborhood Great Harvest Bread Co. Whole grains make the best bread on the planet, and that has been their forté for the last 25 years. Five pure and simple ingredients are all it takes to make a great, healthy loaf of bread. Tom and Sally believe in finding the highest quality ingredients for their bread. They even grind all of the wheat they use on the premises. For the best whole-wheat taste, it is important to rush flour from the mill to the mixing bowl. You have never really tasted the true flavor of wheat until you have tasted it this fresh. Great Harvest Breads have never been made with preservatives or artificial additives of any kind. Their special made-from-scratch process keeps bread fresh for up to ten days. Great Harvest is also a huge community supporter. Each year Tom and Sally hold a contest to choose the nonprofit group that will serve as Baker for a Day. Every group that fills out an application for the contest is put onto a ballot. Over a two week period, customers come in and cast their vote. It is a great way to get the whole community involved in the business, as well as lending support to a worthy cause. They have also sponsored many races such as the Twin City Marathon. Great Harvest Bread Co. is truly a neighborhood bakery operated by people that care about the health and well-being of their loyal customers.

4314 Upton Avenue S, Minneapolis MN
(612) 929-2899
www.greatharvestmn.com

B & W Specialty Coffee

Wherever the folks at B & W Specialty Coffee go looking to buy their coffee beans, their request is the same. "Show me the best that you've got," they say. Since 1992, B & W has roasted the highest grade coffees from around the world, which can be savored at coffeehouses and restaurants throughout the Minneapolis/St. Paul area. How will you know if you are drinking B & W Specialty Coffee? The superior taste will be the first clue. On top of that, most establishments are eager to let customers know that they get their coffee from B & W, because the company has such a stellar reputation. B & W congratulates those coffee shops that have won the Golden Cup, an award of excellence presented by the Specialty Coffee Association to operators who meet strict brewing standards. As of the last time the awards were handed out, B & W was the only roaster in Minnesota to have Golden Cup winners. In addition, B & W provides brewing equipment plus training in everything from making the perfect cup of coffee to getting one's business Golden Cup certified. B & W gets its beans from the major coffee-producing countries of the Americas, including Colombia, Bolivia and Guatemala, as well as from Ethiopia and New Guinea. To taste the most flavorful coffee that the world has to offer, sip a cup of B & W Specialty Coffee.

2010 E Hennepin Avenue # 70, Minneapolis MN
(612) 331-5345 or (800) 331-2534
www.bwjava.com

Peace Coffee

As its name implies, Peace Coffee is not in the coffee roasting business to make a killing. While fair trade coffee is becoming the norm throughout the industry, Peace Coffee goes further than most of its competitors by paying extra for their coffee to ensure farmers receive a livable wage. Peace Coffee ships more than 5,000 pounds of coffee in a typical week, most of it to Minnesota grocery stores and coffee shops. Its biodiesel van is part of its environmentally friendly delivery fleet. Every day, even in winter, Peace Coffee bikers deliver about 900 pounds on large rigs, which consists of a bike pulling a seven-foot custom trailer. Stops on their routes include several co-op grocery stores and the office of the Minneapolis mayor. Like all Peace Coffee employees, even the bikers can talk intelligently about the goods, though for breadth of knowledge, no one can approach the roasting team's collective coffee knowledge. They are getting to the point where they can tell you what's happening on the farm by tasting the coffee. Of course, there's no better way of knowing how the farm is getting along than to drop by for a visit. Peace Coffee employees regularly travel to Mexico, Ethiopia and elsewhere. It's part of the company's commitment to building trusting relationships with its growers. Support stores and coffeehouses that carry Peace Coffee, the company that's working for social justice one cup of coffee at a time.

2801 21st Avenue S, Minneapolis MN
(612) 870-3440
www.peacecoffee.com

Che Bella Boutique

Che Bella Boutique offers everything a girl could want, from fashion handbags, vintage-inspired jewelry and French imported body products, to its award-winning custom bridal accessories. Founders Jennifer Meyer and Jenn Bresee have been designing bridal accessories since 1996. *Minnesota Bride* magazine bestowed Best Of awards in 2003, 2004 and 2006, and noted, "Their creations are the perfect way for brides to add glamour from head to toe." Che Bella's work, which blends yesterday's classic styles with today's elegant trends, has won national awards and has been featured in *Weddings in Style*, *The Knot* and *City Pages*. Che Bella's specialty is handcrafted veils, headpieces and jewelry for the bride and bridal party. The boutique also offers shoes, handbags, bachelorette party essentials and much more. For timeless accessories and handmade items, consider Che Bella Boutique—and if you're about to become a bride, head there immediately.

3826 Grand Way, St. Louis Park MN (952) 746-2561
www.chebella.com

dugo

Short for Dress Up Go Out, dugo is a women's clothing store that's ideal for intelligent, modern women looking for clothes that offer extra, effortless panache and style. Owner Nancy Shank has held a respected place on the Minnesota fashion scene for many years. She uses her expertise to cut through the thicket of high fashion options and deliver a one-of-a-kind selection for just about any occasion. The sportswear, outerwear and accessories at dugo provide European flair. The shop offers a special selection of hand-dyed Thai silk separates, which become colorful wardrobe extenders as well as gorgeous gowns that can be custom-ordered in many colors. Nancy aims to equip women both with business attire and dresses for special occasions such as charity balls, summer parties and weddings. The shop can outfit a bride and the mother of the bride as well. Fit is a vital part of fashion, and Nancy handles proper fit with a house fitter from Finland and a commitment to her clientele that extends well beyond the sale. To insure perfect fit, garments are ordered using your measurements, rather than by size. The colors and styles at dugo mix and match beautifully. The trunk shows are popular events that draw many women to the Galleria. Take satisfaction in dressing well with fashions from dugo.

3601 Galleria, Edina MN
(952) 746-4440
www.dressupgoout.com

The Foursome

When a clothing store has been in business since 1935, you can be sure it's been changing with the times to meet the needs of its customers. The original Foursome, a project of four schoolteachers who played golf together, was a small men's clothing store. Husband and wife team Ron and Lucille Engel became part-owners of the shop in 1955, with Ron in sales and Lucille in alterations. The Engels became sole owners in 1965, joined by their son Gordy, and moved the store into the new enclosed Wayzata Bay Shopping Center. Since then, the Foursome has blossomed into five separate family stores, all located in the shopping center—a men's store, a ladies' store, a big and tall men's store, a children's store and a family shoe store. Among them, the stores can meet just about any apparel and shoe need you might have. The Engels stick with classic styles and avoid short-lived trends. Their stores feature quality brand names such as Ralph Lauren, St. Croix and Cole Haan. You can even buy clothing from the Foursome online, but you would miss the friendly salespeople who get to know their customers by name. Over the years, the Foursome has been featured in local publications and often cited for its community involvement. In 1998, *DNR*, a trade journal for men's retail fashion, named the Foursome one of the top 30 specialty stores in the country. For business and casual wear from a clothes-savvy family, visit the Foursome.

841 E Lake Street, Wayzata MN
(952) 473-4667
www.thefoursome.com

J.B. Hudson Jewelers

J.B. Hudson, Minnesota's oldest jewelry store, has been an enduring tradition since 1885. Located on Nicollet Mall, it is a downtown destination. Upon entering the gates of J.B. Hudson, you'll view exquisite collections, from the traditional Mikimoto cultured pearls and precious gemstones by Oscar Heyman, to cutting-edge contemporary designs by Mattioli, H. Stern and Valente. J.B. Hudson has always been known for its one-of-a-kind global treasures, including a large selection of fine estate jewelry. J.B. Hudson is the exclusive retailer of Swiss and French timepieces such as Cartier, Girard-Perregaux, Jaeger-LeCoultre and Rolex. How do you even begin to set the table without hand-painted china from Herend or Anna Weatherley, or beautiful crystal from Daum or Baccarat? The great team of knowledgeable sales associates is always eager to help. J.B. Hudson Jewelers' signature silver boxes are sure to create special memories that last a lifetime.

770 Nicollet Mall, Minneapolis MN
(612) 338-5950 or (800) 388-8234
Ridgedale Center, Minnetonka MN
(952) 591-0737
www.jbhudson.com

Judd Frost Clothiers

When your trouser hem brushes the heel of your shoe and the cuffs on your shirt reach below your wrists, you are on your way to the kind of meticulous fit you can expect from Judd Frost Clothiers. Owner Judd Frost opened his clothing store 13 years ago in downtown Wayzata with the aim of making customers for life. He knows that when clothes fit properly they feel as comfortable as loungewear. The shop specializes in custom-made clothing; you can also find designer lines, such as Italy's Ermenegildo Zegna and Canada's Samuelsohn. Nothing is typical here, from the bowl of ginger snaps for nibbling to the services of such professionals as Butch Davidson, visual director, and Warren Lester, custom clothing and shirt specialist. You can find everything from underwear through jackets, coats and shirts to suit any occasion when looking good matters. The shop devotes one wall to 60,000 fabric samples. Judd and his staff put a combined 135 years of tailoring know-how to work for you. When designing a wardrobe for a man, they consider build, stance and even facial structure right along with style and fit. They also keep a detailed record of your purchases, right down to swatches of the fabrics used and a record of alterations. With this kind of attention to detail, it's easy to understand why even customers who have moved away from the area still come to Judd Frost Clothiers for their apparel. Treat yourself to the kind of attention that gets attention at Judd Frost Clothiers.

339 Barry Avenue S, Wayzata MN
(952) 473-4633
www.juddfrost.com

Martin's

Being a mom does not have to spell the end of fun and funky fashion, especially if you know where to shop. Your teenage daughter might actually agree to be seen with you in public if you let Martin's help you with your wardrobe. Whether you seek a breezy summer look or something to keep out winter drafts, Martin's puts the focus on clothing that's cute and hip as well as comfortable and well-made. Larry and Jill Martin opened their first clothing store in Forest Lake 34 years ago and moved to Wayzata 18 years back. At one time they stocked clothing for men, women and children, but eventually they changed the focus. Today, the Martin's shop caters exclusively to women. This is not your teenager's store, but the clothes are so darling and youthful that your teenager might be tempted to borrow them. Larry and Jill's daughter Erin does the buying personally. She knows the clothes and her customers, who get her personal attention. Erin will call you when items come in that she knows you will like. She's even made visits to customers' homes to analyze their closets, with an eye for putting old clothes together with new ones for an updated look. Shake up your style with the trendy outfits you'll find at Martin's.

1155 E Wayzata Boulevard, Wayzata MN
(952) 473-0238
www.martinswayzata.com

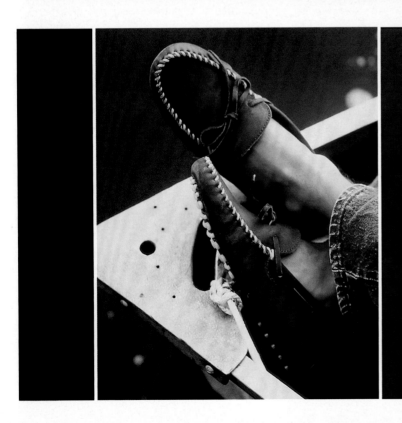

Minnetonka Moccasin

The American Indians could not have predicted that moccasins would someday be a fashion statement. Even Phillip Miller, founder of Minnetonka Moccasin, could not have known that his moccasins would survive the fashion whims of six decades. Today, a third generation of the Miller family carries on Phillip's legacy. David Miller, his grandson, acts as president of the company. Operating from Minneapolis, the company ships all-leather moccasins to markets throughout the country and beyond. In earlier days, resorts and gift shops bought moccasins from street vendors, but today you are just as likely to find Minnetonka moccasins in a fashion boutique or upscale national chain store. Such magazines as *Elle*, *Glamour* and *Vogue* have been known to pair the beaded Thunderbird model, developed in the 1950s, with a shearling coat or a faux fur hat. Moccasins may go through phases but they just don't go out of style. The fringed ankle-length models from the 1960s are still top sellers, and sales of the Thunderbird tripled in 2004. In the late 1980s, Minnetonka Moccasins created the comfortable Driving Moc with its long-wearing nub bottom. For practical footwear favored by vacationers, celebrities and even your grandmother, look for the Minnetonka Moccasin brand.

www.moccasinhouse.com

Über Baby and Expecting Über Baby

Lynne Gonsior believes that you're never too young—or too pregnant—to be fashionable. This is the simple but revolutionary concept behind Über Baby and Expecting Über Baby, the twin boutiques that have become landmarks for new and expecting mothers everywhere. MTV has called Über Baby the hippest baby store in the Midwest. Lynne was dreaming of her own business and shopping for her first child when she noticed there was nothing different or funky in the baby clothes and accessories. After scouring the world and conjuring a few designs herself, she unveiled Über Baby in 2004. The store was an instant smash with its sassy baby clothes, unusual toys and snazzy diaper bags. Lynne thought carefully about new fashion-forward colors for both boys and girls. Mothers can now buy specially designed paint colors for the nursery. Within two years, popular demand led Lynne to open Expecting Über Baby right next door. *Mpls.St.Paul Magazine* has called Expecting Über Baby the best maternity store in the metro area. Offering sexy maternity clothes, private label lines and local designer exclusives, Expecting Über Baby accommodates the fashion and figure needs of women even into their so-called fourth trimester. You'll find denim, great weekend wear and basics with body-hugging silhouettes in must-have black. There's even a play area for kids and Über Garage for dads. Whether you're expecting, nursing, or simply on your way to a baby shower, don't miss the fun and inspiring selection at Über Baby and Expecting Über Baby.

6001 Lyndale Avenue S, Minneapolis MN
(612) 869-0930
www.myuberbaby.com

The Elegant X

Women with classic builds have been finding classic fashions that fit and flatter their figures for 36 years at the Elegant X, located in the Wayzata Bay Shopping Center. The store covers the fashion bases with dresses, sportswear separates and outerwear as well as lingerie, sleepwear and accessories. The fashion-forward clothing, available in sizes 14W to 30W and 0X to 4X, is colorful, tasteful and fun to wear. The staff is happy to help you put together a custom fashion look to suit your figure. You can even make an evening or Sunday appointment that fits your schedule and assures you get just as much attention as you need. The clothing designers represented at the Elegant X specialize in styles for plus-size women. You will find classics by Eileen Fisher, denim by French Dressing and the cotton comfort of Ezze Wear. For hip T-shirts, you can turn to Mona Lisa; for slinky knits, to Vikki Vi; and for natural linen ensembles, to Flax. Owner Jim Burnett came to the Elegant X with a retail background in menswear and a strong desire to own his own business. He appreciates the plus-size woman, understands her needs and carries clothing to accentuate the beauty of each customer. Turn your plus size into a plus with clothing from the Elegant X.

931 E Lake Street, Wayzata MN
(952) 473-1393
www.wayzatabaycenter.com

Cynthia Rae/Dress Code

Whatever your age, your clothing can be a creative expression as individual as you are. To get that just-for-you look, turn to Cynthia Rae's Dress Code, a boutique for girly girls. Cynthia designs her own line—Cynthia Rae—and also stocks trendy, affordable new styles from other designers. Cynthia is also proud of her Revamp line of vintage feminine slips embellished with scarves and lace. Cynthia calls her wearable art *young contemporary.* It's not just for young people, though, but for any woman looking to put some fun into fashion. Cynthia's touch shows up in everything from the fashions to the handmade flower boxes and lampshades that decorate her shop. She opened her first Minnesota shop in 1992 and moved to her present location four years ago. Let Cynthia and her staff find a look for you at Dress Code. Attitude is everything.

244 Water Street, Excelsior MN
(952) 401-4484

Muddy Paws Cheesecake

Usually a bride would gasp if she saw muddy paws at her wedding. However, cheesecakes from Muddy Paws are always a welcome sight. Owner Tami Cabrera provides her luscious creations to approximately 400 weddings a year in the Twin Cities area. When Tami opened Muddy Paws in St. Paul in 1993, it was the first cheesecake bakery in Minnesota. Since then, she has moved her business to Minneapolis and has been featured on the Food Network while constantly expanding her repertoire. At last count, Muddy Paws offers 170 different flavors of cheesecake. There are two dozen chocolate choices alone and many fruit flavors, such as pineapple, strawberry and mango. Cinderella has a cheesecake named after her at Muddy Paws, and so does Elvis. You'll have to ask Tami how the ingredients, peanut butter and banana, relate to the King of Rock and Roll. Ordering the Sampler Cheesecake allows you to try different flavors as you share nibbles with your friends. All cheesecakes are made in small batches using only the freshest all-natural ingredients. You will find cheesecake by the slice or whole, plus fresh bread, espresso and a full deli menu. Muddy Paws ships cheesecake anywhere in the nation and delivers door-to-door anywhere in the metro area as well. Keep Tami in mind for all of your special events and fundraisers. Feast your eyes at the display case and then place your order for creamy rich cheesecake at Muddy Paws.

2528 Hennepin Avenue S, Minneapolis MN
(612) 377-4441 or (763) 545-7161
(business, wedding and delivery)
www.muddypawscheesecake.com

Sebastian Joe's Ice Cream Café

Sebastian Joe's Ice Cream Café was one of the first businesses to bring super-premium ice cream to Minneapolis. Sebastian Joe's has new flavors every day, all of them made with the highest quality all-natural ingredients. Top selling flavors include raspberry chocolate chip, Oreo and Pavarotti (so good it will make you sing). The shop also bakes fresh muffins, scones, cookies and croissants daily and offers coffee, including lattes and espressos. Sebastian Joe's has a sound reputation as a neighborhood coffee shop, but it is the homemade ice cream that truly brings in the crowds. The café was started in 1984 by three brothers, Tim, Todd and Michael Pellizzer. They named the store after their grandfather Sebastiano, who was nicknamed Joe after arriving here from Italy. Minneapolis locals and visitors can thank Joe for descendents that dish up some of the best ice cream anywhere. Many of the finer restaurants in town also serve Sebastian Joe's ice cream. Come to Sebastian Joe's Ice Cream Café at either of its two locations to satisfy your ice cream cravings.

1007 Franklin Avenue, Minneapolis MN
(612) 870-0065
4321 Upton Avenue S, Minneapolis MN
(612) 926-7916

Simply Nuts & More

Chris Carney started selling his nuts, dried fruits and old-fashioned candies at festivals 20 years ago. Today, Simply Nuts & More is still popular at community celebrations and the Minnesota State Fair, but you don't have to go to a festival to get the great snacks. In 2000, Chris opened a retail store where all the company's mixing and packaging takes place. You can also order these healthy snacks online or by mail. Chris' devotion to quality means he roasts nuts at exactly the right temperature. He makes the mixes to order rather than roasting in advance, so whether you desire butter toffee peanuts, jumbo cashews or pecan pralines, you can be sure your purchase will be fresh and flavorful. You can pick up the morsels in an acrylic designer canister and have the wooden top engraved with a message or logo. A wooden collector's box or a private label holiday tin in red or green makes a thoughtful gift. The store is on Excelsior's Water Street, a hub for hotels, restaurants and stores since the city's founding in 1853. Remember candy dots and candy cigarettes? Simply Nuts carries these old-fashioned items as well as snack mixes. For nuts and other specialties that pack a flavorful punch, visit Simply Nuts & More.

217 Water Street, Excelsior MN
(952) 401-8699 or (888) 449-NUTS (6887)
www.simplynutsandmore.com

Jean Stephen Galleries

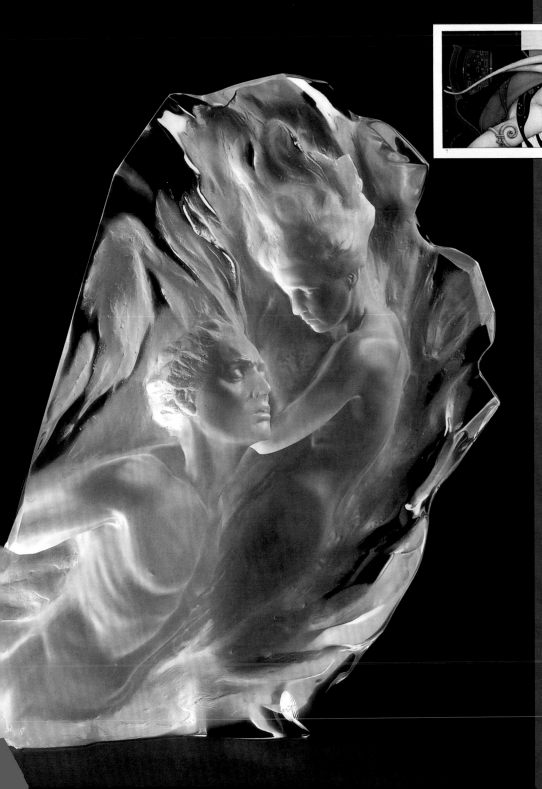

Nicollet Mall is rife with art and sculpture, but the best place to enjoy it is inside Jean Stephen Galleries. The collection of art exhibited by Jean Stephen Galleries reflects an outstanding range of talent. From the traditional classic bronze and acrylic sculptures of Frederick Hart, the creator of the *Three Soldiers* at the Vietnam Veterans Memorial and the *Creation Sculptures* at the National Cathedral, to the magical realism of Michael Parkes, Jean Stephen Galleries represents a full spectrum of the art world. The art of Dr. Seuss is a rare opportunity to get a glimpse into his private life. Secret Art, the art created for his personal enjoyment, the illustration works from his books, and his sculptures are shown together for the first time. Yuroz, the creator of the 2005 *Peace Mural* at the United Nations, is shown in all his glory with a comprehensive display of unique and graphic works. The rich colors of Jennifer Markes' works provide a dramatic contrast to the bronzes by Brian McMullen and the animal and abstract works of local polyresin artist Louis Von Koelnau. Processions of gifted visionaries create an unforgettable ambience at Jean Stephen Galleries. A trip through this gallery is always enlightening and inspirational. Prices start in the low hundreds, making some items accessible to almost any collector with an appreciation of fine art. From humor to sadness, from passion to pure joy, Jean Stephen Galleries has the kind of art you are looking for.

917 Nicollet Mall, Minneapolis MN
(612) 338-4333 or (800) 336-9924
www.jeanstephengalleries.com

Frank Stone Gallery

Art-lovers congregate at Frank Stone Gallery. With a wide selection, everything from pottery and art glass to paintings, the gallery has something for everyone. Each weekend, the gallery puts on a new show with new artists, who are often present to discuss their work. Frank Stone started the gallery to exhibit his own creations. He soon realized there was an unmet demand for more gallery space, and he began to show art from all over the map, from classical pieces of the highest quality to experimental pieces that define innovation. Despite the gallery's growing popularity, Stone keeps the prices affordable and the atmosphere congenial. Everyone can enjoy the art showcased each weekend, even the struggling art student living on a shoestring. Every Friday night, Frank Stone Gallery hosts opening parties that afford art aficionados a chance to mingle. The space, which accommodates 100 people, can be rented out for weddings, parties and meetings. It features an outdoor courtyard that displays pieces that can withstand the elements, such as brass sculpture and artist-made tables, benches and fountains. Whether you fancy a quick glance at the captivating art or to meet the artists and make new friends, a visit to Frank Stone Gallery is sure to please.

1224 NE 2nd Street, Minneapolis MN
(612) 617-9965
www.frankstonegallery.com

Your Art's Desire

Husband and wife team Kenneth Herren and Melissa Williamson-Herren have put their custom framing expertise and their passion for the local art scene together at Your Art's Desire. They fell in love after meeting and working together in a Wayzata frame shop. "Framing is our element. While the art thing is new to us, we are approaching it with a certain zeal and the community has really responded positively to what we are doing here," says Melissa. The eclectic and unpretentious Minnetonka Mills art gallery features mostly local artwork, including paintings, glass, sculptures, ceramics and much more. Ken and Melissa designed the space to give visitors a comfortable place to see what's happening within the local art scene. Equally committed to community service, the pair used the opening of their gallery two years ago to raise funds for nonprofit art organizations in the Twin Cities. Many people think that mixing marriage and business is a formula for trouble, but Ken and Melissa disagree. They worked together for 10 years before starting Your Art's Desire and continue to enjoy the closeness. "I'm working with my best friend," says Ken. For creative framing and a vision of what artists in the Twin Cities have on their minds, visit Your Art's Desire.

12928 Minnetonka Boulevard, Minnetonka MN
(952) 988-9772

"Feel the Spirit"

Northland Native American Products

Northland Native American Products is a gallery and retail space where you can find treasures of the land—original items by native peoples from Minnesota, the Dakotas, Wisconsin and Canada. When Ken Bellanger started the business in 1996, it dealt entirely in gift products, such as hand-crafted birch bark baskets or canoes and rare gourmet foods of the Northlands. These products are still available, and they come with stories of their origins: the Ojibwe people harvest the wild rice in the traditional way. Northland sells this wild rice, along with wild berry syrups and jellies in many rare and mouth-watering flavors such as chokecherry, hawthorn, highbush cranberry, rose hip and wild plum. In 1999, Northland moved to the Ancient Traders Market and added a gallery. You enter to the soothing sound of the native flute, the gentle scent of sage and cedar, and a warm greeting from the staff. Then, drink in the beauty and spirit of the art. You'll see pottery, jewelry and beadwork. There are sculptures of elders, horses, eagles and the White Buffalo Spirit. The gallery has dance sticks, drums of all sizes and blankets of many colors. The names of the prints and paintings offer only a hint of their visual poetry: *Buffalo Dancer, Grandfathers Tears, Wolf Song* and *Keeper of the Plains*. Some of the art is traditional, and some of it is quite contemporary. Bellanger is eager to tell the story of each artist. Come to Northland Native American Products for the best the land has to offer.

1113 E Franklin Avenue, Minneapolis MN
(612) 872-0390
www.northlandvisions.com

Clay Squared to Infinity

Josh Blanc and Layl McDill founded Clay Squared to Infinity in 1996. Located in a section of an old brewery in the Northeast Minneapolis Arts District, Clay Squared is a multi-functional ceramic studio, a handmade tile showroom and a gallery dedicated to advancing the public's knowledge of tiles, clay and mosaics. Here, many artists display tiles for use in kitchens, bathrooms, fireplace surrounds and anywhere else the imagination craves color. Josh himself finds inspiration in natural forms to create tiles with such titles as Smoky Landscape and Autumn Forest. Layl brings whimsical characters to life out of polymer clay. Magical fairies, benevolent monsters and funky cats make enchanting decorative pieces, which can also be incorporated into functional objects such as light-switch plates and mirrors. *Mpls. St. Paul Magazine* has named Clay Squared to Infinity a Best of the Twin Cities for handmade tiles. Many local and national publications have highlighted the gallery as well. You will find an enormous selection when you visit, and you can watch designers creating new pieces. Rotating and seasonal shows highlight beautiful works throughout the year. The shop offers classes in tile, mosaic and polymer. Find just the right touch to add whimsy or color to your home at Clay Squared to Infinity.

34 13th Avenue, Minneapolis MN
(612) 781-6409
www.claysquared.com

Icebox Quality Framing & Gallery

Fine art photography comes into full view at Icebox Quality Framing & Gallery. Owner Howard Christopherson opens the walls of his gallery to photographers from many schools—a broad range of artists from all over the world. The photographs, which run from candid portraits to allegorical dreamscapes, are united only by their originality, vision and energy. Successful recent exhibits were as diverse as the series of black-and-white photographs of the young Bob Dylan by John Cohen and color seascapes and underwater images from the Seychelles by artist/scuba diver Margo Cavis. Howard's own photographs of everything from sensual nudes to stone ruins in Peru reveal his unceasing urge to explore all aspects of life through his lens. He is always happy to explain the background of his photographs or to assist customers who seek masterful picture framing. The gallery takes its unusual name from an old refrigerator in the gallery's original space in downtown Minneapolis. Since 2003, Icebox has been in the Northrup King Building, which provides studio and gallery space for the greatest concentration of artists in Minnesota. Be sure to include Icebox Quality Framing & Gallery on your itinerary when you are gallery hopping in Minneapolis or shopping for the perfect frame to enhance a photograph or work of art.

1500 Jackson Street NE #443, Minneapolis MN
(612) 788-1790
www.iceboxminnesota.com

Fusion LifeSpa

If you seek a fusion of East and West, Fusion LifeSpa is ready for you. This cutting-edge center offers the best of two worlds, a place where two time-honored healing traditions and life philosophies join in a new concept wellness. Donna and Tim Duffy have fused their own talents—she's an esthetician and he's a designer—into one inspired undertaking. A holistic approach to beauty and health are offered in an Asian-inspired, ecologically sensitive environment by highly trained therapists who combine methods from across the globe, from Thailand, Bali, Japan, France and elsewhere. You can enjoy the Japanese soaking tub or other water therapies before indulging in one of the many other body treatments Fusion LifeSpa offers. Everything here is 100-percent organic. Even the nail products contain no toxic chemicals, making Fusion a completely healthful environment for both its clients and staff. There is a Traditional Chinese Medicine Clinic on-site that offers acupuncture and herbal medicine, as well as a Feng Shui practitioner, a natural health clinic, a whole foods nutritionist, and an R.N. who is board-certified in internal anti-aging medicine. The spa also offers a comprehensive selection of organic and natural products for your skin, body, home and life. In Fusion's relaxed and beautiful environment, you will find a unique and truly meaningful health and relaxation experience. Let Fusion LifeSpa create a new world of health and beauty for your body and your life.

18142 Minnetonka Boulevard, Deephaven MN
(952) 345-3335
www.fusionlifespa.com

Pull Out a Plum
Salon & Gallery

Plum (n.): desirable object or reward—Reward yourself! This beautiful salon and gallery employs a play on words to support and drive home its message of the value and importance of investing in yourself. Housed in a renovated warehouse dating back to the 1800s, this full-service salon and spa encompasses an upscale cornucopia of pampering services, trend-setting styles, incredible jewelry and gift items. Pull Out a Plum Salon & Gallery is located in the heart of 50th and France, an enchanting neighborhood filled with special shops and wonderful culinary temptations all connected by cobblestone walkways and plenty of complimentary parking. Upon entering Pull Out a Plum Salon & Gallery, you are immediately enveloped in a genuine warmth and camaraderie that grants you the mental oasis necessary in your busy, stressed life. Interwoven in the salon's surroundings are various art pieces, many of which are created by local artists. The salon couples the creative energy and talents of local artists with those of its salon and spa professionals. When you visit for a new haircut and style, you can receive a consultation for, perhaps, a new color or highlight to compliment your style. Learn how to properly care for your skin, as well as the benefits of regular massage and the value of frequent manicures and pedicures. If scheduling allows, you are treated to complimentary chair massage or, if you so desire, a hand massage and paraffin dip. Both men and women will find many reasons to visit. This salon truly knows how to show its clients they are valued. "Our concept was born out of a desire to pull together the works of those creative around us," says Michele Gatien, owner. The salon opened in 1997 with a "passion for creativity and appreciation for art and handcrafted pieces," says Gatien. The result is an experience unlike any other. Pull Out A Plum Salon & Gallery offers frequent client events, promotions and trunk shows to further enhance your experience. The salon has become known for its exquisite jewelry. In addition, it features luxurious body care items, as well as great gift books, bags, belts, candles and home accessories. Shop the gift gallery while you visit for that distinct gift perfect for yourself or someone important in your life. The salon's mission is further enriched by its work in supporting the community. Frequently throughout the year staff members participate in varied philanthropic efforts such as clothing drives and cancer research, and campaigns for schools, the theater and more. Each year the salon hosts a client appreciation event in which clients are treated to samplings of pampering services and local artist trunk shows, all while enjoying the sounds of phenomenal local musicians. This event inspires clothing donations for a local women's shelter, which helps the women put a wardrobe together to rejoin the work force. "It takes each of us coming together, working together to create the type of community we all wish to be a part of," says Gatien.

4946 France Avenue S, Edina MN
(952) 922-0634 *www.pulloutaplum.com*

Prairie Massage & Bodyworks

The massages on the service menu at Prairie Massage & Bodyworks are state-of-the-art. It all started when the owner got in an accident that led her on a personal crusade to find a massage therapist who understood medical conditions. As a result, she began training to become a massage therapist herself, knowing that she wanted to help people who had met with frustration in their attempts to free themselves from pain. In all, the owner and her staff offer 14 different types of massage, from a 15-minute chair massage to deluxe body treatments lasting 90 minutes. Prairie Massage provides specialty massages, such as sports, pregnancy, heated stone therapy, trigger point therapy and ear candling, just to name a few. While all massages are designed to relax muscles and reduce stress, some target specific problems. For example, the lymphatic drainage massage can help prevent colds and flu by increasing the production of white blood cells and stimulating the immune system. At Prairie Massage you can enjoy a calming massage with your favorite fragrance by adding an essential oil for a nominal fee. The waiting room at Prairie Massage is warm and inviting. You are always welcomed and offered a complimentary beverage of your choice. This environment and excellent service has made it the dedicated massage service provider for Medica employees. The Minnesota Cancer Society also lists Prairie Massage as a resource for current or former cancer patients. Begin living a healthier and happier life by booking an appointment with Prairie Massage & Bodyworks today.

16315 Terrey Pine Drive, #300, Eden Prairie MN
(952) 465-7799
www.prairiemassage.com

Spalon Montage

Spalon Montage, a full-service day spa and salon, brings customers the kind of service that has grown an original team of 25 highly trained and educated members to 350 professionals serving three locations. Owners Shelley Engelsma and Mitchell Wherley developed Spalon Montage 15 years ago with the aim of providing the most effective treatments available. Forefront in their minds was a singular goal: to give you an environment where you can relax while having your personal needs met. Treatments include care for your hair, body, face and nails. Spalon's hairstylists employ color and cut to give you a signature look that complements your features and personality. They excel at updos and hair extensions, too. Your body will feel rejuvenated and moisturized following such treatments as massage, reflexology, body polishing and wraps. Spalon's estheticians can assess your skin and recommend an ongoing care program. Skin treatments range from all-natural facials to microdermabrasion. Men find specialized skin help here, too. The Montage Retreat package offers a full day of pampering, complete with massage and body polish, a facial, paraffin treatments for hands and feet and a shampoo and styling. Lunch comes with this package. Readers of the *Star Tribune* named Spalon Montage their favorite day spa and favorite all-around spa to visit. Treat yourself to personal care at one of Spalon Montage's three locations—in Edina, Woodbury and Chanhassen.

3909 W 49 ½ Street, Edina MN
600 Market Street, Suite 270, Chanhassen MN
8375 Seasons Parkway, Woodbury MN
(952) 915-2900
www.spalon.com

Ridgeview Seasons Medical Spa

The philosophy of Ridgeview Seasons Medical Spa is that your skin should be a mirror reflecting your good health, self-confidence and inner beauty. Under the direction of Dr. Gene Tseplaev, physician and internal medicine specialist, Seasons offers the latest skin techniques to enhance your personal appearance or address specific problem areas. Services include Botox, dermal injection, acne treatment, laser hair removal and sclerotherapy as well as photorejuvenation, microdermabrasion and chemical peels. Most procedures require no recovery time, with treatment sessions lasting about 30 minutes. Because the medical spa is affiliated with Ridgeview Medical Center, clients can be confident in the quality of care. Dr. Tseplaev and his staff follow safety precautions and procedure protocols typically found only in medical clinics. Ridgeview Seasons carries a full line of skin care products to complement its services. A certified massage therapist provides hot stone and prenatal massage and many other therapeutic massage treatments. Call Ridgeview Seasons Medical Spa to schedule a complimentary consultation, your first step to refining and improving your personal appearance.

675 Water Street, Excelsior MN
(952) 906-7877
www.seasonsmedicalspa.org

Bella on the Bay

Hairstylists Pamela and Kiko Cruz and business executives Paula and Bryce Johnson shared a partnership and a vision. In 2006, that vision produced Bella on the Bay, a salon and spa built around a top-notch professional staff and a special home-like atmosphere. Paula drew from firsthand knowledge of the world's spas and a knack for assembling successful teams to bring the partnership together. Pamela and Kiko, with 40 years of combined salon industry experience and a passion for their craft, have put together a team to deliver outstanding style to clients. The spa salon offers the full range of hair, nail, beauty, tranquility and revitalization treatments out of a historic home in Excelsior. Whether you're in need of hair or makeup design or a treatment to smooth, contour or stimulate your skin, Bella on the Bay has you covered. Guests can design custom packages of three or more services for a special discount. After your massage, scrub or wrap, rinse off in the warm-water Vichy hydrotherapy shower, a perfect ending to a perfect afternoon. You can't always change the world, but you can change your look and your outlook with a visit to Bella on the Bay.

474 2nd Street, Excelsior MN
(952) 474-5005
www.bellaonthebay.com

Rodica Face & Body, Inc.

Rodica Face & Body opened in 1974 as the first salon in Minnesota specializing in skin care. From the beginning, Rodica designed its treatments using a holistic approach, and as a result, the effects are much more than just skin-deep. The Rodica philosophy is to address stress and the balanced life during the treatments, which mesh mind, body and spirit. The result is a feeling of well-being, lightness and joy. The salon offers signature facials along with peels, collagen, oxygen, peptide, vitamin C, placenta and live-cell treatments. The salon is named for its founder, Rodica Stern, and is run today by her daughter, Mariana Lippa, who helped her open it 32 years

ago. Mariana spent the first 18 years of her life in Romania. Not surprisingly, her spa has the feel of a European home. Mariana is well traveled and fluent in several languages and also organizes tours of Italy that include a spa experience. Through these tours, Mariana keeps herself immersed in European culture and introduces it to others. The Italian trip offers the stuff of dreams, such as a day trip to one of the oldest Etruscan spas in Tuscany, more than a week in a villa hotel (with breakfast included) and a trip to the Chianti wine region. Travelers who accompany Mariana say that the trip is a life-changing experience. Whether you find rejuvenation in downtown Wayzata or in Italy, the results will amaze you. Call Rodica Face & Body and plan your own moments in paradise.

681 Lake Street E, Suite 257, Wayzata MN
(952) 475-3111

Revessence Skin Enhancement Center

Revessence Skin Enhancement Center offers the latest in laser and skincare treatments in an environment that is both calming and medically sound. The private reception area, a comfortable waiting room and individual treatment rooms create a soothing experience. The center is owned by Dr. Gregory Mesna, a local plastic surgeon certified by the American Board

of Plastic Surgery. All procedures here are performed by licensed medical professionals who have advanced training in lasers and skin care that assures safe and effective treatments. The staff of skin care specialists use the latest techniques, technology and modern-day cosmeceuticals to create a personal skin fitness plan that offers lasting results for years to come. This talented team is committed to helping you select the best treatment options to meet your individual goals and lifestyle. Revessence is passionate about offering you the best skin enhancement technology available, and presents each client with the opportunity to receive a computerized skin analysis. You can restore a smooth, healthy complexion that brings back the youthful appearance of your skin. Raise your spirits, enhance your outlook on life and revitalize your essence at Revessence Skin Enhancement Center.

Eden Prairie MN (952) 829-SKIN (7546)
Minnetonka MN (952) 745-4624
Edina MN (952) 925-4161 or (952) 893-9100
Shoreview MN (651) 483-8483
Vadnais Heights MN (651) 783-5910

reVamp! salonspa

reVamp! salonspa is not just a place to get your hair and nails done, but a place where you can get a total image makeover to bring your inner spirit into full view. Christopher Hopkins founded reVamp! more than 10 years ago and remained true to his vision of a salon and spa where customers would feel like guests of the whole reVamp! team. The staff here is upbeat, full of team spirit and happy to be here. Their customers adore the team and the personal attention they get during customized spa services, such as facials, massage, waxing and body treatments. The reVamp! team is a trusted source for customers looking for a flattering hair style, the right hair color and the best makeup choices. You can also discover what necklines, skirt lengths and dress styles work best on you. reVamp! treats the whole person by offering silhouette analysis, wardrobe consultations and image development along with wellness services. The salon and spa has been featured on *Oprah* and HGTV. *Glamour* magazine named reVamp! one of the top 10 salons, and *Minneapolis/St. Paul Magazine* featured it in the *Best of the Twin Cities*. When you're ready to let your outer being reflect your inner being, come to the experts at reVamp! salonspa and let them give you a new look to present to the world.

**2910 Hennepin Avenue S,
Minneapolis MN**
(612) 341-0404
www.revampsalonspa.com

Bachman's

When Henry and Hattie Bachman started growing potatoes, lettuce, onions and squash on a plot in south Minneapolis in 1885, they little suspected that their heirs would be managing a floral empire more than 100 years later. The Bachman story begins in 1914 when one of Henry's sons decided to grow flowers in his father's greenhouse to earn some pocket money. The experiment was so successful that the family spent the 1920s replacing their vegetable operation with flowers. Today, the original vegetable farm is the site of Bachman's flagship store, one of 19 retail locations in the Twin Cities metro area. Members of the fourth and fifth generation of Bachmans are now running the business. They oversee six full-service floral, home and garden centers, a seasonal garden and landscape center called Cedar Acres, and floral stores in downtown Minneapolis and at all Byerly's locations. The business also includes indoor and outdoor landscaping divisions, a nursery wholesale center, seven acres of greenhouses and a 513-acre growing range near Lakeville. Bachman's purple wrapped packages are instantly recognizable and a fleet of vans delivers about 5,000 of them every week. If you are looking for ideas for a beautiful world, start with a visit to the legendary Bachman's.

6010 Lyndale Avenue S, Minneapolis MN
(612) 861-7600 or (866) 222-4626
www.bachmans.com

Go Home

In the heart of Uptown on the corner of Lake Street and Hennepin Avenue, shoppers will find a delightful home furnishings store called Go Home. Rick Olinger, proprietor of this inspiring boutique, has created an enchanting wonderland filled with ever-changing home décor items, gifts and accessories that will quickly get you addicted to decorating. Go Home carries an eclectic mix of contemporary upholstered furniture, unusual wall art, fabulous lighting including hand-blown Venetian and Murano glass pendants and an extensive collection of wall clocks. Great gift items such as imported European soaps, coffee table books and fragrant candles can be found here as well. Olinger's background in art and design shine through in the intriguing pieces that make up his inventory. Nothing here is likely to be found at your local

mall. Other items worth noting are colorful, jeweled drawer pulls and a choice selection of witty greeting cards that will leave you laughing on the way out the door. "We sell items that are unique and original, and attract people who are looking for individuality," says Olinger proudly. While Go Home caters primarily to the local community, other customers worth noting are Bette Midler, Winona Rider and Minnesota's own Prince. Go Home is the ideal place to shop for your next housewarming or holiday gift and is the perfect place to pick up a little something for yourself.

1408 W Lake Street, Minneapolis MN
(612) 824-8732

A Wreath of Franklin

You'd be hard-pressed to find another store as well decorated as A Wreath of Franklin anywhere. Each of the rooms of this home décor marketplace is done up in its own style to best set off its collections. You'll find intriguing lamps, mirrors and artwork. Furniture includes desks, sofas, chairs, dressers and more. Floral design is one of owner Sue Anderson's signature services. She'll fill planters, urns or baskets with silk flowers, dried flowers or dried fruit. Other household items include vases, candles, picture frames and bookends. Interior design is a major share of Susan's business. She has more than 25 years of experience in residential decorating and has furnished

some of the most expensive homes in the Twin Cities area, incorporating furniture, rugs, pillows mirrors, lamps and all accessories. Susan has gathered her eclectic collection from near and far and refreshes the selection constantly. Prices range from the easily affordable to the seriously luxurious—there is something for everyone. Susan's expertise is visible at her store. The staff is as pleasant as the décor, and regular customers find shopping to be a joyful experience. Stop by A Wreath of Franklin for beauty, good cheer and items you'll just have to buy.

11 E Division Street, Buffalo MN
(763) 682-0188
www.awreathoffranklin.com

Minnehaha Falls Nursery & Landscaping

Whether you seek one tree, a dozen flats of flowers or a garden design for your house or business, Minnehaha Falls Nursery & Landscaping is prepared to help you. Not everyone is prepared to tackle their own garden project, which is why this store offers installation and design services in addition to outstanding plant selection. The creative Minnehaha Falls landscape designers can add distinctive features to your property and personalize the grounds around your home in ways that add value, usefulness and year-round beauty. A patio of brick pavers or flagstones adds entertainment space in summer, while shoveling in winter gets easier when you use these materials on walkways and driveways. Minnehaha Falls stocks plants, soils, mulches

and garden tools. The bird feeders, pottery and statuary are always in demand. In winter, the nursery carries Christmas trees and poinsettias as well as bird food and firewood. Garden design preferences and plant varieties have changed since Robert Sr. and Shirley Lindgren launched the company 50 years ago, but the commitment to be a one-stop garden shop remains strong for the Lindgrens' son Robert Jr. and his wife, Jennifer, who bought the business in 2001. Freshen up your out-of-doors with a visit to Minnehaha Falls Nursery & Landscaping.

4461 Minnehaha Avenue, Minneapolis MN
(612) 724-5453
www.minnehahafallslandscape.com

Schulte's Greenhouse & Nursery

Schulte's Greenhouse & Nursery is a family-owned business located 30 miles northwest of Minneapolis. The greenhouse was established in 1963 by Larry and Roseanna Schulte. Now, along with their sons Dave and Dan and a friendly, knowledgeable staff, they operate the greenhouse, garden center and nursery. Schulte's has built an excellent reputation based on customer satisfaction and high-quality plants. The majority of the plants sold are grown in the nursery and greenhouse. With more than 1,200 varieties of perennials, trees, shrubs and evergreens, including many unusual, ornamental and common varieties, Schulte's has the largest selection in the area. In addition, you can expect a huge assortment of annual, vegetable

and fruit plants. Known for carrying many unique and specialty plants, along with all the old favorites, these greenhouses are overflowing with color. Customers enjoy strolling through the gorgeous array of plants. You can also look for houseplants, birdseed, seasonal plants and decorations for fall and all of the various holidays. Certified nurserymen and horticulturists are on staff year-round to provide answers to all your questions about your garden, lawn or landscape, and will help you find the perfect plant for any need.

2960 LaBeaux Avenue NE, St. Michael MN
(763) 497-3747
www.schultesgreenhouse.com

Polly Berg

For 39 years, Polly Berg has been furnishing Minnesota and the world with the finest in bed linens, tableware and delicate lingerie. Customers come from all over to hand-select heirloom-quality linens, to buy extravagantly beautiful, hand-embroidered lingerie or simply to accessorize their bedrooms, bathrooms or trousseaus. The environment of this upscale shop is intimate, yet the array of materials, textures, colors and sizes is impressive. The variety of accessories, designer wares and fashions is equally vast. Oscar de la Renta, Ralph Lauren, Carole Hochman and Fernando Sanchez are among some of the featured names. Berg personally ensures that all her customers find exactly what they need. If a size or color is not in stock, the attentive staff will try to order it for you. The items Berg features in her shop reflect her creative spirit. From luxurious Egyptian cotton sheets, including 1,020 thread count cotton satin, to romantic silk nightgowns, anything from Polly Berg is an instant classic. Whether you're visiting from New York or anywhere in the country, Berg's exquisite taste and superior service will make a lasting impression.

712 E Lake Street, Wayzata MN
(952) 920-0183
www.pollyberg.com

Brothers Meat & Seafood

Welcome back to an old-fashioned, family-run butcher shop. Brothers Meat & Seafood has been offering the freshest meat and seafood, the old-fashioned way, for the last four years. Owners Jerry and Joel both have 25 years experience in cutting everything to their customers' satisfaction. Specialty cuts are welcome. The brothers believe in lean and extra lean same-day ground beef. Just like rural butcher shops, they have giant freezer pack and grill pack meats, beef sticks, large packages of burgers and do deer, elk, bear and moose processing. They also have high-end items such as lamb, elk and venison. The owners are justifiably proud of their smokehouse. They have a huge selection of beef jerky in all sorts of different flavors, such as barbecue spice, lemon pepper and garlic dill. They have fantastic turkey jerky plus the Brothers specialty, Old Country Jerky, which has four flavors to choose from. Brothers makes a fine selection of smoked sausages and snack sticks. You'll find a tasty variety of link sausages, including three flavors of bratwurst. There's a large selection of smoked hams, chicken and three flavors of bacon. Don't forget about the seafood counter. It's the freshest fish you will find next to catching it yourself. Brothers is a great place to come for your fundraisers, too. The shop is able to package cuts of meat in any combination for raffles. Brothers Meat & Seafood is a huge supporter of community and is willing to go to any lengths to support your group. Customers come from all over the city and from out of state just to get their meat exactly the way they like it, fresh and served with a smile.

13545 Grove Drive, Maple Grove MN
(763) 416-1901
www.brothersmeatandseafood.com

Sam's Washington Avenue Wine Shop

The menu is planned, the guests have been invited. All that's left is choosing just the right wine. A quick trip to Sam's Washington Avenue Wine Shop will put an international array of wine options at your fingertips. Sam, the owner, has 15 years of experience as a wine expert. All of his employees have a broad knowledge of wine and new trends in wine from around the world. They are eager to assist you in finding the perfect wine for your special occasion. If you are a wine novice, feel free to ask for information on any wine-related topic. At Sam's Washington Avenue Wine Shop, there are no stupid questions. Participate in the wine tasting offered three days a week to discover new favorites. If your hectic schedule makes wine shopping difficult, place your wine order online and have it delivered two days later to your home within the Twin Cities metropolitan area. Pick up your order in person and take advantage of free parking in the lot adjacent to the shop. Sam's Washington Avenue Wine Shop is located in the historic warehouse district of downtown Minneapolis. Stop by and see what tempts your palate.

218 Washington Avenue N, Minneapolis MN
(612) 455-1045
www.mywinecart.com

101 Market

Welcome to 101 Market. The Market started out in a pole building in 1997 with a temporary greenhouse. In 2003, it moved into the current building with two greenhouse bays. The spring of 2005 brought the addition of the courtyard and remaining greenhouses you can see today. The 101 Market is like the ever-changing seasons in Minnesota. Spring in the greenhouse comes in full bloom with custom-planted hanging baskets and one-of-a-kind container designs. Summer brings tasty Minnesota homegrown produce, picked daily. The Market is well-known for mouthwatering super-sweet sweet corn. The winds of fall bring the fun of pumpkins, mums, gourds, corn stalks and a five-acre corn maze. During winter, smell the pine of Christmas trees, custom decorated spruce tips and wreaths. Spark your imagination with cut flower arrangements in the floral department. Beauty and nature radiate fabulous color, texture and movement. From weddings and funerals to everyday bouquets, 101 Market has what you are looking for. The delight of home décor and gifts follow all the seasonal changes for your home—during Christmas and every day, indoors and out. Stop in and experience why 101 Market is Simply the Best.

8980 NE Quantrelle Avenue, Otsego MN
(763) 441-4487
www.nathes101market.com

Forster's Meats & Catering

When the son of the prime minister of Denmark married a Minnesota lass, Forster's Meats & Catering catered the wedding. For many years, people planning a bash have found that the easy way out is to order a pig roast and steak fries from Forster's. At its store in Plymouth, customers gaze in awe at display cases full of beautiful chops and steaks. The cold-smoked, dry-aged rib eye steaks are a specialty. Locals know that Forster's is the place for delicious homemade sausage, too—more than 70 kinds in all. Tour the world with sausage links by ordering German bratwurst, Irish pork sausage, Cajun andouille and other ethnic varieties. The hams and bacon that Forster's makes in-house are also something special. Forster's has been around since 1947, when it opened as a slaughter plant that served the needs of local livestock farmers. The current owner, Cynthia Forster, took over the business from her father who, in turn, learned it from his father. The store, at its current location since 2001, offers not only a meat market but a café where customers can enjoy breakfasts and lunches featuring Forster's meats. Drop by Forster's to grab a bite or to do some shopping, or please the crowd at your next event by having Forster's handle the catering.

11255 Highway 55, Suite 40, Plymouth MN
(763) 559-5775
www.forsters.us

Canterbury Park

Canterbury Park is Minnesota's premier entertainment and gaming destination. With the excitement of live horse racing all summer and 24/7 action in the card club, Canterbury Park offers fun and games like no place else in Minnesota. Canterbury Park's live horse racing meet runs from Kentucky Derby Day in May through Labor Day. It's Minnesota's only thoroughbred racetrack, and more than 350,000 visitors pour through the gates each summer to experience a thrill of the stretch run as the horses turn for home. Of course, you can watch and wager on America's biggest races year-round in Canterbury Park's newly remodeled Racebook. The action in the Canterbury Card Club never stops. Canterbury Park is home to the largest poker room in the upper Midwest, dealing Texas Hold 'Em, Seven-Card Stud and Omaha. Each fall, poker players from around the country converge on Canterbury Park for its signature tournament, the Fall Poker Classic. Canterbury's Casino Games room features traditional favorites such as blackjack, Four-Card Poker, Pai Gow Poker, Caribbean Stud and more. Canterbury also hosts several special events throughout the year, including the Midwest's largest arts and crafts show and championship snowmobile racing. As a member of the Minnesota Keystone Program, Canterbury Park contributes five percent of its pre-tax profits to the community each year. Canterbury Park is located in the southwest of the metro area, just 25 minutes from downtown Minneapolis. Visit the website for more information. Canterbury Park truly offers fun and games like no place else.

1100 Canterbury Road, Shakopee MN
(800) 340-6361
www.canterburypark.com

Safari Island

Before 2001, residents of Waconia had to travel to neighboring towns for an athletic workout. Responding to the community's needs, the city of Waconia opened Safari Island, an impressive $18 million, 57,000 square foot facility. Safari Island is so thoroughly and imaginatively equipped that neighboring townspeople now come to Waconia. With more than 5,000 members, Safari Island caters to exercisers of every age and stripe, from the most serious to the most playful. Safari Island also offers day rates for guests. Childcare is available. Kids can crawl, climb and slide in the four-level indoor play structure called the Lion's Den. Gorilla Ridge is a four-court gymnasium that hosts batting cages, basketball, volleyball and shuffleboard games. Walkers can enjoy Rainforest Trails, a tenth-mile three-lane suspended track that circles the gymnasium. The Iron Forest features a wide range of strength and cardio equipment and overlooks the aquatics facilities. Wildcat Bay is a 277,000 gallon, 75-foot lap pool. The Raging Falls is a 175-foot water slide that plunges into Amazon Bay, a 57,000-gallon pool with a zero-depth-entry area and water fountains. Naturally, there's a full menu of swimming lessons. Guests can also enjoy a variety of fitness classes, dance lessons and instruction in self-defense and scuba diving, or birthday party packages. Come and enjoy a wild and watery expedition at Safari Island. Visit the website for daily fees and special offers.

1600 Community Drive, Waconia MN
(952) 442-0695
www.safariisland.net

Sundance Golf & Bowl

Sundance Golf & Bowl has it covered, whether it's a genteel day on the greens or a night of pizza and bowling with buddies. Golfers will delight at the 18-hole par 72 course. It offers plenty of fun and challenge for both novices and experienced players. Sundance offers a fully stocked pro shop, PGA-certified teaching pros and power carts. The club also offers company tournament outings and daily leagues. The Sundance Men's Club is one of the most highly regarded men's golf clubs in the state. The bowling alley has 24 hardwood lanes, automatic scoring machines and bumpers for kids. Sundance offers leagues for everyone, including men, women, seniors and youths. Parents can book bowling birthday parties for children, and the club holds special bowling events with music and prizes. You can work up an appetite while golfing and bowling. The Sundance Grill offers meals ranging from salads to burgers and pizzas, with daily specials and a prime rib dinner. Enjoy drinks and dancing at the 19th Hole at the clubhouse. Poker enthusiasts can dive right in to Texas Hold 'Em tournaments, which are held every Monday. This combined entertainment center has been open for more than 36 years. The Robert H. Allen family has owned it since 1980, and Brian Allen is the current president. Come to Sundance Golf & Bowl for golf, bowling and fun for all ages.

15240 113th Avenue N, Dayton MN
(763) 420-4700
www.sundancegolfbowl.com

Crostini Grille

The owners of Crostini Grille never tire of hearing guests say that they can't believe a restaurant this good is in such a small town. Since opening on Valentine's Day 2003, Crostini Grille has brought Italian and American favorites with a touch of sophistication to Monticello. Crostini Grille is an independent restaurant with true atmosphere. Taste what it does best by ordering the Tuscan pork chops topped with marinated tomatoes, spinach and bleu cheese. Loyal customers swear the dish never disappoints. The restaurant cooks all pan-tossed pastas to order in individual pans. Fresh cream, garlic and spices create signature dishes such as seafood *pomodoro* and artichoke spinach ravioli. Staples on the menu include spaghetti with meatballs, fettuccini Alfredo and lasagna, not to mention pizzas cooked in a stone-slate oven. For a satisfying lunch, try the sausage minestrone with a walleye sandwich or the bruschetta chicken wrap. A special wine dinner, served four times a year, is a much anticipated event. It's the chef's chance to shine as he creates fabulous five-course meals paired with specific wines. Folks are still talking about the Tour of Italy dinner. Choose Crostini Grille for lunch or dinner, and be prepared to tell your city friends about the fine meal you had halfway between Minneapolis and St. Cloud.

254 W Broadway, Monticello MN
(763) 295-8898
www.crostinigrille.com

Origami

Located in the Market Hotel in the heart of the warehouse district in downtown Minneapolis, Origami serves some of the finest sushi in Minneapolis as well as traditional Japanese fare and American favorites. The Market Hotel, built in 1867, was remodeled into office space in 1985 after functioning as a hotel for more than a century. When the first floor remained vacant in 1990, Kiminobu "Ichi" Ichikawa seized the opportunity to introduce sushi to the people of Minneapolis. With the help of partners Del Francis and Tatsuya Saji and the carpentry skills of friend Dan Bartel, Ichi's vision of Origami unfolded. Opening in 1990, Origami's success allowed Ichi to buy out his partners in 1993 and to purchase the entire Market Hotel building in 1995, where he expanded Origami into the building's second floor in 1997, adding a new lounge and dining area. Origami has earned scores of laurels, including multiple awards from *City Pages*, *Gourmet* magazine, the Zagat Survey and *Mpls. St. Paul Magazine* for Best Sushi and Best Japanese Restaurant. In addition to Asian cuisine, the restaurant features a sensational sake selection and an extensive menu of martinis, wine, Scotch and beer. Both the original downtown location and Origami West at Ridgedale Mall offer patio seating. Stop in and treat yourself to fabulous Japanese cuisine for lunch or dinner or just grab a quick bite at the sushi bar.

30 N 1st Street, Minneapolis MN (612) 333-8430
12305 Wayzata Boulevard, Minnetonka MN (Origami West) (952) 746-3398
www.origamirestaurant.com

Christo's Greek Restaurant

If you are looking for Greek cuisine, Christo's is the place to find it. Gus and Carol Parpas opened the original Christo's in 1988 in a space that had been a furniture store in the 1920s and was a hardware store when it closed in the 1980s. Nicollet Avenue, the site of the building, was once the main artery to downtown but had become dilapidated, despite the presence of several successful businesses. When Christo's arrived, the area experienced a renaissance. At first, Christo's offered classic Greek cuisine with a few specialties from the island of Cyprus. Today's menu combines many contemporary dishes with traditional ones. New dishes are developed every year from what Gus and Carol's discover on their travels. The restaurant is spacious and reminiscent of an island taverna. Prices are intentionally affordable, service is attentive and personable, and the wine list features products from five Greek wineries in addition to domestic selections. Christo's also offers a wide range of catering services and can supply anything from pick-up to delivery or a full-service meal planned and presented at any site you choose. In 2000, Christo's was voted Best Greek Restaurant by the readers of City Pages and DINE.com. They were also the overwhelming choice of a panel of Twin Cities food critics for best Greek restaurant. Come taste Christo's unique brand of Greek hospitality.

2632 Nicollet Avenue S, Minneapolis MN
(612) 871-2111
www.christos.com

Biella and Ravello

The names Biella and Ravello sound like characters from a fairytale, perhaps a beautiful princess and her handsome prince. In fact, they are pair of restaurants. The romantic names, however, are most fitting. These are small and intimate spaces, ideal for a quiet evening with that special someone. The chef-driven menus feature northern Italian cuisine with some Swiss and French influences. The fresh food is made completely in house and is complemented by lists of exquisite wines. Housed inside an 1880s building on Excelsior's historic Water Street, Biella is a sophisticated marriage of Old World charm and chic ambience. Ravello, in Long Lake, is as captivating as the Italian coastal city for which it is named. Owner Mark Christian Nazigian, who has been in the business since the age of 12, is living his dream of owning his own restaurant twice over. His joy shows as he drops by each table and visits with his guests. He is used to hosting local and national celebrities, who appreciate the outstanding cuisine and discreet atmosphere. Chefs Andrew Suthers and Phil Byrd are the stars of the kitchen at Biella, while Chef Jeremy LaFond develops the menu at Ravello. Come and experience why one critic called these romantic restaurants "the best thing to happen to the west suburban dining scene in ages."

227 Water Street, Excelsior MN
(Biella) (952) 474-8881
www.biella-restaurant.com

1935 W Wayzata Boulevard, Long Lake MN
(Ravello) (952) 473-7373
www.ravello-restaurant.com

D'Amico & Partners

With more than 20 years of experience in Minnesota and Naples, Florida, D'Amico & Partners has gained a local and national reputation and has become one of the most highly regarded restaurateurs in Minnesota. From catering to cafés to full-service restaurants, D'Amico's award-winning food and wine consistently garner the praise of critics and patrons alike. D'Amico never stops with a great menu. The beautiful interiors of its restaurants add sophistication and elegance to every dining experience. Local and national publications have lauded D'Amico's carefully crafted interior designs.

www.damico.com

D'Amico & Sons

D'Amico & Sons is a family of European-style delis and cafés that offer creative, high-quality casual Italian food for eat-in, take out and catering. The first of these popular establishments opened in 1994, and demand has grown ever since. Today, you can choose from among 17 D'Amico & Sons locations in the Twin Cities.

www.damicoandsons.com

D'Amico Catering

Since its inception in the early 1990s, D'Amico Catering has risen to the top in the Twin Cities. Featured exclusively in some of the most sought-after locations, D'Amico Catering has a well-deserved reputation for gourmet food programs, outstanding service and unparalleled sophistication. In 1995, D'Amico Catering opened the Metropolitan, a sprawling 10,000 square foot event facility with stunning décor and a state-of-the-art media system. In 2003, D'Amico took over the stunning space in the International Market Square, featuring a multi-story atrium and peaked glass roof 72 feet above a sun-washed space. Dishes from D'Amico Catering continue to appear at the area's most prestigious homes and events.

275 Market Street, Suite C25, Minneapolis MN (612) 238-4444
www.damicocatering.com

D'Amico Cucina

In 1987, brothers Richard and Larry D'Amico opened D'Amico Cucina in downtown Minneapolis. The restaurant was to become the flagship for D'Amico & Partners. This acclaimed gourmet Italian restaurant has been featured in the *New York Times*, the *Wall Street Journal* and many other local and national publications. As one of the best fine dining restaurants in Minneapolis, Cucina's inventive cuisine continues to inspire critics and entice customers.

**100 N 6th Street, Minneapolis MN
(612) 338-2401**

Campiello

Campiello is an authentic Tuscan-style restaurant featuring rustic Italian dishes, wood-fired pizzas and rotisserie meats in a casually elegant setting. For more than 10 years, Campiello has attracted a loyal following to its two Twin Cities locations. Campiello's Tour di Italia campaign presents a rotating selection of cuisine from the diverse regions of Italy, offering patrons a continually changing menu.

**1320 W Lake Street, Minneapolis MN (612) 825-2222
6411 City West Parkway, Eden Prairie MN (952) 941-6868**
www.campiello.damico.com

Café and Bar Lurcat

Opened in 2002, Café and Bar Lurcat is housed in a restored historic building off Loring Park in Minneapolis. The menu features innovative American cuisine and an award-winning wine list. With beautiful décor that complements the historic 9,000-square-foot space, Lurcat is a favorite spot for patrons looking for dining or cocktails.

**1624 Harmon Place, Minneapolis MN
(612) 486-5500 or (612) 486-5900**
www.cafelurcat.com

Masa

The newest addition to the D'Amico family of restaurants is Masa. This contemporary Mexican restaurant opened its doors in 2005 to much anticipation. Masa's high-end authentic Mexican cuisine quickly gained local and national attention. The sunny restaurant features glass tile mosaics, hand-painted murals and a glowing back-lit bar. Located on Nicollet Mall in downtown Minneapolis, Masa caters to today's urban food-savvy crowd.

**1070 Nicollet Mall, Minneapolis MN
(612) 338-6272**
www.masa-restaurant.com

Escape Ultra Lounge

Everything about Escape Ultra Lounge is dramatic, from its 12,000 square feet of space to its state-of-the-art multimedia sound and lighting systems for live entertainment. Open seven days a week, this hot Minneapolis club showcases some of the best artists in today's music, from rap and rock to rhythm & blues and dance. Escape also serves as a stage for CD release parties, product launches and fashion shows. You can choose to host a corporate conference or executive meeting here. Escape's trendy interior design features a color scheme in vibrant cobalt blue, rich chino orange and molten bronze with funky furniture and a decidedly cosmopolitan feel. With a capacity for 1,000 guests, the sheer size of Escape adds to the other-worldly atmosphere. The lounge features two distinct VIP bars, with comfortable lounge areas and oversized seating, along with nine large plasma television screens to catch all the sports action. The main bar area offers an extensive selection of beer, wine and spirits, private tables and lighting that washes the leather couches in changing colors. State-of-the-art fiber optic lighting plus uplighting that changes color with the beat of the music radiate sizzle and a positive vibe. Looking for the ultimate escape? Come experience the energy, upscale décor and powerful music at Escape Ultra Lounge.

600 Hennepin Avenue S, Suite 200,
Minneapolis MN
(612) 333-8855
www.escapeultralounge.com

Bellanotte

In February 2004, Bellanotte brought an unprecedented late night experience to the Twin Cities. Inspired by restaurateur Piero Filpi's Miami restaurant, Mezanotte, David Koch teamed up with Randy Norman to bring the South Beach experience to Minneapolis. Bellanotte combines fine dining and superior service in an energetic and sophisticated late night atmosphere. The award-winning interior design is the perfect backdrop for enjoying music and relaxing with friends over cocktails and conversation at the onyx-lit bar. To fully experience Bellanotte, indulge in the imaginative cuisine and excellent service up until midnight. Executive Chef Amber Severtson, a Cordon Bleu graduate, presides over an Italian-inspired menu that also includes such signature seafood specialties as lobster linguini and seared salmon in lobster cream sauce. You'll find a daily seafood feature, too. The best seller, however, is Bellanotte's succulent signature filet, a beef tenderloin grilled to order and topped with Maryland jumbo lump crab and a honey bourbon butter sauce. Sous and pastry chefs creates an array of delectable desserts from scratch, including crème brûlée, cannoli, Bellanotte Lava Cake and tiramisu. Add a well-chosen wine list and impeccable service, and you're sure to agree that the cuisine deserves your undivided attention. For sophistication without pretense, join the lively scene at Bellanotte for lunch, dinner or happy hour. In keeping with the name *Bellanotte*, have a beautiful night.

**600 Hennepin Avenue S, Suite 170,
Minneapolis MN**
(612) 339-7200
www.bellanottempls.com

Peninsula Malaysian Cuisine

Visiting an authentic Malaysian restaurant is like exploring another country. The flavors challenge the palate; the names challenge the tongue. Peninsula Malaysian Cuisine lets Minneapolis diners approach authentic Malaysian food in a stylish, contemporary setting. Mei Yip, Chang Hu and Kelly Sim opened the restaurant at the beginning of 2006 and have inspired enthusiastic reviews in the *Star Tribune*, *Minnesota Monthly* and the *Rake*. Malaysian food is heavily influenced by cuisine from India, China, Thailand and Singapore, which accounts for such offerings as *roti canai*, an Indian flatbread served with a chicken and brown potato curry, and Hainanese chicken from China. Thailand contributes Thai green curry and *tom yum* hot and sour soup. The majority of the dishes are traditional Malaysian. They can be spicy and are characterized by a mix of complex flavors produced by cinnamon, ginger, cardamom, kaffir lime leaves and hot peppers, along with lemongrass, fermented shrimp paste and cloves. The Peninsula's spicy and salted golden tofu, made in-house, attracts a loyal following. Other specialties include slow-cooked beef *rendang* and curry lamb shank. Beverages, such as the green bean and grass jelly freeze, are equally unusual. Take your taste buds to Southeast Asia with a visit to Peninsula Malaysian Cuisine.

2608 Nicollet Avenue S, Minneapolis MN
(612) 871-8282
www.peninsulamalaysiancuisine.com

Nancy's Landing Restaurant

Nancy's Landing Restaurant, nestled on the south shore of Lake Waconia a block from downtown, boasts one of the loveliest settings around. This laid-back family-owned restaurant features four separate dining areas, including a deck overlooking the water and an indoor dining room with beautiful window views year-round. The Fireplace Room and the Captain's Room create a warm and inviting atmosphere that is perfect for smaller private gatherings. The full bar has an excellent wine selection. Nancy's Landing is operated by husband and wife chefs Paul and Laura Laubignat. Laura, a Minnesota native, and Paul, originally from France, have together created a simple yet original menu that has been hailed by food magazines and local papers. Nancy's Landing was once

featured on the Food Network's *The Best Of*. The internationally themed Sunday brunch, featuring a different country every Sunday, is especially famous. It was voted Best Brunch by the *Minneapolis Star Tribune*. You can check out the schedule of brunch themes on the website given below. Nancy's Landing also offers lunch buffets and catering. In 2005, the Laubignats undertook a thorough restoration of the building, which was once Weinzierl's Boat Livery. Come relax and enjoy the ever-changing view at Nancy's Landing Restaurant.

318 E Lake Street, Waconia MN
(952) 442-4954
www.nancyslanding.net

Nye's Polonaise Room

With its authentic 1950s décor, entering Nye's Polonaise Room is truly like walking into an old movie. Just across the Mississippi river from downtown Minneapolis, Nye's offers authentic Polish cuisine as well as supper club favorites such as prime rib, lobster tails and many tasty Polish delights. Owners Rob and Tony Jacob and General Manager Joe Stouffer encourage

their customers to partake in many of life's great activities: eating, drinking, dancing and singing. To this end, Nye's features a piano bar seven nights a week and a polka band. The lounge atmosphere in the restaurant hasn't changed since it opened in 1949. Rob and Tony know that once you experience Nye's, you'll be a regular for life. Their restaurant has been the recipient of many awards, including AOL Best Bar Minneapolis 2005. In 2006, Nye's was named Best Bar in America by *Esquire Magazine*. For pleasurable entertainment and delectable entrees, have dinner at Nye's Polonaise Room today.

112 Hennepin Avenue E, Minneapolis MN
(612) 379-2021
www.nyespolonaise.com

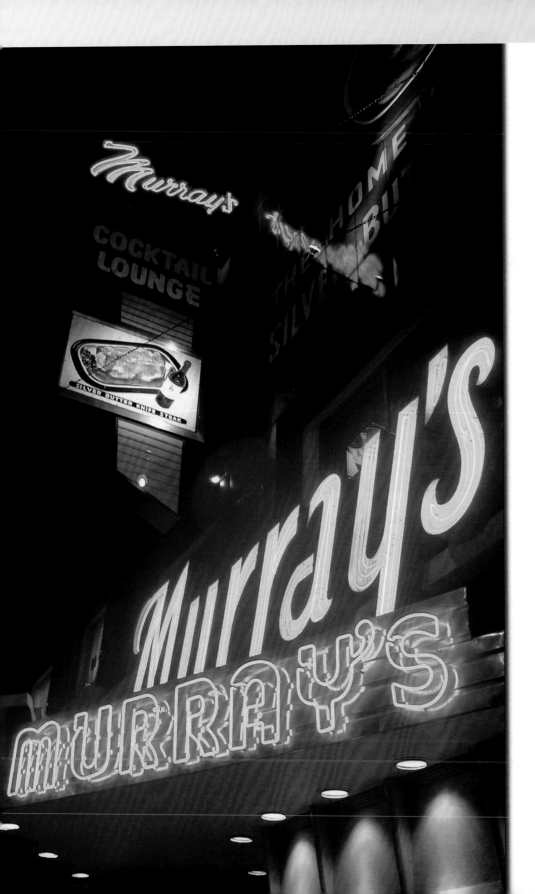

Murray's Resturant

Art and Marie Murray opened Murray's Restaurant in 1946. These days, their descendants Pat, Tim, Jill and Jamie Murray co-manage the restaurant the same way Art and Marie did. A fourth generation of dedicated and faithful clientele still come to Murray's because Murray's knows how to treat people right. For over 50 years, Murray's Restaurant has been an unofficial Minnesota landmark, home of the mouthwatering and famous silver butter knife steak. Murray's menu was popular with the meat and potatoes generation that grew up in the 1940s and 1950s and the restaurant has no intention of changing what works. The food is the wonderful kind you remember from your childhood. Garrison Keillor's tribute to Murray's says in part, "Murray's . . . is the sort of grand old joint you find in any big city, restaurants with pink drapes and a 70-year-old coat-check girl and a pianist who plays 'Deep Purple'. The waitresses have names like Agnes and Gladys and the menu harks back to the Age of Steak. A place where a fiftyish couple can enjoy a Manhattan and tuck into a chunk of cow and au gratin potato. . . . I have gone back about once every three or four years, and the magic seems never to wear off. . . . Some glories remain. You for sure, and me perhaps, and absolutely, Murray's." Go to Murray's while the glory remains. Go and enjoy, so you can remember it, too.

26 S 6th Street, Minneapolis MN
(612) 339-0909
www.murraysrestaurant.com

FireLake Grill House

There are many reasons to eat at the FireLake Grill House, including its convenient location in the Radisson Plaza and Chef Paul Lynch's dedication to using local produce, but the main draw is that the food is fabulous. FireLake has been celebrated in more than a dozen publications, ranging from the *Minneapolis Star Tribune* to *Bon Appetit*. The beef, chosen for its tenderness, won Chef Lynch the Minnesota Beef Council's Beef Backer award in 2006. Lynch's philosophy that fresh is better is demonstrated in the delicacies emerging from his kitchen. Diners can watch Lynch and his team deftly coax the mesquite flames that lick at thick-cut chops, steaks and fresh fish. Meanwhile, prime rib and chickens turn lazily on the hickory wood burning rotisserie. Fine wine or a cocktail complete your dinner. FireLake serves lunch and breakfast as well. The *Star Tribune* has called its breakfast menu "one of the most varied and imaginative in town." Lynch is a leading member of the Heartland Food Initiative, a network of farmers, chefs and distributors that brings the freshest regional produce to local restaurants. This novel organization makes it easy for restaurants to buy locally rather than relying on distant shipments that sap flavor. Lynch is also the talent behind Business Class to Go, which provides gourmet carry-on meals to hungry travelers tired of standard or non-existent food. For the freshest upscale Midwestern fare and a relaxed yet sophisticated ambience, come to FireLake Grill House.

31 S 7th Street, Minneapolis MN
(612) 216-FIRE (3473)
www.firelakerestaurant.com

Lyon's Pub

Authorities differ over whether lions purr, but you certainly will when you visit Lyon's Pub. Dining, drinking and dancing are just three of the experiences you'll have. The Minneapolis restaurant and bar has been satisfying customers for more than 23 years. Chris Rodgers saw the need for a casual place where friends can enjoy good, inexpensive food and drink amid the surrounding upscale restaurants. Since then, customers have been coming to Lyon's Pub for rip-roaring fun. Chris and his staff have earned a reputation throughout the area as congenial hosts who make guests feel right at home. You'll find many pub grub favorites here, including home-cut French fries and the signature Chesapeake chicken wings. Lyon's Pub is especially renowned for its smothered chicken sandwiches and Philly cheesesteaks. With happy hour specials and a wide variety of beers and ales, including Guinness, Bass and the pub's very own Lyon's Lager, which is brewed by the Schell's Brewery in New Ulm, you'll find plenty of ways to quench your thirst. Dance the night away on the dance floor any night to the best music of the past 30 years. Cheer on your favorite sports teams on the multiple television screens. If you're looking for a den where you can hang with friends, come to Lyon's Pub, the friendly neighborhood pub in downtown Minneapolis.

16 S 6ᵗʰ Street, Minneapolis MN
(612) 333-6612
www.lyonspub.com

Papa's Pizza & Pasta

Owner Mick Brogan sets the rules at Papa's Pizza & Pasta, and you'll find them easy enough to follow. The rules are come often, eat well and stay as long as you like. Folks in the Victory neighborhood of Minneapolis have warmed to Mick's open-hearted attitude, turning his little pizza and pasta place into a popular community gathering spot. It helps that he serves a tomato pie so good that he could probably be elected mayor if he promised a free slice to everyone when he won. A tomato pie is a little different from the pizza you might ordinarily eat. For starters, it doesn't use sauce and it's not smothered in cheese. Mick makes his by drizzling olive oil over the crust and then adding a layer of crushed tomatoes. He applies a sprinkling of cheese, not a bucket load, before the finishing touch of one more drizzling of olive oil. Mick is from New Jersey, and he says that his is as close to a genuine East Coast tomato pie as you are likely to find. Papa's Pizza & Pasta is more than a one-trick wonder. If you'd like to try something besides the tomato pie, Mick offers delicious pasta dishes, Philly cheesesteaks, hoagies and a velvety cheesecake like no other. Enjoy your meal on the patio in nice weather as you bemoan not having a place like Papa's Pizza & Pasta in your hometown.

4159 Thomas Avenue N, Minneapolis MN
(612) 521-PAPA (7272)

The Lookout Bar & Grill

Come for Food . . . Stay for Fun. The Lookout Bar & Grill has been Maple Grove's place for food, fun and family gatherings since 1958. It is known as the best kept secret in Maple Grove. There is never a cover charge for the live entertainment you can enjoy Wednesdays through Saturday evenings. The music ranges from classic rock to acoustic jams. You can catch a game—football, baseball, hockey, basketball—whatever you choose, anytime you visit. The food is fantastic, and with nightly specials at very reasonable prices you will be tempted to come every night just to taste the mouthwatering delights. The Lookout is known for its Broasted Chicken with jojos, barbecue ribs and au gratin potatoes. The Lookout specializes in banquets, private parties and catering on-site or off for all of your special events, such as weddings, company picnics, anniversaries or graduations. The Lookout also boasts the fact that it has the largest outdoor patio around with a play area for the kids to enjoy when the weather is warm and it's fun to be outside. Bob Kinnan originally opened the business as Bob's Lookout in 1958 with a 3.2 beer and set-up license and a seating capacity of 55. He was soon hosting live country music seven nights a week. The Kinnan family expanded the operation over the years, and today, the restaurant seats 260. Mike and Brenda Kinnan, the second generation, welcome you to The Lookout Bar & Grill.

8672 Pineview Lane N, Maple Grove MN
(763) 424-4365

Bella

Newly opened in Blaine, Bella introduces the community to the same sublime blend of fine dining and energetic nightlife that Minneapolis has experienced in the Bellanotte restaurant. Bella offers fresh handmade pastas, fresh seafood, steaks and chops in a lively atmosphere. David Koch, owner of Bellanotte and Escape Ultra Lounge, brought his vision to life with the help of David Shea, owner of Shea, Inc., one of the Twin Cities' premier restaurant design firms. Meeting by chance at Bellanotte during one of Koch's group food tasting and brainstorming sessions, the two soon realized that Shea's design skills were the perfect complement to Koch's customer-focused restaurant vision. Bella's dazzling décor and energetic ambience magnify guests' enjoyment of the fine Italian-inspired cuisine. Open for lunch, brunch, happy hour and dinner, Bella offers a tempting selection of salads, homemade soups, appetizers and pizza. Entrées include steaks, a selection of signature ravioli and lasagna dishes and chicken in plain or fancy versions. The carefully considered wine list provides the perfect accompaniment to each dish. Looking for a little drama with dinner? The outdoor patio provides a striking setting with a stunning water feature, fire torches and an outdoor bar. For exquisite food and lively ambience, bring your friends, family and colleagues to Bella, where you can count on a beautiful experience.

10950 Club W Parkway, Suite 270, Blaine MN
(763) 746-9990
www.bellablaine.com

Salsa a la Salsa

At Salsa a la Salsa, Lorenzo Ariza and his wife, Elvia, have reinvented Mexican chic. Lorenzo and Elvia's children help serve the food, which is artfully presented, fresh and authentic. Yes, the chile relleno is real and the lettuce is romaine, but there is also character. Jicama, cactus and banana leaves are among the extra ingredients you may find on your plate. Lorenzo also enjoys incorporating Midwestern flavors into the mix, and his walleye tacos have become a local favorite. Located in the Midtown Global Market, Minneapolis's internationally-themed shopping district, the restaurant sports a friendly fireplace and exposed brick walls hung with vibrant artwork from the Trujillo Gallery. Lorenzo honed his restaurant skills in the demanding community of Beverly Hills for 24 years. With this experience, he was able to create the synthesis of cuisine, ambience and service he now offers at Salsa a la Salsa. Born in Mexico near the volcanoes Popocatépetl and Ixtacclhautl, Lorenzo began his career working at the heart of the California cuisine revolution. He learned to cut calories and add pizzazz to classic ethnic dishes at businesses that serve the Hollywood elite. Find out why this fun, inventive restaurant has *Mpls.St.Paul Magazine* and its readers talking. Stop by Salsa a la Salsa.

1420 Nicollet Avenue S,
Minneapolis MN
(612) 813-1970
www.salsaalasalsa.com

Rudolphs

The word for ribs around Minneapolis is Rudolphs. Since 1975, this restaurant has built its reputation on serving flavorful ribs hand-rubbed with spices and slow-cooked in a custom pit. Rudolphs has taken home top honors twice in the National Rib Cook-Off in Cleveland and has been voted the local favorite 17 times. Once you've tried the ribs, you'll want to come back to check out the barbecue chicken, burgers or other treats from the menu. There was no shortage of barbecue in the Twin Cities when Jimmy Theros lit the first flame in his pit more than 30 years ago. But Jimmy thought he could build something better than the typical barbecue joint. Why not open a full-fledged restaurant that brought a touch of class to the lip-smacking ribs? Ask folks who have eaten here why they like it so much, and they'll tell you that it's a nice place without being pretentious. You can dress up a bit or go casual with jeans and still feel comfortable. A Hollywood motif provides a little kitschy glamour. Rudolph Valentino, dashing legend of the silent screen, receives special honor. Take the family, bring a date or join your friends at Rudolphs, where the barbecue can't be beat.

1933 Lyndale Avenue S, Minneapolis MN
(612) 871-8969
www.rudolphsribs.com

Santorini Taverna & Grill

At Santorini Taverna & Grill, you are treated to famous Greek hospitality honed over the decades. Owner Tony Nicklow creates an authentic Mediterranean atmosphere at Santorini. "We wanted guests to picture the cobalt blue of the Aegean Sea with the sheer white cliffs", says Tony. The Nicklow family serves favorites such as traditional stuffed grape leaves and the flambéed *saganaki*—Greek casseri cheese that could almost make a meal alone. It's virtually impossible to have a bad meal at Santorini Taverna & Grill. The entrées include many Mediterranean specialties such as lamb moussaka, a Greek variation of lasagna. The Nicklows use only the freshest cuts of meat and fish as well as pastas. Santorini offers nightly specials, a pasta bar with more than 25 items and weekly half-priced bottles of wine. In just the right location, Santorini's has multiple rooms available for special events. Sunday brunch at Santorini's features incredible food as well as bottomless cocktails. At Santorini Taverna & Grill, the Nicklow family is proud to serve you the most amazing Greek food in the Twin Cities area.

9920 Wayzata Boulevard, St. Louis Park MN (952) 546-6722

The Sample Room

As its name implies, this Northeast Minneapolis restaurant excels at sampling. In the 1800s, the Sample Room rolled kegs over from Gluek Brewery for tastings. Today, you can sample from sophisticated combinations of veggies, meats, cheeses and seafood as well as flights of fine wine or flights of Scotch, bourbon or tequila. The laid-back atmosphere with indie tunes, imported beer on tap and servers in T-shirts and headscarves will make every day seem like a long, lovely summer night. The menu changes seasonally, so there's always something new to tempt you. Nosh on such delights as tangy baked goat cheese with oven-dried Roma tomatoes, crispy walleye strips, seared tuna with wasabi aioli or three-meat meatloaf. The house-made sausages and the seasonal oven-roasted vegetables are local favorites. Ordered in individual portions or combined to make platters, you can nibble on these samples or continue with sandwiches, salads, homemade entrées or desserts. The nightly specials are particularly attractive. Sunday brings pot roast, Monday pasta, Wednesday risotto and Thursday means a fresh fish dish. The Sample Room is an inviting space in a century-old landmark. Enjoy the outdoor patio or the comfortable contemporary interior in warm hues under a restored tin ceiling. The bar glows in the candlelight, creating an easy world of shared pleasure with friends and neighbors.

2124 Marshall Street, Minneapolis MN
(612) 789-0333
www.the-sample-room.com

Gianni's Steakhouse

Tom Webster opened Gianni's in the fall of 1996 following in the tradition of his father, Eddie Webster, a name in the restaurant industry in Minnesota for more than 60 years. Gianni's is a continuation of Eddie Webster's with an emphasis on the finest food and drink, a great classy relaxing atmosphere and a fun professional staff. Gianni's features great steaks, fresh seafood entrées, creative appetizers and side dishes, and a large wine and cocktail selection. Every entrée comes with Gianni's signature spun Caesar salad, prepared tableside. Diners can customize their salads by adding any or all of 10 extra ingredients. The enticing appetizer menu offers fare as varied as baked brie and escargot Bourguignonne. With nine steak options, each offering a host of variations, the choices for steak lovers are virtually limitless. The seafood menu is well-rounded, and the homemade pasta choices are equally inviting. Be sure to try the *papallete* (stuffed hash browns) or the Oprah spuds (sweet-cream potatoes with a mayo, horseradish and sour cream dressing). Gianni's is a perfect blend of old-fashioned steakhouse atmosphere and casual elegance. For entertainment to accompany your meal, a magician performs Thursday and Friday evenings and can be booked to perform tableside. Gianni's is a true Minnesota steakhouse: great food, relaxed atmosphere and superlative service. For an unforgettable evening, enjoy Gianni's Steakhouse.

635 E Lake Street, Wayzata MN
(952) 404-1100
www.giannis-steakhouse.com

Babalu

For Latin cuisine, live music and a chance to linger and enjoy your evening, come to Babalu in the Minneapolis Warehouse District. Owner and concept developer Terrence Large has created a hot spot where elegance and the eclectic meet. The culinary creations are five-star, the surroundings are opulent and the music is Latin and jazz. Menu selections include tapas, Cuban mojitos and entrees ranging from chicken and game to seafood and pork. Appetizers can be unique or traditional. There's always a house special, and less expensive selections are available for lunchtime in order to accommodate busy professionals. Babalu's spacious lounge area offers live entertainment every day of the week, with music from Spain, Cuba, Brazil and Puerto Rico. The gregarious bar staff is happy to serve you classic, retro or eccentric cocktails, as well as *cervezas* (beer) and wines from Chile, Argentina and Spain. Babalu exists to infuse you with Latin culture in a comfortable yet high-energy atmosphere. Make your reservation for dinner and immerse yourself in an authentic culinary adventure—feel the rhythm, taste the flavor, live the life.

800 Washington Avenue N, Minneapolis MN
(612) 746-3158
www.babalu.us

Trocaderos Nightclub & Restaurant

Trocaderos Nightclub & Restaurant in the trendy Warehouse District is both a fine dining establishment and one of Minneapolis's hottest entertainment spots. Troc's features five bars, balcony views of the 8,000-square-foot dance floor and live music on Thursdays, Fridays and Saturdays. A state-of-the-art sound system and hip décor provide a stylish, upscale vibe. The dining room, open for lunch and dinner, features a variety of delectable dishes ranging from coconut shrimp and calamari to fabulous steaks, seafood and pastas. Do you have an upcoming event? Troc's is your all-inclusive stop for parties of up to 1,400 guests offering in-house catering and private bars. The Boardroom, located on the top floor, features a private party space for groups of up to 100. This beautiful space offers a full bar, independent sound system, flat screen televisions, lounge areas, wireless Internet and a fireplace. Boardroom memberships can be purchased and feature VIP status at the door, preferred seating in the restaurant, pre-sale access to tickets for national acts and free private party access. Whether you're looking for a happy-hour gathering spot, an exciting dining and dance experience or private event space, come to the place that has it all, Trocaderos Nightclub & Restaurant.

107 3rd Avenue N, Minneapolis MN
(612) 465-0440
www.trocaderos.com

Brit's Pub

If you've been yearning for a plate of bangers and mash, or have a deep longing for a pint of stout, then jump in your lorry and point it toward the Nicollet Mall in Minneapolis, home of Brit's Pub. Brit has been serving the finest foods and spirits in true British style since 1990. This five-time Diners Choice Award-winning pub provides a warm and welcoming atmosphere that's ideal for a pint with your mates, an intimate meal with the missus or a knees-up with the chaps from work. With a famous Scotch and Port menu, a range of draught beers that would make a connoisseur weep with delight and a bevy of rich stouts, creamy ales, and crisp lagers, Brit's has what people want to drink. At Brit's Pub, the staff takes two things quite seriously: libations and lawn bowling. The Brit's Bowling Club currently has a ten-year waiting list for new teams who wish to join. This popular sport takes place outside on the roof of the pub, where there is room for over 300 guests to sit, eat, drink and watch the fun. Brit's Pub also hosts events throughout the year, such as the Bastille Day Celebration or the Summer Film Series that runs every Monday evening in August. Even without a passport, you can stop by the gift shop where you will find imported gifts such as glassware, custards, malt vinegar and other English gourmet goodies you can't pick up at the local market. Lift your spirits and drink to health at Brit's Pub.

1110 Nicollet Mall, Minneapolis MN
(612) 332-3908 *www.britspub.com*

Erté Restaurant and the Peacock Lounge

Rich hardwood floors offset the high ceilings trimmed with crown moldings and decorative tin inlays to create a feeling of comfortable elegance at Erté Restaurant and the Peacock Lounge. Chefs Josh McKenzie and Lissa Michalsky have created menus intended to tease and tempt your palate. Dry-aged Black Angus beef is the secret to the Erté's quality steaks and brisket. The restaurant is not only a Parisian steak salon, but also prides itself on such specialties as Bowstring Walleye and Star Prairie Trout. You can enjoy both lunch and dinner—lunch prices range from $5 to $10 and dinners from $15 to $25. The management recommends reservations for dinner. Erté offers wines from its extensive wine list either by the glass or by the bottle. The Peacock Lounge extends the warm feel of the dining room with a handcrafted zinc and mahogany bar along one wall. It would take many visits to try out all the martinis. Consider a martini with a hint of caramel and apple, chocolate or watermelon. On Friday and Saturday evenings, Erté features live music, everything from jazz to New Age instrumentals, always at a comfortable volume. Owner Patte Kraske invites you to enjoy fine dining, easy elegance and good company at Erté Restaurant and the Peacock Lounge in the heart of the historic Northeast Minneapolis Arts District.

323 13th Avenue NE, Minneapolis MN
(612) 623-4211
www.ertedining.com

View Restaurant & Lounge

Clean, modern lines, healthy portions and upscale menu options have diners talking about the View Restaurant & Lounge, on the first floor of the newly redesigned Calhoun Beach Club in Minneapolis. The restaurant is the only restaurant on Lake Calhoun, and as its name implies, it has spectacular views of the lake. Owner Farzad Freshtekhu opened the doors in 2006. Executive Chef Joe Gentile brings 30 years of restaurant experience to the contemporary menu of fresh, light offerings with Pan Asian and California influences. Seafood, gourmet pizzas and pasta are favorites. You'll also find such specialties as ahi tuna and stuffed portabella mushrooms for appetizers and such entrées as grilled pork tenderloin with pecan demiglaze and rosemary-encrusted filet mignon. Joe's menu changes frequently, and his desserts are worth your consideration. Try one of his specialty cobblers or see what dreams the Chocolate Dreams will inspire. You can enjoy lunch or dinner and a European-style brunch on the weekends. Beyond an excellent selection of beers and wine, look for such specialty drinks as the Blood Orange Martini and the signature Viewtini. In the summer, patio seating brings the views still closer. The restaurant can also accommodate private parties and small groups. For healthy dining in a scenic setting, come to the View Restaurant & Lounge.

Hubert's Bar & Grill

After a visit to Hubert's Bar & Grill, happy hour will never feel the same. Located near the Hubert H. Humphrey Metrodome, Hubert's is the watering hole of choice for Minnesota Twins and Vikings fans. Naturally, it's decorated with an extensive collection of sports memorabilia. On game days, fans pack the place to down pre-game drinks or celebrate after a big win. The beer washes down the signature burgers, homemade corn tortilla chips served with salsa and nachos with cheese, salsa and jalapenos. Hubert's offers several beers brewed right in Minnesota, plus a selection of domestic and imported lagers, ales and stouts. Those who can't catch the game across the street are welcome to settle in one of the roomy booths and watch it on one of the big-screen televisions. You don't have to be a sports nut to have a good time at Hubert's. It's known locally as a meeting place for businesspeople and caters to private parties of up to 300. The menu boasts fare that falls outside the sports-bar box, such as garden burgers, an array of fresh green salads and even Thai peanut pasta salad. Whether you're heading out to the game or just kicking back with good food and good company, Hubert's Bar & Grill is sure to fit the bill.

601 Chicago Avenue, Minneapolis MN
(612) 332-6062

Eli's Food & Cocktails

After 50 years, Eli's Food & Cocktails remains a popular gathering spot that puts special twists on traditional American favorites. With long hours and lots of menu variety, the Minneapolis restaurant is a good place to go both before and after a show. It holds a four-hour happy hour, from 3 to 7 pm on weeknights, making it an ideal place to stop after work. It's classy enough for a special dinner date. Eli's seats 70 people and provides a menu with everything from Vienna dogs and burgers to filet mignon. Other menu favorites provided by Executive Chef Jeff Webber include a steak sandwich, topped with blue cheese crumbles, sautéed onions and mushrooms, and Eli's Mac & Cheese, a tasty mix of parmesan, mozzarella, Asiago and American cheese, topped with *panko* bread crumbs and baked with penne pasta. Eli's has a reputation for its

honey-soy wings with *sriracha aioli* and jumbo lump crab cakes, served over sautéed spinach with a spicy mustard mayo. Tai Ipsen and John McKenney took over Eli's in January of 2005 and continue the long-standing tradition of good service, food and cocktails. Eli's is open until 2 am every night with food available until 1 am. For outstanding food and drink in a neighborhood bar and grill setting, visit Eli's Food & Cocktails.

1225 Hennepin Avenue, Minneapolis MN
(612) 332-9997
www.elisfoodandcocktails.com

Harvey's Bar & Grill

Once you've seen that Harvey's Bar & Grill does a good lunch, you'll want to come back for dinner, perhaps for the full rack of ribs on Tuesday or the homemade sloppy Joe's on Wednesday. After dinner, there's no need to move on for a little nightlife. Harvey's features live acoustic sets every Thursday night and a DJ and dance floor on Friday and Saturday nights. Entertainment on other nights includes karaoke and Texas Hold 'Em. Nightly specials on tap beer and mixed drinks add to the party atmosphere. Happy hour at this upscale but casual spot in the warehouse district is 180 minutes of discounted drinks and half-price appetizers to put you in a relaxed

mood. The clock starts ticking on the great deals at four in the afternoon. Don't be surprised if you become a regular. If you do, you'll appreciate the consistently great food and the comfortable prices. With lots of friendly people, plus six televisions broadcasting the daily news and the sports action, Harvey's is practically the neighborhood living room. Whether you're looking for a great place for lunch, dinner, happy hour or after-hours entertainment, consider Harvey's your all-purpose bar and grill.

106 N 3rd Street, Minneapolis MN
(612) 343-5930
www.harveysmpls.com

Rockwoods Grill & Backwater Bar

Old-fashioned service with a smile, favorite foods both old and new, and spacious comfortable surroundings create a winning recipe at Rockwoods Grill & Backwater Bar. The sight of whole chickens turning on the rotisserie, flames from the sauté chefs in the display kitchen and the wood burning in the wood-fired oven start your mouth watering as you enter the restaurant. The menu combines comfy classics such as slow-cooked pot roast and old-fashioned chicken pot pie with an array of wood-fired selections such as the popular cedar-planked salmon. There are also several varieties of hand-tossed wood-fired pizzas and pastas to choose from, not to mention an indulgent 32-ounce Porterhouse steak. All dishes are served to you by a fast and friendly staff. The warm atmosphere at Rockwoods makes it an ideal place for family meals. Children as well as the young-at-heart will delight in the G-scale model trains—the circus train that actually runs through the dinning room, the freight train that pours a beer as it goes through the bar or the dueling coal trains that turn on the power plant in the lobby. If you're looking for a late night bite or a drink with friends, try the Backwater Bar. It has an impressive selection of beers and cocktails along with happy hour twice daily, seven days a week. Rockwoods Banquet & Conference Center is the area's premier location for all of life's events. Whether it is a wedding reception or a corporate business meeting, the catering staff is eager to assist you with all of the details. Come to Rockwoods Grill & Backwater Bar for smiling service, fabulous food and drink.

9100 Quaday Avenue NE, Otsego MN
(763) 441-6322 or (763) 441-6375 (banquets)
www.rockwoodsgrill.com

The Malt Shop Restaurant

The Malt Shop Restaurant has offered family fun dining since 1973. It has everything you would expect from a malt shop and much, much more. You can pair juicy burgers and specialty vegetarian entrees with your choice of more than 30 flavored malts. The restaurant makes all the malts with premium ice cream, and they draw rave reviews from customers. The malts come in seasonal and specialty flavors, such as apple cider and fig banana. Fresh fruits add a luscious kick to the fruit malts. Stained-glass windows and wooden booths enhance the aura of a bygone era, and the malts are served frosty-cold in old-fashioned oversized metal malt tins. The Malt Shop makes all of its soups and salad dressings from scratch using the finest ingredients. The hamburgers are made daily from fresh ground beef. Great new menu items include the wild Alaskan salmon dinner, the Jamaican jerk chicken sandwich and the Aegean turkey burger. The Malt Shop offers tasty vegetarian entrees such as ratatouille and the incomparable mushroom and spinach lasagna. You can wrap up the meal with The Malt Shop's own cheesecake or carrot cake. The restaurant is a heaven for kids, with games on the children's menu and a monthly coloring contest. For a great lunch or dinner that will bring back memories, stop by The Malt Shop Restaurant.

809 W 50th Street, Minneapolis MN
(612) 824-1352
www.themaltshoprestaurant.com

The Independent

The Independent, a hip place for dining and cocktails at the Calhoun Square Mall, has been making its mark since 2003 with a martini list named Best in the Twin Cities. The Independent has even earned praise in *Cosmopolitan*. A huge list of appetizers greets patrons during happy hour, which actually lasts for four hours, except on Wednesdays when it lasts even longer. The full menu offers American bistro fare with some European and Asian influences. Hand-patted burgers and the surf 'n turf are popular. The seafood is fresh, and everything is homemade, right down to the dressing on your salad. Vegetarians find a bounty of delicious menu choices.

The Independent gives you two reasons Sunday should be your favorite day of the week: brunch early in the day and the Alaskan king crab feast in the evening. Patrons mingle well into the night, enjoying local DJs and the lounge vibe. The kitchen stays open until 2 am. Owner James Nelson is a proud Minnesota native, and the Independent is part of the community. "Support your independent everything," he urges. Join the rest of the free spirits that gather there.

3001 Hennepin Avenue, Suite A201, Minneapolis MN
(612) 378-1905
www.theindependent-uptown.com

Lucia's Restaurant

Lucia's Restaurant opened on Valentine's Day in 1985 as a 36-seat bistro. Today, it has grown into an intimate 72-seat neighborhood restaurant still committed to a weekly changing menu that focuses on the highest quality seasonal ingredients. Over the years Lucia's has earned a reputation as one of the top chef-driven restaurants in the Midwest, but its mission remains the same, to offer amazing food for a reasonable price in an environment that is simple and friendly. The atmosphere at Lucia's has an elegance and warmth that is unpretentious and inviting whether you are having a romantic dinner for two or a casual night out with friends. Friends of the restaurant say you can read a Lucia's menu and tell what month of the year it is. The wine list is short yet sophisticated and changes weekly to pair with the entrée selections. The service

is polished yet informal and friendly. In 1991, the second addition, Lucia's Wine Bar, was added to give customers a place to have a glass of wine while they wait for a table in the restaurant. This comfortable, cozy and inviting space has since developed its own clientele. Lucia's also has recently added Lucia's To Go, located right next to the wine bar, where you can eat-in or grab something on the run. If you haven't already, stop in and check out the most recent addition to the Lucia's family.

1432 W 31st Street, Minneapolis MN
(612) 825-1026
www.lucias.com

Lord Fletcher's Old Lake Lodge

For almost 40 years, owner Bill Naegele has been the host of Lord Fletcher's Old Lake Lodge on Lake Minnetonka, providing the area with exceptional food, wine, service and fun. Year-round you can put together an unforgettable get-together at Lord Fletcher's for gatherings of 10 to 180. The establishment has won national awards for its fabulous regional Minnesota cuisine, outstanding wine selection and individualized service. These include the *Wine Spectator* Award of Excellence and the coveted Dirona Award. Lord Fletcher's has seven different dining rooms, each with its own flair, flavor, personality and seasonal specialty. In the summer, ask anybody in Lake Minnetonka where to go for a good time. They'll tell you it's either the Wharf, Granddaddy's or the Paddle Club at Lord Fletcher's. The Wharf is a huge deck the size of a football field right on the lake complete with boat slips, so you can dock and dine in the sun. It's only open in summer, when you can hear live music on Saturdays and Sundays after a long day and a good catch out on the lake. The rest of Lord Fletcher's consists of the Chart Room, Wine Cellar, Old Lake Room and the Old English Pub. They are all available for enjoyment throughout the year, and feature dining rooms with stone fireplaces and beautiful lake decor. Summer or winter, come to Lord Fletcher's Old Lake Lodge and enjoy beautiful Lake Minnetonka in all its splendor.

3746 Sunset Drive, Spring Park MN
(952) 471-8513
www.lordfletchers.com

Town Talk Diner

The new owners who bought Town Talk Diner in 2006 intended to serve seriously upscale food, but they wanted to leave a little of the past behind. Aaron Johnson, Tim Niver and Chef David Vlach therefore retained the neon and the retro décor while they turned the old counter into a bar. They still serve burgers and first-class pancakes, but most of the taste combinations are far from standard fare. Vlach excels at daring combinations, such as the sweet potato risotto, or frickles, lightly battered pickles served with a mustard dill sauce. A forest mushroom tart marries caramelized onions, roasted mushrooms and fontina cheese, while a chocolate ganache tart makes a finale out of white chocolate mousse and poached pears. A carefully chosen wine list promises to add a perfect complement to your meal. The beverage list also includes beer, classic cocktails and innovative liqueur-based malts and floats. A reviewer for *Minneapolis Monthly* described a fish special featuring poached halibut as embodying "the deftness of haute cuisine and the emotional heft of Mom's chicken soup." For foods that are often organic and always imaginative, visit Town Talk Diner.

2707½ E Lake Street, Minneapolis MN
(612) 722-1312
www.towntalkdiner.com

Victor's 1959 Café

Victor's 1959 Café is a Cuban oasis in South Minneapolis. Victor moved from Cuba in 1961. His father was a chef and taught Victor everything he knows about good, authentic Cuban cooking. Then Victor taught his Greek-Cypriot wife Niki how to cook the Cuban specialties, and the legacy continues. Niki and Victor take great pleasure in sharing these special foods with you. They also love to talk with you about Cuba. With only eleven tables—a coveted handful—you'll likely get to meet at least one of the two during your dining experience. A sign at the front entrance confirms that *you are now leaving the American sector* and when you enter this most unusual little café, you will understand. The authentic Cuban memorabilia on the walls keeps you occupied as you wait in line or while sitting at one of the tables. The décor is bright and colorful and, combined with the Cuban music and friendly service, you will feel like you have found a little piece of Havana in Minneapolis. The writing is on the walls, literally. Ask for a Sharpie and you can contribute your own impressions of the café on the walls. Breakfast is as popular as dinner at this authentic Cuban restaurant. The colorful official café T-shirts are *muy* popular and loved for their clever Cuban-themed slogans. Check the website for breakfast, lunch and dinner menus. Then make your way over to this gem to taste the delightful food of Cuba. It's located on the corner of 38th Street and Grand Avenue.

3756 Grand Avenue S, Minneapolis MN
(612) 827-8948
www.victors1959cafe.com

Ted Cook's
19th Hole Bar-B-Que

The steamed-up windows tell passersby that there's some real cooking going on inside Ted Cook's 19th Hole Bar-B-Que. If you've got a hankering for cherry and hickory-smoked spare ribs, beef ribs, chicken and rib tips, then you are about to enter paradise. One local expert calls the barbecue here "the real deal." As for the sauce, a connoisseur issues this advisory: "If you like it hot, try the medium, and, if you dare, ask for the hot—it's wicked." If sauce isn't your thing, yet another pro says, "Don't be afraid to order your ribs dry, because their crusty mantle has all the great charred pork flavor that makes memorable barbecue dreams." Ted Cook's consistently ranks among the top spots for barbecue in Minneapolis. Some claim it's the very best. "Just the way God intended," gushes one reviewer. As one of the oldest African American-owned businesses in Minneapolis, Ted Cook's offers a list of side dishes that is synonymous with soul food, including collard greens, black-eyed peas and red beans and rice. For dessert, there's peach cobbler and sweet potato pie. All food is take-out at Ted Cook's, so you'll need a place to eat your food once it's in your hands. If you choose to eat in the open, you might be amazed at how quickly people stop and want to become your friend. Try the lip-smacking barbecue at Ted Cook's 19th Hole, a Minneapolis tradition since 1968.

2814 E 38th Street, Minneapolis MN
(612) 721-2023

Cottage Chicks

Cottage chic is one of the hottest decorating trends today. It creates an inviting atmosphere that makes you want to hang out with friends over a warm cup of tea and home-baked cookies amid overstuffed upholstery, soft florals and painted woods. It mixes new and worn, elegance and ease, but above all, it is individual, cozy and comfortable—and on display at Cottage Chicks. If you've got a penchant for cottage chic, Kim Banyard and Kaye Benson have it all for you at their store. This quaint shop reflects its surroundings: it is nestled in the charming old village of Deephaven on Lake Minnetonka, one of the largest glacial lakes in the state. "We seek out new home décor and gifts as well as antiques that will bring a feeling of a simpler time back to our customers," says Kim. Cottage Chicks has painted furniture, primitives, new and vintage linens, hooked rugs, barkcloth, garden items and French soaps. Feast your eyes on the vintage jewelry, candles, clocks, prints and gifts. The shop carries treasures in all price ranges, so there's something for everyone on your list. If the holiday season is closing in, Cottage Chicks has a huge variety of vintage and vintage-style Christmas décor. Both Kim and Kaye strive for that cottage feeling in everything they buy, whether it is old or new. Stop by and soak it in.

18128 Minnetonka Boulevard, Deephaven MN
(952) 476-1565
www.cottagechicksmn.com

Creative Kidstuff

Creative Kidstuff in Minneapolis is a store with a mission, and it's not just a mission to sell toys. It's a mission to save childhood. To get a sense of the passion and intelligence behind this true gem of a business, log on to its website and read the blog posted by the store's founder, Cynthia Gerdes. "I'm a toy store owner who loves to sell toys," Gerdes says. "But I was once also a teacher, and I know early childhood experts are shaking their heads in dismay. The importance of play in development cannot be underestimated. We need to balance our nine-year-olds' experiences with play. Our kids need to be free a little longer. Don't let your kids miss the joy of books, the delight of beating a parent at Scrabble, the satisfaction of finishing a sophisticated beading art project or the creativity of figuring out, by themselves, what to do when they're bored." Creative Kidstuff, which is billed as a hands-on, do-touch store, is packed floor-to-ceiling with toys, books, art supplies and more. It is staffed by teachers, parents and kind-hearted people who like kids. They have won praise and more than 50 awards from admirers such as *Minnesota Parent, Minnesota Women's Press, City Pages* and *Child* magazine. The shop steers clear of violent toys. It doesn't sell Barbies. It sells toys that last and that live up to the claims on the packaging. This is a store that every parent in America should know about, so pass the word. There are five stores in the Twin Cities area, and six stores in airports around the country. Make it a point to visit one of their locations, and share the store's web address with every parent you know.

4313 Upton Avenue S, Minneapolis MN
(612) 927-0653 or (800) 353-0710
www.creativekidstuff.com

Blanc de Blanc, Ltd.

Located near the shores of beautiful Lake Minnetonka in Wayzata, Blanc de Blanc, Ltd. was established in 1988 to express the charm and fascination of all things white. Blanc de Blanc is a refreshingly unique and distinctly exquisite shopping experience that is celebrated for its tasteful style. Each item in the shop is chosen to add beauty and distinction to your lifestyle and home. Blanc de Blanc's window displays always draw the attention of pedestrians. Upon entering, you are struck by the many textures and by the array of items in white and cream, with splashes of color to intrigue and entice. Eclectic dinnerware, attractive serving pieces, vases and frames abound. A playful mix of women's and children's clothing and accessories can be found in every price range. Luxurious robes, sleepwear, throws and aromatic essences delight your senses and soothe your soul. There's also that one-of-a-kind specialty item or collectible. Holidays are especially festive with gifts and whimsies that are sure to bring joy to every celebration. Blanc de Blanc offers the utmost in attentive customer service and provides unrivaled attention to detail. The shop is an favorite among women, but everyone has discovered that a gift or personal luxury from Blanc de Blanc is a pleasant delight and well-received treasure.

691 Lake Street, Wayzata MN
(952) 473-8275
www.blancdeblancltd.com

Whymsy

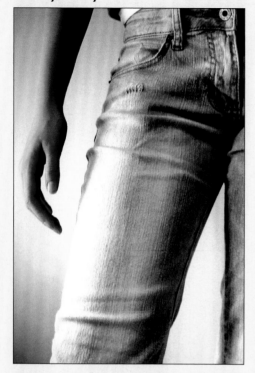

The mother-daughter team of Jannine and Lindsey Primus work hard to make Whymsy a fun place to shop. Playfulness is the general mood at this cute store, where the owners call themselves purveyors of seriously whymsical nonessentials that you can't live without. Located in Edina's seriously upscale Galleria shopping mall, Whymsy is brimming with creative accessories and clothing for women, including Tummy Tuck jeans and Sweet Romance jewelry. Baby gifts and clothing from Bunnies by the Bay are other popular items, along with seasonal décor and gifts. Jannine and Lindsey bring everything together in one attractive package, adding a focus on customer service. Their efforts begin with clever window displays that draw in the curious. How does a store with this much merchandise manage not to feel cluttered? The answer is that the owners have taken care in arranging it all to provide an easy flow throughout the sales area. Have some serious fun shopping at Whymsy.

3360 Galleria W 70th Street, Edina MN
(952) 924-4176
www.whymsy.com

Nihonto.us: Japanese Swords and Tsuba

In Japan, and increasingly throughout the world, the Japanese sword and its fitting are recognized as high art. The beauty and utility of the Japanese sword is unparalleled. Its design has adapted through time in response to military and social changes. Andrew Quirt has collected Japanese swords and their accoutrements for more than 40 years and has been a full-time dealer in antique Japanese militaria for the past 30 years. Through his constantly changing website, Nihonto.us, Quirt offers a panoply of swords and fittings. The selection of swords dates from the Heian period (794 to 1185) to modern times. Fittings range from *Nambokucho jidai* (1333

to 1393) to the 20th century. Quirt served on the board of directors of the Japanese Sword Society of the U.S. for eight years. He has been a member of the *Nihon Bijitsu Token Hozon Kyokai* (NBTHK), the Society for the Preservation of the Japanese Art Sword, Tokyo, for 30 years. He was vice president in charge of the Americas for the European section of the NBTHK for three years. In 2002, he helped form an American branch of the NBTHK and is now on its board of directors. At Nhinto.us you'll find a varied selection catering to differing tastes and budgets. All items are authentic and many are illustrated in Japanese texts. Whether you are a collector or just curious, visit Nihonto.us.

Edina MN (952) 920-0471
www.nihonto.us

Midtown Global Market

Midtown Global Market celebrates ethnic diversity with products from 50 small business owners brought together in a bazaar-like setting. The Market opened in the spring of 2006, and brought new life to a once-vacant Sears building. Here, you can sample Mexican baked goods, discover Tibetan jewelry and pick up a fresh bouquet of flowers for your home. You can even get a massage or have a suit altered by a tailor. The market is a place of discovery, where neighbors learn about each other's cultural backgrounds. You can rent space for a special event or sit back and enjoy free live entertainment. The Midtown Global Market is truly a unique experience. No passport is needed, so there's no reason to miss it.

920 E Lake Street, Minneapolis MN
(612) 872-4041
www.midtownglobalmarket.org

Photo by Fernando Weberich

La Veranda Floral

La Veranda Floral in Minneapolis has been providing the community with fresh, quality flowers and exemplary service since 1999. This charming shop carries a full array of fresh flowers, green plants, silks and dried arrangements that are sure to please everyone. A full service European-style floral design service offers patrons more that 24 years of total floral experience, ensuring that every flower and bouquet you order is picture perfect. Owner Sharon Knutson and her friendly, cheerful and knowledgeable staff are always on hand to offer suggestions or help you pick the ideal gift. La Veranda Floral is also a full-service event specialist which can help you on your special occasion, no matter how large or small the event. Another special service that La Veranda offers is cemetery maintenance. For a modest annual fee, La Veranda will maintain your loved one's gravesite, replant grass and provide fresh bouquets or wreaths thrice yearly. Delivery is available for both domestic and international destinations; fees vary. If you would like to say you care with more than flowers, La Veranda carries a choice selection of designer gift baskets that can be delivered with your flowers. Whether you are searching for a corporate gift for your prized assistant or that extra special bouquet for your extra special someone, take your floral needs to La Veranda Floral, where the staff excels in fine floral design.

3001 Hennepin Avenue, Minneapolis MN (612) 825-1991 *www.laverandaflowers.com*

Northland Poster Collective

The creative folks at Northland Poster Collective take to heart the words of Tom Joad, a character in John Steinbeck's *The Grapes of Wrath*. Joad vows to be there in spirit wherever the battle for justice is fought. The Northland collective applies its artistic talents to making posters, T-shirts and bumper stickers that raise awareness for any number of causes. Since 1979 it has supported justice for immigrants, workers and underrepresented ethnic groups and has worked to promote peace, education and a clean environment. Co-owner Ricardo Levins Morales is himself a prolific poster artist. His work is featured at the store and in the collective's popular catalog along with that of many other talented and committed individuals, such as Betsy Raasch-Gilman, Richard Kees and Janna Schneider. The items typically use wisdom and humor to get their message across. What teacher wouldn't enjoy a bumper sticker proclaiming No Teacher Left Behind? Who can object to a T-shirt that says Food for Everyone? Many items pay tribute to past leaders, such as Martin Luther King, Cesar Chavez and Mahatma Gandhi. All T-shirts sold at Northland Poster Collective are union made and come in a variety of sizes to fit even the infant and child activist. Find support for your cause at Northland Poster Collective.

1613 E Lake Street, Minneapolis MN
(612) 721-2273
www.northlandposter.com

Down in the Valley

Whether you love pop, rock, rap or jazz, Down in the Valley carries the tunes that appeal to you. Steve Hyland has been selling cool music and hip merchandise at his Golden Valley shop since 1972. You can also experience in-store performances here. Now with shops in Wayzata, Maple Grove and Crystal, Down in the Valley is sure to be located near you. Need a lava lamp to rock 'n' roll you back into the 1960s or a Grateful Dead T-shirt? Down in the Valley has it, along with body jewelry, collectibles and a selection of books, including the *Corky Rock-n-Roll Biography*, that can only be found Down in the Valley. Customers can find used vinyl, CDs and video games to round out their collections. Steve started by working out of his basement, where he

sold hundreds of items for national vendors—from waterbeds to LPs. Over the years, he focused in on music and the specialty products that define individual lifestyles. He's become the largest independent store of this type in the Minneapolis area, with a website for still more convenience, but he still stands by a level of service not found in chain stores and seeks to create a comfortable and enjoyable shopping experience for his customers. For music and gifts from a store that understands what you want, visit Down in the Valley.

8020 Olson Memorial Highway, Golden Valley MN
(763) 544-0033
www.downinthevalley.com

Heritage II— Scandinavian & British Isles Shops

Heritage II has served the Minneapolis/St. Paul metro area with Scandinavian, Celtic and British gifts, tableware and apparel for more than 32 years from two old lake villages, now suburbs: White Bear Lake to the east and Excelsior to the west. You'll find a range of gifts, from Orrefors crystal vases and bowls to Kosta Boda art glass from Sweden. Discover fun gifts such as Guinness décor from Ireland, plus trolls, *tomtes* and Dala horses from Scandinavia. You'll find flags, caps, tees and books. The shop has traditional Norwegian and Irish sweaters and, for denim folks, contemporary Original Blues sweaters from England. Come visit Heritage II, open seven days a week.

50 Water Street, Excelsior MN
(952) 474-1231
www.heritageii.com

Patina

With its finger on the pulse of trends, Patina has something for everyone and every occasion. When you open the door, you're treated to an eclectic blend of fragrance and fashion. Hip housewares range from stylish furniture and luxurious chandeliers to kitschy kitchen gadgets and inspirational quotables. Don't be afraid to laugh out loud—you won't be alone. Patina has a knack for offering its customers the latest in humorous merchandise. You can also indulge yourself or someone you love in a wide array of bath and body products that soothe your senses and relieve your stress. Patina is known for its extraordinary jewelry collection, with a price range that will make anyone smile. Other Patina favorites are its wide selection of office goods, from the practical to the hysterical, plus a stationery selection that will have you sending your sentiments with style. The first Patina opened in 1993, and you can now visit any of four Patina locations. All are known for high-quality customer service. This is a shop that offers Accessories for a Good Life.

5001 Bryant Avenue S, Minneapolis MN (612) 821-9315
1009 W Franklin Avenue, Minneapolis MN (612) 872-0880
2305 18th Avenue NE, Minneapolis MN (612) 788-8933
2057 Ford Parkway, St. Paul MN (651) 695-9955
www.patinastores.com

Let's Cook

Each season gives Margaret McDonald any number of reasons to prepare a special meal at her cooking classroom and cookware store in Minneapolis. The place is called Let's Cook, and Margaret typically greets the New Year there with a demonstration cooking class for those determined to break their resolution and for those who didn't bother to make one in the first place. The Chinese New Year provides Margaret and her guest chefs with a chance to conduct a hands-on class in Hong Kong-style cuisine. Let's Cook will inspire you to lick your lips whenever you glance at the calendar. In addition to presenting the cooking classes, Let's Cook sells knives, pots and everything else you need to cook like a magician at home. Let's Cook also hosts private events that bring folks together in its state-of-the art kitchen. Whether or not your group chooses to participate in the cooking, you can be assured that many culinary delights and a truly memorable experience await you. All the staffing, equipment and ingredients are provided if you do wish to participate. Imagine preparing a smoked duck salad, a pork tenderloin in dried cherry-red wine and a chocolate and cashew tart, and then sitting down and enjoying it all with everyone who helped. These events are popular not only with families but with gourmet clubs, book clubs and office teams as well. What will Margaret be cooking for Cinco de Mayo or Halloween? Drop by Let's Cook and find out.

330 E Hennepin Avenue, Minneapolis MN
(612) 623-9700 *www.letscook.com*

Manitoba

Debra Gangelhoff and Jim Bates started out working for a small nursery and gift shop. Together, they came up with the idea for Manitoba, a shop that offers much more than gifts. The elegant and understated store carries affordable, handcrafted items for visitors to take home to friends and family members. Manitoba provides the perfect place to while away an afternoon browsing through a charming collection of products, which range from plants and home accessories to hats, handbags, linens and bath and body products. Local artisans craft many of the other items you'll see. Offering jewelry, candles, cards, sweaters and beautifully crafted journals, this shop really has something for everyone. With ever-changing displays of local artists' work, Manitoba has earned itself a place of honor in the community. Come to Manitoba—the shop is a lot closer than the province—where you'll be sure to find a treasure to take home for yourself or a loved one.

306 Manitoba Avenue, Wayzata MN
(952) 476-5856
www.manitobagifts.com

Something Different

Sitting at the confluence of the Rum and Mississippi Rivers is the historic town of Anoka, where visitors can come to enjoy a bounty of recreational opportunities. These include outdoor adventures, skating at the Anoka Ice Arena and shopping in fabulous stores such as Something Different on East Main. This delightful shop opened in 1992 and is currently owned and operated by Ann Packer-Smith, who took over the shop from Cheryl Karpen, the original owner and a popular writer. Karpen's wonderful book series Eat Your Peas is available at Something Different, along with a multitude of other whimsical and charming gifts for all ages. The store offers visitors and the community a gathering place where folks can come together to socialize and talk while they examine and shop the stores latest inventory. Together with the gift books, cards and complimentary gift wrap, Something Different also offers a terrific selection of specialty gifts and collectibles, such as hand-painted wine and martini glasses from the Talk by Leslie collection and Demdaco Willow Tree figurines. The staff's hands-on, old-fashioned customer service gives patrons a refreshing change from the hustle and impersonal service of some department and chain stores and makes customers feel like friends. Whether you are searching for the perfect hostess gift or something special for your someone special, you are sure to find it at Something Different.

209 E Main Street, Anoka MN
(763) 421-2255
www.somethingdifferentanoka.com

Antiques Riverwalk

Photo by Brandon Powell

Since 1985, Antiques Riverwalk has been a destination for people seeking 19th and early 20th century American and European furniture, Oriental rugs, lighting and other fine antiques. Its selection of silver, jewelry and original sculptures and paintings is also strong. *Mpls.St.Paul Magazine* has named the business the best in the Twin Cities. The world of antiques includes all kinds of people, but few are as well-educated in the field as Charley Bathke, owner of Antiques Riverwalk. Current president of the Minnesota Antiques Dealers Association, Bathke knows quality. The many dealers who share Bathke's 6,000 square feet of show space meet his high standards. The booths in which the dealers display their goods are like rooms and are eye-catching marvels of design. Advertising stylists and theater companies in need of authentic period pieces for their sets rent from Antiques Riverwalk. Hollywood actors and other celebrities have shopped its booths. Located in the Warehouse District, Antiques Riverwalk also offers related services such as consigning and appraising, and conducts estate sales. You can scour the flea markets hoping to find a hidden gem, but be sure to go to Antiques Riverwalk, where you will always find treasures.

210 3rd Avenue N, Minneapolis MN
(612) 339-9352
www.antiquesriverwalk.net

42nd Street Gifts

For whimsical jewelry, unusual cards and original, sometimes humorous gifts, there's no shop like 42nd Street Gifts. Owner Annie Hines and manager Sue Perry have lived in South Minneapolis their whole lives and care about the community. Their love of where they live and what they do shows in the wide selection of fanciful items featured in their store. Here, you can pick out a pair of silk slippers or browse the broad array of cards for all occasions. You can

sample a box of chocolates or chat with some of the loyal customers Hines and Perry have befriended over the years. The two have worked hard to provide a quaint gathering place in their neighborhood, a respite from busy everyday life. Whether your taste is quirky or down-to-earth, there is something for you here. Stop by 42nd Street Gifts. You'll be sure to find exactly what you're looking for, and you may be pleasantly surprised to spot something you never knew you wanted.

4165 Minnehaha Avenue,
Minneapolis MN
(612) 721-4151
www.42ndstreetgifts.com

Brighton Collectibles

Brighton Collectibles showcases the Brighton line of personal and home accessories. This diverse assortment of products is known for its signature silver embellishments. The mother and daughter team of Ruth Jackson and Gini Rowland opened the Bloomington shop in 1998. After several moves and name changes, the store settled into a permanent location at Bloomington's Mall of America in 2000. The shop is one of only a few privately owned Brighton Collectibles stores. The expansive line of women's accessories includes casually chic denim jackets, silver jewelry and watches, plus fashionable and functional eyewear. Brighton's handbags, belts and

shoes, from Italy and Brazil, feature decorative silverwork and sumptuous leathers. You can coordinate everything in your purse with the shop's handbag accessories, which include checkbook covers, mini photo albums and cell phone cases, as well as card cases and passport covers. You'll find rugged men's belts and wallets here, too. Locating a gift becomes a pleasure when your choices include silver pens, a silver jewelry box or glassware with silver bases. Even the luxurious bath and body products are packaged with silver accents. This intimate boutique offers the kind of exceptional service that turns first time shoppers into loyal customers. For beautiful accessories meant to last, visit Brighton Collectibles.

224 South Avenue, Bloomington MN
(952) 854-8043 or (877) 525-8043
www.brighton.com

Ingebretsen's Scandinavian Center

Since 1921, Ingebretsen's Scandinavian Center has been providing traditional Scandinavian gifts and food to the Twin Cities and establishing its reputation as a connection to Scandinavian tradition and culture. Family-owned and operated for more than 85 years, Ingebretsen's is more than a store. In a part of the United States that is known for Scandinavian traditions, Ingebretsen's stands out as a local institution and a connection to another place and time. Ingebretsen's is the Twin Cities' oldest retail establishment dedicated exclusively to Scandinavian and Nordic products, including wares produced locally in the Scandinavian tradition. Founded by Norwegian immigrant Charles Ingebretsen, the current generation of the family and the friendly, knowledgeable staff are dedicated to providing everything Scandinavian. You'll find lingonberries, pickled herring, pickled beets and chocolates. The shop is never without potato sausage, meatballs, lefse, lutefisk or Scandinavian cheeses. For the holidays and cookie baking, it carries marzipan, cardamom and all the utensils for traditional foods. You'll find Nordic sweaters and knitting yarns and quality Danish needlework. If a gift of lasting value is on your list, you might consider fine Swedish glassware, traditional or contemporary jewelry from Norway or stylish tableware from the Nordic nation of Finland. The excellent craftspeople of Scandinavia are well represented and the selection of books and music is unparalleled. Whether you visit in person or just want to leisurely drop in on-line, Ingebretsen's can make you feel like you've traveled to the old country.

1601 E Lake Street, Minneapolis MN
(612) 729-9333 or (800) 279-9333
www.ingebretsens.com

Al's Farm Toys

Model tractors, trucks and other tough, old-fashioned farm machinery in miniature are the specialties at Al's Farm Toys, located in the Mall of America in Bloomington. Owner Al Batzel proudly points out that his selection "represents real America." His store has been celebrating the Midwest's farming traditions since 1978. Anyone who appreciates models will be delighted by the selection. Al's Farm Toys has memorabilia such as T-shirts, playing cards, gloves, caps, tin signs and more by John Deere, Farmall, Moline, Oliver and Allis Chalmers. Al's Farm Toys stocks farm animals by Schliech and horses from Breyer for collecting or just playing. It has a large selection of Cow Parade and Painted Ponies figurines by Westland. It continues the American theme with model cars, ranging from the popular Dukes of Hazard collection to larger, more advanced models from Corgi, ERTL and the Franklin Mint. Al's Farm Toys also carries model ships, helicopters and military airplanes. The shop has a large selection of construction toys and cranes from Caterpillar, Conrad, NZG and Bruder. It also has plenty of cement trucks, snow plows, roll-offs, semis with box trailers, reefers and lowboy trailers from the world-famous Tonkin and First Gear. For classic American toys, come to Al's Farm Toys in the Mall of America or visit it online.

370 W Market, Bloomington MN
(952) 858-9139
www.alsfarmtoys.com

CorAzon

No matter how sophisticated or jaded you are, you will find something at CorAzon that will induce you to take it home. Susan Zdon was warned that she would starve to death if she pursued her dream of blending the best of a multifaceted gift shop with an art gallery. Fortunately, she ignored the warnings and opened CorAzon, a fresh and exciting boutique gift shop and gallery that has had remarkable success. Susan believes in supporting local talent, and nearly half of the goods in the shop are created or made by artists and artisans from the surrounding area. The beautiful exposed-brick walls display artwork along with imported and regional crafts, cards, books, candles, homegrown bath and body products, and clothing. Susan knows the story and the artist behind every painting, sculpture, book, earring and bar of soap because she carefully chooses only those items that she would select for herself. She carries an unusual and universally

appealing assortment of items such as mittens and hats made from recycled cashmere sweaters and purses made—believe it or not—from tires. Susan holds Gallery Grooves exhibitions and conducts seminars in the back of her converted warehouse shop. For a truly diverse experience of the local art scene that takes eclectic to a whole new level, visit CorAzon.

204 Washington Avenue, Minneapolis MN
(612) 333-1662
4646 E Lake Street, Minneapolis MN
(612) 276-0198
www.corazononline.com

The Country Look in Antiques

You can find the charm of Colonial New England in the quaint village of Excelsior on beautiful Lake Minnetonka. The Country Look in Antiques enjoys a solid reputation for legitimate antiques of superb quality. The store offers space to knowledgeable dealers, and most of them have been with the Country Look for years. The mix is eclectic, but never cluttered. The shop features primitives, painted and refinished furniture, lamps and lighting. You'll see Oriental, loomed and braided rugs, plus quilts and folk art. A wonderful selection of lake lodge and cabin décor, along with vintage English, sports and nautical memorabilia are also available. Widely considered one of the top antique stores in the state, The Country Look invites you to come visit, browse, and enjoy warm conversation and some of the Twin Cities' finest antiques and vintage collectables. The Country Look in Antiques— 28 Years and Still Setting the Standard.

240 Water Street, Excelsior MN
(952) 474-0050

live, laugh, love

As its name implies, the shop named live, laugh, love encourages life, laughter and loving. Owners Kevin and Kary Shaw offer gifts, home accessories, cards and paper products not previously available in Edina. They strive for distinction with an inventory that changes frequently and is sure to delight you and the special people in your life. The shop is an exclusive dealer for Pandora Jewelry and offers silver and gold Danish-designed charms that can be set into the bracelet in any order you desire. Homeowners adore the Parisian Lampe Berger line that not only perfumes the air but actually purifies the air and destroys odors. The Life Is Good clothing collection brings upbeat good taste to casual wear. The store is a premier dealer for Peggy Karr fused glassware and fragrance candles by Tyler Candles, known for even and long-burning jar candles. Kevin and Kary have invested their hearts and souls into the store, and the result is a feel-good atmosphere. Everything, from the attitude of the Shaws and their staff to the store's décor, is designed to put a smile on your face. Lighten your day with a visit to live, laugh, love.

5019 France Avenue S, Edina MN
(952) 929-0701

Max's

Exclusive jewelry, gifts and heavenly chocolate come together at Max's in St. Louis Park. Ellen worked as a business consultant for most of her adult life, but her true loves were always retail and jewelry, so when the opportunity arose in 2006 to bring her passions together, she jumped at the chance. Ellen personally selects the men's and women's jewelry sold in the store, most of which is handmade and exclusive to the store in the Twin Cities. The pieces, which represent the work of leading artisans from around the world, have a modern, architectural quality and sensual appeal. Beyond individual works of jewelry art, Max's carries a generous selection of art for the home, including fused glass plates, porcelain serving bowls and metal candle holders. Artistry also extends to quality chocolates, including Sweet Bliss (whose owner was formerly Ralph Lauren's personal chef), Chocolat Moderne, V Chocolates, Galler and Pralus. Imported chocolates come from Belgium, Italy and France. The cocoa beans come from places such as Venezuela, Madagascar, Jamaica and Trinidad. Stock changes frequently, so you will want to visit often. Ellen goes the extra mile to ensure customer satisfaction. In fact, if you can't find what you need, just ask Ellen and she will do what she can to find it for you. Ellen named the store for her grandfather, a prominent jeweler and the owner of Max's Jewelry Company in Detroit for more than 50 years. For a shopping trip that will reveal sensory delights not found elsewhere in the Twin Cities, come to Max's.

3831 Grand Way, St. Louis Park MN
(612) 922-9405
www.stylebymax.com

The Woods

The Woods gift store in Maple Grove is the perfect place to find distinctive gifts for your home, garden or cabin in the woods. Linda and David Looney, owners of The Woods, have been furnishing rustic and sophisticated homes and gardens alike since 1985. The Woods has an ample supply of Northwoods furnishings, accessories and home and garden gifts, and a visit will equip even the pickiest of shoppers with something perfect. Visitors to The Woods are offered a free, fresh cup of delicious flavored coffee as they explore the varied gift items kept in stock, including scented candles, silk-screened or embroidered T-shirts, Woolrich blankets, handmade carved wooden bears, exotic wood jewelry boxes and imaginatively crafted

kaleidoscopes. You can decorate the house with fresh, seasonal accents or stock up on unique Minnesota souvenirs before the big trip. The Woods offers custom-made sandblasted stones, free gift wrapping and will ship anywhere in the United States and Canada. You can even browse through the merchandise on the web. For a piece of Maple Grove and the small-town relaxation you'll find here, be sure to stop by The Woods gift shop on your next visit.

15825 95th Avenue N, Maple Grove MN
(763) 416-WOOD (9663)
www.davlinswoods.com

N'Tice Home Furnishings & Gifts

At N'Tice Home Furnishings & Gifts, owners Al and Bobbie Miller enjoy providing customers with unusual and one-of-a-kind furnishings, home décor and boutique items, a service they dreamed of for many years. Al previously worked as a merchant for a department store and could only order standard items that were in large demand. When Al and Bobbie opened N'Tice in 2004, they let creativity take top billing. As a result, many of the items are handcrafted and one-of-a-kind. The store proudly carries lines from the award-winning Sticks furniture company, which offers delicately hand-painted and etched pieces. Al and Bobbie say that their hope is to bring smiles to the faces of their customers, and their whimsical wares are sure to do just that. Examples in glass are the topsy-turvy Rainbow Sculpture and the Splatter Bowl, which gives the illusion of a raindrop as it hits the pavement. Pamper yourself with a long soak in the tub and a scoop of Bath Ice Cream, which comes in tantalizing flavors such as chocolate, pomegranate and gin martini. Massage oil candles come in a variety of fragrances. Gadgets include wind-up

radios and wine caddies. N'Tice carries stunning jewelry from designers such as Zivot. You'll marvel at the elaborately decorative adornments by Michal Golan. Everywhere you'll see gifts any friend would be happy to receive. Visit N'Tice Home Furnishings & Gifts to add a little fun to your life.

6547 York Avenue S, Edina MN
(612) 861-0016 or (877) 861-0072
www.nticehome.com

"Feel the Spirit"

Northland Native American Products

Northland Native American Products is a gallery and retail space where you can find treasures of the land—original items by native peoples from Minnesota, the Dakotas, Wisconsin and Canada. When Ken Bellanger started the business in 1996, it dealt entirely in gift products, such as hand-crafted birch bark baskets or canoes and rare gourmet foods of the Northlands. These products are still available, and they come with stories of their origins: the Ojibwe people harvest the wild rice in the traditional way. Northland sells this wild rice, along with wild berry syrups and jellies in many rare and mouth-watering flavors such as chokecherry, hawthorn, highbush cranberry, rose hip and wild plum. In 1999, Northland moved to the Ancient Traders Market and added a gallery. You enter to the soothing sound of the native flute, the gentle scent of sage and cedar, and a warm greeting from the staff. Then, drink in the beauty and spirit of the art. You'll see pottery, jewelry and beadwork. There are sculptures of elders, horses, eagles and the White Buffalo Spirit. The gallery has dance sticks, drums of all sizes and blankets of many colors. The names of the prints and paintings offer only a hint of their visual poetry: *Buffalo Dancer*, *Grandfathers Tears*, *Wolf Song* and *Keeper of the Plains*. Some of the art is traditional, and some of it is quite contemporary. Bellanger is eager to tell the story of each artist. Come to Northland Native American Products for the best the land has to offer.

1113 E Franklin Avenue, Minneapolis MN
(612) 872-0390
www.northlandvisions.com

Shinder's

With its massive selection of newspapers, comic books, magazines and sports cards, Shinder's is a Minneapolis landmark. The original location, at 8th Street and Hennepin Avenue, was opened in 1916 by Russian Jewish immigrants Al and Harry Shinder. In the more than 90 years since then, Shinder's has become a local institution, with 12 locations throughout the state. Shinder's started out as a New York-style newsstand, and you'll still find a huge number of newspapers here, including editions from as far away as Germany and Israel. Minneapolis was at the center of the comic book collecting boom in the 1970s and 1980s, and Shinder's quickly became a leader in that market. Whether you are looking for the slam-bang adventures of your favorite DC and Marvel superheroes or the latest sensations on the indie scene, you're guaranteed to find them at Shinder's. The store also purchases old comic books and offers many back issues. Sports card collectors are in for a home-run experience here, with many hard-to-find cards available for purchase. Shinder's offers a lively magazine selection, with topics ranging from fitness to arts and crafts. You may even find a best-seller you've been meaning to read here. Vintage toys and games are other attractions of this quirky, fun store. For collectibles, games and all sorts of reading matter, visit Shinder's.

733 Hennepin Avenue, Minneapolis MN
(612) 333-3628
www.shinders.com

Melrose Antiques

Finding exquisite pieces from the past to adorn you and your home is easier than ever, thanks to Melrose Antiques. Peggy Kouri, a former nurse and 29-year resident of northeast Minneapolis,

and her colleague Barb Schneider opened this antique resource in 2002. The shop is fittingly located in the 1860 Melrose Flats building, which is listed on the National Register of Historic Places. You will find a terrific selection of hard-to-find pieces with a focus on items that have decorative appeal. *Mpls.St.Paul Magazine* honored the shop for its vintage baubles in 2004, and for the best vintage clothing in the area in 2005. Peggy and Barb both have extensive experience collecting and selling antique and vintage home accessories and décor items, and they put that experience to work for their customers. The two pride themselves on providing exceptional customer service to help you find just what you need from their inventory of fine antiques and collectibles. Whether you are an antique fanatic or just in search of unique gifts or décor, you are sure to find the items you seek at Melrose Antiques.

13 NE 5th Street, Minneapolis MN
(612) 362-8480

Shorty's Loft

Louise Otten founded Shorty's Loft in 1996 in an upstairs office space in Long Lake with a wonderful collection of bronze sculptures, Native American jewelry and black and white artwork. Louise also threw in a fabulous, yet small, selection of hand-tooled belts for both men and women, and an eclectic gathering of folk art from the Southwest. By 1999, Louise thought a change was in store and brought on co-owner Nancy Sherman. With Nancy, the shop went on the road as Shorty's Loft Mobile Store. From 2000, Nancy traveled to show jumping horse events all around the country 10 months out of the year. This boutique on wheels led to a much larger selection of items, including beautiful ladies apparel, hats, belts, children's items and much more. Keeping its Southwestern flair, Shorty's evolved into a boutique that carried collections from the antique to the cutting edge. Traveling became tiresome for Nancy, who really just wanted a

corner shop in a cute town. In 2005, that exact kind of place was up for lease in Saint Louis Park. In May 2006, Shorty's Loft opened its doors to the streets again. Louise and Nancy pride themselves on providing a friendly shopping experience to all who walk through the door. If you are looking for beautiful apparel and home accents, be sure to stop by Shorty's Loft.

4590 Excelsior Boulevard,
St. Louis Park MN
(952) 473-0404
www.shortysloft.net

Ross Hall—*Casting on Clearwater*, 1950
Photograph

Soleil Brule Importers

In late 2006, a new store named Soleil Brule Importers opened in Wayzata. *Soleil Brule* means burning sun, a name inspired by a collection of paintings owner Jennifer Vervoort-Smith purchased from the renowned Haitian artist, Jean-Claude "Tiga" Garoute. The brilliant saturated colors and exotic flavor of the paintings characterize the kind of imported goods that Jennifer most appreciates. "I'm drawn to the shape of the pieces, how they stand architecturally," says Jennifer. "But it's the color and intimacy that determines whether or not I will purchase it." Jennifer has turned her travels to the West Indies, Africa and Europe into a store filled with chandeliers, lamps, hand-painted glassware, china, textiles and furniture. About 70 percent of the shop's offerings come from Morocco. The artistic displays of clothing, fine art and much else give the shop the look of a museum. The baskets, tableware, vases and other home accessories at Soleil Brule show a quality and design you'll find refreshing. Boxes, pillows and tassels are next to jewelry and soaps. The vividly colored home décor and craftsmanship is utterly charming, but no less memorable is the contagious enthusiasm of Jennifer and her staff. Jennifer wants customers to feel welcome and have fun. She offers cooking classes and provides free delivery and installation services. Put some vibrant colors into your décor with a visit to Soleil Brule Importers.

726 E Lake Street, Wayzata MN
(952) 476-9600
www.soleilbrule.com

Minnesota State Fair, St. Paul

St. Paul Metro

The Outing Lodge at Pine Point

The Outing Lodge at Pine Point is a European-style, 19th century country home surrounded by lawns and gardens, plus 300 acres of wooded park land. It is a place where people go to get away from modern city life. Pine Point was founded in 1858 as Minnesota's second poor farm, a home for the chronically indigent or those temporarily down on their luck. Stillwater was a wealthy community in 1850 and the territorial capital. In this abundant atmosphere, a desire to help the less fortunate culminated in the construction of this poor farm. The prize-winning dairy farm became both a home and a workplace to thousands of needy for almost 100 years. When the farm was closed in 1957, the land was planted in pine trees and became Pine Point Park. The house continued as a rest home for 20 years. In the 1980s, to save it from proposed demolition, Lee Gohlike began its renovation. He gutted its interior with a reverence for its historic past. Today, wide-planked wooden floors cut from old pine beams provide a perfect setting for the many elegant antique furnishings, numerous candelabra and massive fireplaces. Featured in *Midwest Traveler*, the *Star Tribune* and other local and national publications, this beautiful Georgian home is a destination for exclusive retreats and events. Guests enjoy the cross-country skiing, horseback and biking trails that connect to the metro system. Check out the calendar of culinary outings on the website.

11661 Myeron Road N, Stillwater MN
(651) 439-9747
www.outinglodge.com

The Saint Paul Hotel

The Saint Paul Hotel, a historic hotel in the lovely Rice Park District, offers unmatched hospitality to business and leisure travelers. This legendary landmark, consistently rated among the country's top hotels, has provided luxurious accommodations and unsurpassed service since 1910. The hotel's 254 elegant rooms and suites, completely renovated in 2005, feature down pillows and comforters, premium mattresses and sweeping views. Luxurious bathrooms pamper guests with premium bath products, thick towels and robes plus invigorating showers. Corporate guests appreciate the business center, concierge service and a convenient downtown location close to business and pleasure. You won't go hungry at the Saint Paul, where dining choices include two distinctive restaurants. Enjoy the M ST. Cafe for breakfast, lunch and private dining, or see and be seen at the St. Paul Grill, which features American-style grill entrées in an upscale yet casual environment. The Lobby Bar, a new addition to the hotel, features lighter fare as well as beer, wine and cocktails. The Saint Paul offers 13,000 square feet of event space, including eight multifunctional meeting rooms. The legendary Promenade Ballroom, a Minnesota institution for 95 years, accommodates up to 300 guests and is an ideal place for a wedding or other important gathering. Come see for yourself why the Saint Paul Hotel has earned AAA's Four Diamond rating for 24 consecutive years.

350 Market Street, St. Paul MN
(651) 292-9292
www.saintpaulhotel.com

The Elephant Walk Bed and Breakfast

Romance, relaxation, rejuvenation, reconnection and quiet. If these words are soothing to you and stir up a longing to get away from it all, then it's time to slip away and enjoy peaceful repose in Stillwater. This quaint, yet vibrant, town is home to The Elephant Walk Bed and Breakfast, which is dedicated to ensuring that you and your mate have time to unwind and reconnect. Enjoy dinner at one of Stillwater's many restaurants. This popular, award-winning bed and breakfast is housed in a stunning 1883 stick-style Victorian home that has been lovingly restored and filled with innkeeper Rita Graybill's collection of antiques. The antiquities were accumulated during more than 20 years of diplomatic and military service by her late husband, Jon. Rita's magnificent collection features antiques and collectibles from Europe, the Far East and America. The Elephant Walk provides two first floor parlors, one with a large fireplace. Luxuriate in the fresh Minnesota air while you lounge on the wrap-around porch, snuggled up comfortably in one of the peacock chairs. Enjoy Rita's renowned four-course gourmet breakfast. In the evening you can chat with your hosts and get to know your fellow visitors while nibbling on tasty cheese served with fresh, homemade crackers and your choice of wine, champagne or a non-alcoholic beverage. This fabulous inn features four beautiful internationally themed rooms, each with a refrigerator containing complimentary water and soda, a gas fireplace, air conditioning, double whirlpool bath and a complete CD sound system. Give your self over to the serenity you deserve with a stay at The Elephant Walk.

801 Pine Street W, Stillwater MN
(651) 430-0528
www.elephantwalkbb.com

The Wildwood Lodge St. Paul

The Wildwood Lodge in metro St. Paul takes extra steps to ensure guests receive superior service while enjoying all the attractions of the Twin Cities. The 99-room boutique hotel is a sanctuary of pleasures and is equipped with a large atrium pool, a whirlpool, a game room and a 24-hour fitness center. The hotel's lobby invites you to linger in front of the fireplace and enjoy the original artwork. Once you are settled in, you can order lunch or dinner at the award-winning Machine Shed restaurant. This is also where you will come for the hotel's complimentary breakfast. A goose down, seven-layer sleep system promises every guest a restful night's sleep. You'll also experience spa-style pampering with a bathroom stocked with Aveda bath products and plush, over-sized towels. Banquet facilities are available for groups of up to 250 people, making the Wildwood an ideal location for weddings and holiday parties. Business travelers find two complimentary business centers and executive rooms with large desks, extra lighting, phones with data ports and high-speed Internet access. Professional staff will help you make arrangements for a private or business function in one of the hotel's 11 meeting rooms. Food service is available with cuisine prepared by an outstanding staff chef. Shopping and a golf course are nearby. For a hotel with the options you most desire, visit the Wildwood Lodge St. Paul.

8511 Hudson Boulevard, Lake Elmo MN
(651) 714-8068 or (866) 294-6250
www.thewildwoodlodge.com

Rivertown Inn

Visit a world of Victorian splendor where the primary mission is to make your stay the ultimate experience in luxury, privacy and romance. From the moment you step inside the Rivertown Inn, you will be surrounded by European-style elegance and outstanding personal service. Built in 1882 at the height of Minnesota's logging boom, this lumber baron's mansion is located three blocks above historic downtown Stillwater and the picturesque St. Croix River. Owners Jeff and Julie Anderson have meticulously restored the Rivertown Inn to its original grandeur while retaining its Victorian charm and elegance. Touted as one of the finest inns in the St. Croix River Valley, the Rivertown Inn features a large collection of stained-glass windows, 10 working fireplaces set in carved Victorian-era mantels, crystal chandeliers, 100-year-old parquet floors, Oriental rugs, hand-painted wallpapers, lush gardens and a carved Gothic wall in the dining room. The inn boasts extraordinary details and furnishings that will exceed even the most discriminating visitor's expectations. The Rivertown Inn offers five suites and four bedchambers, each with a private bath featuring a double whirlpool tub, live-flame gas fireplace and a sumptous décor that pays homage to a great romantic poet or literary figure of the 19th century. Each night, guests are invited to a social hour with complimentary wine and hors d'oevres in the parlor or, weather permitting, on the grand, wrap-around porch. Sumptious and original three-course gourmet breakfasts are prepared for guests each morning by their European chef, who chooses the finest and freshest ingredients available for his culinary creations. If you can bear to leave your room, Stillwater offers riverboat excursions, trolley tours, antique shopping and fine restaurants among its many activities. Come and enjoy.

306 Olive Street W, Stillwater MN   (651) 430-2955   *www.rivertowninn.com*

Wet Paint

The Wet Paint staff of 15 is well-known and respected for its knowledge of art and for its hands-on experience with the art supplies it sells. The business has been serving St. Paul for 32 years and has belonged to Beth Bergman for the past 21 years. Beth refuses to allow Wet Paint to develop the look or feel of a chain store. She also campaigns to keep independent businesses open in her neighborhood. One way she ensures that her store stands apart from large self-service stores is by having her employees lead patrons through the narrow aisles to help them find exactly what they need. Wet Paint sells an array of art supplies, including many items not easily found in other stores. It offers supplies for serious, professional artists, for those with a heartfelt avocation and for students. Merchandise includes decorative paper by the sheet and more than 10 manufacturers' lines of oil paint. The store also offers an outstanding selection of writing instruments, stationery, photo and scrap albums. Art books and magazines here appeal to art lovers with varied tastes, and in-store demonstrations introduce customers to techniques and specialty products. You'll also find framing services. Whether you are a serious artist or a hobbyist, for an independent store that understands you, come to Wet Paint.

1684 Grand Avenue, St. Paul MN
(651) 698-6431
www.wetpaintart.com

Bear Patch Quilting Company

Quilting is a truly American pastime that became popular in the 1840s when the textile industry had grown enough to support a large distribution of fabrics. The quilting craze has endured and today, quilters have Bear Patch Quilting Company to supply all of their quilting needs. Owners Debbie Engh and Laurel Riter opened Bear Patch in 1997 to provide top-quality supplies and hands-on customer service. The largest quilting shop in the Twin Cities, Bear Patch offers an extensive selection of fabrics, patterns and supplies. Learn how to make heirloom quilts or add to your knowledge with classes designed for quilters of all skill levels. Classes in rug hooking, sewing, embroidery, needlepunch and garment construction are available. Bear Patch also serves as a meeting place for sewing and quilting clubs. Debbie and Laurel are dedicated to

their community and show this support through donations and special classes for volunteer groups that create quilts for charity. In 2001, *Better Homes and Gardens* honored Bear Patch Quilting and its commitment to excellence by naming it one of the country's top 10 quilting shops. Learn more about this historical and creative pastime with a visit to Bear Patch Quilting Company.

2199 4ᵗʰ Street, White Bear Lake MN
(651) 429-1039
www.bearpatchquilting.com

The Yarnery

The Yarnery, knitted into the fabric of St. Paul for more than 30 years, abounds with natural fibers. Knitters thrill at the yarns and accessories found in this quaint house, located in the bustling Victoria Crossing area. Basic wool, cotton, silk, alpaca or mohair and a wide selection of novelty yarns offer enticing possibilities for creative clothing and crafts. Whether you are new to knitting or an old-timer, a child or an adult, the Yarnery can further your knowledge with an assortment of classes. The Yarnery's owners, the Kreisman-Maddux family, think globally by supporting suppliers such as Lantern Moon that make a difference in their own communities. Lantern Moon, a supplier of needles and baskets, works directly with Vietnamese producers

to provide income, education, and self-reliance to Vietnamese women and their families. In 2004, Lantern Moon established an educational trust fund for children while continuing to nurture and revive the traditional handicrafts of Vietnam. The Yarnery seeks out such innovative companies, including those marketing sustainable alternative fibers and environmentally responsible goods. The shop is an excellent place to connect with other knitters, and staff can help you untangle a knitting or crocheting problem. Discover a knitter's paradise with a visit to the Yarnery.

840 Grand Avenue, St. Paul MN
(651) 222-5793
www.yarnery.com

2007 Winter Carnival
Photos by Michael Hicks

St. Paul Festival & Heritage Foundation

The St. Paul Winter Carnival is the coolest celebration on earth for reasons that go far beyond the chill of the season. Chief among these is the hard work of the St. Paul Festival & Heritage Foundation, which puts the event on each year. The annual Winter Carnival began in 1885, when a New York reporter called St. Paul "unfit for human habitation." In response, the people of St. Paul came up with a festival to prove how amazing the city was. The carnival's activities including snow and ice carving competitions, a torchlight parade and the famous 5K and a Half Marathon. Have a blast slipping down the giant snow slide or losing yourself in the frozen ice maze. Look for King Boreas, whose court includes the Queen of Snows and the sassy Klondike Kate. The mission of the foundation is to foster a sense of community pride and celebrate St. Paul's unique history with fun and educational experiences. The St. Paul Festival & Heritage Foundation invites you to the Winter Carnival to celebrate the beauty, climate and people of St. Paul.

**429 Landmark Center, 75 W 5th Street,
St. Paul MN**
(651) 223-4700
www.winter-carnival.com

Minnesota Wild

In 1997, the National Hockey League awarded Minnesota an expansion franchise to begin in 2000. The announcement electrified thousands of Minnesota hockey fans, who poured in suggestions for the name of their new home team. Six months later, a sellout crowd gathered for the official unveiling of the Minnesota Wild hockey team. Jack Sperling, team CEO, said that the name "represents what Minnesota hockey fans hold most dear—our rugged natural wilderness." In the years since, Minnesota has embraced the Wild as its own. The Minnesota legislature voted to fund half of the projected expenses of building the Xcel Energy Center, the team's home arena in St. Paul. The arena is a landmark that features a transparent glass exterior and strategically designed seating for great hockey sightlines. *ESPN: the Magazine* named it the number-one stadium in the nation in 2003 and the number-one stadium experience in the nation in 2007 according to their Ultimate Standings survey. The Minnesota Wild has sold out every single game at Xcel Energy Center through the team's first six seasons. The 274 sellouts include 246 regular season games, 18 preseason contests and 10 playoff games. Visit Xcel Energy Center to cheer on St. Paul's own Minnesota Wild and experience what Minnesota hockey pride is all about.

199 W Kellogg Boulevard, St. Paul MN
(651) 602-6000
www.wild.com

Minnesota Museum of American Art

Founded as the St. Paul School of Art in 1927, the Minnesota Museum of American Art, or MMAA, has undergone six name changes and a dozen moves in its long history. The School of Art began collecting works of art for instructional purposes in the 1930s and expanded its collection over the years through the acquisition of additional paintings, sculpture and other artwork. In 1969 the school was renamed the Minnesota Museum of Art, and by the 1980s the museum's emphasis had shifted to research and exhibitions. The museum added *American* to its name in 1992 to reflect its commitment to representing the diversity of American art and artists. Today the central mission of the MMAA is the support and recognition of Minnesota artists. The museum also sponsors the Patio Nights summer music series, an outdoor concert series for all ages that features all types of music from jazz to jug bands. For the past seven years, MMAA has presented three to four exhibitions per year as well as displaying selections from its permanent collection. Past exhibitions have included *Speak Soft and Carry a Beagle: The Art of Charles Schulz*, *Norman Rockwell's 322* Saturday Evening Post *Covers* and *On the Road with Thomas Hart Benton: Images of a Changing America*. Awaken your senses with a visit to the Minnesota Museum of American Art, where there is always something new to experience.

50 W Kellogg Boulevard, St. Paul MN
(651) 266-1030
www.mmaa.org

James J. Hill House

James J. Hill, builder of the Great Northern Railway, was a key figure during America's age of expansion. His massive stone home, sturdy as a fortress, is open to visitors who would like to know more about Hill's life and times. With its 13 bathrooms, 22 fireplaces, 16 chandeliers and a 100-foot reception hall, this was the home of a man who clearly lived big. James J. Hill amassed his great wealth pursuing a range of business interests, including mining, shipping and banking, but it is for the railroad that people remember him most. Branches of the Great Northern pushed up to the Canadian border, and the main line crossed the Rockies to the Pacific at Seattle. When the mansion was completed in 1891, it was the largest and most expensive house in Minnesota. As you walk its halls and stand in its rooms, you can't help but imagine the lives of the Hill family members and their servants, while you marvel at the early mechanical systems that provided central heating, indoor plumbing, gas fireplaces and electrical security. The two-story, sky-lit art gallery features exhibits by Minnesota artists and highlights the Minnesota Historical Society's extensive art collection. The Hill House hosts dramatic programming throughout the year, including Victorian ghost stories, chamber concerts, gaslight tours, a Victorian poetry slam and summer walking tours of the historic Summit Avenue neighborhood. Tour the James J. Hill House, a symbol of the wealth and power of America's Gilded Age.

240 Summit Avenue, St. Paul MN
(651) 297-2555
www.mnhs.org/hillhouse

Science Museum of Minnesota

For nearly 100 years, the venerable Science Museum of Minnesota has been offering exciting lessons about the world of science. With cutting-edge technology, inventive hands-on exhibits and a world-class collection of fossils and artifacts, there's much to explore. A good place to start is the Collections Gallery, showcasing popular museum treasures such as Native American artifacts, an Egyptian mummy, a two-headed turtle and antique medical devices (which may not have done patients much good). For your next stop, at the Dinosaurs and Fossils Gallery, you'll meet all manner of bony beasts reconstructed to their full size and glory. Don't miss the Omnitheater, a breathtaking domed theater with the world's largest video projection system that supports IMAX and other giant-format films. Another theater shows films in 3D. Looking for something more interactive? The Experiment Gallery offers a host of hands-on activities for investigating the laws of nature. You can explore the mechanics of light and sound, operate a steam engine or watch a tornado form from a cloud at your feet. Outside, a 1.2-acre outdoor exhibit gallery features nine holes of science-themed miniature golf. You can climb aboard an authentic Mississippi River towboat, pan for gemstones and fossils in a giant sluice or view a 3D spherical map of the world. The museum offers youth and family education programs, including a summer camp. Discover the world we live in as you've never seen it before at the Science Museum of Minnesota.

120 W Kellogg Boulevard, St. Paul MN
(651) 221-9444
www.smm.org

Photo by Ryan Clausen
Courtesy of the Minnesota Zoo

Photo by Jashua Lemon
Courtesy of the Minnesota Zoo

Photo by Ryan Clausen
Courtesy of the Minnesota Zoo

The Minnesota Zoo

Where in the state of 10,000 lakes can you see 408 different species of animals? If the first answer that comes to mind is a zoo, then you are on the right track. The Minnesota Zoo is no ordinary animal park, however. With over a million annual guests, the Minnesota Zoo specializes in connecting people, animals and the natural world. The staff is dedicated to inspiring people to act on behalf of their environment and they work to accomplish this lofty goal by providing award-winning recreational, educational and conservation programs at the local, national and international levels. The unique Zoomobile program goes on the road each year, and last year the zoo sent 200 ambassadors to present a variety of programs at more than 700 schools, nursing homes, hospitals, churches and county fairs in Minnesota, Wisconsin and Iowa. More than 600 individuals volunteer in different programs at the zoo, and after your visit you'll probably want to join the volunteer ranks too. The zoo offers presentations to interest visitors of all ages, including bird shows, dolphin programs and zookeeper talks, along with simulated environments. Set out for a wild visit and enjoy the amazing animals and entrancing educational programs at the Minnesota Zoo.

13000 Zoo Boulevard, Apple Valley MN
(952) 431-9200 *www.mnzoo.com*

St. Paul Saints Baseball Club

The St. Paul Saints have provided St. Paul with outdoor family entertainment since 1993. One of the most famous franchises in minor league baseball, the independent Saints play 96 games per season as members of the American Association. Tickets have been tough to come by since the club's inception, because the Saints draw nearly 300,000 fans each year to the 6,069-seat Midway Stadium. A record crowd of 9,251 fans attended on July 7, 2006. The team's eclectic ownership group includes Marv Goldklang, baseball and marketing maverick Mike Veeck and actor/comedian Bill Murray. The Saints have adopted a Fun is Good attitude that keeps fans smiling, laughing and cheering every game night. Famous for outlandish promotions, the Saints are the only team in baseball with a live pig as its mascot. In 2006, the pig's name was Bud Squealig; past swine have included Hammy Davis, Jr., Notorious P.I.G. and Kevin Bacon. You won't find another team with an 80-year-old nun who gives massages in the stands and haircuts behind home plate. Tickets start at $3 for kids and $4 for adults. Among the baseball stars who have played with the Saints are Darryl Strawberry, Jack Morris, J.D. Drew and Kevin Millar. *Baseball America* named the Saints as the 2006 Independent Baseball Organization of the Year. Buy your tickets early and make the St. Paul Saints part of your summer fun.

1771 Energy Park Drive, St. Paul MN (Midway Stadium)
(651) 644-6659
www.saintsbaseball.com

Como Park Zoo & Conservatory

For more than 100 years, the Como Park Zoo & Conservatory in St. Paul has charmed, educated and entertained millions of children and adults while fostering an appreciation of the natural world. Owned and operated by the City of St. Paul, Como Park Zoo & Conservatory boasts free parking and is one of the last remaining free zoos in the country. The Como Zoo opened in 1893 and provides a caring and safe habitat for all its occupants including gorillas, lions, orangutans, giraffes, polar bears and more. One of the highlights of your visit is the Sparky Show, as well as a journey through the all new Tropical Encounters exhibit. The Marjorie McNeely Conservatory opened in 1915 and contains the largest glass domed garden in the region—about one-half acre under glass. Five themed flower shows take place each year in the popular Sunken Garden. Como Park Zoo & Conservatory has won many prestigious awards and is a true Minnesota treasure. Bring your family on an adventure into the world of nature.

1225 Estabrook Drive, St. Paul MN
(651) 487-8200
www.comozooconservatory.org

Padelford Packet Boat Company, Inc.

Captain Willian D. Bowell, Sr. founded the Padelford Packet Boat Company in 1969 with a single authentic steam sternwheeler, the *Jonathan Padelford*. He added to the fleet until it now consists of the *Anson Northrup*, the *Betsey Northrup* and the *Harriet Bishop*, all of which ply the waters of the Mississippi with daily public excursions that have entertained more than 4,000,000 passengers. You, your family or group can delight in one of the specialty packages, such as the Prime Rib Dinner Cruise or the Sunday Brunch Cruise. These magnificent boats can be privately rented for special events such as weddings, dances and anniversary celebrations. Always committed to the community, Captain Bowell and his company have made reduced rates available to schools in the Twin Cities area, so that almost 600,000 children have enjoyed educational field trips on the river. One of Captain Bowell's proudest accomplishments was rebuilding the *Minnesota Centennial Showboat*. When the University of Minnesota's theatre department lost the showboat that had been their student theatre in an accidental fire, the University could not replace it. Captain Bowell volunteered to oversee the design and construction of a new vessel, in large part at his own expense. In gratitude, the University gave the company the contract to manage the boat. The *Centennial Showboat* is the summer home of the University's Showboat Players and the home of the Actors Theatre the rest of the year. Let the Padelford Packet Boat Company offer you and your family or friends a wonderful riverboat cruise and a terrific show.

Harriet Island, St. Paul MN
(651) 227-1100 or (800) 543-3908
www.riverrides.com

Wabasha Street Caves

Downtown St. Paul provides a striking contrast between modern skyscrapers and historical landmarks. Located below the skyscrapers and antique-style lighting of this city, along the Mississippi River, are the Wabasha Street Caves, human-made caves that were a haven for gangsters in the 1920s and 1930s. The caves were the site of a notorious Prohibition-era nightclub called the Castle Royal, which hosted such gangsters as John Dillinger, Babyface Nelson and Machine Gun Kelly. Today, you can host a banquet, convention or special event here. You can also take a family-friendly tour of the 12,000-square-foot space and learn about the gangster ghosts that are said to haunt it. Donna and Steve Bremer bought the property in 1992 and restored it to its 1930s appearance with the original brick walls and stucco ceilings. You'll think you are back in Prohibition days during your guided tour of this historic site. "We make history fun," say the Bremers. "Out-of-towners find a new place to visit, and locals find out new things about their city." A 60-foot bar, theatrical stage, large hardwood dance floor and ample dining and meeting space make this a superior location for a private function as well as the Bremer's weekly Big Band swing dances. For a memorable encounter with the past, visit the Wabasha Street Caves. Just remember the password: "Gus sent me."

215 Wabasha Street S, St. Paul MN
(651) 292-1220
www.wabashastreetcaves.com

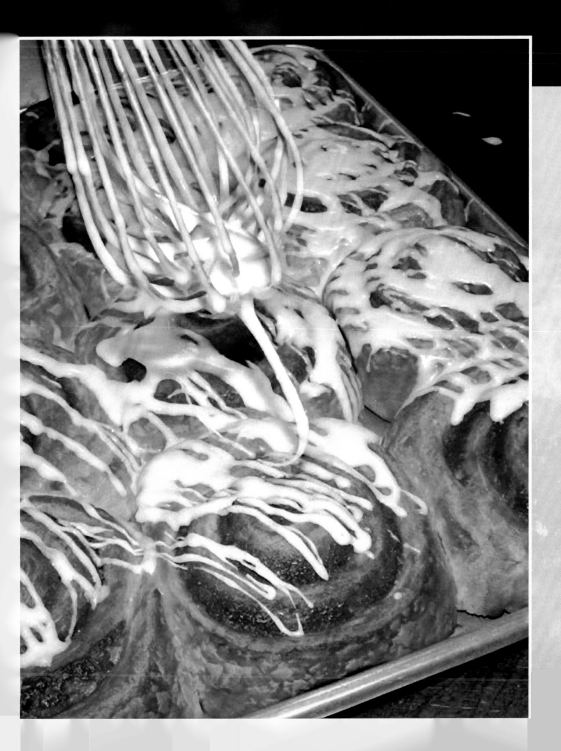

Bread & Chocolate

For the past 25 years Bread & Chocolate has been the destination for a light breakfast, a quick lunch or a sweet snack and latte drink. In the mornings it's all about fresh baked muffins, scones, cinnamon and caramel rolls, assorted croissants and a variety of breakfast panini sandwiches. Lunch means sandwiches on Café Latte's excellent fresh-baked breads with a side of salad or chips. Bread & Chocolate's bakery cases overflow with wonderful desserts and filled croissants baked fresh daily—ham and cheese croissants are a favorite. The award-winning brownies, fabulous fudge bars, fresh baked warm cookies and a changing selection of special bars are irresistible. The espresso bar serves fresh roasted Fair Trade coffees and espressos from locally owned Morningstar Coffee Co. Bread & Chocolate's expert baristas will be happy to make your favorite latte.

867 Grand Avenue, St. Paul MN
(651) 228-1017
www.cafelatte.com

Baglio's of Afton

Baglio's of Afton offers both classic and modern fashions for women. Since Lisa and Bill Baglio opened the store in 1986, styles have become much more diverse and individualized, which meets with Lisa's approval. "Its not much of a trend-driven fashion world anymore. Now it's about what works for a particular individual . . . Go with whatever style and color looks good and makes you happy," says Lisa. With that in mind, the Baglios have gathered together a diverse collection of casual styles. You'll find tailored clothing, soft, loose-fitting styles and such fun accessories as mod handbags or a string of magnetized hematite beads. Something new is always showing up to tweak customer interest. Baglio's is famous for its style shows, which have been attended by thousands of Twin Cities women. Lisa and Bill will work with any group or organization to create a comfortable and entertaining venue for fundraising events or for bringing awareness to worthy causes. They entertain groups from 50 to 500 in locations ranging from church basements to the Minneapolis Hilton Hotel. People come from all over the metro area to shop and all the way from Duluth and Wisconsin to attend Baglio's fashion shows. For more information on the luncheons and reviews hosted by these purveyors of good taste, visit the Baglios in person or on their website. For practical fashions from professionals who know what works, come to Baglio's of Afton.

3290 S St. Croix Trail, Afton MN
(651) 436-1506
www.bagliosofafton.com

Trade Winds International

Roxanne Sullivan was working as a geologist in remote areas of South America when she fell in love with the artistry and spirit of the local people. She decided to help the talented artisans she met by developing a way to market their unique goods. She started by connecting craftspeople with American businesses, then she decided she wanted to do more, so she opened Trade Winds International in St. Paul in 1990. Trade Winds sells high-quality, long-lasting women's and children's clothing made by women in developing countries. Most of the products are made from natural, environmentally friendly materials. Trade Winds also offers jewelry, accessories and other items that reflect the individuality and spirit of the artisans Roxanne supports. Her goal is to connect humans globally. She is devoted to the concept of fair trade, aligning herself with cooperatives, artists and businesses devoted to global sustainability. The next time you are in St. Paul, make it a point to visit Trade Winds International, a shop that is making a difference for people around the world.

857 Grand Avenue, St. Paul MN
(651) 293-9275

Charlemagne Fine Jewelry

Charlemagne Fine Jewelry is the passion of designers and owners Charles and Harriet Fogarty. They form a design team that produces world-class jewelry, with a focus on premium diamonds, natural colored gemstones and astonishing South Sea, Akoya and Freshwater pearls. Some of the Twin Cities' top movers and shakers wear the Fogarty's nationally recognized designs. Every step of the jewelry-making process takes place in-house, providing complete control over the final product. Each handcrafted piece, whether it comes from the huge collection of original designs or is custom-made to reflect your personality, will help you stand out from the crowd. The staff at Charlemagne treats each customer like royalty, and close personal attention guarantees your satisfaction. Charles and Harriet's jewelry designs have been featured in a video produced by the American Gem Trade Association that highlights their outstanding work and includes them among the nation's top designers. You will find more treasures in the home accessory department at Charlemagne, which offers gifts of hand-blown glass, carved stone and porcelain that are handpicked by the designers with the same care and discerning eye that they devote to the jewelry. Charlemagne has been a landmark destination in St. Paul's Grand Avenue shopping district for more than 30 years, and shopping here is an experience like no other. Personal service, unparalleled quality and pioneering designs will keep you coming back time and again.

1262 Grand Avenue, St. Paul MN (651) 699-1431
www.charlemagnefinejewelry.com

Sven's Comfort Shoes

Built for comfort and durability and loved for their traditional style, clogs are shoes with a Scandinavian connection. You can get them at Sven's Comfort Shoes, a dealer of high-quality, handcrafted clogs for more than 30 years. The products of several nations go into the making of these shoes. The wood bases come from Austria and Sweden; the leathers, from the United States and the Netherlands; the sheepskin for the slippers and clog boots, from Australia. Where are the parts put together to make a whole, perfect shoe? Well, that happens at the Sven's factory right in Chisago City. Sven's came to the area because of the beauty of the lakes and the close Swedish connection. "What better place to make Swedish-style clogs," say owners Marie and Jeffrey Rivers, "than where the Swedish immigrants came to settle so many years ago." An array of clothing, including Dale of Norway sweaters and Norwegian blankets, adds to the Scandinavian theme at Sven's retail location. Dazzling Swedish crystal and whimsical Scandinavian gnomes are among the gift items that you will find. Sven's also carries other shoes besides clogs from such leading brands as Red Wing, Clarks and Birkenstock. All feel as good to your feet as your favorite pillow does to your head. Shop for gifts and slip into your next pair of clogs at Sven's Comfort Shoes.

10,000 Lake Boulevard, Chisago City MN
(651) 257-4598 or (800) 243-7836
www.svensshoesandgifts.com
www.svensclogs.com

Grand Jeté

No matter what kind of dancing gets your feet moving, Grand Jeté provides the shoes to keep them happy and healthy. Owner Ruthena Fink, a dancer in her own right, started her store in 1983, specializing in all sorts of dance shoes and bodywear. Shoes for children, men and women are available to satisfy a variety of dancing passions, from tap and jazz to ballroom and ballet. Ruthena understands the importance of fit in pointe shoes and specializes in fittings that help prevent injuries. Ballet slippers by such industry notables as Capezio, Bloch and Freed assure quality and performance. You'll also find name-brand clothing and accessories, including leotards, tights and children's tutus by such names as Capezio, Danskin, Mirella and Body Wrappers. Ruthena believes that every customer counts, and she proves this with the kind of personalized attention that has made her store famous. Customers come from all over Minnesota and from Wisconsin to let Ruthena's knowledgeable staff —which has 50 years of combined experience in dance—fit their feet. Dance teachers, professional dancers and leaders of dance teams often qualify for discounts. Whether dancing is a profession or an avocation, get the fit and advice you need to keep your feet in tip-top shape with a visit to Grand Jeté.

975 Grand Avenue, St. Paul MN
(651) 227-0331
www.grandjete.com

Just Truffles

Take one bite through the crisp, chocolate coating and into the smooth, creamy ganache center of a truffle from Just Truffles. You will discover the pure chocolate bliss that keeps people coming back for these heavenly morsels, even when they live halfway across the world. Once upon a time, Kathleen O'Hehir-Johnson made truffles for family and friends at Christmas. She brought the tidbits to work, and coworkers begged for more. After receiving orders for several dozen, the idea for the business blossomed, and almost 20 years ago Kathleen and Roger Johnson opened their shop. Now, the two fill orders for people from every continent. Just Truffles' loyal customers include Yo-Yo Ma, Hillary Clinton and Luciano Pavarotti, who wore the gold ribbon from his truffle box onstage. The truffles are completely hand-created, using only the finest chocolate, fresh butter and cream. Kathleen starts from the inside of the truffle, creating the smooth center first, and then the crisp chocolate coating, rather than pouring a filling into a mold. Luscious flavors include Bailey's Irish Cream, Key lime, pecan turtle and nearly 30 other choices. The shop's signature treat remains the Just Chocolate truffle, a piece of pure chocolate goodness. Visit Just Truffles to experience the ultimate chocolate treat.

1363 Grand Avenue, St. Paul MN
(651) 690-0075 or (877) 977-9177
www.justtruffles.com

Candyland

People have been driving a few extra miles for Candyland's popcorn and sweets for almost 75 years. Candyland's popcorn is legendary. In 1932 the shop opened under the name Flavocorn. Arnie Kelsy bought it in 1938 and ran it for 40 years, turning it into Candyland along the way. Doug Lamb worked at Candyland after school and on weekends when he was a teenager. In 1981, he and his wife Brenda bought the shop and soon expanded to other locations. The couple continues to maintain the 75-year-old traditions, recipes, customers and mom-and-pop feel of the place. They only use the surest, freshest, richest ingredients in their mouthwatering array of treats. Candyland carries old-fashioned flavors of popcorn, gummies, sours, jawbreakers, jelly candies, salt water taffy and suckers. Look for brittles and barks of chocolate, bulk chocolate, fine chocolate, and of course chocolate-filled and chocolate-covered treats. Have we mentioned that they carry chocolate? Candyland specializes in wholesome, old-fashioned sweets and treats, lovingly prepared and beautifully packaged. The famous Chicago Mix popcorn blend has even been patented. Candyland specializes in sweet treats for every holiday and event and will ship your order anywhere in the country. So, be sure to visit Candyland, where you will be taken back to a time when life was simple and sweet.

435 N Wabasha Street, St. Paul MN
(651) 292-1191
www.candylandstore.com

Grand Ole Creamery

The Grand Ole Creamery scoops up handcrafted American ice cream right like you remember it. Open seven days a week in two locations, the shop features 31 flavors sure to satisfy every judicious dessert licker. Its tried-and-true flavors, plus a few newcomers, represent a 150-year-old tradition of secret recipes, blended to perfection and rotated for continual surprise and satisfaction. As the Twin Cities' oldest homemade ice cream store, the Grand Ole Creamery consistently honors its ole-time promise of crafting super-premium homemade ice cream. Just look for the giant neon ice-cream cone. If you need a meal first, the Hastings shop serves delectable soups, sandwiches and hot dogs made to order, along with an assortment of fine chocolates. Both locations offer a wide array of old-fashioned candy and novelty desserts. Grand Ole Creamery stays open late on Friday and Saturday nights. Indulge your loved ones, yourself included, with some of the finest handmade flavor ever creamed in the Twin Cities.

750 Grand Avenue, St. Paul MN (651) 293-1655
919 Vermillion Street, Hastings MN (651) 437-9111
www.grandolecreamery.com

Regina's Candy Shops

It's a legacy, it's a tradition and it's wonderful. Regina's Candy Shops are a family affair, a legacy from Grandfather Frank. Frank came to America from Greece in 1906 and opened his first shop, the Central Candy Company, in downtown St. Paul in 1926. In 1954, he re-named the shop to honor his wife, Regina. Present owner Mark Elliott is Frank's grandson, and many children and grandchildren have worked in the shops over the years. Today, Mark's mother and his three sisters are essential parts of the longtime successful business. Quality has no substitute in the Regina's legend. Founder Frank Elliott's tradition of excellence and his original recipes are maintained. The shop uses the same marble tables and copper kettles, and candies are still cooked in small batches using the finest ingredients. There is no skimping on the fresh fruits, sweet cream butter, real whipping cream, and nutmeats that go into Regina's candies. Regina's *truffes* have won rave reviews, and the English toffee and brittles have no equal. Other favorites are Grecian mints, solid chocolate figurines, peanut brittle, caramels, pecanettes, sweet cream fudge and sugar-free chocolates. One of Regina's trademarks is the pictogram that comes with the boxed chocolates, but feel free to hand-pick a box of your own choices. As the slogan has it: handmade confections for your enjoyment. It's a tradition at Regina's Candy Shops.

Factory & Retail Shop: 2073 St. Clair Avenue, St. Paul MN (651) 698-8603
Shop: 1905 S Robert Street, West St. Paul MN (651) 455-8864
www.reginascandies.com

Muddy Paws Cheesecake

Usually a bride would gasp if she saw muddy paws at her wedding. However, cheesecakes from Muddy Paws are always a welcome sight. Owner Tami Cabrera provides her luscious creations to approximately 400 weddings a year in the Twin Cities area. When Tami opened Muddy Paws in St. Paul in 1993, it was the first cheesecake bakery in Minnesota. Since then, she has moved her business to Minneapolis and has been featured on the Food Network while constantly expanding her repertoire. At last count, Muddy Paws offers 170 different flavors of cheesecake. There are two dozen chocolate choices alone and many fruit flavors, such as pineapple, strawberry and mango. Cinderella has a cheesecake named after her at Muddy Paws, and so does Elvis. You'll have to ask Tami how the ingredients, peanut butter and banana, relate to the King of Rock and Roll. Ordering the Sampler Cheesecake allows you to try different flavors as you share nibbles with your friends. All cheesecakes are made in small batches using only the freshest all-natural ingredients. You will find cheesecake by the slice or whole, plus fresh bread, espresso and a full deli menu. Muddy Paws ships cheesecake anywhere in the nation and delivers door-to-door anywhere in the metro area as well. Keep Tami in mind for all of your special events and fundraisers. Feast your eyes at the display case and then place your order for creamy rich cheesecake at Muddy Paws.

2528 Hennepin Avenue S, Minneapolis MN
(612) 377-4441 or (763) 545-7161
(business, wedding and delivery)
www.muddypawscheesecake.com

The Grand Hand Gallery

At the Grand Hand Gallery in St. Paul, owner Ann Ruhr Pifer showcases crafts that reveal the hand of the artist at work. A strong sense of authenticity is important to Ann, who brings together an earthy contemporary collection of functional pieces, including pottery plates, bowls and vases. Beyond work in clay, metal, wood and glass, the gallery has vibrant fiber art, including dolls, rugs and blankets. The clothing and jewelry here promise to adorn the wearer in ways possible only with handmade pieces of great quality and power. The gallery, which opened in 2004, carries pieces from across the country but specializes in work by Minnesota, Wisconsin and Iowa artists. Ann says she selects her artwork in precisely the same way she hopes her customers will. "When I see something that I absolutely love, it is as if it hits me physically in the center of my chest and makes gasp," she says. Ann believes that when customers find a piece that hits them that way, they should take it home right away, because it will make them happy every day. The opportunities for that type of happiness are abundant at the Grand Hand Gallery. The Grand Hand represents some of the finest artisans in the Midwest, including the cream of Minnesota's clay artists. Collectors from across the country converge here to find museum-quality work at reasonable prices. Bring home artwork that speaks volumes about its maker from the Grand Hand Gallery.

611 Grand Avenue, St. Paul MN (651) 312-1122
www.thegrandhand.com

Grand Hill Gallery

St. Paul artist Douglas Nielsen shows his art at his Grand Hill Gallery. He also restores oil paintings and offers exemplary picture framing services. Douglas is an associate member of the Oil Painters of America, an organization founded in 1991 to emphasize the lasting value of fine drawing, color and composition, and the appreciation of light. The gallery displays plein air and studio paintings by numerous artists, predominately landscape and nature scenes. Doug's picture frames hang in the Minnesota State Capital building and in the Governer's Mansion. Doug has 30 years of experience as a picture framer. He lends a signature style to his framing, and displays more moldings than you are likely to find elsewhere in St. Paul. Visit with an artist who is knowledgeable about artistic display at Grand Hill Gallery.

333 Grand Avenue, Suite 101, St. Paul MN
(651) 227-4783
www.grandhillgallery.com

New Beginnings face and body spa

Life tugs at your peace of mind. New Beginnings face and body spa offers a vacation from life with treatments designed to restore your body and soul. From full massages to slimming wraps, dozens of signature treatments address your well-being. Brides appreciate the makeup services and so do celebrities. New Beginnings' reputation is national. A local radio station calls New Beginnings the diva spa, because it has gone on-site to help celebrities prepare for big events, such as Oscar night. Back home, packages group some of the spa's favorite treatments together. For example, Escape offers a full day of services, including a green tea manicure, a makeup application, a hot stone massage and a shampoo. Owner Melissa Sanchelli-Gabriel and her staff understand that spending time with friends is good for your spirit and have devised several spa party packages, such as the Sweet Sixteen and the Bachelorette Relax Bash. At Death by Chocolate, you'll sip a chocolate martini while enjoying a chocolate almond pedicure and a chocolate mousse massage. You'll also find treatments specifically for couples, teens and men. In addition to luxury spa services, experts offer acupuncture, hypnotherapy, dermatology and chiropractic services. For programs and treatments that address your health, visit New Beginnings face and body spa.

1672 Grand Avenue, St. Paul MN
(651) 698-1867
www.faceandbodysolutions.com

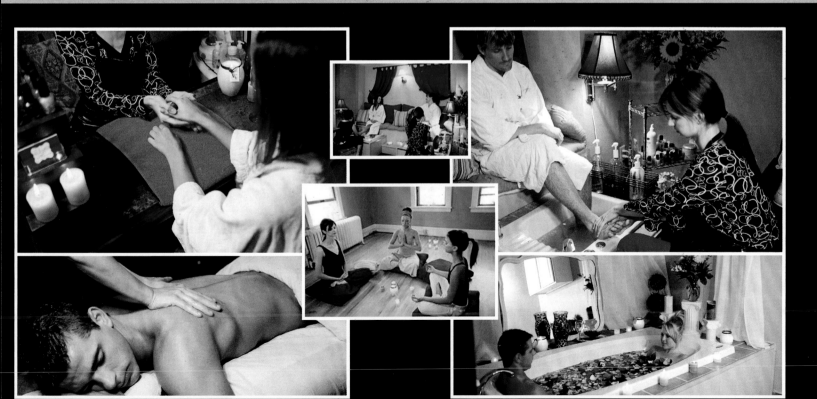

Ambiance Spa & Salon

Designed as a healing retreat, Ambiance Spa & Salon's private and inviting atmosphere blends Greek architectural romance with today's most sophisticated full-service spa experience. Highly trained technicians at Ambiance specialize in the latest hair services, skin and beauty treatments, massage techniques and nail services. With 20 hair designers trained in the latest trends and styles, Ambiance's guests know they'll be treated to the best cut, color and foil to accentuate their individual features. A 30 to 90 minute Ambiance facial treatment provides luxury and subsequent beauty enhancements that are unsurpassed. For longer lasting results, an esthetician may recommend a facial sculpting treatment. Known as the fountain of youth by satisfied clients, facial sculpting lifts sagging skin and tightens tissue by using radio frequency technology to release collagen and reduce fine lines and wrinkles. Similar results may be achieved through microdermabrasion treatment, which effectively reduces the appearance of fine-line wrinkles, acne scarring, superficial blemishes and age spots. Known for invigorating massage therapy services, Ambiance's team of therapists combine the latest ancient healing practices to soothe away tension and improve circulation. Manicures and pedicures are one of life's simple pleasures. From French manicures to full acrylic sets, Ambiance manicurists provide exquisite nail services. Whether you're looking for the perfect gift for a spouse, friend or colleague, Ambiance Spa & Salon has just the right gift of beauty and relaxation. Conveniently located in Burnsville, access to one of the most rejuvenating spa and salon experiences is just a phone call away.

13911 Aldrich Avenue S, Burnsville MN (952) 435-3300
www.ambiancespasalon.com

Just for Me—The Spa

Heidi Rosebud has strong beliefs about personal health and balance as key components to the quality of life, and her "political beauty beliefs" led her to create that reality at Just For Me—The Spa. This facility is an award-winning and nationally recognized top spa and salon. Heidi and her expert staff take pride in offering an array of treatments and services that are guaranteed to improve your sense of well-being, your appearance, and through that, your own personal growth and self-confidence. Heidi's goal is to help you look and feel your best, and she has staffed her spa/salon with top professionals in both the beauty and body treatment fields. In her salon, the stylists are both artists and highly trained professionals with international Aveda training in color, style and cutting techniques. Whatever your beauty needs, from eyelash and eyebrow tinting to makeup to exquisite hair color, cuts and Great Lengths hair extensions, the professionals at Just For Me can create your signature look. The spa provides a calm, relaxing environment where guests can leave cares behind as Heidi's top therapists ease stress, restore and rejuvenate body and mind with various types of soothing massages that address specific issues. The spa also provides foot reflexology, hot stone therapy, sea clay wraps, detoxifying body wraps, water treatments, rejuvenating facials and peels, and a full line of nail services and waxing. Just For Me is your relaxation destination.

110 S Greeley Street, Stillwater MN
(651) 439-4662
www.justformespa.com

eq-life

Health reformers in bygone eras once preached that the key to wellness was a rigid diet and restrained lifestyle. For evidence of how far we have progressed since then, you need only visit an eq-life store. Here, folks enjoy good food in the organic café, pamper themselves with a stress-reducing massage at the day spa and meet new friends in a yoga or Pilates class. Since 2003, eq-life has been helping people live healthier, happier and more balanced lives through products, services and classes. Consider it a one-stop wellness emporium. You can shop for skincare products and diet supplements or just drop by to enjoy a delicious and healthful snack. Guides stand ready throughout the store to answer questions about the products. Interactive displays invite you to pause and educate yourself about key health conditions that are impacting the American population, such as heart disease and diabetes. Workshops and classes emphasize holistic approaches to good health, while providing opportunities to meet other health-focused individuals who are pursuing their personal journeys to improved health, well-being and balanced living. The road to wellness passes through eq-life. Make a stop there soon.

870 Grand Avenue, St. Paul MN
(651) 225-2880
5803 Neal Avenue N, Oak Park Heights MN
(651) 275-2600
www.eq-life.com

Our Gang Salon and Day Spa

Styles have changed many times since Our Gang Salon and Day Spa opened in 1976, down the street from its current location. Through every style phase, the loyal clientele has counted on Our Gang to provide a great cut that matches an individual's face shape and lifestyle. "Although we keep abreast of current trends, you don't have to be under 25 years old to appreciate our services," says owner Pat Swinney, who leads a friendly and energetic staff that offers texturing and coloring in addition to its haircuts from women, men and children. The St. Paul spa provides an array of pampering as well as therapeutic treatments. You'll feel ready to take on the world at the end of your treatment session. The name of the business reflects that the professionals who work here consider themselves a family. They practice an open-door policy in this lovely old home on historic Grand Avenue. "So many salons nowadays are either very trendy or intimidating," notes Pat. Although scores of customers have been coming here for years, first-time visitors sense right away that they are welcome. Let the family vibe put you at ease as you enjoy head-to-toe indulgence at Our Gang Salon and Day Spa.

770 Grand Avenue, St. Paul MN
(651) 222-8507

Gertens

Discover the wonder of the most beautiful flora and foliage available in the Twin Cities by visiting the family-owned and operated Gertens nursery and landscape supply center. Only 10 minutes south of downtown St. Paul, this is a business known for its fresh, high-quality plants and accessories. Gertens is owned by Lewis and Glen Gerten and Gino Pitera. Since the early 1900s, Gertens has been committed to providing its customers with the best products available. The center only sells plants and trees that perform well in Minnesota's climate. Gertens also wants its customers to have fun. This is easy when the center provides landscape design services and has a friendly staff with excellent product knowledge. You can rely on several landscape designers, master gardeners and horticulturists. Gertens has such confidence that you will succeed with its plants and trees that it warranties your deciduous and evergreen trees and shrubs for one year from the date of purchase. If the plant fails to perform within the first year, Gertens will replace the tree or shrub. For beginners or those still growing a green thumb, educational seminars and clinics are available throughout the year. From bird accessories to lawn and garden products and grilling accessories, this nursery is stocked. During the holidays, Gertens transforms itself into one of the biggest Christmas shops in the Twin Cities. With the widest selection of annuals, perennials and nursery items around, combined with an expert level of service and product knowledge, Gertens makes shopping fun.

5500 Blaine Avenue, Inver Grove Heights MN
(651) 450-1501 or (866) GERTENS (437-8367)
www.gertens.com

Linder's Garden Center

The St. Paul landscape wouldn't be the same without Linder's Garden Center. The business has been around for almost a century, and it has helped enhance the beauty of countless local homes and businesses. A mark of Linder's integrity is its two-year guarantee of all trees, shrubs, perennials and hardy roses. Albert Linder founded the three-generation family-owned business in 1910. Albert grew celery and other vegetables to take to market. The vegetable business was slow, so he began to grow flowers. Albert's new line of business proved to be phenomenally popular. Today, Linder's 110 greenhouses and large outdoor planting area grow some 13 million bedding plants and a half-million perennials in 800 varieties. Linder's 50,000 poinsettias make the Christmas season festive, and the center also grows a variety of Easter plants, including lilies. In all, Linder's grows enough trees, plants and flowers to support its retail garden center and 46 seasonal satellite nurseries, called Flower Marts, located throughout the metro area. Linder's Garden Center is staffed by happy, friendly and knowledgeable folks who are kept in line by Baby, an Amazon parrot who lives in the store and has served as the company's spokesbird for 20 years. You'll want to shop at Linder's, the garden center that stands for generations of quality.

270 W Larpenteur Avenue, St. Paul MN
(651) 488-1927
www.linders.com

Pahl's Market

Pahl's Market has been a family owned and operated farm since the early 1900s. Owners Brian and Gary Pahl are fifth-generation farmers, and they take pride in growing and selling quality products on their 1,100 acres. In the early days, the family sold its products out of the back of a truck in Bloomington. By the 1980s, they had constructed a simple pole building in Apple Valley, and by 1996, the enterprise included a greenhouse. The experts at Pahl's Market can help you beautify your little piece of the world at the market's full-service garden center. You'll find 14 acres of annuals, perennials, trees and shrubs. Look for fertilizers, plant food, fountains and statuary, as well as professionals prepared to help you design a landscape. Fill up a basket with sweet corn, green beans and other summer vegetables or stop by in the fall for squash or a pick-your-own pumpkin. The kids love Pahl's Halloween haunted house and straw maze. Pahl's Market takes you into the winter holidays, too, with Christmas trees, gifts and seasonal decorations that would put a smile on Scrooge himself. The Pahl brothers continually strive for great selection, quality and low prices. Their staff is knowledgeable and ready to answer your questions. The market sponsors a frequent buyer's club to reward repeat customers; it also offers discounts to seniors. For four seasons of garden supplies and decorative solutions, visit Pahl's Market.

6885 W 160th Street, Apple Valley MN
(952) 431-4345
www.pahls.com

St. Paul Farmers' Market

St. Paul loves its fresh foods, and nowhere is this love more apparent than at the St. Paul Farmers' Market, which offers a downtown location and 17 seasonal satellite locations throughout the metro area. You'll find locally grown produce plus baked goods, cheeses and poultry. You'll also find such popular specialties as bagel sandwiches, buffalo meat and trout. Flowers, plants and shrubs are popular, too. Growers sell directly to the public, and third-party brokering is not allowed. The first St. Paul Farmers' Market opened for business in 1853 as the result of an editorial in the *Minnesota Pioneer*. It was a two-story market at 7th and Wabasha Streets that offered fresh produce in season, along with dairy products, flour, cakes and candies throughout the year. The market continues this long tradition, but has changed its main location as space requirements grew. The flagship market remains open throughout the year. During the growing season, farmers also set up in parking lots and other accessible venues throughout the city. Customers should telephone the recorded hotline for up-to-date details on hours and locations. The St. Paul Growers' Association operates the market. Association members can only sell products from Minnesota or western Wisconsin. These policies assure fair prices and freshness. When freshness counts, shop at the St. Paul Farmers' Market.

290 E 5th Street, St. Paul MN (651) 227-8101 or (651) 227-6856 (hotline)
www.stpaulfarmersmarket.com

El Burrito Mercado

Since 1979, El Burrito Mercado has been setting the standard for Mexican and Latino business in the Twin Cities. The authentic atmosphere at El Burrito Mercado is as close to a Mexican experience as you'll find this far north. From the moment you enter this combination supermarket/café, your senses are immersed in Mexican flavors, sounds, smells and sights. Owners Tomas and Maria Silva provide award-winning Mexican fare that includes everything from piñatas to furniture. Their attention to detail and progressive business practices have garnered awards from numerous critics, including *City Pages*, *Minneapolis/St. Paul Restaurant Guide*, *CitySearch*, *Pioneer Press*, *Star Tribune*, *La Prensa* and *Nuestra Gente*. The store carries everything you need to make a gourmet Mexican or Latin American dinner from scratch, ranging from hard-to-find spices to Mexican cheeses to maseca for homemade tortillas. The shop stocks Mexican imported candies, corn husks, canned peppers, baking ingredients, beverages and frozen entrees. You can also find household items like tamale steamers, tortilla warmers and Mexican soaps. To stock your pantry with the most authentic Mexican foods available in the Twin Cities, visit El Burrito Mercado in St. Paul's District Del Sol.

175 Cesar Chavez Street, St. Paul MN
(651) 227-2192
www.elburritomercado.com

Afton Alps

Looking for a winter vacation destination that includes skiing, snowboarding and snow tubing all in one convenient place? Pack up your parka and head to Afton Alps, where you'll get the most variety for your dollar. Located adjacent to a state park, Afton Alps features more than 250 acres of ski terrain, 18 chair lifts and five chalets. Paul and Robert Augustine and Tom Furlong, three farmers from Hastings, loved to ski the area's scenic hills so much that they started Afton Alps in 1963. Boasting the largest ski school and one of the largest ski areas in the Midwest, Afton Alps welcomes 250,000 visitors every year. Many area schools and churches make day trips to the Alps, and folks stream in from neighboring states for the weekend. Planning a special event? Afton Alps can host weddings, anniversaries and corporate events in several facilities sized to accommodate small or large gatherings. Not just for winter fun anymore, Afton Alps features eight miles of challenging mountain bike terrain overlooking the gorgeous St. Croix River Valley. The 18-hole golf course, opened in 1989, and the Pitch & Putt Par 3 course lets golfers enjoy a great game in beautiful surroundings and then relax over cocktails and conversation at the Club House Bar & Grill. For a variety of year-round vacation activities, come to Afton Alps, where acres of fun await your arrival.

6600 Peller Avenue S, Hastings MN
(651) 436-5245 or (800) 328-1328
www.aftonalps.com

A Rebours

A Rebours is French and means against the grain. The name is an appropriate description of the popular A Rebours restaurant in the historic Hamm Building on St. Peter Street. This fabulous restaurant bypasses the typical Americanized French cuisine that one has come to expect of Parisian-style restaurants. Instead, it offers the look and feel of a traditional bistro while providing a menu that is simply fabulous. The truly contemporary French menu offers an array of entrées that are unpretentious yet thoroughly delicious, including cocoa-scented duck with fig sauce or homemade lamb cassoulet. Additional favorites include velvety and flavorful butternut squash soup, lightly laced with sage oil, and the tempting steamed mussels, swimming in a savory bath of subtly curried butter. A Rebours is also recognized for its eclectic wine list that features a cornucopia of perfectly chosen wines that will highlight any dish. From the exceptional service to the incomparable cuisine, A Rebours is the place to go for a fantastic French experience.

410 St. Peter Street, St. Paul MN   (651) 665-0656

The Bierstube

Since 1962, delicious German and American food and drink, plus fabulous service, have been family traditions at The Bierstube. Larry Yanz opened the first Bierstube in Hastings in 1962. Originally from Germany but now living in Hastings, Hilde thought she could add some German flair and applied for a job at the Bierstube. Before long, Hilde became Larry's bride. The rest, as they say, is history. Since then, the Yanz family has opened four more locations. The Bierstube menu is loaded with German and American favorites, such as sauerbraten, marinated roast beef served Bavarian-style with spätzle and red cabbage. For a full experience of German cuisine, try the Taste of Deutschland platter, which includes a variety of The Bierstube's German dishes, including Wiener schnitzel and bratwurst. The celebrated Reuben is a favorite. For true German authenticity, try Hilde's German meatballs, served on the first Saturday of the month. Bierstube means beer parlor, and you can expect excellent cold beers on tap. The Bierstube makes a fine gathering spot for television viewing of all major sporting events, including the Minnesota Twins, Timberwolves, Wild, Vikings and all Minnesota Gophers games. A big Oktoberfest bash is the highlight of the fall season. Today, a second generation of the Yanz family follows in the footsteps of Larry and Hilde, who have passed on. The members of the third generation, still toddlers, have given their names to menu items: the Max Burger, Sammy's Steak Sandwich and Maci's Mega Grilled Cheese. It's the sense of family that makes each Bierstube restaurant such a congenial place to have a meal or a drink with friends. Larry and Hilde's sons, Mike and Jim, and Jim's wife Jodi co-own the Hastings and Inver Grove locations, while Jim and Jodi own the Oakdale restaurant, and Mike owns the Red Wing branch. Jim and Jodi, along with Jim and Shelly McArdle, preside over the White Bear Lake site. The restaurants are active supporters of youth sports and participate in many charitable functions in their respective communities. Let the Yanz family serve your family and friends at The Bierstube.

109 W 11th Street, Hastings MN (651) 437-8259
233 Withers Harbor Drive, Red Wing MN (651) 385-8852
6434 Cahill Avenue, Inver Grove Heights MN (651) 451-8073
7121 10th Street N, Oakdale MN (651) 731-8381
2670 E County Road E, White Bear Lake MN (651) 773-5854
www.thebierstube.com

Boca Chica Restaurant

The oldest Mexican restaurant in the Twin Cities celebrates Mexican culture not just through food, but through music, art and history. At Boca Chica, beautiful murals depicting key moments in Mexican history decorate the walls. Live music plays at Sunday brunch and on two Saturday nights a month. Gloria Frias started the business in the 1964 with her late husband Guillermo. Together they have created flavorful, authentic Mexican food with recipes from different regions of Mexico. Boca Chica was named the Best Mexican Restaurant for 2005 and 2006 by *Mpls. St. Paul Magazine*. It has won many awards for its homemade salsa and Margaritas. Some highlights from the menu include *Guisados de Puerco*, rich and satisfying stews of pork in either chipolte or tomatillo sauce. The *Pescado a la Boca Chica* marries Mexico and Minnesota with a walleye fillet topped with Gloria's own poblano sauce. There are varieties of enchiladas as well as sopes, tamales, carnitas, *mole poblano* and *carne asada*. Choose from the Tex-Mex section for more familiar favorites such as tostadas, tacos and burritos. The weekday lunch buffet and Sunday brunch buffet offer a delicious sampling of menu favorites. For the tastes, sights and sounds of Mexico near downtown St. Paul, try Boca Chica Restaurant.

11 Cesar Chavez Street, St. Paul MN
(651) 222-8499
www.bocachicarestaurant.com

Café Cravings

Café Cravings lives up to its name by serving delicious breakfast, lunch and dinner, fine fresh-roasted coffee and delectable desserts in a relaxed atmosphere. One visit to this popular café and you'll be craving a return visit. The Rick family opened the first Café Cravings in White Bear Lake in 1995, then went on to open a St. Paul location. They began selling fine espresso well before the current coffee craze started. The rich and smooth coffee found here is made from fine Arabica beans and roasted freshly every week. You can buy it by the cup or take home whole beans for fresh-ground home preparation. Breakfasts here are so magnificent that you'll want to skip dinner to make room for them. Consider Bananas Foster, a waffle or French toast topped with the house's rum caramel sauce, sliced bananas, whipped cream and toasted pecans. Other breakfast fare worth lingering over includes omelettes, croissants and bagels. Delicious soups and salads as well as hot and cold sandwiches promise a satisfying lunch or light dinner. The café also specializes in pasta entrées, including white chicken spinach lasagna. If these aren't enough to develop a craving, dive into cookies and cheesecakes. Everything's made from scratch at Café Cravings. The St. Paul location features live music on the weekend. Café Cravings is so popular that the Ricks are opening two more cafés, in Maplewood and Blaine. Develop a habit you won't want to kick with a visit to Café Cravings.

1600 E County Road E, White Bear Lake MN
(651) 482-7742
271 W 7ᵗʰ Street, St. Paul MN
(651) 224-1554
www.cravingsmn.com

Cafe Latté

Cafe Latté has been serving customers reasonably priced, gourmet quality food, fresh-baked breads and scones, and award-winning desserts for more than 20 years. Cafe Latté has been endorsed for Best Desserts by *Mpls.St.Paul Magazine* for the past 15 years. Cafe Latté is actually three restaurants in one. First, it is a gourmet cafeteria serving an ever-changing selection of soups, stews, chilis, creative salads and design-your-own sandwiches. Second, it is a retail bakery specializing in fresh-baked hearth breads and scones, wonderful cheesecakes, tortes, cupcakes and the famous turtle cake. Finally, it is a wine bar serving creative pizzas, bruschetta and salads and an extensive list of reasonably priced wines by the bottle or glass. Owners Peter and Linda Quinn continually strive to improve product quality and customer service while maintaining a tradition of giving back to the community they serve. If you're looking for a hearty meal or just care to relax with a latte and slice of dessert, Cafe Latté is waiting to serve you.

850 Grand Avenue, St. Paul MN (651) 224-5687
www.cafelatte.com

Axel's

For more than 10 years, partners Linda Young and Charlie Burrows have been changing the landscape of casual fine dining in the Twin Cities area with their wonderful collection of Axel's restaurants. At Axel's, patrons can enjoy fabulous lunch and dinner entrées as well as sensational Sunday brunches. Menu favorites include perfectly prepared walleye and mouthwatering steaks. Axel's adheres to the philosophy that if employees are well taken care of and happy that the customers will be well taken care of and happy. This philosophy has served it well. The warm and welcoming atmosphere and personable staff members make for an ideal backdrop to the fabulous cuisine of this popular family of restaurants. It all began when the two partners purchased their first restaurant, formally the Parker House, in 1996 and opened Axel's River Grille, the first of five Axel's locations. Young, who received a Woman to Watch award, began working with her parents at the Parker House when she was just 11 years old. In the mid-1990s, Young and her good friend Charlie Burrows chose to join forces to fulfill their joint dream of restaurant ownership. With the help of family and friends, Young and Burrows opened the doors to their dream eatery, renaming the Parker House after Young's father, Axel, who was a well-known and beloved member of the community. The restaurant was an instant success and as popularity grew, Young and Burrows began expanding. Come by today for a terrific meal and an unbeatable dining experience at Axel's.

1318 Sibley Memorial Highway, Mendota MN (651) 686-4840
560 W 78th Street, Chanhassen MN (952) 934-9340
9555 Wedgewood Drive, Woodbury MN (651) 294-3160
2540 N Cleveland Avenue, Roseville MN (651) 367-3967
130 W Railway Street, Loretto MN (763) 479-1788
www.axelsbonfire.com

Axel's Bonfire Wood Fire Cooking

Savor the flavors of Americana at Axel's Bonfire Wood Fire Cooking. This popular, family-oriented restaurant offers patrons a distinctive Southwestern menu filled with delicious entrées such as wood-fire prepared steaks, pizzas and chicken. Additional menu favorites include perfectly prepared walleye and Bull Bites appetizers, along with desserts that are made from scratch daily. Kids will especially enjoy building their own pizzas and sundaes. Axel's Bonfire's primary goal is to provide a warm, caring and respectful atmosphere where all of its guests will feel comfortable. The owners, Linda Young, Charlie Burrows and Mike Gehlen, opened their first Axel's Bonfire Wood Fire Cooking restaurant in 2001, before expanding to what is now six locations. Young, Burrows and Gehlen operate on the principal that if the employees are happy then everything else will fall into place. This is certainly true of Axel's Bonfire, where the service is always excellent and friendly. Come by today for a terrific meal and an unbeatable dining experience at Axel's Bonfire Woodfire Cooking.

1555 Cliff Road, Eagan MN
(651) 452-0200

1424 Weir Drive, Woodbury MN
(651) 735-0085

850 Grand Avenue, St. Paul MN
 (651) 312-1299

14120 S Highway 13, Savage MN
(952) 447-1122

4365 Pheasant Ridge Drive NE, Blaine MN
(763) 398-2475

3000 Harbor Lane, Plymouth MN
(763) 398-7408

www.axelsbonfire.com

Village Bistro

The Village Bistro remains what it has always been, a place where working people and families find meals worth their time and money. Some customers who have frequented the restaurant all their lives remember getting their first job here as kids. They still find the selections and memories they cherish. You can choose from a large breakfast menu any time of the day. Burgers and sandwiches remain mainstays. Dinners can be downright special with such selections as a simple but delightful walleye dish, steak or pasta. You might find lobster cakes or breaded quail offered as a change of pace. The home-cooked flavors are the result of starting from scratch, applying care and using quality ingredients in the cooking. This classic American bistro offers an inviting interior with old wood on the walls and softly lit booths. In 2002, Corbin Lacina and Steve Gerber purchased the Highland Park restaurant, which has gone by various names since it opened in the 1950s. The two gave it a new name, a much-needed face-lift and some updated menu selections. Otherwise, history prevails. For a restaurant in tune with its neighborhood, come to Village Bistro.

2012 Ford Parkway, St. Paul MN
(651) 698-6335

Margaux, A Brasserie

Margaux, A Brasserie is an intimate and romantic restaurant that manages to be both upscale and casual. Margaret Doran first opened Margaux Limitee in White Bear Lake before moving her restaurant to downtown St. Paul, opening at the present location on Valentine's Day 2005. Her menu features contemporary American cuisine, plus extensive French and Belgian selections and a comprehensive fine wine list. This neighborhood brasserie serves starters, sandwiches and full entrées until 10 each night, and the bar stays open until midnight. Drinks are wonderfully interesting, whether you are ordering a martini from a full menu of martinis, one of the many Belgian beers, a glass of wine or a Jamaican Ginger Ale. Some folks come in just for the dark roast coffee and freshly made desserts. Margaux is French and fun with loft style dining and a friendly atmosphere. A lovely Van Gogh mural sets a bright and cheerful tone. Margaux is just the spot for a variety of occasions, from a casual night out to a special celebration. Margaret offers catering and makes the restaurant available for private parties. For an atmosphere and a menu full of European character and charm, plan a visit to Margaux, A Brasserie.

486 Robert Street N, St. Paul MN
(651) 407-6438

Casper and Runyon's Nook

Casper and Runyon's Nook in St. Paul knows more about hamburgers than almost anyone. This well-loved neighborhood restaurant has been serving up burgers and fries since 1938. Ted Casper and Mike Runyon, the current owners, continue building on the traditions begun so many years ago when the place was known simply as the Nook. Ted and Mike bought the restaurant in 2000. Before that, a friend of Ted's family, Mickey Brausen, owned it for nearly 30 years. Long before Ted and Mike knew each other, they shared a love for the Nook. Both attended high school right across the street from the restaurant and came into the Nook just about every day for hand-cut fries and burgers served on fresh buns that were made daily by a bakery down the street. Much of the menu is the same today, and the famous burgers are still made on a seasoned grill. Additions to the original menu include steaks, sandwiches, salads and seasonal soups. You can also purchase beer and wine with your meal. Even the walls of this Minnesota landmark speak to its history. You'll find many local awards, including an award for Best Fries from *City Page*'s Best of the Twin Cities. A photo and handwritten note from patron Barbra Streisand occupies a special place on the wall. Babs loves it here and so will you. Treat your taste buds to the old-fashioned burgers, fries and fun atmosphere of Casper and Runyon's Nook.

492 Hamline Avenue S, St. Paul MN (651) 698-4347

Chart House Restaurant

The Chart House Restaurant, on the shores of Lake Kingsley, has offered guests award-winning cuisine and unsurpassed service since 1968. Long favored by Twin Cities residents both for fine dining and special events, Josh and Matt Ruppert's restaurant boasts one of the most scenic lakeside patios in the area. Executive Chef Matt Ruppert contemporary American menu includes his signature champagne chicken and succulent prime rib as well as weekly specials incorporating Latin American and Mediterranean influences. The Sunday brunch is also a hit. The newly remodeled dining room is dressed with elegant white linens. Musicians play live for your dining and dancing pleasure on Friday and Saturday. Looking for a place to celebrate the weekend? Relax with friends or colleagues over cocktails, conversation and casual food in the Lounge or Lakeside Patio. For a change of pace, experience outdoor dining under the lakeside pavilion or near the fountain, then take an after-dinner stroll through the manicured grounds and enjoy the view of the koi pond from the bridge. The perfect place to host your special event, the Chart House offers customized menus, beautiful indoor and outdoor reception sites and convenient valet parking for your wedding or other celebration. Come enjoy memorable dining, impeccable service and spectacular garden and lakeside views at Chart House Restaurant.

11287 Klamath Trail, Lakeville MN
(952) 435-7156
www.charthouserestaurant.com

Cesare's Wine Bar, Wine Shop & Marketplace

The Cesare's locations are a labor of love for their four owners, Robert and Leslie Alexander, Richard Lay and Kirsten Lysne. Robert is an artisan cabinet maker and former home builder, and Rich is an architect. The two teamed up to design and create stunning spaces in which to enjoy a bottle of wine or a fine dinner. Leslie, in addition to being the pastry chef, is a painter whose work is displayed throughout the restaurant and shops. Cesare's Wine Bar carries a list of 450 carefully selected wines, priced reasonably and served flawlessly by a staff that knows its stuff. The same wines are available for purchase in the Wine Shop. Cesare's Wine Bar features an exceptional seasonal menu. The simple selection of entrées changes every other week, on a menu that also includes small plates, pizzas, salads and scrumptious desserts. The Marketplace carries a smaller menu of pastas, tasting plates and sweets. To say that the food complements the wine is an understatement, but then again, most things you could say about Cesare's would be an understatement. The food is beautifully presented and flat-out delicious. Many of the gourmet food items that go into Cesare's dishes are sold in the Marketplace for you to enjoy at home. While it is true that sophisticated wine environments can be intimidating, Cesare's is anything but. The atmosphere is warm and comfortable, creating a non-threatening ease that makes an evening at Cesare's delightful for both wine geeks and wine novices. At last, the Twin Cities has a complete resource for delicious wines and foods that you can either take home or enjoy during a night out of fabulous dining.

Cesare's Wine Bar:
102 S Second Street, Stillwater MN (651) 439-1352
Cesare's Wine Shop:
610 N Main Street, Stillwater MN   (651) 439-7111
Cesare's Marketplace:
610 N Main Street, Stillwater MN   (651) 439-1332
www.cesareswinebar.com

Copper Bleu

Suburban Lakeville added a classy new restaurant in 2006 that has everything a diner could want, from stylish surroundings to well-prepared updates of American classic dishes. Owner Scott Winer brings 16 years of experience to the restaurant, which is a sleek, modern version of an old-fashioned supper club, but is also open for lunch and a weekly brunch. Local Chef Tobie Nidetz designed the menu, which features sophisticated steak and seafood selections, burgers and salads. The gourmet Maytag blue cheese appears in dishes throughout the menu, from the Copper Blue Wedge Salad to the Blue Velvet Burger and the Bleu Cheese Fondue. Popular fish dishes include the pecan-crusted walleye and the blue cheese crusted filet. The sandwich known as the Walleye Slider appears on both the adult and kids' menu. Make way for out-of-this-world desserts and such specialty coffees as the Copper Coffee, a blend of Frangelico liqueur and French Vanilla Royale coffee. Freshly squeezed juices and wines poured at your table are welcome touches, as is the build-your-own mashed potatoes cart. The restaurant flaunts a copper and stone exterior and rich earth-toned interior with lots of natural light and glints of copper. A friendly staff excels in putting you at ease. For a dining experience that brings good taste to the food and the surroundings, visit Copper Bleu.

17516 Dodd Boulevard, Lakeville MN
(952) 431-5050
www.copperbleu.com

Borderline Bar & Grill

Borderline Bar & Grill is a sports bar with a NASCAR theme. This Lakeland Shores bar and grill attracts a friendly mix of people, including families, with everything from typical bar food to classy entrées. Owners Greg Briggs and Rod Graf have put together an irresistible mix of homey atmosphere, varied entertainment and dining options. Start with the fresh food. Borderline makes the sauce for the pizzas itself. The burgers and onion rings are extremely popular. If you are looking for a tidbit or a starter to a larger meal, consider the coconut shrimp, mini tacos or sirloin bites. If you're still hungry, choose from grilled sirloin, soup, salad or such pasta dishes as ravioli or fettuccini. You can cozy up to the bar's fireplace with the beer, wine or

hard liquor of your choice. Or choose the outdoor patio or an indoor dining room fitted with 17 televisions for watching the big game with friends and family. A live band often plays in the evening. When the weather cooperates, the outdoor area features sporting games and entertainment. Kids enjoy the indoor game room. No matter what your age or interest, Borderline Bar & Grill invites you to join the fun.

157 St. Croix Trail N,
Lakeland Shores MN
(651) 436-7560

Dixie's on Grand

Dixie's on Grand serves up a 20-year tradition of down-home Southern comfort food with award-winning barbecue and smokehouse specialties. A master of Southern hospitality, the head chef consistently delights his guests by mixin' Old World charm with New World flavors. The St. Paul classic delights customers with a downright diverse menu of savory fixin's, from tantalizing jambalaya to coconut fried shrimp and black bean salsa. With a full bar, extensive wine list, and frothy array of 15 beers on tap, Dixie's serves up sensational seafood gumbo, blackened catfish and Carolina crab cakes in homey dining rooms or on a heated outdoor patio. Ya'll better save some room for the key lime or butterscotch-pecan pie. While you're here, bring home some of Dixie's beef jerky to your next-o'-kin. If you're bringing a crowd, you can reserve Dixie's Key West Room for up to 60 people. If y'all can't come on down, Dixie's will be happy to cater your la-di-da occasion. Start you Sunday Creole-style with Dixie's Southern brunch. You'll like the

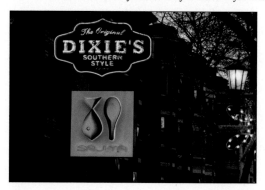

heapin' portions, made-to-order omelettes, champagne and smooth jazz. For your foot-stompin' delight, expect a spicy mix of rock, zydeco or jazz on Fridays and Saturdays, with valet parking to boot. Dixie's keeps long hours seven days a week with a three-hour happy hour. Load up your kith and kin and come on over to Dixie's on Grand.

695 Grand Avenue, St. Paul MN
(651) 222-7345
www.dixiesongrand.com

Cossetta

Everybody in St. Paul who loves Italian food has heard of Cossetta. The business has been around since 1911, when a young man from Calabria, Italy named Michael Cossetta opened a food market in a tiny building in the Italian neighborhood known as the Upper Levee. The Cossetta family didn't always wait for customers to come to the store but would sell its famous sausages out of pushcarts. Several expansions and moves to new locations followed throughout the years until Cossetta became what it is today: a pizzeria and Italian market with a deli that is much beloved by everyone who has been there. In the last few years alone, *Mpls.St.Paul Magazine* has recognized Cossetta for Best Pizza, Best Deli and Best Sausage in addition to inducting it into its Hall of Fame as Best Eatery. Add awards for Best Italian Food and Best Family Friendly Restaurant from online sources such as AOL City Guide and City Pages, and you soon get the idea that your appetite will never forgive you if you don't eat at this St. Paul institution or take some of Cossetta's meats, breads and cheeses home with you. Visit Cossetta, the place that has been bringing Italy to St. Paul for four generations.

211 W 7th Street, St. Paul MN (651) 222-3476
www.cossettaeventi.com

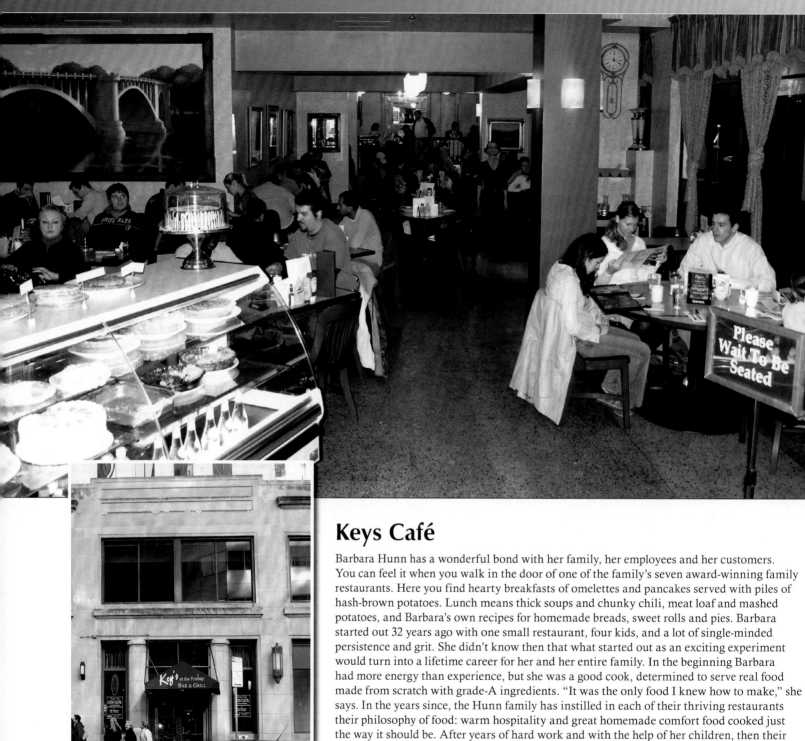

Keys Café

Barbara Hunn has a wonderful bond with her family, her employees and her customers. You can feel it when you walk in the door of one of the family's seven award-winning family restaurants. Here you find hearty breakfasts of omelettes and pancakes served with piles of hash-brown potatoes. Lunch means thick soups and chunky chili, meat loaf and mashed potatoes, and Barbara's own recipes for homemade breads, sweet rolls and pies. Barbara started out 32 years ago with one small restaurant, four kids, and a lot of single-minded persistence and grit. She didn't know then that what started out as an exciting experiment would turn into a lifetime career for her and her entire family. In the beginning Barbara had more energy than experience, but she was a good cook, determined to serve real food made from scratch with grade-A ingredients. "It was the only food I knew how to make," she says. In the years since, the Hunn family has instilled in each of their thriving restaurants their philosophy of food: warm hospitality and great homemade comfort food cooked just the way it should be. After years of hard work and with the help of her children, then their spouses, and now her grandchildren, the string of Keys Cafés are now the most award-winning family restaurants in the St. Paul area. Barbara and her children are the reason behind Keys Café's reputation for some of the best breakfasts and comfort food around.

767 Raymond Avenue, St. Paul MN (651) 646-5756 *www.keyscafe.com*

Ho Ho Gourmet

The greatest sign of approval for Sum and Kaling Wong comes when Chinese people tell them how good the food at their restaurant is. The place is called Ho Ho Gourmet, and it has been a St. Paul favorite for Cantonese-style dishes since 1990. Sum and Kaling say that Cantonese is the tastiest of the many regional cuisines of China. Of course, they might be a bit partial, but then again, the lines of people at the buffet speak for themselves. The lunch buffet is an everyday affair at Ho Ho, while the dinner buffet is offered on Friday and Saturday. Customers may always order from the menu, and takeout is popular as well. A casual atmosphere complements the savory, moderately priced food. Sum and Kaling never tire of hearing people tell them that their food is fantastic. In fact, it challenges them to maintain the level of excellence that folks have come to expect. Is Cantonese the tastiest? Decide for yourself when you eat at Ho Ho Gourmet.

1985 Old Hudson Road, St. Paul MN
(651) 731-0316

Glockenspiel

The best German cuisine is famous for its hearty richness and flavor. It conjures up visions of robust, happy laughter, rosy-cheeked friends and family, and huge tables filled with tankards of beer and fantastic food. That is exactly what you will find at Glockenspiel: authentic German food, beer, atmosphere—even a terrific waitstaff that speaks German. This German restaurant does it right with its tall ceilings, polished brass, and gingerbread décor. You can polka, foxtrot and two-step to live music every Wednesday night and enjoy a strolling accordion player on Fridays. The extensive menu is laden with German dishes such as *Bratwürste*, *Käsespätzle* and *Weisswürste* accompanied by onion tarts, hearty soups, sauerkraut, cabbage and a plethora of potato dishes. For every mouthwatering meal there is a fine imported German, Austrian, Russian or Lithuanian beer or ale to keep it company. A month after the restaurant opened in 2000, a restaurant reviewer brought a friend visiting from Germany to Glockenspiel. Clearly impressed, the German friend said, "Wow, this smells like a German restaurant. I mean, it smells like a real restaurant, in Germany. …This is so right, this is exactly what my parent's friends would have when they got together." What better recommendation could anyone want?

605 W. 7ᵗʰ Street, St. Paul MN
(651) 292-9421
www.glockenspielrestaurant.com

Grand Shanghai

Have you ever tried Shanghai-style food? You may have eaten at dozens of Chinese restaurants, but Chinese cuisine is so diverse that it's possible you have yet to explore the specialties of Chef Tak Yeung at Grand Shanghai. Since 1991, he has been offering his own take on egg foo yung, moo shu pork and many other popular favorites while inviting guests to try Shanghai soups and delicious Hong Kong noodles. You will find many familiar choices on the extensive menu as well temptations for more adventurous appetites. In the latter category, try the steamed or deep-fried walleye. The steamed dumplings are the most popular item from the appetizers menu and could easily make a small meal in themselves. A perennial favorite is the Peking duck. For a bargain-priced feast, go to Grand Shanghai for the lunch buffet on Monday through Saturday. Trained in Hong Kong, Chef Yeung enjoys creating new dishes and says that if customers love his food, that is his reward. Everything is cooked fresh. Yeung promises that even your take-out order will be made to order and handled quickly, even if you don't call ahead. For a Chinese lunch or dinner Shanghai-style, eat at Grand Shanghai.

1328 Grand Avenue, St. Paul MN
(651) 698-1901

The Lexington

Established in 1935, the Lexington restaurant is a unique spot with timeless style. Whether you are a twice-a-week regular or a first-time diner, the staff and management at the Lexington will make every effort to ensure that your needs are met. After more than 70 years, this restaurant's reputation for superior food and excellent guest relations is well-established. The fabled steaks, fresh salmon and walleye almondine are perfect choices for lunch or dinner. If your tastes turn to more home-style dishes, try the award-winning short ribs, chicken pot pie, pot roast or St. Paul's finest hamburger. The restaurant itself is a masterpiece of carved wood, chandeliers and Old World charm. The private banquet rooms boast an antique bar, a fireplace and stained glass windows sure to make any occasion that you may celebrate memorable. The Lexington has been an integral part of St. Paul tradition for generations. Visit it and you will feel like you have come home.

1096 Grand Avenue, St. Paul MN
(651) 222-5878
www.the-lexington.com

La Grolla

Anyone who has had the privilege of eating in Italy knows that there's a difference between true Italian food and American reproductions. It's not the complexity or the combination of the ingredients but their freshness and purity that makes the difference, whether you're eating at a four-star restaurant or a small village café. At La Grolla, you'll find the atmosphere of the village café with a four-star Italian chef at the helm, located right in the heart of St. Paul. A former personal chef to Donald Trump, Antonio Tattamanzi owned restaurants in Italy, New York and Florida before coming to Minnesota in 1998. At La Grolla, he has created a simple, intimate restaurant emphasizing fresh, local and often organic ingredients in Northern Italian recipes. The restaurant's name, which means *cup of friendship*, suggests the spirit of personal hospitality found here. You can dress up or dress down as the occasion warrants while enjoying handmade pastas, a famous dessert menu and a lovely outdoor eating area. A full-service bar serves Italian wines and beer, and a happy longtime staff with little turnover offers warm and attentive customer service. For a genuine taste of Italy, come to La Grolla.

452 Selby Avenue, St. Paul MN
(651) 221-1061

Jensen's Supper Club

The 1940s and 1950s were the glory era of supper clubs, classy places where people went to celebrate stylishly with family and friends. Doron and Derek Jensen opened Jensen's Supper Club in 1996, dedicated to their grandparents. Al and Mabel Jensen started their own café 50 years ago and introduced both of their grandsons to the restaurant business. Doron and Derek wanted to carry on the restaurant business in the grand old tradition of the supper club. Jensen's has a traditional supper club menu of wonderful steak and seafood entrées, family-style side dishes and a selection of martinis that would take Dean Martin's breath away. Try an appetizer of supper club frog legs or coconut shrimp and follow it with a king cut of prime rib. Or impress your group with a juicy porterhouse steak big enough for two, Alaskan king crab legs and, because you're in Minnesota, a walleye fillet deliciously prepared any number of ways. Steaming sides of garlic mashed potatoes, Jensen's hash browns, creamed spinach and asparagus with hollandaise sauce are meant to be passed around and shared. If you're looking for that special place to have your wedding rehearsal dinner or business banquet, Jensen's can accommodate up to 100 people for a fabulous meal, accompanied by live music. The warm atmosphere and terrific service hearken back to a simpler time when men always wore suits and a hat, women wore gloves and going out to dinner at a supper club was a just little bit glamorous.

3840 Sibley Memorial Highway, Eagan MN
(651) 688-7969
jensenssupperclub.com

La Cucaracha

La Cucaracha has been serving authentic Mexican food for 40 years in the historic Crocus Hill area on Grand and Dale, a district of great dining and shopping. Cozy private booths compliment the colorful atmosphere in every room. Owners and sisters Nina Turner and Gina Acevedo grew up in this business, where their mother stressed the importance of tradition. They learned their lessons well, because La Cucaracha is a down-to-earth, neighborhood-style restaurant where people come to come to eat, celebrate and have a good time. Culinary specialties include Nina's pepper cactus stew, shrimp tacos and hot green pork. Enjoy award-winning soups, such as the house chicken soup with *pico de gallo* and grilled shrimp soup. Your visit here will be a happy, memorable experience in a unpretentious environment.

36 S Dale Street, St. Paul MN
(651) 221-9682

O'Gara's Bar & Grill

O'Gara's is one of the finest entertainment establishments in the Twin Cities, a place of nostalgia, charm and good humor. O'Gara's is everything you can imagine and more. Not only does O'Gara's offer a truly Irish experience in décor and ambience, but it's menu encompasses the best Irish and American cuisine. Perhaps your mouth waters at the thought of perfectly prepared corned beef and cabbage. Items such as the Selby Chicken Sandwich or the Snelling Melt make O'Gara's a real find. In 1941, James Freeman O'Gara first opened the doors of his tavern to the local residents who fought in the World War II homefront by manufacturing supplies and munitions for those overseas. You could even get a haircut from Carl Schulz, whose son, Charles, gained international fame with the cartoon strip Peanuts. Schulz's original shop was located in what is now the game room. Since then, O'Gara's has been an integral part of the St. Paul community, now arguably the busiest spot in town on St. Patrick's Day. The O'Gara tradition continues with James's grandson, Dan, and his wife, Kris, who now run the family business with the same passion as their grandfather. Visit a piece of history. Head three blocks south of I-94 to find O'Gara's, located on the corner of Snelling and Selby.

164 N Snelling Avenue, St. Paul MN
(651) 644-3333
www.ogaras.com

Photos by Todd Buchanan/Metropolitan Media Group

McHattie's Victorian Times

The conversion of an 1850s farmhouse eight years ago provided not only a new home for Joe and Roxanne Kielbasa, but a restaurant that goes beyond expertly prepared food to provide a bridge of sorts between the slower paced 19th century and the non-stop present. McHattie's Victorian Times, surrounded by six acres of flowers, herbs and vegetables, is the result of the Kielbasa's desire for a simpler, country-based life and Roxanne's love of cooking. The restaurant began as a teahouse, serving special teas and luncheons, then developed elaborate five-course wine dinners on pre-scheduled weekends. All seating is by reservation only. "We're a world away from ordinary dining," says Roxanne, referring to the ambience as well as the extraordinary food quality and presentation. Roxanne delights in using original recipes and prepares everything from scratch with seasonings from her garden. Her signature scones are the best anywhere. Each meal begins with a seasonally inspired starter such as mushroom soup or strawberry spinach salad. The menu changes frequently, but favorites include stuffed pork tenderloin, chicken mixed with lentils, salmon fillets and vegetable quiche, with an appropriate wine accompanying each course. McHattie's offers catering and makes a lovely setting for weddings and private parties with room to seat up to 50 people. Roxanne revels in life's bountiful details and fills her antebellum house with comfortable furnishings, expertly prepared food, friendly service and great wine. Call for a reservation at McHattie's Victorian Times, where body and soul find satisfaction.

10350 Bailey Road, Woodbury MN (651) 768-8753 *www.mchatties.com*

O'Malley's Irish Pub

O'Malley's Irish Pub is a perfect fit for Beth and Todd Hanson and the neighborhood they love. They built the restaurant and bar themselves with the help of a few family members and friends and modeled it after that television bar of fame, Cheers. Like Cheers, they aim to provide a truly local restaurant and bar where everyone knows your name. The food is, of course, Irish in theme. The menu ranges from homemade shepherd's pie to Papa O'Malley's Delight, a dish of corned beef, Swiss cheese and sauerkraut in crisp wontons topped with Thousand Island dressing. Alongside such favorites you'll also find a selection of Americanized dishes, including beef and veggie burgers, Jameson barbecue ribs and children's entrées. O'Malley's features a large and comfortable central seating area with a four-sided fireplace and leather couches. Patrons can enjoy a game of darts or catch major-league sports on one of the large-screen plasma televisions. Employees and customers alike pride themselves on making new friends and welcoming newcomers, so no visitor will leave O'Malley's a stranger. Be sure to stop in at O'Malley's Irish Pub for a glass of wine or beer, an affordable and tasty meal, a game of darts or an evening of talking and laughing.

1775 Radio Drive, Woodbury MN
(651) 578-7007
www.omalleysluckyirishpub.com

Patrick McGovern's Pub

On your next visit to the Twin Cities, bypass the hustle and bustle of downtown and head to West 7th Street, near St. Paul's Irvine Park district, the home of Patrick McGovern's Pub. This neighborhood pub features an atmosphere just right for friendly gatherings and cozy suppers and offers a refreshing change from roadside fare and nouvelle cuisine. Owners Pat and Dianne Boemer and their friendly staff members, many of whom have been with the pub for years, are dedicated to providing exceptional service and serving up a menu of classic pub favorites. Patrick McGovern's first opened its doors in 1982 and has since built a loyal following of customers who regularly come in for its hearty and delicious menu options. The open-faced hot turkey sandwich, made from house-roasted, hand-carved turkey, is one of the most popular items. Other favorites include pot roast, pork chops, a variety of salad selections and the sensational meat loaf, homemade with fresh, quality ingredients. Located in an historic 1888 building, Patrick McGovern's is the perfect place to sit back, relax with friends and enjoy a meal. In warm weather months, the charming, three-tiered stone patio with a spectacular wood-burning fireplace and full-service bar offers outdoor seating amidst lush perennials, trees and a calming waterfall built with Lake Superior rock. Discover your new favorite neighborhood pub when you visit Patrick McGovern's Pub for some great food and good conversation.

225 W 7th Street, St. Paul MN
(651) 224-5821

Tavern on Grand

The Tavern on Grand specializes in walleye, and hungry patrons can have the signature northern fish for lunch or dinner. Walleye enthusiasts and those trying the fish for the first time are all equally welcome. The *Twin Cities Dining Guide* wrote, "Tavern on Grand is the place you should bring your out-of-state friends to give them a true taste for Minnesota." It's easy to spot the Tavern on Grand because it features a giant neon walleye in the window. Meeting the locals is easy at this cozy casual dining restaurant with a log cabin décor. The staff consists of friendly, smiling faces willing to go the extra mile to make your dining experience pleasant. Patrons who pass on the delectable walleye will find plenty of other choices, from classics such as spaghetti or burgers to regional favorites such as the Philly cheesesteak, the B.L.T. or the grilled cheese sandwich. The Tavern offers many varieties of red and white wines from around the world, as well as beers on tap and in the bottle, so diners can easily find the perfect beverage to complement their meal. For an enjoyable dinner and a truly local experience, you can't miss the Tavern on Grand.

656 Grand Avenue, St. Paul MN
(651) 228-9030
www.tavernongrand.com

Grand Thai Restaurant

Grand Thai Restaurant offers diners a fittingly grand Asian dining experience in a comfortable atmosphere. Though the restaurant's name refers to its Grand Avenue location in St. Paul, it could also refer to the excellent food on the menu as well as the superior service. The *Pra Ram Rong Sung* is quite popular. It features your choice of meat served atop steamed spinach and carrots with an authentic coconut milk and peanut sauce. Owner Luan To says people are

always approaching him for his curry recipes, and after you taste the delicious but not too fiery blend of spices, you'll be asking for them too. Another favorite at Grand Thai is the traditional pad thai with noodles, egg, bean sprouts, onion and crushed peanuts. Waiter Ricky Tang and the rest of the friendly staff are always glad to help you pick a dish that will perfectly suit your taste. For a Thai meal that's the next best thing to a trip to Thailand, come to Grand Thai.

758 Grand Avenue, St. Paul MN
(651) 293-9124

Everest on Grand

Padam Sharma is a trained scientist turned restaurateur who educates folks about his native Nepal from the place he calls Everest on Grand. The subject of your first lesson is food, of course. Curries, the national dish of Nepal, are as spicy as you would like. Eggplant, asparagus and cauliflower are some of the featured ingredients in the vegetarian curries. As for the non-vegetarian choices, you can have lamb, goat or chicken, though if you are going to eat just one meal at Everest on Grand, why not try a curry with ground yak? For this dish, the chefs use Tibetan yak raised in a sustainable environment at Hoopers' Christmas Tree Ranch in Cold Spring, Minnesota. Padam invites you to sample other Tibetan delights as well, including the steamed dumplings called *momo*, which are filled with a mixture of vegetables or ground meat, onion, herbs and spices. They are served with *momo achar*, a specialty house sauce of cilantro,

roasted tomato and other spices. To complement your culinary education, Padam, the president of the Empower Nepal Foundation, is always willing to discuss Nepali history and culture with his guests while making them aware of the work that the foundation does. Minnesota's first restaurant serving Nepali and Tibetan cuisine, Everest is open for lunch and dinner every day. Come get an education with your meal at Everest on Grand.

1278 Grand Avenue, St. Paul MN
(651) 696-1666
www.hotmomo.com

Rudy's Redeye Grill

Rudy's Redeye Grill opened in 2003 as a premier fine-dining establishment in White Bear Lake. This fabulous restaurant offers patrons an eclectic and memorable selection of entrées that are beautifully prepared and bursting with flavor. Specialties of the house include pan-fried walleye and perfectly prepared charbroiled steaks, along with barbecue salmon and pork tenderloin. Other menu favorites include fantastic seafood dishes such as coconut shrimp and intriguing, always flavorful side dishes, for example sweet potato hash browns. Rudy's is also well-known for its full-service bar, where martinis are served with the shaker and the gin is never bruised. Rudy's Redeye Grill offers patrons the feel of an old-time supper club while retaining the small-town atmosphere that makes the area so popular. The well-praised eatery was named as the Best New Restaurant in 2003 by *Twin Cities Monthly*, and it has received the AAA Diamond award, a highly coveted benchmark of excellence. Rudy's Redeye Grill caters luncheons, intimate dinners and cocktail parties, as well as picnics, barbecues and other special events. The warm, welcoming atmosphere and friendly, personable staff are ideal accompaniments to Rudy's exquisite cuisine. Treat your family and friends to a rewarding and memorable dining experience at Rudy's Redeye Grill, where the food is surpassed only by the ambience.

4940 N Highway 61, White Bear Lake MN
(651) 653-6718
www.rudysredeye.com

Luci Ancora and Ristorante Luci

Owned by the Smith family since 1987, Luci Ancora and Ristorante Luci both offer fine cuisine in intimate settings, but have two distinct presentations. At Ristorante Luci, you'll find romantic, classically prepared Italian dishes in an intimate bistro setting. At Luci Ancora, you'll find progressive dishes prepared with an eye for experimentation in a lighter atmosphere. Whichever restaurant you choose, all of the food is prepared on-site daily. Many of the ingredients used at the restaurants come from local farmers, guaranteeing each memorable meal is as absolutely fresh as possible. The two Luci establishments, now largely operated by the second generation of Smiths, feature dishes from many regions of Italy with the chefs' special twists. Led by Chef Stephen Smith and assisted by Chef Jim Kohler, the kitchen staff at the two Luci restaurants has dozens of years of experience serving cuisine in the Twin Cities area. Some of the chefs are featured presenters for classes at local cooking schools. You'll find gracious service at both restaurants and a friendly, warm atmosphere as you share a delicious meal with friends or family. For a meal unparalleled in authenticity and freshness, make a reservation at Luci Ancora or Ristorante Luci.

470 S Cleveland Avenue, St. Paul MN
(651) 699-8258 (Ristorante Luci)
2060 Randolph Avenue, St. Paul MN
(651) 698-6889 (Luci Ancora)
www.ristoranteluci.com

Zander Café

The Zander Café is a neighborhood American bistro offering cultural and ethnic food styles. All of the food is deliciously fresh and prepared in-house. This café has innovative renditions of tried and true recipes. You can find three-soup mosaics, which consist of three soups artistically swirled together in one bowl. The restaurant also serves excellent seafood. Zander Café has an impressive wine bar with a fine list of about 300 selections. Owner and Chef Alexander Dixon made the flooring, booths, tables, copper bar and the eclectic light fixtures himself. All of these elements come together in creating a fantastic atmosphere. With the help of Executive Chef Kai Panthavong, Alexander strives to help customers try new foods without intimidating them. Alexander and Kai enjoy preparing creative food, and cook just as if visitor were a guest in their home. Alexander has been in Twin Cities since the 1980s and has spent 30 years in the restaurant business. Open for lunch Mondays through Friday and dinner daily, the café has seating in the bar area and a formal dining area. Come and enjoy your meal at the Zander Café.

525 Shelby Avenue, St. Paul MN
(651) 222-5224

W.A. Frost & Company

When you can count at least 25 top awards and rave reviews, you know the restaurant has to be good. John and Peggy Rupp opened W.A. Frost & Company 30 years ago, against the advice of everyone they knew. They lovingly restored the magnificent old Dacotah Building , constructed in 1889. The wonderful architectural pieces they salvaged from other 19th century gems, such as the old bar and the polished banisters, have given the restaurant its unique and warmly historic ambience. (The décor is award-winning.) The menus at W.A. Frost change with the seasons to take advantage of the freshest available ingredients. The staff tries to use as much organically grown or naturally produced food as it can and is committed to local family farmers and businesses. W.A. Frost's fabulous food is inspired by the many different country cuisines of Europe imaginatively fused with the hearty style and flavors of America's Upper Midwest. (Food: award-winning.) The result is an exquisite dining experience that offers everything from meat to vegetarian dishes, from the haute to the casual. And to top it off, the wine list offers more than 1,000 wines. (Wine: award-winning.) Come in and find out why W.A. Frost has won the Best Award of Excellence from the *Wine Spectator* nine years in a row, won America's Top Table Award from *Gourmet* magazine and is featured in *The Best Restaurants in America* guide. And as we've said, the awards only scratch the surface.

374 Selby Avenue, St. Paul MN
(651) 224-5715
www.wafrost.com

Phil's Tara Hideaway

There were times when decent folks wouldn't go near the place now known as Phil's Tara Hideaway. It's been a shady chicken shack during its days and a speakeasy run by Al Capone and John Dillinger with gangsters bootlegging moonshine in the basement. Now couples on dates and families celebrating special occasions dine by the fireplace while enjoying the mystique of a 1920s roadhouse. Phil's Tara Hideaway looks like a log cabin but lives up to its name by being a little hard to spot. It's located just minutes from the Twin Cities in the historic river town of Stillwater. As a food critic for the *St. Paul Pioneer Press* put it, "The place is barely noticeable from the road, yet once you figure out how to reach it, you'll be amazed." Attribute the amazement to the warm atmosphere and a menu offering a pleasing variety of fine steaks, chops and seafood. An array of Greek favorites reflects owner Phil Barbatsis's heritage. The building was in rough condition when Phil bought it in 1997, but he was determined to save its history and keep the landmark open to the public. He brings a lifetime of restaurant experience to work with him every day. For lunch or dinner with mystique, choose Phil's Tara Hideaway.

15021 60th Street N, Stillwater MN
(651) 439-9850
www.tarahideaway.com

Selma's Ice Cream Parlor, Run-A-Muk and Village Brass

Stopping for ice cream is a century-old tradition in Afton, where Selma's Ice Cream Parlor, housed in one of the oldest buildings in town, turns on the heat with a tropical motif. The parlor adjoins Run-A-Muk restaurant and Village Brass, giving visitors the chance to enjoy a deli meal and ice cream dessert, then pick up a silk screen shirt or other keepsake all at one lively location. For the past 25 years, owner and operator Laine McGee has been bringing pleasure to her customers while preserving Afton history. The outdoor décor is reminiscent of the Florida Keys, right down to the plastic pink flamingos rising from the lush greenery. Run-A-Muk's casual menu includes a choice of deli sandwiches served on bagels or croissants. You can try a vegetarian Reuben or a Muk Burger. A full bar will serve you the drink of your choice to enjoy at tables with market umbrellas that are scattered throughout the garden setting. For dessert, Selma's Ice Cream Parlor offers 10 flavors of premium ice cream. In 1984, Village Brass opened next door. Here, Laine sells custom plaques, trophies and engraving and provides silk screening services. Take a tropical break at Selma's Ice Cream Parlor and Run-A-Muk, then run on over to Village Brass for some custom treasures.

3419 St. Croix Trail S, Afton MN
(651) 436-8067 or (800) 235-8067
www.selmasicecream.com

Lake Elmo Inn

Founded in 1881, Lake Elmo Inn was originally a stage coach stop. It has undergone many changes throughout its rich 120-year history, serving as host to a railroad station, a barbershop, and a couple of bars. In the 1930s, it was called the Blackhawk Hotel and for the first time housed a restaurant. In 1983, Chef John Schiltz began living his dream of owning the inn. He had started his career as the inn's dishwasher and cook in 1971. He then spent many years honing his skills at some of the finest restaurants in the country. Today, he continually strives to provide the finest cuisine available. Experience his creative and expert cooking—enjoy exceptional dining in one of the inn's three beautiful dining rooms or on the seasonal patio. Reasonable prices for more than exceptional food will make you want to come back again and again. Manager Steve Teitlel invites you to check with their excellent catering department that offers a large variety of options for all of your special occasions. When you have finished your meal, browse the collections on display that include paintings from local artists, carved wooden ducks, nutcrackers ranging from six inches to six feet, antique silver, crystal and, unique to the Inn, one of the largest salt and pepper shaker collections in the area. Remember to ask about the Sin of the Inn. Hint: it's the award-winning restaurant's signature dessert.

3442 Lake Elmo Avenue, Lake Elmo MN
(651) 777-8495
www.lakeelmoinn.com

Sunsets

Sunsets vows to provide great service in an upscale yet casual atmosphere, a promise it keeps twice—at its original restaurant in Wayzata and in Woodbury. Brian Prose and his partners started Sunsets on the shores of Lake Wayzata in 1988 and continue to offer chef-inspired breakfasts, lunches and dinners with a spectacular view. In 1999, Sunsets' culinary prowess expanded to include the elegant Woodbury location with its copper, brick and cherry wood interior. A lovely courtyard entices diners to the outdoors during the summer months. Executive Chef Dennis Palma presides over Sunsets' kitchens, where all items are prepared fresh daily. Every day features a sheet of chef's specialties, such as the renowned meatloaf with a sweet Marsala sauce or the broiled walleye with a lobster sauce. Light eaters will appreciate such creative salad choices as Sherrie's Chicken Salad with coconut-fried chicken and vegetables on a bed of mixed greens. Sunsets also offers steak, burgers, pizza and pasta. Sunday brunch is a hit at both locations. With long hours every day of the week, a long list of signature dishes and many more staple dishes, Sunsets can please even the most single-minded diner. For memorable meals in an easygoing environment, visit Sunsets.

700 Commons Drive, Woodbury MN
(651) 735-1997
700 E Lake Street, Wayzata MN
(952) 473-LAKE (5253)
www.sunsetsrestaurant.com

Thanh Truc Restaurant

According to Hai Phan, the soups from his native Vietnam are the best in the world. Also, even if you have sampled egg rolls in dozens of Asian restaurants, you are in for a treat when you try a Vietnamese egg roll, he says. The many loyal customers of his Thanh Truc Restaurant would certainly agree. They count on Thanh Truc for healthful, flavorful Vietnamese food, which is always prepared to order with very fresh ingredients. Hai Phan recommends that you enjoy your lunch or dinner with the jasmine tea or one of the other premium teas on the menu. Life has been an unpredictable journey for Hai Phan, who fled Vietnam and came to America in 1980. After going to college to become an electrical engineer, he worked in the telecommunication industry until that job collapsed. His story continues happily now that he has converted his hobby and passion for cooking into a business that was named the community's Best Ethnic Restaurant by *Woodbury Magazine* in 2005 and 2006. This cute and cozy restaurant feels as fresh and as clean as when it opened in 2004. It is named after a delicate green bamboo that grows in Vietnam. Are the Vietnamese soups the best in the world? Judge for yourself with a visit to Thanh Truc Restaurant.

2230 Eagle Creek Lane, Suite 300G, Woodbury MN
(651) 436-3431
www.thanhtrucrestaurant.com

Kozlak's Royal Oak Restaurant

The Kozlak family first got involved in the restaurant business in 1943, and it's been in their blood ever since. In 1977, the third generation of the family opened Kozlak's Royal Oak Restaurant. Lynn Kozlak-Satt and her husband Mark now operate this landmark spot. For 30 years people have counted on Kozlak's Royal Oak for the consistency of its wonderful cuisine and fine service. Mark Satt, Kozlak's chef, oversees the menu and the standards of excellence for which the restaurant is famous. Properly aged steaks are cut daily and fresh fish is flown in from around the country. The salad bar is popular for the extent and variety of its fresh produce, delicious salads, side dishes and spreads. Voted as one of Twin Cities most romantic spots, the main dining room overlooks the main garden, which has patio seating. Sundays are known for the award-winning New Orleans Jazz Brunch. The Royal Oak has five beautifully decorated private rooms that accommodate 10 to 200 guests. Off-site catering can also be provided for you. Reunions, receptions, business meetings, luncheons, dinners—whatever your special occasion may be—if it calls for excellence, you can be sure that Mark, Lynn and their expert staff will see that it is a spectacular success.

4785 Hodgson Road, Shoreview MN
(651) 484-8484
www.kozlaks.com

Mississippi Pub

Whether you're driving a car or a boat, the place to pull in for a great meal or a good time is the Mississippi Pub, located right on the Mississippi River at the River Heights Marina. Dock it or park it and come on in for a late breakfast or early lunch on the weekend and dinner seven nights a week. Whether it's one of the great daily specials, such as soft-shelled tacos or chicken fettuccine, or their famous Friday night all-u-can-eat fish fry, the Mississippi Pub is a unique family friendly pub that caters to both the locals that are lucky enough to live on this beautiful waterway and visitors who may be passing through for the first time. You can enjoy the river vista from the pub's lovely outdoor patio or from the indoor, four-season glass enclosed dining area. Because it's connected to the River Heights Marina, it is a favorite stop for the boating set as well, who make it one of the river's hot spots and meet for a beverage and a bite while they fuel up. Known for great burgers and friendly, smiling faces, the Mississippi Pub hosts horseshoe leagues and a happy hour every night. You will be able to observe the *Spirit of St. Paul* luxury charter vessel and year-round pub events. Stop by Mississippi Pub to experience the Mississippi River, great food and friendly people.

4455 66ᵗʰ Street E, Inver Grove Heights MN
(651) 455-4975
www.mississippipub.com

Shish, A Mediterranean Grill & Café

Those who have visited the eastern Mediterranean develop an enduring love of the fast food served from street carts in that region. Shish, A Mediterranean Grill and Café inspires this same love with Mediterranean fare that is fast, healthy and not the least bit Americanized. Rashed and Beth Judeh opened their casual eatery in 2006 in the St. Paul neighborhood where they live. Rashed has owned delis in San Francisco with his brothers, but it was his dream to open a restaurant that displayed a part of his culture. Shish offers an alternative to American fast food with gyros, falafel, hummus and tabouli. A chicken *shawarma* comes wrapped in

Lebanese flatbread or in a pita. The Turkish coffee is a refreshing change of pace. One customer called the spicy eggplant dish called *babaganoush* "the best I've had outside Beirut." Others rave over the stuffed grape leaves or the cheese pie with its layers of filo dough and feta cheese. Even the burger choices take on Middle Eastern overtones with such ingredients as fresh ground lamb, hummus and feta. You don't have to leave the Midwest to taste the Mideast—just bring your appetite to Shish, A Mediterranean Grill & Café.

1668 Grand Avenue, St. Paul MN
(651) 690-2212

Mancini's Char House & Lounge

For more than 50 years, Mancini's Char House & Lounge has kept in touch with what St. Paul wants from a great restaurant. Nick Mancini opened the place in 1948 as a beer joint and soon expanded it into a supper club. Though the restaurant has since become more of a Chicago/New York-style steakhouse, it still has that classic supper club feel, with old-style booths that wrap around the table, allowing for the sort of easy table talk every Italian family appreciates. Some of the finest steakhouses in the world exist in Italy, and Mancini's embodies their philosophy with beef that has been carefully raised and aged, then grilled on a huge open charcoal broiler. Mancini's hand-picks and prepares its lobster and other seafood with the same attention to quality. Nick's sons Pat and John continue the family's traditions. Their friendly staff will help you pick the right wine for your dinner from Mancini's extensive list, which features many local vintages. Mancini's is also an ideal location to hold a banquet, with private rooms available

for 30 guests or more. In addition to fabulous food and drink, Mancini's provides entertainment, featuring live music by the restaurant's own Mancini Players and several other musical acts. Nick no longer walks through his restaurant, but his spirit lives on here. Celebrate a St. Paul tradition with a succulent steak at Mancini's Char House & Lounge, where many still raise a glass to Nick.

531 W 7ᵗʰ Street, St. Paul MN
(651) 224-7345
www.mancinis.com

Casper's Cherokee Sirloin Room

Offering the highest quality steaks in the state, Casper's Cherokee Sirloin Room can be found in historic city of West St. Paul. You can enjoy steaks that are aged or prime, and every Wednesday you can take pleasure in all-you-can-eat crab. Every Thursday night is birthday night, where the birthday boy or girl gets a free steak and free dessert. Casper's is famous for its au gratin potatoes. It's also known for its unconventional wine list. The signature dessert is a one-and-a-half-pound chocolate cake, or you can try their one-and-a-half-pound carrot cake instead. The restaurant has been around since 1931, and Rick and Racquel Casper have owned it since 1970. All four of their children have worked at Casper's and Rick's brother Jim is involved as well, making this a true family business. Patrons are always greeted at the door by either the owners or a member of the family. Casper's has a comfortable social club atmosphere. It also hosts many groom's dinners and retirement parties. Rick and Racquel believe that top-notch food and quality service ensure loyalty, so you will always be treated to the best when you come to Casper's Cherokee Sirloin Room.

886 Smith Avenue S, West St. Paul MN
(651) 457-2729
www.cherokeesirloinroom.com

Highland Grill

Highland Grill has been a neighborhood diner and grill with an urban oasis atmosphere since 1993. David Burley grew up in Western Australia in a family hotel/pub business. Stephanie Shimp grew up in a small town in Minnesota. When the two saw a small café for sale, they jumped at the opportunity. They called their investment the Blue Plate Restaurant Company. Highland Grill serves fresh, often organic, made-from-scratch food morning, noon and night. Well-known dishes include the turkey burgers and banana waffles. The menu is full of eclectic offerings such as the delicious sweet potato fries served with chipotle peanut pesto aioli or the calamari tacos.

The success of Highland Grill prompted Blue Plate to open another restaurant, the Edina Grill, in 1999. Located in the Edina business district, this is a more architecturally edgy place with an airy feel, but it has the same made-from-scratch menu.

In 2001, Stephanie's brother Luke Shimp had just completed seven seasons racing in the NASCAR circuit and decided to join the company. In 2005, the trio added their third restaurant, the Longfellow Grill. This restaurant differs only slightly from its sisters. It's still an urban diner serving up comfortable made-from-scratch food, but it also has a full bar, dramatic views of the Mississippi River through almost floor-to-ceiling windows and a large outdoor patio.

Blue Plate now has a fourth restaurant that is completely different from the others. The Groveland Tap is your neighborhood beer and burger joint. The family-friendly dining room serves up chicken wings and burgers to a full house every night. For an evening out with friends, this is the place to be. Groveland Tap serves over 30 types of beer, 14 of which are straight from the tap. It has a game room, juke box and 10 televisions for a full night of entertainment. No matter which restaurant you choose, the feeling is still the same: great food in an urban diner atmosphere.

771 Cleveland Avenue S, St. Paul MN
(651) 690-2102
www.highlandgrill.com

Tinucci's Restaurant

Tinucci's Restaurant in Newport offers a family-friendly dining experience. You can expect superior buffet meals at an excellent price. This welcoming eatery was founded in 1958 by Louis Tinucci, Jr. and his wife, Patricia. Today it belongs to third-generation family members John, Mark and Greg Tinucci. The Tinucci family story began in Asciano, Italy, a small hamlet below towering Mt. Pisano. Patriarch Oreste Tinucci was born there and migrated to the United States in 1909. His eldest son Louis followed him in 1913; his wife and other children, in 1915. Various family members entered the restaurant business and thrived, which inspired Louis with a drive to establish his own restaurant. Since opening nearly 50 years ago, Tinucci's has faced its share of adversity, including a devastating fire in 1972 that completely destroyed the building. Today this favored community landmark offers seating for several hundred diners, including a private dining room for 60, as well as a full-serv deli. Tinucci's specializes in sumptuous buffets, which include fresh salads, a full ra of entrées and side dishes. Look for the fish and chicken buffet on Fridays, the prime rib on Saturdays and a Sunday brunch extravaganza. Tinucci's enjoys a reputation a one of the best caterers in the southeast metro area. Experience a dining sensation a Tinucci's Restaurant, where a satisfied guest is the only reason for continued succes

396 21st Street, Newport MN
(651) 459-9011
www.tinuccis.com

Sociale

Are you perpetually harried by life's little appointment book? Fretting that your family never spends time around the dinner table actually talking? What you need is a good, home-cooked gourmet meal that you can pop out of the oven and onto the table in a matter of minutes. This is the specialty at Sociale. Jason and Lisa Hake, time-starved executives themselves, were tired of struggling with the what's-for-dinner-tonight dilemma. What they came up with is a revolutionary concept of dining. They crossed the time-consuming art of gourmet cooking with the timesaving convenience of take-out and TV dinners, and Sociale was born. Part gourmet store, part meal preparation, Sociale gives you the choice of a mouthwatering selection of gourmet meals that change monthly. Head Chef Ampy Versalles is both a valedictorian graduate of Le Cordon Bleu Cooking Academy and daughter of Zoilo Versalles, a Most Valuable Player for the Minnesota Twins. Chef Ampy is Sociale's MVP, and the monthly menus for each of Sociale's three locations are prepared under her creative direction. You can attend a cooking session and assemble a month's worth of meals for your family, you can pick up chef-prepared frozen meals or you can have everything delivered right to your door. Chef Ampy, Jason and Lisa want to help you prepare and serve great-tasting gourmet meals with a home-cooked feel. Jason and Lisa are striving to bring families back to the table, so step out of your routine and into some very fine cuisine at Sociale. Visit Sociale at any of its Twin Cities locations: Eagan, Edina, St. Paul, Minneapolis, Savage and Northfield.

(651) 944-9000
www.socialegourmet.com

Supatra's Thai Cuisine

The dishes served at Supatra's Thai Cuisine are authentic in every sense of the word. Owner and Chef Supatra Johnson got her training in Bangkok. Supatra's Thai Cuisine is the only restaurant in Minnesota to have been awarded the Thai Select designation from the Thai government. Johnson is not just a restaurateur and chef, but a cooking instructor as well. She offers Thai cooking classes at her restaurant each month. In a natural progression from instructing cooking classes, Johnson is the author of *Crying Tiger: Thai Recipes from the Heart,* a Thai cookbook featuring over 100 easy-to-prepare recipes. Johnson points out that many of the fresh ingredients used in Thai cooking are noted for their immune-boosting properties and, contrary to popular belief, not all authentic recipes are spicy. Her menu offers a wide range of dishes sure to please any palate, along with an extensive wine and beer list. Johnson is providing a commendable (and tasty) service in helping to bring the flavors of Thailand to Minnesota. The best part is you can choose whether to order the dishes from the menu at Supatra's Thai Cuisine or learn to make them yourself under Johnson's expert guidance.

967 W 7th Street, St. Paul MN
(651) 222-5859
www.supatra.com

Wiederholt's Supper Club

A third-generation family business, Wiederholt's Supper Club has been serving some of the same families since opening in 1955. John and Charlie Wiederholt keep the personal touch with their guests by being there to welcome them time after time. Their mother, Harriet, at 82, still serves as hostess on the weekends and pitches in on busy week nights as well. Wiederholt's serves quality, no-miss entrées that generation after generation enjoy, such as steak, seafood, chicken and ribs. If you're simply hankering for a good burger with fries, you'll find that too. Ask about the nightly specials. A full bar serves delicious cocktails and fine wines. Any night of the week, the supper club is full of good food and company. On the weekends, when live music plays, Wiederholt's regularly triples the population of Miesville, a small town south of Hastings—one indication why the Chamber of Commerce named it Small Business of the Year in 2002. The restaurant is located on Highway 61 in downtown Miesville, providing the opportunity to dine in a lovely country setting. Bring your family to Wiederholt's Supper Club to begin a tradition that might be hard to break.

14535 240th Street E, Hastings MN
(651) 437-3528

Collectors Gallery

When you want a gift to celebrate an occasion great or small, you need search no further than the Collectors Gallery. Reward yourself or someone you love with that certain something from this shop. With a wide range of gifts and collectibles, you could easily while away an afternoon browsing here. The Collectors Gallery is proud to carry brands such as Vera Bradley, Swarovski, Armani, Lladro and Brighton, Pandora, Department 56 and others. From beautiful Swarovski crystal representations of sea lions, butterflies and adorable baby penguins to Armani figurines and gorgeous jewelry, there is something to suit every taste and every occasion at the gallery. You'll find rare coins, Pandora jewelry featuring build-your-own-bracelets and artisan-crafted original beads. The gifts suit occasions ranging from a birthday or wedding to a new baby. The Collectors Gallery works closely with each designer it represents. It has attained top dealer status with many vendors due to its dedication to quality, customer service and the highest standards in gift selection. The Collectors Gallery is the place to go for a gift that's sure to please even the friend who has it all.

8306 Tamarack Village #401, Woodbury MN
(651) 738-8351
www.collectorsgallery.com

The Bibelot Shops

Sophisticated, whimsical, elegant and amusing, The Bibelot Shops are very satisfying places to shop and enjoy. Add to that a talented and attentive staff and you will begin to understand why these four delightful shops have become a Twin Cities legend, honored in 2005 as one of the Top 25 Twin Cities businesses owned by women. The first Bibelot was opened by Roxana Freese in 1966. Her stores have been setting the standard for style and trends ever since, offering a lively collection of gifts, clothing, jewelry, stationery and items for the home. Seasonal themes are important at Bibelot, and you are always certain to find that special gift for someone you love. There are gifts and ornaments for every holiday and life event from Hanukkah to St. Patrick's Day, from wedding showers to baby showers. Shop in the clothing departments for a classic, updated outfit, and add an elegant or funky piece of jewelry for yourself. Whether it is books, cards, candles, jewelry, toys, clothing or a truly special something, The Bibelot Shops have the perfect selection to delight their customers. For all locations, check the website given below.

1082 Grand Avenue, St. Paul MN
(651) 222-0321
www.bibelotshops.com

no pics

Goodthings

It's not hard to find good treasures for you and your home in Minnesota. All you have to do is drive to Goodthings, located on 4th Street in White Bear Lake or the Shoppes at Arbor Lakes in Maple Grove. Punchy, interesting, quirky, smart, on the edge but in the groove, Goodthings packs a lot into one's retail shopping experience. Eye candy takes on a whole new meaning in this Minnesota's family's trendy, cutting-edge stores. The concept is one-stop shopping and Goodthings wins hands down with their merchandise mix. Unpredictable homewares, gifts, clothing and shoes for men and women, plus fabulous custom home furnishings you can't find anywhere else await you in this shopper's haven. In 1973, founder Sharon Conrad started the business in downtown White Bear Lake, primarily selling women's clothing. Sharon has been successful in growing her business and has constantly expanded her selection and relocated several times. With a degree in entrepreneurship from the University of St. Thomas and successful ventures of his own, Sharon's son Tyler saw great potential in one of the Twin Cities' best kept secrets—his mother's store. In 1999, Tyler and Sharon merged their talents. Her knack for creative merchandising and his business skills turned out to be the right mix. This dynamic duo carries a magical, trendy mix of women's clothing and shoes, along with unique home furnishings and gifts. Goodthings merchandise is often cited by *Mpls. St. Paul* magazine, *Minnesota Monthly* and *Midwest Magazine*, as well as the Minneapolis *Star Tribune* and the St. Paul *Pioneer Press*. A shopping trip to Goodthings is a discovery of things too good to miss.

2184 4th Street, White Bear Lake MN (651) 426-0625
12139 Elm Creek Boulevard, Maple Grove MN (763) 494-9255
www.seegoodthings.com

Love from Minnesota

Whether you want to spread a little cheer from your Minnesota home to loved ones in other places, or you want to bring a reminder of your Minnesota visit home with you, Love from Minnesota has you in mind. The Roseville shop is one of eight Minnesota-themed shops owned by Steve and Pat Chinader. It's next to the headquarters for Love from the USA (formerly Merchant Moose). You'll find everything from log furniture to refrigerator magnets and bottle openers with Minnesota themes. Minnesota maple syrup, jellies and dressings command attention among gourmets, while recipe boxes sport Minnesota wildlife. Who wouldn't smile at a plush moose, wolf, loon or bear? Look for dozens of books, including volumes on cooking fish, traveling in Minnesota and ghosts of the great North Woods. Why play checkers with standard markers when you can pit the Minnesota Vikings against the Green Bay Packers in markers shaped like football helmets? You'll find Love from Minnesota shops in Minnetonka, Nisswa and the IDS Center in downtown Minneapolis. Bloomington's Mall of America features a Love from Minnesota shop as well as Ron Schara's Minnesota Bound store and Minnesota-ah! Roseville is also home to Wine Time, a Chinader store devoted to local wines. Whatever it is you love about Minnesota, from its lakes and outdoor recreation to its local cuisine, lodge décor and phenomenal sports teams, look for clever expressions of it at Love from Minnesota and its sister stores.

2465 Fairview Avenue N, Roseville MN (Love from the USA headquarters)
(800) 247-3139
www.lovefromtheusa.com

Irish On Grand

Irish on Grand is the place to find all things Irish. The store was established in 1990 to promote Irish culture and provide a place where the Irish community can stop and chat. Open seven days a week, everyone here is happy to fill your ears about Ireland. You might bump into just about anyone on a Saturday morning: musicians, bagpipe players or an author signing books. You can get updates on festivals, concerts and other things happening around town as well as travel information. The store carries a large selection of Irish goods from candy to jewelry. Owners Liam O'Neill and Maeve O'Mara import Claddagh and Celtic jewelry, crystal, Belleek China, books, clothing, Irish groceries, candy and more from their native country. Need a book about Irish wedding traditions or a Claddagh ring for your beloved? Irish on Grand will have it. You'll also find baby clothing and traditional Irish garb. Irish on Grand is the oldest Irish store in the Twin Cities. It's located in a three-story converted residential house that retains its charm with hardwood floors and stained glass windows. Liam and Maeve invite you to shop at Irish on Grand to chat and see what Ireland has to offer you.

1124 Grand Avenue, St. Paul MN
(651) 222-5151
www.irishongrand.com

Stogies on Grand

When a premium, hand-rolled cigar is your pleasure, turn to St. Paul's experts at Stogies on Grand. Owners Eileen and Howard Bream are well-versed in the tobacco industry and offer their customers an extraordinary selection of flavors and products along with a lounge for enjoying the stogie. Whether you seek the unique taste of a Dominican, Nicaraguan or Honduran cigar, the Breams can help. Their shop features a walk-in humidor with hundreds off top-quality brands purchased directly from the manufacturers. You'll also find imported cigarettes, pipes and aromatic house-blended pipe tobaccos. Stogies is a great place to turn when you are looking for a gift for the cigar aficionado in your life—it has cigar cutters, lighters and fine humidors. A visit to Stogies on Grand is more than an opportunity to purchase tobacco products, it's an opportunity to savor them. The turn-of-the-century house on Grand features three lounge areas

where you can smoke, meet, take advantage of wireless Internet or watch a movie on a large screen television. Its owners describe it as a non-alcoholic version of Cheers. An outdoor patio offers still another smoking option. Eileen's father was a tobacco wholesaler, and Howard worked for him. She grew up climbing the boxes in her father's tobacco warehouse and putting tax stamps on cigarettes. For an unparalleled smoking experience, visit Stogies on Grand.

961 Grand Avenue, St. Paul MN
(651) 222-8700
www.stogiesongrand.com

A. Johnson & Sons Florists

When you walk into A. Johnson & Sons Florists, you'll find yourself in one of the most unique flower shops in the world. This fourth-generation family business claims to be the only flower shop in the world to have G-scale model trains traveling through a flower cooler on one of multiple tracks. The trains may make flower buying fun for the whole family, but the large walk-in flower cooler is what really sets this flower shop apart. Filled to the brim with an assortment of more than 300 fragrant fresh-cut flower varieties, including every imaginable color of Minnesota grown roses, picking out a bouquet of your favorite flowers has never been easier. Located on historic Grand Avenue in St. Paul, A. Johnson & Sons has remained family-owned

and operated at the same location for 70 years. Ever since the shop was first founded in 1936, the Johnson family has guaranteed fresh quality arrangements and complete customer satisfaction on every order. Whether you want to pick out your own personal bouquet or search the largest assortment of flower arrangements in St. Paul, the award-winning design staff of A. Johnson & Sons Florists will work to make every floral design exceed your expectations.

1738 Grand Avenue, St. Paul MN
(651) 698-6000 or (800) 959-8010
www.jflorist.com

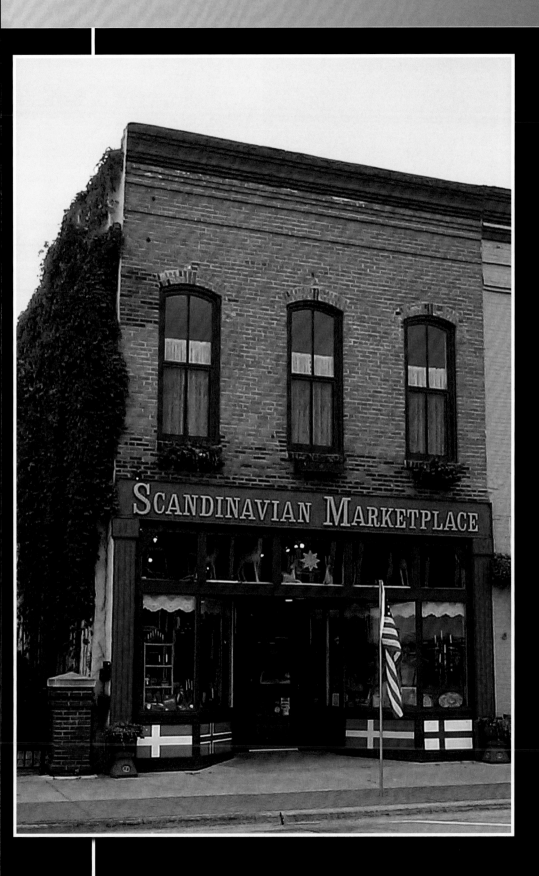

Scandinavian Marketplace

Scandinavian Marketplace in historic downtown Hastings is your source for imports from the countries of Norway, Sweden, Denmark, Finland and Iceland. Scandinavian Marketplace stocks a huge selection of hard-to-find books, Nordic china, jewelry, sweaters, Tokheim stoneware and mugs, Suzanne Toftey trivets and plates, Fjord Design flatware and many other beautiful products. The rosemaled selections include beautiful hand-painted plates, rugs and wallpaper borders. The shop carries many unusual, one-of-a-kind items handcrafted by artisans. The idea for Scandinavian Marketplace dates back 20 years to Janet Martin's mail-order business, Martin House Publications. Martin House Publications received many requests from customers who wanted a shop. In 1997, Janet's daughter and son-in-law, Jenny and Steve Green, purchased the historic 1872 Pitz building and renovated it, uncovering the original wood floors and beautiful brick walls. They commissioned Egil Dahle from Norway to paint a beautiful mural on the side of the building. Scandinavian Marketplace is especially strong in Scandinavian humor books and products, which is natural given the fact that Janet Martin has authored or co-authored 16 best selling humorous books. Her book, *Growing Up Lutheran*, won the Minnesota Book Award for Humor and was recently turned into a successful smashing musical comedy entitled *Church Basement Ladies*. Whether you shop Scandinavian Marketplace through the Internet, the mail-order catalog or at the store in Hastings, you will find lovely items that exceed your expectations.

218 2nd Street E, Hastings MN
(651) 438-9183 or (800) 797-4319
www.scandinavianmarket.com

Minnesota Bound

Ron Schara and his black Labrador, Raven, win the hearts of outdoor enthusiasts on their weekly *Minnesota Bound* television show, which goes out to viewers in several Minnesota cities as well as Fargo, North Dakota. In 2005, Steve and Pat Chinader opened the Minnesota Bound store, which features useful outdoor gear along with items Ron and Raven made famous. At this Mall of America shop, you'll find books by Ron, including a fish cookbook and a fishing guide. A limited edition Raven plush toy resembles the famous dog right down to the red bandana. If you happen to know a hunter who plays chess, you might fancy a chess set featuring turkey hunters versus pheasant hunters. Rapela's Pro Fishing games also are popular. You can pick up birdfeeders and squirrel feeders. Fans of the television show may have seen the Squngee, a gadget that diverts squirrels from the bird feeder by letting them bungee jump for corn. When you visit the Minnesota Bound store, you'll know you are buying products approved by Ron and Raven. "*Minnesota Bound*, the television show, has been a long-running tribute to all who cherish the outdoor lifestyle," says Ron. "We hope to carry on that tradition with this store." For gear from the beloved team of Ron and Raven, stop by Minnesota Bound.

Mall of America, 316 N Garden, Bloomington MN
(952) 854-9100 or (800) 247-3139
www.mnboundstore.com

Heritage II— Scandinavian & British Isles Shops

Heritage II has served the Minneapolis/St. Paul metro area with Scandinavian, Celtic and British gifts, tableware and apparel for more than 32 years from two old lake villages, now suburbs: White Bear Lake to the east and Excelsior to the west. You'll find a range of gifts, from Orrefors crystal vases and bowls to Kosta Boda art glass from Sweden. Discover fun gifts such as Guinness décor from Ireland, plus trolls, *tomtes* and Dala horses from Scandinavia. You'll find flags, caps, tees and books. The shop has traditional Norwegian and Irish sweaters and, for denim folks, contemporary Original Blues sweaters from England. Come visit Heritage II, open seven days a week.

50 Water Street, Excelsior MN
(952) 474-1231
www.heritageii.com

Legacy Art & Gifts

Located in St. Paul's fun and funky Grand Avenue shopping district, Legacy Art & Gifts features affordable treasures created mostly by Minnesota-based artisans. Owned and operated by Betsy Carter, Legacy has showcased a cross-section of art and fine craft since 1994 inside a charming two-story house that was built in 1916. Paintings and etchings of local and European scenes appear alongside gorgeous blown glass and the rich glazes of hand-built pottery. Original photography and hand-designed jewelry make delightful gifts for any occasion, as do the leather accessories, whimsical hanging mobiles and exotic wooden boxes. The homey kitchen area of this shop is filled with functional pottery and decorative glassware. Last, but certainly not least,

Legacy offers lovely three-season scarves and table runners handwoven by Betsy herself. Legacy is named not only as a tribute to the artists and their art, but to Betsy's parents, who encouraged her since she was young to open a shop. Eventually she used her inheritance to pursue this lifetime dream. Betsy Carter has come a long way since peddling her first potholders door-to-door as a child, and she still offers one-of-a-kind artwork at affordable prices. Come browse the enjoyable selection of treasures at Legacy Art & Gifts.

1209 Grand Avenue, St. Paul MN
(651) 221-9094

Sophie Joe's Emporium

For more than five years, owner Shirley Payne has been supplying a fabulous mix of vintage items in her 80-booth antiques mall, Sophie Joe's Emporium. If you're looking for jewelry and watches, clothes and collectibles, Sophie Joe's provides a satisfying shopping experience. Gifts from all over the globe converge at this shop. Look for everything from furnishings and home accents to vintage shoes, canister sets and cookie jars. Clear and colored glassware abounds. You'll find bar and tableware that you could proudly display in your grandma's hutch. Book collectors enjoy browsing through old books and magazines. Shoppers often find themselves reminiscing over the dolls and toys, hat boxes, old bottles and prints. You might recognize a lamp from childhood, a nightlight from your little sister's room or a mirror like the one that was your mother's pride and joy. Sophie's usually has a selection of vintage wedding gowns, too. The shop has been featured in both *People* and *Star* magazines and has been voted the Best of the Best by *Mpls. St. Paul Magazine*. You might see a celebrity here, such as young actress and singer Lindsay Lohan, who has been a regular customer. Whether you're on the hunt for something specific or browsing for a treasure, Sophie Joe's Emporium invites you to have a look around.

453 W 7th Street, St. Paul MN
(651) 224-1357
www.sophiejoes.com

Northern Vineyards Winery

What do the words Prairie Smoke, Lady Slipper and Yellow Moccasin have in common? They are all names of unique wines produced at Northern Vineyards Winery. Members of the Minnesota Wine Growers Cooperative own the winery, which was established in 1983. All of the wines are made in Stillwater and most of the grapes are grown in Minnesota and western Wisconsin near the banks of major rivers. The Cooperative takes great pride in its award-winning wines and regularly enters national and international competitions. Climate, of course, has a tremendous impact on the types of grapes that can be grown in the area. Varieties that ripen early are essential and the vines must receive meticulous care in order to thrive. Generally around Labor Day the grapes begin arriving at the winery and the crush begins. The harvesting and crushing process may last through October depending on the particular season. The winery now has a terrace overlooking the St. Croix River with a tremendous view of the historic lift-bridge that makes a comfortable spot for enjoying a glass of wine with a picnic lunch. The winery offers live music on the deck during the summer months, and it is open for tasting and sales all year around. It can also be rented for special events such as weddings and holiday parties. Put Northern Vineyards on your must-see list while in Stillwater.

223 N Main Street, Stillwater MN
(651) 430-1032
www.northernvineyards.com

Great Waters Brewing Company

If you happen to be in St. Paul on St. Patrick's Day, the Great Waters Brewing Company is the place to go. Fortunately for us, when Sean O'Byrne was downsized by corporate America he decided to open a brewery. It was 1997 and just in time for everyone's favorite Irish holiday. The rest, as they say, is history. Great Waters Brewing Company is fortuitously lodged in the historic Hamm Building, which happens to rest on the original site of St. Paul's Cathedral, a site blessed with a natural spring. This could mean that the secret of the brewery's fabulous handcrafted beers is holy water straight from the well. Great Waters has fantastic views of the beautiful city of St. Paul from the best patio in town. The recent building boom that brought the River Center, the Xcel Energy Center and a thriving theater district into the area has caused the once-sleepy little city across the river to explode into a thriving hub of popping energy and fun. Speaking of beer, the Great Waters Brewing Company's brewmaster, Bob DuVernois, has come up with over 85 flavors. Many of these beers have won awards, including a gold medal from Winterfest for his unique King Boreas Imperial Wit. If you want to experience some great beer, great food, great friends and great surroundings, get yourself over to the Great Waters Brewing Company.

426 St. Peter Street, St. Paul MN
(651) 224-2739
www.greatwatersbc.com

WineHaven
Winery & Vineyard

WineHaven's legacy began three generations ago when the Peterson family first produced honey and fruit in the scenic Chisago Lakes area of east-central Minnesota. Each generation passed the secrets of the earth on to the next, always striving for higher quality. In keeping with that tradition, the Petersons founded WineHaven with a commitment to producing the highest quality grape, honey and fruit wines. Today, WineHaven is recognized as one of the top award-winning wineries in the Upper Midwest. The winery has won more than 100 awards for winemaking excellence and an unprecedented seven gold medals at New York and California wine competitions. WineHaven's specialty wines have caught the attention of wine experts throughout the country, and have earned the winery national acclaim in *Wine Spectator*, *USA Today* and *Simply Wine with Andrea Immer*. WineHaven has grown well beyond the Peterson family's original expectations. However, the winemaking and viticultural team remain small and focused, working in an environment where their talents can be combined to produce elegant wines with distinctive regional character. WineHaven's selection of award-winning wines is available for complementary tastings April through December, Thursday through Sunday (please call for hours).

9757 292nd Street, Chisago City MN
(651) 257-1017
www.winehaven.com

Sunset at Voyageurs National Park

Northeast Minnesota

The Inn on Gitche Gumee

For many, Henry Wadsworth's poem, *The Song of Hiawatha*, was an introduction to Gitche Gumee, the Native American name for Lake Superior. Today's travelers can rediscover the charms of Gitche Gumee at an Inn bearing its name. The Inn on Gitche Gumee offers year-round downtown opportunities for enjoying the "shining Big-Sea-Water" of the lake. It's just nine miles from Duluth and a world away from everyday experience. Butch and Julie Sievert, the owners for 20 years, want your vacation to be a relaxing experience imbued with a sense of the past. Rooms feature handcrafted rustic wood furniture created by Butch. Large windows, glass doors and multiple decks offer views of Lake Superior and the inn's award-winning three-season gardens. Suites and a individual cottage showcase the Sieverts' favorite Northwoods themes. You'll feel like you've fallen asleep inside a tree when you wake up in the king-size four-poster bed made of black walnut trunks in the Three Bears' Cottage. The Anderson Suite, named after Julie's grandparents who had a dairy farm in Minnesota, gets its charm from antiques and antique replicas, while the Dream Catcher-Okabena Suite devotes two rooms to Native Americans with native-made blankets and birch accessories. Expect complimentary tea and coffee in the mornings and plenty of nearby activities both on and off the lake. Make a memorable connection with Lake Superior while enjoying the hospitality and beauty of The Inn on Gitche Gumee.

8517 Congdon Boulevard, Duluth MN
(218) 525-4979 or (800) 317-4979
www.innongitchegumee.com

A Stay Inn Ely

A stay in Ely? What a good idea, especially when you choose one of the five rustic suites at A Stay Inn Ely or rent the whole inn for a group as large as 21. Don Beans and Joan Kjorsvig-Beans remodeled this turn-of-the-last-century house in 2005, using lumber from nearby forests to panel the rooms and pine log furniture for lodge-style comfort in the gathering room. The inn is much like a hostel with a communal gathering room and kitchen, but each suite has its own bath and a Northwoods décor. Rooms glow with such local woods as tamarack, pine, black ash or white cedar. The wide wrap-around porch is a great place for packing or unpacking your Duluth Pack or taking in the fresh evening air with new or old friends. If you would like to dip more deeply into the nearby wilderness, Don is the man to see. He owns a second business, Jasper Creek Guide Service, and can arrange a guided wilderness trip for a day or longer with the focus on canoeing, fly-fishing or camping. Guests at A Stay Inn Ely can often be found discussing the adventures of the day around a big antique table and a roaring fire in the gathering room or out on the covered porch. When you are ready for a little civilization, your location in downtown Ely puts museums, art galleries and restaurants within easy reach. Whether you prefer adventure in remote landscapes or easygoing days, come to A Stay Inn Ely for a vacation you will cherish always.

112 W Sheridan Street, Ely MN
(218) 365-6010 or (888) 360-6010
www.astayinnely.com
www.jaspercreek.com

Bluefin Bay
on Lake Superior

Welcome to Bluefin Bay on Lake Superior— recognized as the gem of America's North Coast. Cozy up to a warm, crackling fire or relax in your own private whirlpool bath. Listen to the waves lapping at the shore. Watch the Seagulls soar. Relax with a massage at the new SuperiorWaters Wellness Center. Savor one of the award-winning meals prepared for you at the Bluefin Grille and the Coho Café. Whether you visit for a getaway, honeymoon, wedding, family reunion or an extended vacation, you'll want to return here again and again to experience this spectacular area, fine accommodations, unsurpassed amenities and the tradition which comes from more than 100 years of hospitality. As one Bluefin guest wrote, "Bluefin Bay has it all—romance, family and tradition." Bluefin Bay was voted Most Romantic Resort in Minnesota by readers of *Mpls. St. Paul Magazine* and Best of Lake Superior by readers of *Lake Superior Magazine*.

Surrounded by the Superior National Forest and five state parks, Bluefin Bay is a gateway to the Boundary Waters Canoe Area Wilderness. The Superior Hiking Trail winds along the ridge-tops, providing spectacular views of Lake Superior. The new Gitchi Gami Bike Trail runs right through Bluefin Bay as it connects with hundreds of miles of trails, paved and unpaved, as well as old logging roads and forest trails. Chartered fishing and sailing boats provide guests the opportunity to get out on the big lake. There are more than 200 inland lakes within 25 miles of each other, along with countless rivers, streams and waterfalls. The Superior National Golf Course, called the Cadillac of Minnesota Golf Courses by *Explore Minnesota Magazine*, is just minutes away. As founder Rob Buntz put it, "We have the best staff on Lake Superior and they enjoy helping our guests to experience Bluefin Bay and America's North Coast—one of the most beautiful spots in the world."

7192 W Highway 61, Tofte MN
(800) BLUEFIN (258-3346)
www.bluefinbay.com

The Ellery House Bed & Breakfast

The 117-year-old Ellery House Bed & Breakfast is a gracious Victorian home that charms the visitor with its rooms, its amenities and its location just blocks from Duluth's Lakewalk on Lake Superior. Jim and Joan Halquist have owned and operated the bed and breakfast since 1988. In 2004, *Arrington's* named the Ellery House the Best in the Midwest. Guests choose from four bedrooms, which all feature private baths, feather beds and bathrobes. Wireless Internet access is available throughout the home. The Thomas Wahl Room features a marble shower, East Lake furnishings and an 1890s gas fireplace, while Lilla's Room delights visitors with a garden view and a clawfoot soaking tub. For spacious accommodations, consider Daisy's Suite with its fireplace and a sun porch with a view of Lake Superior. The luxurious Ellery Suite offers a sitting room with a fireplace, a private balcony and an antique carved walnut bed. You can enjoy breakfast with its signature fresh fruit platter and *souffle du jour* in the dining room or in your private quarters. Special Aveda spa and romance packages personalize your visit and assure a satisfying and relaxing stay. Enjoy golf, skiing or antiques shopping during the day and return to the comforts of the Ellery House Bed & Breakfast at the end of your day.

28 S 21st Avenue E, Duluth MN
(218) 724-7639 or (800) ELLERYH (355-3794)
www.elleryhouse.com

Buckhorn on Caribou Lake Resort

Located on the shores of one of Minnesota's deepest, clearest lakes, Buckhorn on Caribou Lake Resort puts travelers in a wilderness setting while treating them to comfortable lodging. Three spacious hand-crafted log lodges give you the true feeling of the Northwoods, be it in the summer on the deck overlooking the lake, or in the winter by the stone fireplace or in your own Finnish sauna. These four and five bedroom log lodges are ideally suited for family reunions and gatherings of friends and loved ones. The four chalet-like cottages offer a step into the days of the old fish camps, each clean and with fully equipped kitchens and bathrooms. Buckhorn is an ideal retreat for couples and small families. At 160 feet deep and clarity levels of 40 feet, Caribou Lake is host to fantastic fishing with plenty of trout and bass. The resort has boats available to anglers

as well as to those who just want to sightsee from a canoe or paddleboat. You can swim and lounge on the dock, hike the many trails, then try the wood-fired sauna. In the winter, opportunities for cross-county skiing, snowmobiling and ice fishing draw visitors. A central lodge has a library and games for kids and adults. For outdoor pursuits in a place of great beauty, owners Peg Landin and Tim Mangni, with the help of their children Lily and Eli, invite you to come to Buckhorn on Caribou Lake Resort.

45101 Buckhorn Resort Road, Marcell MN
(218) 832-3723 or (800) 450-6628
www.buckhornoncaribou.com

The Firelight Inn on Oregon Creek

As the only property in Minnesota to be listed on the Select Registry of Distinguished Inns in North America, the Firelight Inn on Oregon Creek excels at luxury. The two-person whirlpool and fireplace in each of the five suites are the most prominent indications of this. More subtle signs include the oversized bathrobes, towel warmers and the feather-top mattress on each king or queen bed. Impeccable service is the specialty of innkeepers Jim and Joy Fischer, who invite guests to relax and be soothed by the sounds of Oregon Creek as it flows to Lake Superior. The location of this mansion that you will be calling home for the length of your stay is a secluded street adjoining the creek. It is an ideal spot for a romantic getaway, yet only minutes from Canal

Park and the Aerial Lift Bridge. The large house was built in 1910 for George G. Barnum, a successful businessman who wanted enough space to showcase his art collection and accommodate his frequent guests in comfort. In this spirit of hospitality, guests enjoy breakfast on the creek-side deck in the summer and gather in several tastefully furnished common areas. Sessions with a massage therapist are available. Be sure to ask about special packages and extra amenities. When nothing but luxury will do, consider the Firelight Inn on Oregon Creek.

2211 E 3rd Street, Duluth MN
(218) 724-0272 or (888) 724-0273
www.firelightinn.com

Braun Properties

When you visit Duluth, try a whole new experience by staying in a fully furnished home, right on the sandy shores of Lake Superior, courtesy of Braun Properties. Richard and Nancy Braun offer a vacation experience loaded with extras in their beach home, called Northern Lights. Just say the word and they will have a variety of things to welcome you, from crackers, cheese and salami to chocolate, flowers and wine. Other extras include an outdoor barbecue/fireplace, mopeds, bicycles, kayaks, basketball, volleyball, croquet and horseshoes. You can also arrange for an in-room massage. You'll be staying right on the waterfront of the man-made island of Park Point, located on the far western tip of Lake Superior. You can arrive by land, sea or air to enjoy what locals call the finest beach in the world. All sorts of activities are right outside your door, including beachcombing, sunbathing and swimming in the summer, and in the winter, cross-country skiing, snowshoeing, skating and ice fishing. Any time of year, you will have a clear sky for star gazing. The Braun families have been Park Pointers for five generations and can tell you what to expect in every season from fall colors to a good old-fashioned northeaster or the blizzard of the century. A visit to the island's south end reveals a beautiful public park and hiking trail. Annual events on the island consist of the Park Point Art Fair, what's advertised as the World's Longest and Largest Garage Sale, and Duluth's oldest foot race, the Park Point Five Miler, held in July. You can cross the Aerial Lift Bridge into Canal Park and walk, stroll or take a carriage ride along Duluth's Lake Walk, stopping to check out the small shops, galleries and restaurants. For a one-of-a-kind vacation spot in any season, contact Braun Properties.

3422 Minnesota Avenue, Duluth MN
(218) 722-3502
www.parkpointvacations.com

Northernair Lodge

You'll find Northernair Lodge on the shores of Mitchell Lake, nestled comfortably in Superior National Forest. The rustic log cabins lend a bit of history, updated with today's modern conveniences. As you unwind, the world seems to be put on hold. The calm waters of the private secluded lake offer wonderful fishing for walleye, bass, pike and other species. Northernair Lodge is the only resort on this crystal-clear undeveloped private-access lake. The cabins at Northernair each have distinct personalities. You will find log cabins that date back to the 1920s with the modern conveniences of home, as well as newer cabins. Each cabin has a deck or screen porch that overlooks the lake as well as access to a private or shared dock. The modern kitchens include microwaves and each cabin has an outdoor grill and a fire pit for bonfires.

Mitchell Lake's clear water is perfect for swimming and Northernair Lodge's sandy beach, sauna, water trampoline and beach playground area are favorites for kids and adults alike. Other activities include berry picking when in season, hiking, bird watching and stargazing at the incredible night sky. Northernair Lodge is only minutes from downtown Ely where you can experience shopping, restaurants, golf, movies and museums. There truly is something for everyone. If you and your family need a change of pace from the hustle and bustle of daily life, book a peaceful retreat at Northernair Lodge.

2123 Haapala Road, Ely MN
(218) 365-4882 or (866) 307-8021
www.northernairlodge.com

Blue Heron Bed & Breakfast

Owner Jo Kovach calls the Blue Heron Bed & Breakfast the B & B with a million-acre front yard for a reason—its 10 acres end where the 1.3-million-acre (2,000-square-mile) Boundary Waters Canoe Area Wilderness begins. Each room comes with its own canoe, and adventurous explorers can meander through 1,200 miles of canoe routes. Kovach can plot full, half-day and one-hour routes for you. The area is prime for fishing, bird watching and wildlife spotting. You may see otter, fox, moose, deer and many other animals from the Blue Heron's porch. In the winter, the bed and breakfast provides its guests with snowshoes for exploring the many paths and logging roads that crisscross the area. More adventurous guests can participate in dog sledding days. The wilderness contrasts with the modern and comfortable rooms in the bed and breakfast. Each room boasts a private bathroom. One room even has a Jacuzzi tub, and everyone can enjoy the wood-fired sauna. The Blue Heron has free wireless Internet access. The creative and delicious dinners are prepared on-site by chefs Annie and Tom Walchuk. Kovach and her staff specialize in warm, welcoming hospitality and will gladly accommodate special diets, such as low fat, vegetarian, vegan or gluten or lactose-free. For an unforgettable getaway, make a reservation at the Blue Heron Bed & Breakfast.

827 Kawishiwi Trail, Ely MN
(218) 365-4720
www.blueheronbnb.com

Photo by Pamalot Roberts

The Coates Plaza Hotel

The historic five-story Coates Plaza Hotel, in the heart of downtown Virginia, opened in 1951. This landmark features a three-story glass-ceiling atrium enclosing a pool, spa and sauna. Each of the 43 guestrooms offers all modern conveniences, plus a spacious work area with free local calls and free high-speed Internet service. Three executive suites and an executive conference room featuring oak paneling, stone fireplaces and coffered ceilings occupy the luxurious top floor. The Coates' restaurant, Chestnut on 5th, serves breakfast, lunch and an elegant dinner with linen tablecloths and candlelight. Breakfast options range from blueberry pancakes to eggs Benedict. At lunch, try local favorites such as the Derby Burger and the Jack Daniels Pepper Wrap. At dinner you can indulge in juicy steaks, wonderful pastas or the chef's succulent butter-garlic steak and scallops. After a long day, unwind with friends over your favorite refreshment in the Hob Nob Lounge. Need to get down to business? The hotel's banquet, meeting and conference facilities can accommodate up to 400 people for conferences, banquets or meetings. Planning an event? The Coates' professional team of event coordinators can help. For a relaxing vacation getaway or stress-free business trip, check in to the Coates Plaza Hotel.

502 Chestnut Street, Virginia MN
(218) 749-1000 or (800) 777-4699
www.coatesplazahotel.com

The Olcott House Bed and Breakfast Inn

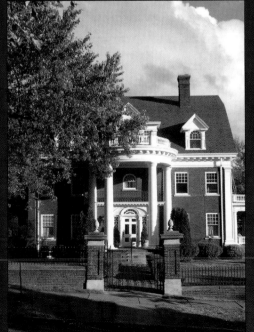

The Olcott House Bed & Breakfast Inn, with more than 100 years of history, is a fanciful, romantic getaway. This exceptional Georgian Colonial mansion, located in Duluth's historic East End mansion district, was built for William Olcott and his wife, Fanny, in 1904. Olcott was president of the Oliver Mining Company, which was later acquired by U.S. Steel, and also presided over the Duluth, Missabe and Northern Railroad. The mansion, surrounded by the original brick and wrought iron wall, stands majestically covering five city lots above Lake Superior. Guests enjoy the original high beamed ceilings, hardwood floors, mahogany paneling, bay windows, fine antiques and fireplaces in every suite. The separate four-room Carriage House Suite features a hand-painted mural of the original outside garden and fountain, a kitchen and a whirlpool tub. The Lake Superior Suite, in the main house, features a hand-carved canopy bed, bay window and a three season porch with balcony. The East Wing Suite feels fit for a president with its rare Birdseye maple floor, antiques and spacious layout. John D. Rockefeller and his family stayed in this house while visiting the Olcotts in 1928. In a home of pure elegance, the innkeepers create a magical environment for guests to relax and renew their spirit. Guests are invited to enjoy the mahogany-lined Library, play the grand piano in the acoustically designed Music Room or feel the soft breezes of Lake Superior on the Grand Porch. The Romance Package adds a special touch to a romantic getaway. The inn is just five blocks from Lake Superior and close to area attractions. Plan to relax and savor a stay at the Olcott House Bed and Breakfast Inn, described in a recently published history work as "the most aristocratic dwelling in the city."

2316 E 1ˢᵗ Street, Duluth MN
(218) 728-1339 or (800) 715-1339
www.olcotthouse.com

Big Lake Wilderness Lodge

Tucked away in the Superior National Forest, far from city lights and noise, Big Lake Wilderness Lodge offers fishermen and their families the chance to experience nature up close. With 1,800 acres of water, 14 islands, and numerous inlets and bays, Big Lake is a place of rugged beauty and the most remote drive-in lodge in Northern Minnesota. Located 23 miles north of Ely on the scenic Echo Trail, this serene resort offers private lakeshore cabins, ranging from cozy studio cabins, perfect for couples, to a spacious three-bedroom cabin that sleeps up to eight. Each cabin has a convenient dock slip, a fully furnished kitchen, full bath with tub and large deck for enjoying the impressive Northwoods scenery.

Outdoor enthusiasts enjoy complimentary use of canoes, kayaks and paddleboats. Guests can take a day trip into the Boundary Waters Canoe Area Wilderness and then come home to hot showers and comfortable beds. Fishermen appreciate the walleye, smallmouth bass, northern pike and perch that fill the clean, pure waters of Big Lake. Marked hiking trails start right at the resort where observant guests often spot local wildlife including moose, black bear, bald eagles, loons and wolves. Summertime visitors can participate in scheduled activities with the in-house naturalist. Three of the cabins, the main lodge and a pontoon boat are wheelchair accessible. Resort amenities include a sauna, laundry, bait and tackle, groceries and a wide variety of souvenirs in the gift shop. Stay at Big Lake Wilderness Lodge and wake up to the sounds of nature.

3012 Echo Trail, Ely MN
(800) 446-9080 or (218) 365-2125
www.biglakelodge.com

Solglimt on the Water

Intimate access to the sandy shoreline of Lake Superior is yours when you stay at Solglimt on the Water. This bed and breakfast takes its name from the Danish word for the jewel-like sparkle that the sun makes on the water. You will catch yourself thinking of this word often on a glorious day as you sit on the deck of the inn and gaze across the water at the nearby lighthouses. Imagine a morning when nothing more pressing engages you than to watch the ships glide under the Aerial Lift Bridge. Your hosts, Brian and Mary Grover, offer Solglimt's three guest rooms as a contemporary alternative to the Victorian theme so common at bed and breakfasts. Brian's love of art shows throughout the house, particularly in Kandinsky's Loft, inspired by 20th century artist Wassily Kandinsky. This loft with its open layout is ideal for a honeymoon or anniversary retreat. The Harbor View Suite features a king-size bed and private deck, while the Lake Superior Suite, sitting just above the water's edge, boasts a four-poster bed beneath a 20-foot ceiling. Brian and Mary pride themselves on their superb attention to detail. Repeat customers claim that each experience here is different. The innkeepers even keep a database showing the three-course gourmet breakfast they served on your last visit. Find the soft sandy beach just feet from your door at Solglimt on the Water.

828 Lake Avenue S, Duluth MN
(218) 727-0596
www.solglimt.com

Lake Breeze Motel Resort

Lake Breeze Motel Resort is reminiscent of lake resorts from the 1960s and is an ideal location for a nostalgic family getaway on Lake Superior. Ken and Paula Hughes, owners of the resort, are on hand to greet you when you arrive. The resort, nestled in the woods just outside Duluth, provides a relaxing atmosphere and a variety of rooms, suites and individual cedar log cabins. You can choose from such amenities as kitchens, a whirlpool for two and a gas fireplace. You can roast s'mores over the open fire pit or plan a picnic using the resort's grills and picnic tables. You can play nine holes of miniature golf, then go on to horseshoes, basketball and more. An outdoor pool and a sauna are favorites. All members of the family find activities to serve their interests. Perhaps you would like to hike along one of the resort's wooded trails, stroll along the shore or simply watch the boats from a deck. This old-fashioned resort is nestled in the woods just outside Duluth. It's typically quiet here by 10:30 at night, promising a tranquil rest. Lake Breeze resort is an excellent way to put the work world far behind you and enjoy a laid-back vacation with family. Get away to the North Shore with a visit to Lake Breeze Motel Resort.

9000 Condon Boulevard, Duluth MN
(218) 525-6808 or (800) 738-5884
www.lakebreeze.com

Ludlow's Island Resort on Lake Vermilion

Ludlow's Island Resort, adjacent to the Boundary Waters Canoe Area Wilderness, offers a vacation experience for families, fishing enthusiasts, and anyone wishing to get away to a private island retreat on one of Minnesota's most beautiful lakes. *USA Today* featured Ludlow's Island and Lake Vermilion as one of the five best vacation spots in the entire world. In 2005, the Minnesota Association of Innkeepers named Ludlow's the Property of the Year, and in December 2006 *Mpls.St.Paul Magazine* named Ludlow's as the Best Family/Kids Resort in Minnesota. Not only is it a special place for families, the property is also perfect for weddings, corporate retreats and romantic escapes to its private, off-island area with secluded cabins. Ludlow's also features gourmet weekends hosted by a variety of renowned chefs. (For details, see the website listed below.) Dream Catcher, the newest cottage, is four stories with tree top views and was featured on the *Travel Channel*. All of the cabins were handcrafted by two generations of Ludlow family members and are situated under canopies of birch and pine trees on the water's edge. Each cottage is distinctively decorated with an emphasis on rustic elegance. All have stone, wood-burning fireplaces, screened porches and decks overlooking beautiful Lake Vermilion. On the island, you will find a waterfront with a safe swimming beach, kayaks, canoes, paddleboats, sailboats and hydrobikes, all for guest use. There is also an inflatable climbing rock known as the Iceburg. The island is a very special place for children, because they can roam freely, play and explore in this protected, private environment. The resort only allows registered guests on the property. For the fishing enthusiast there are weekly fishing clinics and professional guides. The lake is renowned for walleye, bass and northern pike, and it is gaining recognition as a major untapped muskie fishing resource. There are fishing boats from 25 to 115 horsepower available for rent. Family-owned and operated for more than 60 years, the Ludlow's Island Resort experience creates a lifetime of memories.

8166 Ludlow Road, Cook MN
(877) 583-5697
www.ludlowsresort.com

Wendigo Lodge, Golf and Conference Center

Immersed in the scenic backdrop of Minnesota's Northwoods, Wendigo Lodge, Golf and Conference Center offers warm, sophisticated lodging, exceptional dining and premier golfing. All accommodations include complimentary high-speed Internet access, microwave, refrigerator and a continental breakfast. Executive Suites also feature their own kitchen, breakfast bar, fireplace and private balcony or patio. Wendigo's expanded indoor pool area, overlooking the scenic golf course, includes a heated pool, whirlpool and sauna.

There's plenty to do at Wendigo. The award-winning 18-hole Joel Goldstrand golf course was designed to challenge the most seasoned players. The course features dramatic elevation changes, water hazards, huge pine trees, abundant bunkering and large, undulating greens. After a day on the links, you can relax with a cocktail on the deck overlooking the 18th hole or enjoy the handsomely carved bar inside the lounge. Fairways Restaurant at Wendigo is well-known throughout the region for its exceptional casual and fine dining. Wendigo continues to be an exciting destination even when the golf course is covered in snow. Winter visitors enjoy miles of groomed snowmobile trails that lead right from the lodge.

Wendigo is the perfect setting for a conference, business meeting or wedding. Every event, large or small, is treated with the same extraordinary level of service. Professional planners will customize every detail of your event according to your individual requirements, including the menu, ambience and décor. The White Pines Ballroom can seat and serve up to 425 guests. The variety of meeting spaces at Wendigo were all designed with windows, specialized lighting and acoustics, and are equipped with Internet access and audiovisual capability. The serene, natural beauty of Northern Minnesota and its resident wildlife await you at Wendigo Lodge, Golf and Conference Center, where your special occasion becomes a memorable event.

20108 Golf Crest Road, Grand Rapids MN
(218) 327-2211 or (866) 727-7345
www.wendigolodge.com

Fenske Lake Cabins

The scenic road leading to Fenske Lake Cabins only hints at the natural beauty, adventure and solitude you will find at the resort, a small group of very private cabins nestled among tall pines along a pristine shoreline. For more than 75 years, families have returned year after year to these cabins. Owners Chris and Laurie Eilrich offer guests five fully furnished and updated one and two bedrooms cabins, each with its own private dock and use of a boat and canoe for the duration of your stay. Spread out over the grounds to ensure the privacy of guests, the cabins offer cozy knotty pine interiors and modern kitchens. Take in a stunning sunrise from the Trails End cabin or relax in the whirlpool tub at the Basswood cabin. Bass, northern pike and walleye fill the lake. The resort sits on the edge of the Boundary Waters Canoe Area Wilderness, where wildlife vastly outnumbers people. Guests can take day trips into the canoe-only lakes and bring home fresh fish for dinner, or hike one of the many trails. At the end of the day, try a relaxing sauna and jump into the cool, clear, refreshing waters of beautiful Fenske Lake. Alternatively, relax by the fire and just spend a few minutes marveling at how bright the stars are. You can find your own adventure at Fenske Lake Cabins.

3788 Fenske Lake Road, Ely MN
(218) 365-5481 or (877) 365-5481
www.fenskelakecabins.com

Timber Bay Lodge & Houseboats

Timber Bay Lodge & Houseboats offers fun-filled getaways. On Birch Lake deep in the Superior National Forest among the towering birch, pine and spruce, it offers rental houseboats for large and small groups. Equipped with water slides, the houseboats provide fun for the kids, a tranquil sanctuary for adults and a base for swimming and fishing. Owners Ron and Beth Rykken also rent comfortable log-sided cabins that are widely spaced to ensure privacy. The cabins feature wood burning fireplaces, large decks and stunning lake views. All are equipped with kitchen amenities, including a microwave, refrigerator and charcoal grill. The popular Bear Trap cabin features six bedrooms, a spacious great room with fireplace and a fantastic view of Birch Lake. At Timber Bay, activities surround you. Favorite winter sports include snowmobiling, ice

fishing, skiing and snowshoeing. In warmer weather, rent a boat or bring your own and try your luck with walleye, northern pike and smallmouth bass near the Boundary Waters Canoe Area. Enjoy the best fishing in spring and summer, or plan an adult getaway when autumn colors peak. A summer children's program and the game room in the Trading Post give parents free time to golf, fish or just unwind. Come enjoy all that Timber Bay Lodge & Houseboats has to offer, any time of the year.

8347 Timber Bay Road, Babbitt MN
(218) 827-3682 or (800) 846-6821
www.timberbay.com

Sawmill Inn of Grand Rapids

No matter what the season, there's always plenty to do when you stay at the Sawmill Inn of Grand Rapids. Whether you crave the excitement of snowmobiling, skiing, golf and boating, or the relaxation of sitting by a fire or unwinding in the whirlpool, you'll find it here. The Sawmill Inn exhibits the rustic grace of the Northwoods everywhere, from the beautiful hand-carved front desk to the split rock fireplace in the dining room. Comfortable guest rooms offer extra-long double beds and free hot breakfasts on weekdays. Come morning, work up an appetite with seasonal outdoor activities. The sales office can assist with setting up your recreational adventure. Exceptional food and attentive service await guests in the Cedars Dining Room. Bask

in the cozy ambience of the pine log walls and a rock fireplace while enjoying great food ranging from homemade soups to the signature rib eye steak. The Cedars Lounge is a great place to relax and features your favorite drinks, casual food and a big-screen television. After a fun-filled day of outdoor activities, unwind in the sauna, whirlpool or heated swimming pool in the 12,000-square-foot domed and climate-controlled recreation area. The Sawmill Inn also offers event facilities for business or family occasions. For four seasons of family fun, come to Sawmill Inn of Grand Rapids.

2301 S Pokegama Avenue, Grand Rapids MN
(218) 326-8501 or (800) 235-6455
www.sawmillinn.com

Radisson Hotel Duluth Harborview

The first thing that many guests do after checking in at the Radisson Hotel Duluth Harborview is head to the rooftop restaurant for a meal and a spectacular panoramic view. At Top of the Harbor, Duluth's only revolving restaurant, you might begin your dinner while gazing down at the city. As the room slowly spins, you might finish your entrée while admiring Lake Superior and then enjoy your dessert while surveying the countryside beyond the metropolitan area. Even if you aren't staying at the hotel, the Top of the Harbor is an attraction that you won't want to miss, one that is made even more noteworthy by its fine American cuisine. If you are staying here, you should congratulate yourself on making such an excellent choice for lodging. Spacious guest rooms and suites feature such conveniences as the Sleep Number beds by Select Comfort, as well as coffeemakers and hairdryers, while offering high-speed Internet access and other business-friendly amenities. When it's time to unwind, guests enjoy the indoor heated pool, sauna and fitness center. The hotel is connected by skywalks to many downtown Duluth businesses and attractions, including the Duluth Entertainment and Convention Center. With more than 9,000 square feet of flexible meeting space and a location just 10 miles from the airport, the Radisson is ideally suited to host conferences and trade shows. Stay at the Radisson Hotel Duluth Harborview and see how things look from the top.

505 W Superior Street, Duluth MN
(218) 727-8981
www.radisson.com/duluthmn

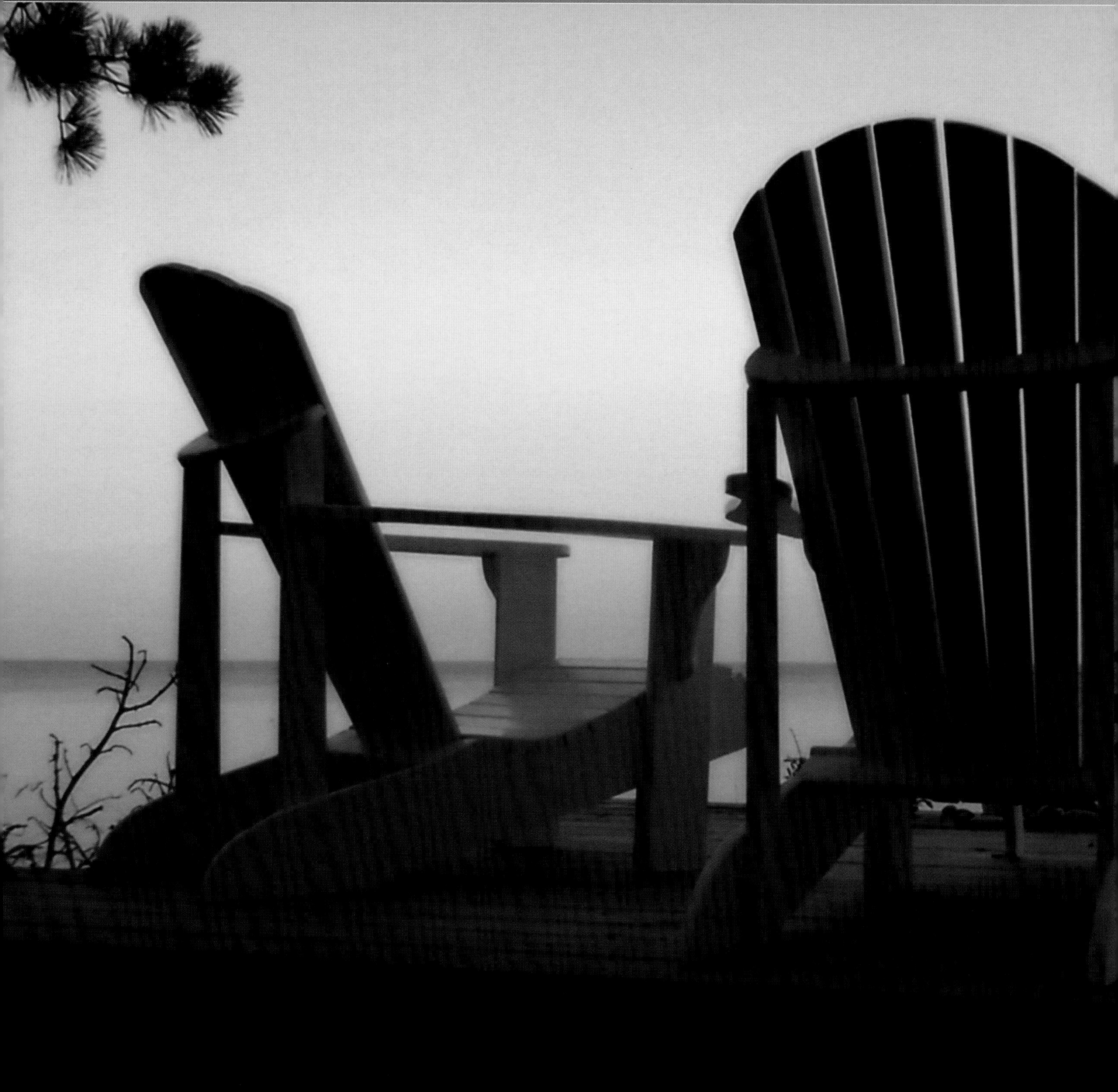

The Inn on Lake Superior

Every night at eight, folks gather around a campfire outside the Inn on Lake Superior to gaze out on the lake and roast marshmallows. Staff members at the Inn pride themselves on such extras as this complimentary campfire. When you turn in for the night, you will experience still another extra, namely the Inn-credible Dream Bed, which features triple sheeting and a mound of pillows. The 175-room Inn on Lake Superior wears many faces. Couples seeking a romantic getaway will love the location between Duluth's shoreline and the Canal Park shops and restaurants, while business travelers will appreciate the high-speed Internet access and conference facilities. Families find the heated pools irresistible. "The water was warm enough even in 15-degree weather," said one mom, "and the kids thought it was pretty cool swimming outside in the winter." The lake commands much of your attention when you stay here. You will enjoy watching big ships from around the globe float by, and the sunset is always dazzling. The complimentary breakfast each morning, another big extra, goes all out to please with scrambled eggs, make-your-own waffles and dozens of other goodies. Come and experience how the Inn on Lake Superior can make your stay in Duluth extra-special.

350 Canal Park Drive, Duluth MN
(888) 668-4352
www.theinnonlakesuperior.com

Split Rock Lighthouse

Standing on a cliff 130 feet above Lake Superior, Split Rock Lighthouse is the most famous landmark on the North Shore. It was built in 1910 during the boom times of the Northern Minnesota iron ore industry as the direct result of a 1905 storm that damaged 29 ships. By 1940, the lighthouse's picturesque image had already made it, by the estimation of the Coast Guard, the most visited lighthouse in the United States. Visitors still find the site an irresistible photo opportunity. By 1970, advanced navigation tools had made the lighthouse obsolete, but it remains as the centerpiece of Split Rock Lighthouse State Park. Restored to its 1920s appearance, the lighthouse offers visitors a glimpse of the isolated life of the lighthouse keeper. Costumed interpreters will take you back in time as you tour the lighthouse, fog-signal building and restored keeper's dwelling. At the visitor center you can view an award-winning documentary and browse a museum store. The 2,075-acre state park offers hiking, picnicking and tent camping. Don't miss the famous Split Rock Lighthouse on Lake Superior's scenic North Shore.

3713 Split Rock Lighthouse Road, Two Harbors MN
(218) 226-6372
www.mnhs.org/splitrock

Grand Rapids

Grand Rapids abounds with opportunities for outdoor recreation, much of it centered on the 1,200 freshwater lakes of Itasca County. Fishing for walleye, northern pike and crappie is popular during the summer open-water season and the winter ice-fishing season. Residents and visitors also enjoy hiking, biking, wildlife watching and snowmobiling on the county's million acres of forest land. Hunting for ruffed grouse is widely regarded as the best in the nation, and the Ruffed Grouse Society National Hunt each October is the highlight of the season. Minnesota's first National Scenic Byway—the Edge of the Wilderness—passes from Grand Rapids to Effie through 47 miles of picturesque countryside and the mixed pines of the Chippewa National Forest. Four championship golf courses, collectively known as Minnesota's Grand Slam of Golf (Wendigo, Sugarbrooke, Pokegama and Eagle Ridge), challenge even the most skilled players.

The area offers attractions with cultural and historical significance. One such stop is the Forest History Center, where costumed interpreters portray life in a 19th century logging camp. One of Hollywood's best-loved stars, Judy Garland, was born in Grand Rapids in 1922 as Francis Ethel Gumm. Her father, Frank Gumm, owned and operated the New Grand Theater. Theater is still a large part of the social life here with the Reif Performing Arts Center presenting a full calendar of events year-round. Grand Rapids is home to art galleries featuring local and regional artists, urban-inspired coffeehouses and many independent shops and restaurants that are all the hallmarks of small town charm and Americana. Visit Grand Rapids invites you to come see all that this community has to offer.

501 S Pokegama Avenue, Suite 3, Grand Rapids MN
(218) 326-9607 or (800) 355-9740
www.visitgrandrapids.com

Comet Theater

The Comet Theater combines a historic movie theater, gift and antique emporium, clothing boutique and coffee house with more pizzazz that is probably legal. Owners Carol Carlson and John Metsa bought the vintage Comet Theater in 2000 and soon began adding more attractions. The movie house dates to 1939 and is the oldest continuously running movie theater in Minnesota. Although Carol and John show first-run movies on the original equipment, the Comet also showcases art films and live music whenever possible. Comet Coffee features Alakef coffee, cappuccinos and lattes as well as specialty teas. You can munch on cookies, muffins or donuts, and enjoy a smoothie or a frozen drink while watching a movie or on the outdoor patio. Inside, you'll find an enormous variety of elegant, whimsical and interesting items, from Tiffany-style lamps to champagne stemware. One-of-a-kind totes and beaded handbags hang from a giant indoor tree, one of John's contributions to the boutique's unique décor. There's something new to see everywhere you look, from art pieces and vases to vintage kitchen collectibles such as salt and pepper shakers. You can also buy selected items online. The theater will continue to evolve, as it has since *The Wizard of Oz* played there in 1939, but as Carol points out, "There's no place like this." If Dorothy were around, she would undoubtedly agree.

102 S River Street, Cook MN
(218) 666-5814
www.comettheater.com

Beaner's Central

If you were to wish your ideal coffeehouse into existence, wouldn't you want one with a full espresso menu, plus freshly baked pastries and homemade soups and sandwiches? Of course, it would be a great place to meet friends and hang out. You could hope for some live music, but that would probably be asking for too much. Guess what? Beaner's Central in Duluth is that coffee house of your dreams. From international touring stars to the best of the local original scene, live music gets served up four to seven nights a week along with the coffee and delicious food. You could even kick back with a beer or glass of wine while listening to the music. Owner Jason Wussow doesn't like to see blank space on his calendar. In addition to booking acts that

perform their own original music, he provides an open mic on Wednesday night, offers Happy Hour specials every day and schedules such special events as wine and cheese tastings. Photography and paintings by local artists fill the walls. Local publications have named Jason's place the Best Coffeehouse and the Best Music Venue in Duluth. For everything you'd want in a coffeehouse, try Beaner's Central.

324 N Central Avenue, Duluth MN
(218) 624-5957
www.beanerscentral.com

Greyhound Bus Museum

Covering nearly a century of time, the Greyhound Bus Museum in Hibbing takes visitors through the history of an industry that helped unite the country. Learn how a new company was born when an out-of-work miner with a 1914 Hupmobile and his own resourcefulness began shuttling miners between the town of Alice and the mine at Hibbing for 15 cents per person. By 1930, after having bought many independent routes, the company became the Greyhound Bus Lines. The museum is home to 14 restored buses and shows off decades of design changes from the 1920s to the 1980s. A lifelike display of a 1916 bus being built and a diorama detailing Greyhound's participation in the war effort demonstrate the impact an industry can have on a country and its people. Changes in building design are also evident in the facades of a 1916 bus flag station and an Art Deco-style 1940s terminal. The Greyhound Bus Museum is the

passion of Gene Nicolelli, the director, designer and caretaker of the restored buses and artifacts. You'll see a VCR presentation of *The Greyhound Story: From Hibbing to Everywhere*. The museum is open from mid-May through September with special group tours available in the off-season. Visit the Greyhound Bus Museum, on the north edge of Hibbing past Bennett Park.

1201 E Greyhound Boulevard (3rd Avenue), Hibbing MN
(218) 263-5814
www.greyhoundbusmuseum.org

Seven of the twelve buses on exhibit

Judy Garland Museum

Minnesota governor Tim Pawlenty officially declared June 22nd Judy Garland Day, but you can pay tribute to this American legend at the Judy Garland Museum in Grand Rapids any day from Memorial Day weekend through September. (Call or visit the website for autumn and winter hours.) The museum offers visitors of all ages a touching glimpse into the life of the artist through such exhibits as the horse-drawn carriage from *The Wizard of Oz*. You can tour the home where Frances Ethel Gumm, aka Judy Garland, lived until she was four. She would perform on the stairway landing while her mother played the piano. You can view Judy's personal collections, remembrances and photographs. The museum is supported by donations from many sources, including the Bob and Dolores Hope Charitable Foundation, the Streisand Foundation and the Blandin Foundation. Private donors have offered up their lifetime collections of memorabilia to help create the most extensive Judy Garland collection in the world. With the tremendous influence this actress had on the film industry and the public, it's fitting that the National Endowment for the Arts deemed *Over the Rainbow* the best song of the 20th century, after conducting a broad poll of journalists, teachers, students and industry professionals in 2001. The performances of Judy Garland still speak to young and old alike, and fans from around the world will love the Judy Garland Museum. Come pay your respects to a true national icon.

2727 US Highway 169 S, Grand Rapids MN
(218) 327-9276 or (800) 664-JUDY (5839)
www.judygarlandmuseum.com

Brewed Awakenings Coffeehouse and Café

Brewed Awakenings Coffeehouse and Café originally opened in a cooperative grocery store in 1996. Cooking delicious vegetarian soups for the patrons of the store, using wholesome veggies, grains, beans and spices, proprietor Joan Foster soon had a following of adventurous connoisseurs. One dear customer commented, "It's like going home for lunch. If you're hungry, you eat what's on the table." Joan now has 60 original recipes written down featuring locally produced foods. In the summer of 2006, Brewed Awakenings moved into a newly remodeled building on Highway 2 East in downtown Grand Rapids. Here, Joan has continued the tradition of using organic and locally grown products for soups, sandwiches, salads and bakery items. She has even added gelato to the menu, which is made fresh daily in small batches in her kitchen, using the same hormone and preservative-free milk that she uses in the lattes and cappuccinos. Joan is proud to brew the finest organic, Fair Trade coffee, which is grown and traded to benefit farmers, communities and their ecosystems—ultimately benefiting us all. Stop by Brewed Awakenings Coffeehouse and Café and let Joan and her husband, John Ostroot, feed you while you take advantage of the free wireless Internet. If you're looking for a marriage partner, let them know. In ten years in business, five marriages have resulted from meetings at Brewed Awakenings, with several more in the wings.

24 NE 4th Street, Grand Rapids MN
(218) 327-1088
www.brewedawakenings.biz

Hepzibah's Sweet Shoppe

Hepzibah's Sweet Shoppe, in Duluth's DeWitt-Seitz Marketplace, answers all your desires for chocolates and other confections in one convenient stop. Owner Tina Anderson has been hard at work selling candy for more than 20 years. Named for early Duluth settler Hepzibah J. Merritt, this old-fashioned candy store is alive with Hepzibah's adventurous and dynamic pioneer spirit. The majority of Tina's products are handmade. She also carries imported chocolates, licorices and hard-to-find candies. You will find all the Jelly Belly jelly bean flavors made. Hepzibah's popular truffles have been featured on *Oprah*, on the Food Network and in *Mpls.St.Paul Magazine*. Expect a generous selection of old-fashioned candies, fudge and caramels as well as sugar-free candy for special diets. Next time your sweet tooth demands its due, bring it to Hepzibah's Sweet Shoppe, where cravings are replaced with satisfaction.

394 Lake Avenue S, Duluth MN
(218) 722-5049

Photo by Michelle Sternberg

Art Options Gallery and Framing

Sue Pavlatos finds endless sources of inspiration in Minnesota's Northland. Original lakescapes, landscapes and cityscapes dominate at Art Options Gallery and Framing. The gallery also carries Sue's prints. Watercolor and acrylics are Sue's media of choice and the way that light interacts with its subject is her main concern. One project features nearly 20 pieces commemorating the 100th anniversary of the Duluth Aerial Lift Bridge. Other paintings, prompted by Sue's travels to Italy, France and New Zealand, include brilliant florals, storybook landscapes and distinct architectural details. Since Sue established her gallery and framing business in 1989, her work has graced the covers of *Lake Superior Magazine* and the Duluth Chamber of Commerce guidebooks. She exhibits regularly and even had a one-person show at the Johnson Heritage Center in Grand Marais. Sue's originals, prints and Artblox can also be found at Art Dock Inc. and The Bookstore At Fitgers. Be sure to visit Art Options Gallery and Framing for evocative impressions of landscapes as viewed by the eyes of a local artist.

207 Avenue C, Suite 103, Cloquet MN (Art Options, Too)
(218) 349-7045
132 E Superior Street, Duluth MN (Art Options)
(218) 727-8723
1500 Jackson Street NE, Room 428, Minneapolis MN
www.artoptions.com

Paintings by Sue Pavlatos

Positive Energy Outdoor (ed) Ventures

A Duluth-based not-for-profit organization, Positive Energy Outdoor (ed) Ventures offers fun outdoor activities ranging from kayaking to dog sledding. The organization is led by the husband-and-wife team of Blake Cazier and Stephanie Love. Blake and Stephanie have a combined 30 years of professional experience leading outdoor activities for people of all ages and abilities. Positive Energy's programs emphasize teamwork, learning new skills and the benefits of an active lifestyle. You'll experience firsthand the power of teamwork during winter dog sledding programs as you learn to harness and drive a team of friendly Alaskan husky sled dogs. Take that fabled one-horse open sleigh ride or learn to hitch and drive a team of draft horses. Those looking for even more of a challenge will enjoy the ice climbing introductions. Summer activities include sea kayaking, driving draft horses and rock climbing. All equipment is provided and no experience is necessary. Positive Energy offers youth-sized equipment, mukluk rentals and customized programs and trips. Proceeds from adult and family programs help support agencies that serve children in Northeast Minnesota. For outdoor fun that will charge you with positive energy, come to Positive Energy Outdoor (ed) Ventures.

15 miles N of Duluth MN
(218) 391-0147 or (218) 428-5990
www.outdooredventures.org

Spirit Mountain Recreation Area

"Objects in motion tend to stay in motion. Objects in front of the television tend to go nowhere." So reads the brochure of Spirit Mountain Recreation Area, which has hosted many a skier since opening in 1974. Its 22 downhill runs are the perfect antidote for the winter blues. What's more, if you're visiting Duluth, you won't have to drive far to get there. It's right at the south end of town in a city filled with lodging, dining, events and activities. Alpine skiers of every skill level have a blast on the slopes, which overlook Lake Superior and the St. Louis River Bay. Nordic skiers love the area, too, because Spirit Mountain offers as much cross-country skiing as you could ever hope to find in Minnesota's beautiful North Woods. Boarders, meanwhile, flock to the Big Air Terrain Park. The largest of its kind in the Midwest, it offers a super pipe, a rail park and plenty of variable terrain. Spirit Mountain has partnerships with many local hotels that offer outstanding Stay and Play packages. In the summer months, the Spirit Mountain Campground is very popular, offering secluded, wooded campsites suitable for tents and RVs. Located directly at the top of the mountain, the campground attracts local hikers and bicyclists as well as tourists looking for a lovely and economical place to stay. With all this to offer, it's time to turn off the television and head to Spirit Mountain Recreation Area.

**9500 Spirit Mountain Place, Duluth MN
(800) 642-6377**
www.spiritmt.com

Lakeview Castle

You'll feel like royalty that's been let loose to explore casual dining after a meal at Lakeview Castle. The Duluth restaurant and lounge offers live musical entertainment, wine, beer and spirits and a mix of premium to casual entrées. It's North Shore location affords fine views of Lake Superior. Owner Mary Yount has traveled the world and brings her experiences to her diners, offering a premium family dining experience laced with a hint of elegance. Mary and her children have a way of putting their guests at ease so they can better enjoy the restaurant's many offerings, which include the famous *saganaki* appetizer, a cheese-based Greek specialty. You'll find everything from burgers and pizza to walleye pike, fillet mignon, and cold water lobster. Enjoy the slow roasted prime rib special every Thursday, Friday and Saturday. The restaurant's wireless Internet access means you can finish up work here, hold a business dinner or surf the Net while watching a game in the lounge. Lakeview Castle's banquet room seats up to 400 people, and the restaurant's beverage professional is on hand to help organize wine tastings or make recommendations from the restaurant's bottle shop. The banquet menu is varied, providing everything you need for sit-down meals, buffets or appetizers. Plan a night out with family or business associates at the lovely Lakeview Castle Restaurant.

5135 N Shore Scenic Drive, Duluth MN
(218) 525-1014
www.lakeviewcastleduluth.com

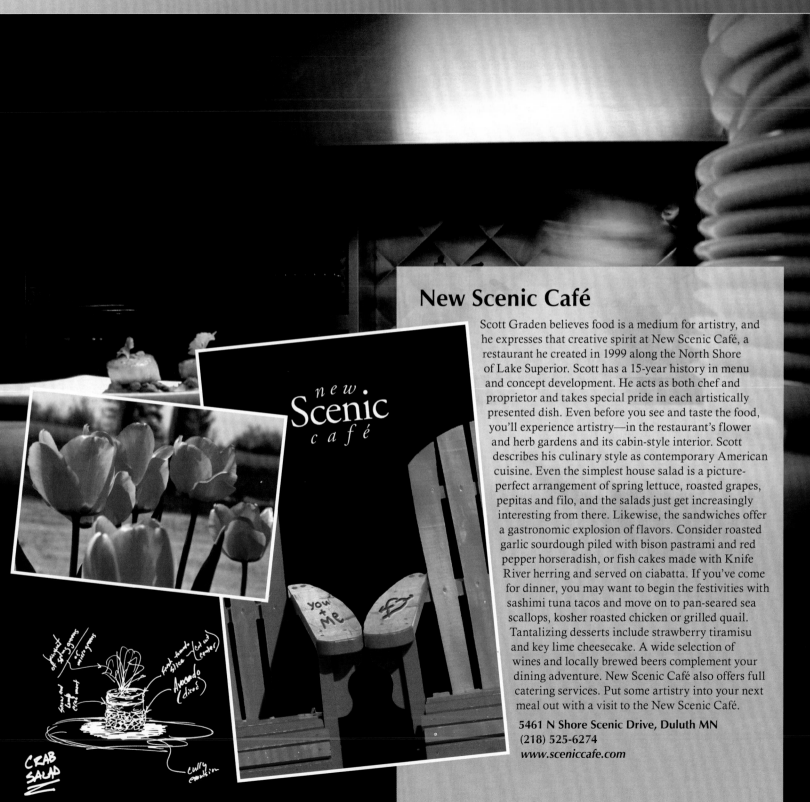

New Scenic Café

Scott Graden believes food is a medium for artistry, and he expresses that creative spirit at New Scenic Café, a restaurant he created in 1999 along the North Shore of Lake Superior. Scott has a 15-year history in menu and concept development. He acts as both chef and proprietor and takes special pride in each artistically presented dish. Even before you see and taste the food, you'll experience artistry—in the restaurant's flower and herb gardens and its cabin-style interior. Scott describes his culinary style as contemporary American cuisine. Even the simplest house salad is a picture-perfect arrangement of spring lettuce, roasted grapes, pepitas and filo, and the salads just get increasingly interesting from there. Likewise, the sandwiches offer a gastronomic explosion of flavors. Consider roasted garlic sourdough piled with bison pastrami and red pepper horseradish, or fish cakes made with Knife River herring and served on ciabatta. If you've come for dinner, you may want to begin the festivities with sashimi tuna tacos and move on to pan-seared sea scallops, kosher roasted chicken or grilled quail. Tantalizing desserts include strawberry tiramisu and key lime cheesecake. A wide selection of wines and locally brewed beers complement your dining adventure. New Scenic Café also offers full catering services. Put some artistry into your next meal out with a visit to the New Scenic Café.

5461 N Shore Scenic Drive, Duluth MN
(218) 525-6274
www.sceniccafe.com

Zimmy's Restaurant

Hibbing, Minnesota, celebrates its most famous son at Zimmy's Restaurant. The restaurant is named after Robert Allen Zimmerman, the Hibbing native who was going by the name of Bob Dylan by the time he hit New York City in the early 1960s. The memorabilia displayed throughout Zimmy's pays homage to Dylan. The menu will also have you humming your favorite Dylan tunes with its array of choices named after songs from every phase of the performer's phenomenal career. The lengthy menu includes everything from burgers and pizza to seafood and steak. Stir-fries, pasta and Southwestern specialties are also available. The gift shop sells Dylan items, including hard-to-find photo prints and the documentary *Tangled Up In Bob*, in addition to Zimmy's original clothing and collectibles. Zimmy's is the birthplace of the annual Dylan Days Celebration every May in Hibbing. This event has grown over the past decade to include songwriting, visual arts and literary contests, plus tours, movie screenings and a concert at the historic Hibbing High School auditorium where Dylan performed in the late 1950s. When you're traveling down Highway 61 or just blowin' in the wind, you can always find a piece of Bob Dylan at Zimmy's.

531 E Howard Street, Hibbing MN
(218) 262-6145
www.zimmys.com

Whistling Bird Café & Bar

At Whistling Bird Café & Bar, JoPat and Toney Curtis have been treating customers to a taste of the Caribbean for eight years. This award-winning restaurant features authentic Jamaican jerk house specialties and Caribbean cuisine as well as traditional favorites such as steak, pasta, seafood and fish. For starters, try the stuffed mushroom caps, filled with bubbly hot feta cheese, parsley and fresh lemon. Chicken wings come in seven versions to suit your taste. Pasta fans will enjoy the Rasta Pasta with Jamaican spiced peppers, red onion, mushrooms and spinach finished in a coconut-lime curry sauce, or the always-popular linguine with garlicky shrimp and lobster. Fish and seafood choices include Tangerine-Kissed Mahi Mahi, shrimp scampi and coconut shrimp, or try the meltingly tender filet mignon, expertly cooked to your liking. Jamaican jerk cuisine uses a combination of spices, onions and peppers to add a mouthwatering sweet and hot flavor to chicken, seafood and pork. Try the Jamaican rum barbecue jerk chicken, served with Jamaican rice and beans and fried corn bread. The full-service bar offers an extensive wine list as well as cocktails and specialty drinks. The Whistling Bird Café & Bar treats customers like friends coming over for dinner, so make reservations to enjoy the tropical decor, friendly service and great food.

101 N Broadway Street, Gilbert MN
(218) 741-7544
www.whistlingbirdcafeandbar.com

Bennett's on the Lake

Everything about Bennett's on the Lake, from its view of Lake Superior and walls decorated with work by local artists to its carefully prepared and reasonably priced breakfasts, lunches and dinners invites your attention. You'll enjoy fresh seafood entrées, such as the salmon roulade, or such regional dishes as Peppered Superior Lake Trout. "Plain, good and fresh food is always in," says owner Bob Bennett, who prefers variety to staying on top of trends. Bob and his wife, Kathy, opened the first Bennett's in 1992 and moved to their present location in the Fitger's Brewery Complex in 1997. Bob is a graduate of the Johnson & Wales culinary school in Rhode Island and served as executive chef at the Crescent Hotel in Phoenix and the Palm Valley Country Club in California before returning to his wife's hometown to open Bennett's. His preparations are so popular that he also teaches cooking classes. To keep his guests completely entertained Bob not only presents daily specials, but special dinner theater events. Change of Pace Productions may present a murder mystery or a Broadway hit. Bennett's offers four event rooms and a 140-seat theater to accommodate various gatherings. Heather Steinbach, Bennett's catering director, can help create the perfect menu for your special occasion or meeting. For a memorable meal on the shores of Lake Superior, visit Bennett's on the Lake.

600 E Superior Street, Duluth MN
(218) 722-2829 (restaurant)
(218) 722-DINE (3463) (catering)
www.bennettsonthelake.com

Duluth Athletic Club Bar & Grill

Owners Peter and Michael Emerson opened the Duluth Athletic Club Bar & Grill five years ago in the same spot occupied by a men's club in the early 1900s and later known as the Chinese Lantern restaurant. This is a come-as-you-are restaurant, where you can enjoy a televised sporting event in the bar or bring a date to the restaurant and then upstairs to the 21 North nightclub. The menu is varied and creative, and everything is made in-house, including freshly cut fries, burgers, steaks and salads. Start off with a creamy artichoke cheese bake appetizer or prehaps the beer cheese soup with popcorn garnish. Cambazola stuffed chicken is a popular main course, or you can take a bite out of history with the Chinese Lantern prime rib. Mike brings 20 years of restaurant experience to his venture and knows how to grow a loyal clientele with quality, house-made selections. The restaurant offers a nightly drink special and can accommodate banquets for large groups either upstairs or down. Catering is available, courtesy of the on-site Coco's Catering, an enterprise which can match a theme to your palate and budget. The Duluth Athletic Club is out and about town, thanks to four separate D.A.C. Deli locations, which provide a somewhat shorter menu, but quicker fare that you can grab on the run. For a restaurant that successfully marries sports and fine dining, visit the Duluth Athletic Club Bar & Grill.

21 N 4th Avenue W, Duluth MN
(218) 720-4445 or (218) 740-3039 (Coco's Catering)
www.duluthathleticclub.net

Coppola Art Imports

Coppola Art Imports is one of the largest importers of Italian goods in the Midwest. Some family businesses do so well that the owners decide to open a second store on the other side of town. Coppola Art Imports offers a somewhat different twist. The shop is a branch of a ceramics store that Antonino Coppola's grandmother started more than 50 years ago in Sorrento, Italy. The most popular line of wares at the store is a dinnerware pattern called Decora Enza, designed by Antonino's mother. In all, the shop has ceramics representing 25 painters from Sicily, Deruta, the Amalfi Coast and Tuscany. The dinnerware is made from a chip-resistant red clay that is prized for its durability as well as its beauty. A selection of Murano glass complements the striking ceramics. Antonino himself crafts the inlaid wood objects in the store, many of which feature the Aerial Lift Bridge, Split Rock Lighthouse and other scenes from his adopted home of Duluth. Antonino grew up working in the family store in Sorrento. The location of his Duluth shop, perched over the Lakewalk and shoreline, reminds him of home. "Sorrento is by the water," he says. "I wanted to be by the water in Duluth." Occasionally folks drop by who have visited his grandmother's store and tell Antonino that his shop takes them right back to their Italian holiday. Visit Coppola Art Imports and you too will feel as if you have been transported to Italy.

728 E Superior Street, Duluth MN
(218) 722-0433
www.coppolaartimports.com

Mealey's Gift & Sauna Shop

Located in Ely's historical business district, Mealey's Gift & Sauna Shop is known for its award-winning garden, one-of-a-kind product line and friendly staff. Unlike typical souvenir shops, Mealey's prides itself on offering quality goods from all over. Mealey's chooses only the finest products from local Minnesota artists and exotic handmade artwork from around the world. With diverse collections of handcrafted pottery, glassware, copper, wood, wall art, jewelry and more, the shop provides its customers with items of the highest quality. Beginning as a small gift shop in 1987, Mealey's has since expanded its inventory to include a furniture and lighting gallery with a large selection of home décor for a variety of tastes. Mealey's also carries a vast supply of fine sauna products including pre-fabricated and custom-cut sauna kits, wood and electric sauna stoves, pre-hung doors and accessories. To better meet customer demand, Mealey's recently began a website where customers can find many of its products and great deals. Next time you are in Northern Minnesota, be sure to stop by this little shop. You'll certainly find something you can't live without, and maybe something you didn't even know you were looking for at Mealey's Gift & Sauna Shop.

124 N Central Avenue, Ely MN
(800) 922-3639
www.mealeysinely.com

Angie's Home Sweet Home

Angie's Home Sweet Home offers customers a vast selection of quality products. Come and explore the seven themed rooms, including the main room, nautical room, Christmas and holiday room, and the rooms with the themes country kitchen, Northwoods, shabby chic, and cards and books. Angie's carries products from many local artists, authors and crafters. Some of the most popular items are made by Caldrea, Votivo, American Expedition and Marianne Richmond. You will also discover homemade Knudsen Caramels, Honey and Me, Briar Patch

Primitives and Simply Irresistible teddy bears. With this great selection, you will be sure to find something for everyone on your list. In the 2006 season, Angie's welcomed guests from 42 different states and 23 different countries. Be sure to sign the guest book, because Angie's tries to beat its record every year. Angie's is open seven days a week from April first—be sure to call for winter hours. For a pleasant chance to browse and chat with owner Angie Locker in her enchanting surroundings, plan a trip to Angie's Home Sweet Home. Angie and her staff can't wait to meet you.

5103 N Shore Scenic Drive, Duluth MN
(218) 525-3122
http://homesweethome.visitduluth.com

Auntie Byrl's Attic

Tucked away at the end of a narrow, tree-lined lane lies Auntie Byrl's Attic, a quaint little shop brimming with handcrafted gifts and antiques. The shop showcases one-of-a-kind ladies' jackets that are handmade from vintage fabrics and home décor items such as pillows made from vintage chenille, old quilts and aged linens. Collectibles include a variety of snowmen, angels and dolls. Whether you're a novice cook or an expert, you'll find kitchen collectibles and an assortment of cookbooks that make wonderful gifts for yourself or someone special. Remember to set an attractive table to show off your favorite recipes. Byrl's has lovely dishes and sparkling glassware to suit any style. Fun and functional garden items round out the shop's

offerings. Owner Byrl Norlander inherited many of her antiques and collectibles from her mother, Beth White, and her paternal grandmother, Rose. Since starting her business 16 years ago, Byrl has begun antiquing herself and also handcrafts the items for sale in her shop. Byrl's is open Wednesdays, Thursdays and Fridays from May through October. For a fascinating selection of handcrafted gifts, collectibles and antiques, come browse awhile at Auntie Byrl's Attic.

6735 Lady Slipper Lane, Virginia MN
(218) 749-4891

Reed Drug

Don't let the name fool you—some of the most delightful shopping in Grand Rapids is at Reed Drug. So much more than a drugstore, Reed Drug tantalizes browsers with a wide selection of gifts, cards and souvenirs. Many paths meet at Reed Drug, located downtown across from the Old Central School. If you are on the trail of tickets for an event at the Reif Center, you can purchase them at this bustling shop. If you are on vacation and have a lot of digital photos, you can bring them in and process them at the picture station. Of course, you can also have your prescription filled efficiently at the pharmacy. Customers find the shelves well stocked with vacation treasures, including rustic North Woods gifts and sporty T-shirts and sweatshirts. If you have fallen in love with the region's natural beauty, you may want to take home artwork that will always remind you of the wildlife and scenery. A cosmetics and fragrance counter adds a boutique touch to the store. Free gift-wrapping makes shopping at Reed Drug even more enjoyable. It's easy to see why so many Grand Rapids residents consider Reed Drug not only a pharmacy they can trust but also their favorite store. Bring your shopping list and have fun.

417 NW 1st Avenue, Grand Rapids MN
(218) 326-3453 or (877) 326-3453

Waters of Superior

Waters of Superior, located in the heart of Duluth's Canal Park, provides an upscale collection of regional art, handmade jewelry, contemporary women's clothing, natural modern gifts and home furnishings. With a discriminating eye, the owners have selected items that reflect their inspiration, Lake Superior and the surrounding northern heritage. In the gallery, regional artists and artisans display a variety of distinctive works including one-of-a-kind paintings, pottery and large format photography by Craig Blacklock. They offer unique necklaces, bracelets and earrings individually chosen from more than 35 jewelers. The pieces at Waters of Superior make beautiful accessories, whether you're at play ar attending the dressiest affair. Waters of Superior also specializes in classic women's clothing that reflects the changing seasons. Quality garments, including those from Eileen Fisher and Geiger of Austria, add timeless style to any wardrobe. Discover the art of living through exceptional gifts and accents for your home. Influenced by traditional and modern Scandinavian design, Iittala dishware from Finland and Ekelund linens from Sweden will inspire the entertainer in you. Experience Waters of Superior, where you'll find a marriage of elegant function and visual interest.

395 Lake Avenue S, Duluth MN
(218) 786-0233 or (877) 387-9766
www.watersofsuperior.com

Minnesota Gifts by Sandra Dee

Sandra Dee Rothman opened Minnesota Gifts by Sandra Dee in 1985 as a place where visitors to Duluth's North Shore could find souvenirs suitable for adults and children. She placed her business on the second floor of the Dewitt-Seitz Marketplace, a historical building that was newly renovated in 1985. The location has proven a good one and attracts those who are visiting the Canal Park area. Sandra knows just what kind of mementos best capture this beautiful country and enjoys helping people find that special something that will best represent their

experience of the area and its history. A blanket can serve as a cozy reminder of your visit, or you might want to bring home an afghan that depicts the area's historic sites. You will find mugs and souvenir spoons to commemorate your trip along with post cards, magnets and T-shirts in all sizes. The Northwoods inspires many local artisans, whose work can brighten your cabin or home. Minnesota Gifts carries the work of local artist Dena Rothman, who created the watercolor painting and resulting commemorative print that celebrates the 2002 North Shore Inline Marathon. Next time you pass through the Canal Park area, come visit Sandra at Minnesota Gifts by Sandra Dee.

394 Lake Avenue S, Duluth MN
(218) 722-3746
www.minnesotagiftsduluth.com

Purple Pinecone

A visit to the Purple Pinecone is an opportunity to see exciting products from many small Minnesota companies. Serving utensils and glass products embellished with colorful glass beads bear the label of a successful Minnesota business, Pizzazz-Ware. Plates and bowls from Front Avenue Pottery evoke the region with their moose, bear, caribou and fish motifs. Jeans, jackets, skirts and tops from FDJ French Dressing blend sumptuous colors and fabrics that reflect the

inner confidence of the women who wear them. Cugino's, a Minnesota purveyor of gourmet foods, supplies the Purple Pinecone with sauces, dressings, soups and chili. For your listening pleasure, Minnesota Mornings CDs soothe the soul with fresh, instrumental arrangements of timeless songs of love and faith. In short, the Purple Pinecone is a great place to shop for all sorts of things. From furniture and clothing to wildlife art, fragrant candles and gifts for every occasion, you will find it at this shop. Visit the Purple Pinecone, located at the heart of Grand Rapids' Central Square Mall.

201 NW 4th Street, Grand Rapids MN
(218) 327-8119

Fitger's Brewhouse

Fitger's Brewhouse opened in 1995 after its owners discovered the brewpub scene while skiing in Washington, Oregon and Colorado. Combining the relaxed ambience of a high mountain brewery with the uncompromising dedication to quality and the pioneering spirit of the original Fitger's Brewery, the Brewhouse continues to carry on a tradition of handcrafted beer, fantastic food and excellent entertainment. Between the Brewhouse and Red Star, the attached club, 16 lines of beer are featured simultaneously. Duluth's sole brewpub, Fitger's Brewhouse earns a loyal following for many reasons, not the least of which is its tasty quaffs, which range from English-style ales to oatmeal stouts to dark German lagers. The kitchen staff has garnered numerous accolades from regional publications for its great food. Terrific live music adds to its overall appeal. Join the lively crowd of young professionals and college kids that flocks to Fitger's Brewhouse.

600 E Superior Street, Duluth MN
(218) 279–BREW (2739)
www.brewhouse.net
www.redstarclub.us

Snowy Owl hunting mice

Northwest Minnesota

Birch Villa Resort

In today's fast-moving world, it's important that you choose your vacation spot carefully. At the Birch Villa Resort, owners Mark and Karrie Nelson offer a slow-paced, relaxing vacation. Built on the shores of Cass Lake in the Chippewa National Forest, Birch Villa is a paradise for the fisherman in need of an ideal getaway. The resort features luxury cabin accommodations in all sizes, including a brand new six-bedroom cabin with a fireplace, a gourmet kitchen, a 40-inch television and outstanding views. You'll find a deluxe harbor with boat rentals, a bait shop and fish-cleaning facilities. The fishing buff who wants a little tutoring can hire a guide who will know where to catch walleye, northern pike and muskellunge. If you've come to the lake for something besides the fish, the resort is prepared for you, too. Birch Villa offers boat rentals, courts for basketball, volleyball and horseshoes, as well as a sand beach and miles of pristine shoreline to tempt the explorer. The winter landscape is equally enticing with opportunities for ice fishing, snowmobiling and cross-country skiing. You can build a fire on the shores of the lake and watch a beautiful sunset followed by a spectacular display of the northern lights. Delight in the splendor of unspoiled nature with a visit any time of year to Birch Villa Resort.

16364 60th Avenue NW, Cass Lake MN
(218) 335-6795
www.birchvilla.com

Big Rock Resort

Your chances of catching the big one are better at Leech Lake, dubbed the Muskie Capital of the World, than probably anywhere else. Big Rock Resort hugs the shoreline of Leech Lake, and owners Jerry and Sandy Emery, along with managers Marty and Mary Andreasen, hope you will spend your next family vacation here. Muskie aren't the only prize game fish in this sparkling, tree-lined lake. You'll find walleye and a large population of northern pike to make each cast exciting. Jumbo perch get very active and hungry in the fall. You can dock at Big Rock's 50-boat marina while staying in one of the resort's deluxe cabins. You bring the towels and soaps, and the staff provides the rest, including a fully equipped kitchen with a microwave, a Weber grill and picnic table. Cabins range in size from one to three bedrooms. Relax at the outdoor heated pool and spa or on a large sunning deck. Opportunities for activity include courts for tennis and basketball as well as volleyball and horseshoe pits. The lodge is a popular gathering spot, especially when there is a fire blazing in the large stone fireplace. Big Rock Resort received a Minnesota Preservation Award in 2006 for initiating a new ownership model and assisting in the drafting of new resort-area zoning to preserve the resort for future generations. For 60 years, guests have been making Big Rock Resort their vacation home on Leech Lake. This season, make it yours.

7860 Hawthorn Trail, Walker MN
(218) 547-1066 or (800) 827-7106
www.bigrockresort.com

Sand Bay Resort

Anyone who loves the natural world will appreciate Sand Bay Resort, established in 1883 on the Shores of Battle Lake, a lake so clear you can see the bottom through 15 feet of water. Bass, crappie, walleye and muskie are just waiting for the fisherman. Resort owner Wade Mills will be glad to guide you to his favorite fishing spots, or you just can rent a boat for a day out. The fisherman in the family isn't the only one who will enjoy Battle Lake. No one can resist the haunting call of the loons. You can also relax in the sun or plan a canoe trip. The lodge offers arcade and video games, billiards and tables for board and card games. Still other opportunities for vacation pleasure exist in the nearby town of Battle Lake, where you will find golf courses and horseback riding stables. State parks for bird watching and hiking are also nearby. You can walk the short distance from the resort to a downtown area of specialty and antiques shops. You'll find historical markers and possibly catch a turtle race. Wade and Hollie Mills provide everything you need for a comfortable stay. Their resort offers 15 modern cabins with kitchens and private bathrooms with showers. Each cabin has cable television and a deck with patio furniture. For a vacation where you can get away from the busy city and still find plenty to do, come to Sand Bay Resort.

405 Washington Avenue N, Battle Lake MN
(218) 864-5244 or (800) 546-9316
www.sandbayresort.com

Prairie View Estate Bed & Breakfast

Phyllis and Lyle Haugrud share the warm and inviting atmosphere of a lovingly restored Norwegian-inspired farmhouse with guests who enjoy the pleasures of a country setting. Three hundred acres of woods, pastures and fields surround the 1927 home, which features several generations of antique family heirlooms. The three guest rooms have a homespun turn-of-the-century look, and each has its own bath to assure cozy evenings and relaxing weekends. The experience at Prairie View is one of serenity. A country dining room, peaceful parlor and sunny porch invite you to sit for a spell. Prairie View is just one mile north of Pelican Rapids, where you can indulge in gift and antique shopping, try out exceptional restaurants or sample the nightlife. The wonders of nature are equally close at hand. You may want to spend a day fishing, picnicking or swimming at nearby Maplewood State Park. Several golf courses are also in the

vicinity. Winter visitors will find themselves close to miles of marked snowmobile and ski trails. Much has changed since the Egstad family homesteaded here in 1876 and built this house in 1927, but the serene surroundings remain as lovely as ever. It's clear to see why four generations made this their home. For a tranquil, country getaway, visit Prairie View Estate Bed & Breakfast.

43581 County Highway 9, Pelican Rapids MN
(218) 863-4321 or (800) 298-8058
www.prairieviewestate.com

Maplelag Resort

Jim and Mary Richards started in 1973 with a 65-acre maple syrup farm. Today, they've expanded their holdings to create Maplelag Resort, a 600-acre wonderland that boasts 63 kilometers of exceptionally well-groomed ski trails. In 2003, their resort was named the best cross-country ski resort in North America by a national poll. "Skiing is something to do to pass the time in between meals," said one guest, referring no doubt to the fresh ingredients and homemade preparation that produces memorable entrées, desserts and breads. Some of the local bounty used in Maplelag's kitchen includes pure maple syrup on Norwegian pancakes, locally harvested honey and lingonberries. You'll also find imported Swiss chocolate, Scandinavian cheeses and flatbreads. Just like Maplelag's bottomless cookie jars, meals here are all-you-can-eat. You'll find an impressive main lodge and comfy accommodations for up to 200 guests. With no televisions or telephones in the rooms, guests find ample time to ski, bird watch, sled,

Photo courtesy of Mapleag Resort

snowshoe or ice skate. Ski rentals and lessons are available. Ask your hosts about taking The Plunge. The experience begins in the old-fashioned wood burning sauna and climaxes with an exhilarating splash into the icy waters of Little Sugarbush Lake. Evening dances and the services of professional massage therapists are also part of the fun. For the quintessential winter holiday, get away to Maplelag Resort.

30501 Maplelag Road, Callaway MN
(218) 375-4466 or (800) 654-7711
www.maplelag.com

Brindley's Harbor Resort

Staying at Brindley's Harbor Resort definitely has its perks. For example, when you pull into the marina with your boat weighed down from all the walleye and jumbo perch you caught, the staff meets you, cleans the fish and assists with fuel, ice and other needs. Now that's service. Brindley's Harbor Resort is a traditional family resort on Leech Lake, one of Minnesota's top fishing lakes. In addition to the 37-slip marina in the protected harbor, the resort features lakeside cottages, a lodge and a store set on 22 acres of mature forest. Minnesota's third largest inland lake, Leech Lake stretches along hundreds of miles of undeveloped shoreline within the Chippewa National Forest. Bird watchers know the Chippewa as the home of the largest population of nesting bald eagles in the lower 48 states. Expect your cottage within this natural wonderland to be sparkling clean with a knotty pine interior, full kitchen and deck or screen porch. Cottages vary in size from one to four bedrooms. For luxury accommodations suitable for family reunions, business meetings and large fishing groups, stay at a spectacular log home at the resort. For sensational fishing, inspiring scenery and outstanding service, choose Brindley's Harbor Resort.

9530 Pine Point Road NW, Walker MN (888) 547-5477
www.brindleysharbor.com

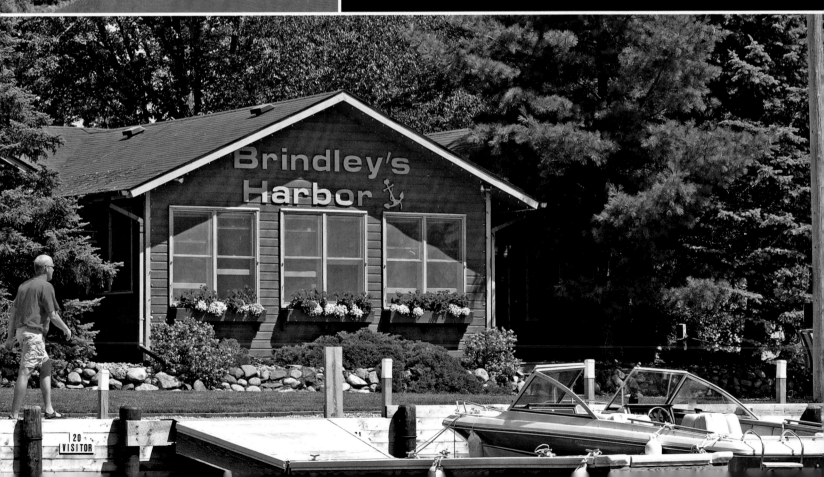

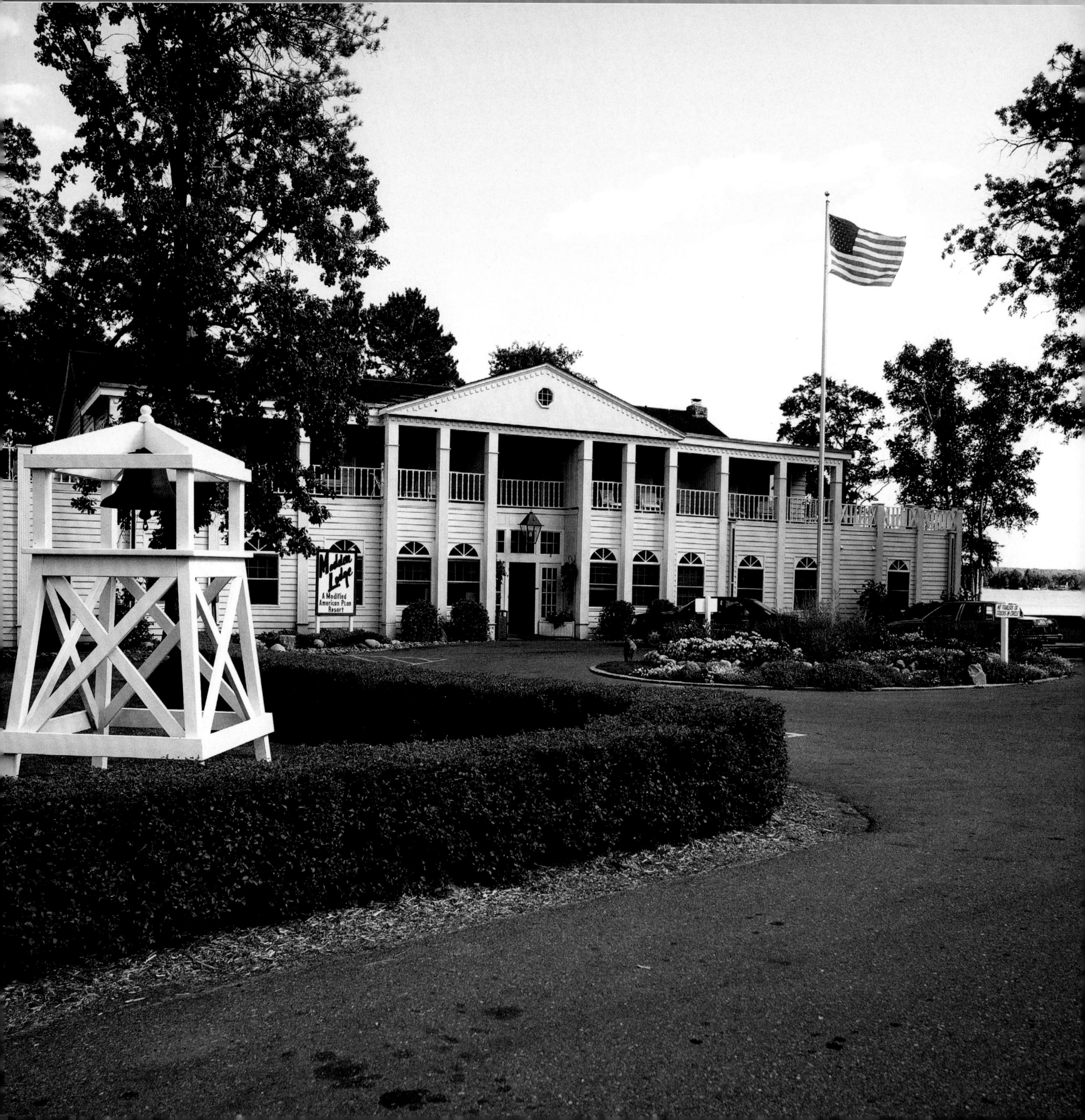
Madden Lodge
A Modified
American Plan
Resort

Madden's on Gull Lake

Madden's on Gull Lake offers more recreational amenities than any other resort in the Midwest. The classic resort offers recreation for every age and ability with more than 1,000 acres, nearly two miles of shoreline and three sandy beaches. The 63 holes of golf include Pine Beach East and West, and The Classic, a premier course that *Golf Digest* honored in 2006 with a five-star rating. Whether you're improving your skills at the Chris Foley Golf School or simply enjoying the Social-9, you can look forward to your day on the links. It could take days just to try Madden's five swimming pools along with whirlpools and saunas, a kid's wading pool and a fitness facility. Other activities include tennis, croquet, bicycling, hiking, shuffleboard and trapshooting. You can rent a power boat or borrow a canoe at Madden's fully equipped marina. You can even take lessons in water skiing. Hungry after all that activity? Madden's features three casual eating areas and three full-service fine dining restaurants with choice and quality for every taste. The newest addition to Madden's list of amenities is the Panache Spa, which provides Zen-like ambience and a relaxing setting for a wide variety of spa therapies. Choose from historic hotel rooms, cozy cottages, or luxury villas on the lake or golf course. From weddings to weekend getaways, corporate conferences to family get-togethers, for a glorious time on Gull Lake, visit Madden's.

11266 Pine Beach Peninsula, Brainerd MN
(218) 829-2811
www.maddens.com

Cedar Rapids Lodge

Choosing a resort the entire family will appreciate isn't always easy, but the folks who have discovered Cedar Rapids Lodge agree that every family member loves this place. Cedar Rapids is the only resort on pristine Medicine Lake, a location that offers unrivaled peace and solitude in the great Northwoods. You'll have 45 acres and a half-mile shoreline at your disposal. The lake-level cabins are clean and comfortable with fully equipped kitchens that include microwaves, cookware and coffeemakers. Picnic tables, grills and lawn chairs are standard equipment, and many units feature fireplaces. Pat and Steve Addler, the fourth owners of the 74-year-old resort, have watched their four children grow up here for the past 19 years and offer plenty of activities kids will enjoy. What child wouldn't thrill at a campfire, a swimming pool and a well-equipped playground, not to mention movies and popcorn? Guests have gathered at the lodge for potluck dinners every Monday night for the past 50 years. You can expect to swap fishing stories, enjoy hand-scooped ice cream and play all sorts of games. If your child heads straight for the candy store, you might want to tag along, since you'll find T-shirts, cookbooks and gift items there, too. The fisherman in the family will have ample opportunity to catch walleye, crappie and largemouth bass, and everyone delights in the sandy beach that slopes gently toward the lake. For the time of your life, plan a trip to Cedar Rapids Lodge.

25387 Everts Road NE, Tenstrike MN
(218) 243-2487 or (800) 233-8562
www.crlodge.com

Point of Pines Resort

If trophy walleye and pike fishing, a crystal clear lake and a cabin right at water's edge are your idea of paradise, then do what folks have been doing for 56 years and get yourself to Point of Pines Resort. Awake in the morning to the call of the loon in your cabin on spring-fed Kabekona Lake. Nestled among towering Norway pines and white birch, the resort is located at the edge of Paul Bunyan State Forest. If you get tired of reeling in big fish, you'll find golf courses and miles of hiking and biking trails close by. Swimming, jet skiing and canoeing are favorite activities at the resort. Away from the lake, guests play volleyball, badminton and horseshoes in addition to the fun at the playground and game room. The lakeside cabins are nicely furnished and come with fully equipped kitchens. Bring binoculars if you enjoy viewing wildlife, because birds are abundant. In addition to the loons, bald eagles, geese and many species of ducks call Kabekona Lake home. Whether your goal is a fishing expedition, family vacation or both, make Point of Pines Resort your destination in the beautiful Northwoods.

27930 County Road 37, Laporte MN
(218) 224-2227 or (800) 840-7038
www.pointofpinesresort.com

Lost Lake Lodge

You'll find Lost Lake Lodge on a tranquil piece of land between Lost Lake and the Gull Lake Narrows. Open mid-May through mid-October, the resort features 13 one, two and three-bedroom cabins with wood-burning fireplaces, air conditioning and private decks. One-bedroom cabins include a living room with a fireplace and a Murphy wall bed, a well-stocked bookcase, small refrigerator and two beds in the bedroom. Larger units are equally comfortable, and all come with full bathrooms stocked with toiletries and towels. The newly remodeled lodge provides telephones, cable television and wireless high-speed Internet access. It's also home to a restaurant, a gift shop and a small bar. Stop at the front desk and the friendly and experienced staff will help with special requests, such as golf, horseback riding or an in-room massage. The Bistro dining room will treat you to fresh, flavorful food in a woodsy ambience. The restaurant's breads are made daily from flour ground at the lodge's own gristmill. All rates include breakfast and dinner, resort amenities and daily housekeeping service. You're sure to enjoy the outdoors, thanks to the equipment the lodge provides at no extra charge, such as bicycles, life jackets, kayaks, canoes and rowboats. Grab a picnic basket and explore the nature trails or try fishing, swimming or boating on Gull Lake. Whether your idea of a good time is lounging around a campfire or landing a big fish, when you are ready to make memories, come to Lost Lake Lodge.

7965 Lost Lake Road, Lake Shore MN
(218) 963-2681
www.lostlake.com

In-We-Go Resort

Lots of pictures of happy people holding big fish have been taken at In-We-Go Resort. Guests who may have caught their first fish on the lake here are now bringing their kids. "Some families have been coming for more than 30 years," say owners Ed and Sara Becker. "They make it their annual trip." In-We-Go is located on the 8th Crow Wing, the most popular fishing lake on the Crow Wing Chain. Ed and Sara describe it as "not too large and not too small, two and a half miles long and a mile wide." Walleye are the big fish in the lake, which is also teeming with crappies and bluegill. Don't worry about not catching any. "We can almost guarantee stringers," say the Beckers. Lodging at In-We-Go is in cabins with charming knotty pine interiors. The modern kitchen in each is fully equipped and complemented by an outdoor charcoal grill.

You'll find plenty to do between fishing jaunts, such as swimming in the pool and playing games in the game room. The area offers miles of bike trails. Popular Itasca State Park, site of the Mississippi River headwaters, is nearby. While summer is the busiest season at the resort, folks come for the snowmobile trails in the winter and the gorgeous colors in the fall. To create some memories for your family photo album, head to In-We-Go Resort.

27385 County Road 33, Nevis MN
(218) 652-3536 or (800) 347-2480
www.inwegoresort.com

Cedar Rose Inn

When you step into the Cedar Rose Inn, you may forget you're on vacation and feel instead like you've just come home. Owners Aggie and Florian Ledermann want you to fall in love with their hometown of Alexandria and experience all it has to offer. It is very possible you will fall in love with this beautiful historic home as well. Wake up refreshed in a room filled with antiques and treasures. Borrow one of the innkeeper's classic novels and begin your day with a good book as the morning sun streams through your window. You won't stay in bed long, though, because the smell of Aggie's homemade caramel rolls will eventually waft up to your room, calling you to the big country-style breakfast downstairs. If you're not too full from your meal, take the short walk to Lake Winona, one of the 200 lakes in the county. Work off your

breakfast by hiking on miles of nearby nature trails or just take the walk into downtown and enjoy the shops and restaurants. In summer, plan to attend a concert; in winter, try skiing or ice skating. Whether you plan a romantic weekend or seek a little slice of heaven as part of your next business trip, let Cedar Rose Inn help you get away. You'll enjoy vintage hospitality in a beautiful lake country setting.

422 7th Avenue W, Alexandria MN
(320) 762-8430 or (888) 203-5333
www.cedarroseinn.com

Hiawatha Beach Resort

You stay at the lake known as the Muskie Capital of the World when you rent a cabin or houseboat at Hiawatha Beach Resort. Leech Lake is its official name. Famous for its clear waters and great fishing for walleye, pike and perch, in addition to muskie, Leech Lake is located in the heart of the Chippewa National Forest. Boats and boats with motors are available for rent at the resort. If canoeing or sailboating are your pleasures, you can use those for free. That's just one of the extras provided by a friendly staff determined to keep you happy and your social calendar full. For example, the wieners are free at the get-acquainted wiener roast on Monday nights. There's bingo on Tuesdays and a fish fry potluck on Friday evenings, when you can swap recipes and fish stories with your neighbors. Children's planned activities Monday through Wednesday include scavenger hunts, lawn games and model rocket launching. Add a sandy beach, a water trampoline on the lake and an indoor heated swimming pool, and you have all the makings for a fabulous family vacation in the Northwoods. Cabins of various sizes house the guests. A popular option is to rent a houseboat. You'll also find a tent campground. Come for the lake and make a few new friends at Hiawatha Beach Resort.

10904 Steamboat Loop NW, Walker MN
(218) 547-1510 or (800) 442-3224
www.hiawathabeach.com

Kavanaugh's Sylvan Lake Resort

Kavanaugh's Sylvan Lake Resort offers all the variety you could hope to find at a resort without sacrificing personalized service. This four-season family resort, owned and operated by John, Dave, Tom and Mark Kavanaugh, offers deluxe accommodations along Lake Sylvan, featuring fireplaces and private lakeside decks. The resort is just minutes from 18 world-class golf courses on the Brainerd Golf Trail, so you'll find ample opportunity to improve your skills or simply enjoy a friendly game. The clean water and beaches here will make you want to rediscover your family's favorite water sports and try an afternoon in a kayak, canoe, sailboat, paddle boat or pontoon. A campfire area gives your group an opportunity to toast marshmallows and tell stories, while a playground and volleyball, tennis and basketball courts provide active good times. Walkers, bikers, nature lovers and photographers will appreciate the trails available at the resort and in the surrounding area. The recreation complex includes an indoor and outdoor pool, plus a fitness room, game room and self-service laundry. When the pines are bowed with snow, winter activities beckon. Get your blood pumping with cross-country skiing on groomed and tracked ski trails, or take a snowmobile over hundreds of miles of trails, including the Gull Lake Lighted Trail. Whether you're looking for a romantic weekend or an extended family vacation, let Kavanaugh's Sylvan Lake Resort show you how to get the most from your getaway.

1685 Kavanaugh Drive, Brainerd MN
(218) 829-5226 or (800) 562-7061
www.kavanaughs.com

The Lodge on Lake Detroit

The Lodge on Lake Detroit is an upscale inn featuring modern amenities and unrivaled views of the lake that bears its name. Owners Chris and Scott Mehlhaff opened the lodge in 2006. All rooms here are lakefront, and many feature private balconies or patios for enjoying the sunsets over the lake. One choice for extraordinary pampering is a Renewal Spa Suite. This suite features a two-person therapeutic aromatherapy whirlpool and a gas fireplace. Other features available in all rooms and suites include DVD and CD players, free Internet access and 32-inch flat-panel high-definition televisions. Guests delight in such details as granite countertops and bathroom vanities, the Northwoods pine, and paintings by local artist Bracken Rourke. You will find a business center, an indoor pool and a fireside lobby piano bar with daily grand piano sunset serenades. Guests have access to a private beach and dock, a 24-hour fitness center and a free daily breakfast buffet. Dinner events and live music are scheduled frequently. The lodge is a popular place for banquets and meetings and offers special events catering services and a full bar in a 1,400-square-foot space. A vacation here is certain to be refreshing, and it can be rejuvenating as well with the pampering services of the Spa Within, a full-service day spa on the premises. The hotel is close to restaurants, shops and golf. For a luxurious vacation, come to the Lodge on Lake Detroit.

1200 E Shore Drive, Detroit Lakes MN
(218) 847-VIEW or (800) 761-VIEW (8439)
www.thelodgeonlakedetroit.com

Just Like Grandma's

The Good Old Days are alive and well at Just Like Grandma's, a bed-and-breakfast, tea room, and collection of craft and antiques stores. In 1984, current owner Carol Mihalchick converted this 1902 home into a complex, featuring accommodations, a gift shop and gardens. A restaurant is open for breakfast and lunch. Accommodations are comfortable and quiet and easily found, not too far from the Interstate. Grandma's Village includes Antiques Oasis, a converted furniture store, located just down the street. This antique hot spot quickly grew to become a 20-dealer antique mall. You'll find more shops featuring handcrafted gifts, home décor and clothing, and an ice cream counter in a converted barn on the property. An old school house is now the Tea Room restaurant and Just Like Grandma's offices. Those who would prefer to go fishing can arrange for a day trip to nearby Lake Osakis. The complex is open May through September and reopens as a Christmas boutique throughout October and weekends in November. Put away the cell phones and spend some quality time with your family enjoying ice cream and simple pleasures at Just Like Grandma's.

113 W Main Street, Osakis MN
(320) 859-4504 or (320) 859-3823

Bakketopp Hus Bed & Breakfast

From decks facing Long Lake, guests at Bakketopp Hus Bed & Breakfast enjoy the relaxing benefits of nature, from the melodious call of loons to eagles soaring overhead. *Bakketopp* is Norwegian for hilltop, a fitting name for this lovely property, situated at the top of a wooded lane. Your seasoned hosts, Dennis and Judy Nims, are the proud owners of this 35-year-old home with a bed and breakfast tradition established back in 1989. Sunken flower gardens and fountains calm weary travelers, who will find complimentary beverages waiting on the counter. Bakketopp Hus offers three enchanting guest rooms, each furnished with family antiques. A leisurely breakfast allows guests to sample lavish homemade creations while enjoying lake

views and conversations with fellow lodgers. Each season holds special wonder, from the maples that color the hillsides in the fall to the migratory birds of spring. Maplewood State Park is nearby, and outdoor enthusiasts will find abundant biking and birding trails in the area as well as numerous golf courses. You can return from your adventures to the cozy comfort of the Bakketopp Hus fireside. For a revitalizing place to rest and rejuvenate, come to Bakketopp Hus Bed & Breakfast.

20571 Hillcrest Road, Fergus Falls MN
(218) 739-2915 or (800) 739-2915
www.bbonline.com/mn/bakketopp

Huddle's Resort

For five generations, Huddle's Resort has been a family tradition for owners and customers alike. On the south shore of Leech Lake, this family-run vacation resort has acquired a loyal clientele with its true North Country hospitality. Guests can enjoy paddleboats and canoes on the lake, as well as great fishing—Leech Lake is *the* muskie lake in Minnesota, and the Minnesota Department of Natural Resources regularly re-stocks other lakes with Leech Lake muskellunge. The lake also has walleye, northern, bass and perch. For still more fishing opportunities, you can easily access the more secluded Linda Lake. Launches and guides are available for fishers old and new, as well as

fishing contests to liven things up. Families will find plenty of entertainment: Huddle's has a heated swimming pool, a playground area and many activities for the youthful set, everything from bonfires and dances to turtle races and scavenger hunts. Over the years, Roy Huddle has taught more than 3,000 kids how to water-ski. The modern furnished cabins are well-spaced for privacy. Townhouses are available as well. The lodge provides a dining room, lounge, store and conference facilities. Start your own family tradition at Huddle's Resort and let the memories begin.

1696 Whipholt Beach Road NW, Walker MN
(800) 358-5516
www.huddlesresort.com

Mille Lacs Resort & Marina

Perhaps some time in your life you intend to scale a peak or otherwise challenge yourself amidst the extremes of the wild. If for your next vacation, however, you seek only a gorgeous setting where you can co-exist with nature, then Mille Lacs Golf Resort & Marina is an excellent choice. The resort has a beautifully maintained 18-hole golf course carved through the hardwood forest of Minnesota's lake country. This course of 6,309 yards is known for its variety of scenic holes and exciting elevation changes. A new clubhouse and pro shop were added in 2006. Pleasure on the lake awaits you between rounds of golf. On the western shores of spectacular Lake Mille Lacs, the resort provides access to the water with a harbor and dock facility. A 50,000-square-foot water park, coming in 2007, promises a wet and wild time for the whole family. For lodging at the resort, you can choose between the Greenview Villa Townhomes, located on the 10th fairway, or a cozy 1,500-square-foot log cabin. As a resort guest, you can ride the shuttle to Grand Casino Mille Lacs, Old Town and Paul Bunyan Land. Garrison and Kathio State Park is just a five-minute drive away. For a golf and lake vacation, consider Mille Lacs Golf Resort & Marina.

18517 Captive Lake Road, Garrison MN
(800) 435-8720 *www.millelacsgolf.com*

Nordic Inn Medieval Brew and Bed

Come to the Nordic Inn Medieval Brew and Bed, where Steinarr the Kraze E. Viking, host and owner, will introduce you to the Viking world. Steinarr was inspired to create his Viking Inn after he became a Viking mascot for his son's football team. Steinarr ended up remodeling a church into an inn and, in true Viking warrior style, refused to surrender to the town's objections to the format, finding one solution after another. Guests here enjoy a morning feast of medieval meat pie and parsley toast, along with oatmeal apple tarts and Viking hash browns with carrots and parsnips. Group reservations receive an evening performance by local actors called the Nordic Players. There are many types of entertainment available. Interactive dinner theater evenings may include dinner and basking in a rock waterfall spa, or you might be a Viking for an evening in the Viking Mystery. New this year is a Viking adventure dinner and game, where you can try your luck with a spin of the wheel of misfortune. If you're in luck, you'll conquer other lands and take home the booty. For just a few Kroner (coins), guests can buy Viking-approved beer, wine, ale or mead. Weary guests retreat to such accommodations as Odin's Loft, where you sleep in a Viking longship suspended over Asgard. Or you can try out the Jarl's Den with its deer antler décor and large Jacuzzi. The ladies will adore Freya's Boudoir with its frills and fluff, while fans of the Minnesota Vikings may prefer the Locker Room with its Astroturf carpet and double beds fitted with goal posts. Find some spare time to relax in Asgard with its bar, games table and library on Viking lore. Visit the Nordic Inn Medieval Brew and Bed for an unabashed good time in the Viking tradition.

210 1ST Avenue NW, Crosby MN
(218) 546-8299
www.vikinginn.com

Pine Peaks Lodge

It's not always easy to explain the motivation for a business, but when the co-owners of Pine Peaks Lodge in Crosslake decided to build a boutique style hotel with special attention to detail, they knew just what customers were seeking. Joe and Sonia Slack, Paul and Carole McCulloch, and Dick Fischer each own other businesses near the Whitefish Chain of Lakes. After five years of discussion, they came together to make their shared idea a reality. They decided on four different styles for the Lodge's 38 rooms, furnished them with locally made log furniture, and equipped each with a microwave, refrigerator and free high-speed wireless Internet access. The hotel offers an indoor pool, hot tub and free Continental breakfast. The adjacent Pine Peaks Restaurant features casual dining in a room tastefully decorated lodge-style as well as a gift shop brimming with intriguing collectibles, jewelry and home décor with woodland flair. Kids 12 and under stay and eat free at the Lodge. The hotel is located across the street from the Army Corps of Engineers Park, which has a swimming beach, boat launch and fishing area. Opportunities to rent skis, wakeboards, boats and personal watercraft are nearby, or you may purchase books or bait and tackle on the premises and find a quiet picnic spot. The hotel is also located on the east loop of the Paul Bunyan Scenic By-Way for easy access to walking, bicycling and bird watching. In the winter, Crosslake is a central spot for snowmobiling and ice fishing. Experience the joys of staying in a well-placed boutique hotel with a visit to Pine Peaks Lodge.

14047 Swann Drive, Crosslake MN
(218) 692-STAY (7829) or (888) 488-STAY (7829)
www.pinepeakscrosslake.com

Fair Hills Resort and Wildflower Golf Course

Why should kids have all the fun? Fair Hills Resort and Wildflower Golf Course let the whole family go to summer camp together. The Kaldahl family has owned and operated this fun-packed getaway for five generations. You are sure to appreciate their hospitality as well as the opportunities to learn such sports as tennis, waterskiing or sailing. PGA Pro Bill Hensel presides over the Wildflower Golf Course, located just down the road. The 18-hole championship course, given four-and-one-half stars by *Golf Digest*, was designed by Joel Goldstrand in the tradition of seaside golf in Scotland. The rolling course offers spectacular views. A vast expanse of prairie grass and 86 bunkers and combine to make this one of the state's most challenging courses, and four sets of tees accommodate varied skill levels. Old-fashioned basics are a big part of the Fair Hills charm, where the water quality of pristine Pelican Lake remains as it was in the early days of the resort, which was founded by the Kaldahl family in 1926. After a fun-filled day of swimming, fishing, hiking, boating, fine dining and evening entertainment, you can rest comfortably in one of the resort's 93 lodging units. Fair Hills' self-contained cabins and cozy motel units can easily accommodate family reunions as large as 250 people. Recapture the traditional summer delights of family recreation at its finest with a vacation at Fair Hills Resort and Wildflower Golf Course.

24270 County Highway 20, Detroit Lakes MN
(218) 847-7638 (year-round), (218) 532-2222 (summer) or (800) 323-2849
www.fairhillsresort.com

Quarterdeck Resort & Boathouse Eatery

Whether you're planning a fabulous summer vacation or a winter weekend getaway, the Quarterdeck Resort & Boathouse Eatery can turn expectations into reality. This award winning four-season resort on picturesque Gull Lake features three choices of lodging and an almost endless list of things to see and do. Guests will find 14 golf courses within a half hour of the property. With close to 450 lakes in a 15-mile radius, expect an abundance of prime fishing spots, and Gull Lake itself is highly rated for bass and walleye. Horseback riding is nearby, and guests can indulge in tennis, basketball, volleyball, boating, swimming and hiking. Quarterdeck also provides free, supervised children's programs to guests from mid-June through mid-August. Autumn brings crisp weather and spectacular fall colors to the area, easily enjoyed from the vantage point of a nature trail or by car, boat or bicycle. The resort and adjacent Pillsbury State Forest offer chances to view more than 225 varieties of birds and an abundance of wildlife. Winter brings a special magic to Quarterdeck and opportunities to enjoy cross-country or downhill skiing, snowshoeing, ice fishing or snowmobiling. After a day of fun, you'll appreciate the Boathouse Eatery with its delightful choices in steaks, seafood, pasta and burgers. Soups, salads and sandwiches are popular selections, and kids have their own menu. Whether you're planning a romantic getaway, a corporate meeting or family vacation, Alan and Jane Gunsbury invite you to visit the Quarterdeck Resort & Boathouse Eatery on beautiful Gull Lake.

9820 Birch Bay Drive SW, Nisswa MN
(218) 963-2482 or (800) 950-5596
www.quarterdeckresort.com

Lake Le Homme Dieu Bed & Breakfast

Opened in 2000, the peaceful lakeside retreat of Lake Le Homme Dieu Bed & Breakfast, just three miles from Alexandria, offers a relaxing stay in a newly constructed home. Owners Steve and Judy Radjenovich built this country-style structure on property originally owned by Steve's father. The family's first cabin remains on the property. The inn offers modern conveniences and a country charm with family heirlooms throughout and a collection of clocks. The four guest rooms, named after area lakes, feature views of Lake Le Homme Dieu plus private baths with whirlpool tubs. An outdoor hot tub is available to all guests, and so is a full breakfast complete with fresh homemade bread. Books and games in the spacious living area offer pleasant afternoon entertainment, while an evening bonfire is an opportunity to make new friends. Beyond the inn, you'll find Alexandria antique stores, theaters and restaurants as well as such outdoor recreation as snowshoeing, cross-country skiing, golfing and hiking. Bicyclists will appreciate the proximity of the Central Lakes Bike Trail. For a vacation in the lake country, visit Lake Le Homme Dieu Bed & Breakfast.

441 S Le Homme Dieu Drive, Alexandria MN
(320) 846-5875 or (800) 943-5875
www.llbedandbreakfast.com

Ten Mile Lake Resort & Steakhouse

Mike and Linda Schultz represent the fourth generation of the Schultz family to welcome guests to Ten Mile Lake Resort & Steakhouse. Surrounded by trees and blue water, the resort is on an isthmus between two lakes. The Minneapolis *Star Tribune* places Ten Mile Lake among the top 10 walleye lakes in the state, and you'll discover many other species as well. The shallower North Ten Mile Lake is a great spot for duck hunting in the fall. The year-round resort has seen many changes in the past 100 years of family ownership. It offers 12 cabins of varying sizes. Many of the cabins have been remodeled, and one was newly built in 2006 to honor Mike's brother Pat. After Pat's death, 80 volunteers got together to build the three-bedroom J. Patrick Lodge in just one day. Like many of the accommodations at the resort, the lodge has large windows, a fireplace and a roomy kitchen with modern appliances. Beneath the trees, visitors find 92 seasonal campsites. Often, the same family returns to occupy a site for several generations. Guests enjoy a swimming beach, boat rentals, a game room and playground. In 1962, the resort added a steakhouse, which specializes in sirloin, prime rib and barbecued ribs. It's open from May through Labor Day and on weekends through the fall, and offers room for private gatherings of up to 150 people. The Schultz family invites your family to enjoy the vacation opportunities at Ten Mile Lake Resort & Steakhouse.

12303 County Highway 35, Dalton MN
(218) 589-8845
www.tenmilelakeresort.com

Bug-Bee Hive Resort

Every member of the family, including the family dog, will have a blast at Bug-Bee Hive Resort, located on Lake Koronis in the heart of Central Minnesota's lake country. The all-season resort, owned by Paul and Kella Bugbee, offers 30 cottage suites, ranging in size from one to six-bedroom units. All cottage suites include full kitchens, cable television and decks with grills, and most feature scenic lake views as well as ceiling fans and fireplaces. Larger condominium style unites offer flexibility for multiple family gatherings. You can choose from such whimsically named cottages as the Bee Haven, Honey Dew and Ought-To-Bee. Activities center around the water and include swimming, boating and fishing. Stretches of sandy beach, a diving tower and water trampoline contribute to the fun. Your cottage rental includes the use of a 14-foot aluminum boat for exploring the lake. Supervised children's activities, scheduled each weekday, include island adventures, scavenger hunts and nature hikes. Kids love romping in the Busy Bee play-town. For the grownups, Bug-Bee is close to golf, shopping and antique stores. You can also join your kids for horseback riding at nearby stables. Winter weather brings snowmobiling, ice skating and skiing to the resort. Make the whole family happy with a vacation at Bug-Bee Hive Resort.

29659 Queen Bee Lane, Paynesville MN
(320) 243-4448
www.bugbeehiveresort.com

Berries & Marigolds

The owners' children came up with the cute name for the bed and breakfast in Starbuck called Berries & Marigolds, and when you stay here, you truly feel that you are a guest of the family. The four bedrooms in this beautiful Victorian home are indeed named after members of co-owner Jeannie Pladsen's family. Jeannie and her husband Paul invite you to stay in Grandpa and Grandma's room, which is filled with treasures that belonged to Jeannie's parents, who were life-long residents of Starbuck. Aunt Juella's Room, Aunt Sylvia's Room and Aunt Julia's Room are other lodging options. All rooms at Berries & Marigolds have private baths. The Pladsens serve a full breakfast in three parlors and open their eatery to non-guests after the morning seating for lodgers. Popular menu items include quiche and sandwiches as well as homemade

pies and cinnamon rolls. The two-story barn on the property houses a gift shop that specializes in the work of Midwest crafters. Lake Minnewaska, just one mile away, brings vacationers to Starbuck, which is also known for the Rosette Factory and Holly Skogen Park. When you're heading this way, stay with family at Berries & Marigolds.

311 E 7th Street, Starbuck MN
(320) 239-4868
www.berriesandmarigolds.com

Huntington House Victorian Bed & Breakfast

If you're in search of a carefree getaway in peaceful surroundings, you'll find all that and more at Huntington House Victorian Bed & Breakfast. Innkeeper Donna Bahr warmly welcomes guests to her inviting 1886 Queen Anne Victorian home surrounded by beautifully kept grounds. Guests to this Paynesville retreat enjoy a sitting room and parlor, each equipped with its own fireplace, as well as a cheerful sunroom with access to a hot tub. Four beautifully detailed guest rooms boast antique furnishings that complement the period architecture and such amenities as private air conditioners and alarm clocks. Get your day off to a perfect start by enjoying delectable candlelit breakfasts that may include eggs Benedict with sausage and hash browns,

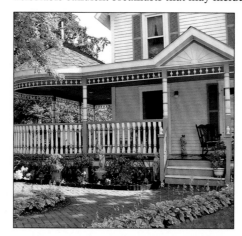

Alaskan waffles with blueberry or strawberry sauce and bacon or French toast with ham and hash browns. In the mood to do not one blessed thing? Enjoy a book on the wraparound porch or soak your cares away in the enclosed hot tub room, complete with heated tile floor, windows all around and a door leading to the outdoor patio. Toast your tootsies in front of a crackling fire, watch a favorite DVD from the movie library or schedule a rejuvenating massage. Time away is precious, so make the most of yours with a visit to Huntington House Victorian Bed & Breakfast.

323 W Hoffman Street, Paynesville MN
(320) 243-3905 or (866) 418-0383
www.huntingtonhousebb.com

Heritage House Bed & Breakfast

Completed in 1904, Heritage House Bed & Breakfast offers the same hospitality you might have expected when it was first built. Owners Jerry and Deb Middelstadt opened the renovated bed-and-breakfast in 1999 with the goal of making it the perfect escape. The Queen Anne style house is listed in the National Registry of Historic Places. The unique eight-foot-diameter leaded glass window in the front parlor is of special interest to architecture buffs. It is thought to be the only window of its kind in the region. Also significant is the carriage house, which was built in 1895. The brick structure with gambrel roof lines on all four faces is also believed to be the last of its kind in the Upper Midwest. Heritage House has been featured in magazines such as *Cloud, Minnesota Moments* and *Among Women.* Jerry and Deb can arrange an afternoon tea and tour for you and your traveling companions. The home has been a popular spot for weddings over the years and two national documentaries have been filmed here, one airing on Showtime and one on ESPN. Guests have the choice of four rooms, each with a private bath and decorated in its own style, English, German, French or Swedish. All rooms have ceiling fans, air conditioning, VCRs and CD players. Amenities in the common areas include a pool table, reading room and video library. Heritage House is a WiFi spot. Stay a night or two at Heritage House Bed & Breakfast and experience the gracious spell of the Victorian era.

402 6th Avenue S, St. Cloud MN
(320) 656-5818 or (888) 547-HHBB (4422)
www.heritagehousebbmn.com

Mantrap Lodge

Whether you're coming with just your honey or with the whole gang, Mantrap Lodge has a cabin your size on crystal clear Big Mantrap Lake. Accommodations in this secluded wilderness setting range from a quaint one-bedroom cabin with full kitchen and bathroom to a five-bedroom version with kitchen, dining room and two full baths. Owners Mike and Dianne Roy provide guests with such extras as free use of canoes, kayaks, paddleboats and bicycles to ensure that they have a pleasant time amidst nature's splendors. If fishing is your sport, you could spend a lifetime getting to know the hot spots on this 1,770-acre lake with its innumerable bays, arms and islands. Boat and motor rentals are available. At Mantrap Lodge, the fun doesn't stop when you take a break from the lake. You can swim in the heated pool, play ping pong in the game room, go on a hayride and enjoy many other activities. Add a large playground and ball courts, and it's easy to see why this resort, only 15 minutes from Park Rapids, is such a favorite for family vacations. Nestled among pine, spruce and birch, it's also peaceful enough to be that special getaway for two. Play for a week or retreat for a weekend at Mantrap Lodge.

20725 Jewel Drive, Park Rapids MN
(218) 732-5405 or (800) 424-0901
www.mantraplodge.com

AmericInn Lodge & Suites of Moorhead

The AmericInn Lodge & Suites of Moorhead offers the location and amenities prized by most travelers. It's just minutes from three universities, which makes it the ideal lodging for families visiting nearby collegians. AmericInn pleases business and vacation travelers with complimentary, 24-hour transportation to Hector International Airport, the Amtrak Station and the Moorhead Convention Center. The hotel recently underwent a renovation costing more than $2 million. AmericInn supports business travelers with 12,000 square feet of conference space that can accommodate up to 600 participants, banquet facilities and free wireless Internet access. All guests appreciate the two-story waterfall that cascades into a courtyard filled with a free-form pool, hot tub, children's pool and nine-hole miniature golf course. The 24-hour fitness center contains cardiovascular and strength training equipment and offers complimentary passes to a nearby racquet club. Courtney's Comedy Club is popular with guests and locals who enjoy the comedy stylings of visiting performers with national reputations. Although the hotel is part of a chain of more than 200 properties, owners Paul and Cathy Cronen have found ways to personalize their services. The fresh Belgian waffles at their complimentary Deluxe Continental Breakfast are perennial favorites. Visit the AmericInn Lodge & Suites of Moorhead for individualized attention and amenities that satisfy your business and vacation requirements.

600 30th Avenue S, Moorhead MN
(218) 287-7100
www.americinnofmoorhead.com

Viking Bay Resort

Owners Dwight and Dianne Droen say that their resort on Lake Miltona has a tucked away feel to it. Located just 10 miles north of Alexandria, it's called Viking Bay, and it's small enough that you won't have to fight the crowds for a spot on the sandy beach. Recreation on the lake takes many forms, from fishing and canoeing to windsurfing and paddle boating. Boat rentals are available. Whether you stay in a cabin or in the lodge, the lake is right outside your door. What's more, the Miltona Golf Course is only a few steps away. The nine cabins at the resort all have kitchens, and they range in size from two to six bedrooms. At the lodge, you can choose between a two-bedroom suite with kitchen, fireplace and living room or a motel room with a refrigerator, microwave and double Jacuzzi tub. Viking Bay has been a favorite spot for family vacations since 1971. It offers several affordable wedding packages as well, whether you are planning an intimate ceremony for just a few people or a grand event for up to 40. A conference room can accommodate meetings of as many as 30 people. Make Viking Bay Resort your getaway on Lake Miltona.

12844 E Lake Miltona Drive, Miltona MN
(218) 943-2104
www.vikingbay.com

Weslake Resort

There's never a dull season at Weslake Resort in Underwood. Tom and Brenda Masloski and their three children are here to greet you every day of the year. They never tire of watching the sunset over West Lost Lake with their guests or participating in the summer campfire and free Sunday night cookout. The resort offers eight spacious cabins comfortably situated under the trees and facing the lake. You'll find cabins in many sizes, including a four-bedroom family cabin and a 3,600-square-foot lodge for large groups. Each comes with heating and air conditioning for year-round comfort. Spring means the arrival of abundant waterfowl, a new fishing season and the opportunity to hike in two nearby state parks. Summer brings a sandy beach on the resort's half-mile shoreline, water toys and volleyball games. You can fish from one of the resort boats. Selected as a state champion fishing lake for the 1990 Bass Master's Classic, West Lost Lake attracts avid fishermen who come for largemouth bass as well as walleye, crappies and northern

pike. Still other ways to spend the day include canoeing on the Otter Tail River or exploring local boutiques and antiques shops. Fall is popular for its brilliant colors and hunting opportunities. During the winter, you can ice fish from an insulated and heated fish house or go cross-country skiing or snowmobiling. You'll find 12 golf courses, numerous restaurants and museums nearby. Whatever your pleasure, take it to Weslake Resort.

28507 County Highway 35, Underwood MN
(218) 826-6523 or (800) 258-9056
www.weslakeresort.com

The Waller House Bed & Breakfast

Scott and Raquel Lundberg understand how details contribute to the charm of a home. That is why they are sure you will love the Waller House Bed & Breakfast, a 110-year-old Victorian house. After purchasing the bed-and-breakfast in 2006, the Lundbergs remodeled, opening afresh in the spring of 2007. The home retains its old charms, such as the stained glass windows, its turret and quaint sitting and dining areas. Guests can stay in any of five appealing bedrooms, including a two-room suite. Each room offers a private bath and a look of its own. Your friendly hosts want to be sure you feel at home, and they strive to provide memorable moments during your stay. Visit with other guests over a hearty breakfast. Your hosts also want you to experience Little Falls, a town that shares the same spirit of hospitality you'll find at the Waller House.

From the inn's quiet neighborhood, you are just three short blocks from the Mississippi River and within walking distance of an art gallery, delightful shops and a bakery. The house is well-suited to small parties and meetings, and offers packages for weddings and anniversaries. A gift shop at the inn features handcrafted jewelry made of sterling silver and semi-precious gems. Take pleasure in the little things that add up to a big difference at the Waller House.

301 3rd Street SE, Little Falls MN
(320) 632-2836
www.wallerhouseinn.com

Red Bridge Inn

At the river's edge in the quaint village of Park Rapids, the Red Bridge Inn is a perfect haven of old-fashioned charm. With its rural setting, Victorian-style architecture and wide wrap-around deck, it has an ambience that is both homey and idyllic. Inside, elegant antique furnishings and marble accents add just a hint of grandeur, while every window offers a soothing view of trees and water. The inn has six picturesque rooms decorated in a country style, all with private baths and some with private decks. The Lady Slipper Suite, equipped with a hot tub and double shower, makes a particularly appropriate getaway for couples. Ask about the elopement package. Guests can access an exercise room, and massages are available for a modest fee. Enjoy one of Red Bridge Inn's wonderful breakfasts either in the dining room or outside on the deck overlooking the river. The lovely grounds include a large gazebo as well as easy access to Fish Hook River and Lake. The Heartland Trail starts right at the door and winds through the scenic countryside. Bring your bike, blades or snowshoes to enjoy nature in every season. Red Bridge Inn is also close to downtown shopping. Guests are driven to dinner or the movies in one of the inn's classic cars. Escape to the Red Bridge Inn, a world where time slows to the pace of the languid river.

118 N Washington Avenue, Park Rapids MN
(888) 733-7241
www.redbridgeinn.com

Whitefish Lodge & Suites

Whitefish Lodge & Suites provides easy access to the Brainerd Lake and Crosslake areas for a vacation that puts the best of Minnesota at your doorstep in every season. The décor is distinctly rustic with cabin-style rooms that offer guests just as much up-north feel as they'll get from the outdoor recreational activities. In summer, you can spend the day waterskiing, lake swimming and fishing. Hiking, biking and golf promise an activity for every outdoor enthusiast. In winter, cross-country skiing adventures start right from your front door. Manicured snowmobile trails offer still more avenues into a frozen winter wonderland. Come on in from the cold to an indoor pool and hot tub in addition to a popular game room. The Lodge's banquet facilities offer intriguing possibilities for hosting a business meeting, wedding dinner or reception. Suites here appeal to many needs, from the Cinema Suite with its 50-inch plasma television and surround sound to a suite that gives kids a sense of being in their own cabin. Whitefish Lodge & Suites is off the beaten track, but still close to shopping and dining. Turn off everyday life and turn on peace and quiet at Whitefish Lodge & Suites.

14150 Swann Drive, Crosslake MN
(218) MY-CABIN (692-2246)
or (800) 692-0727
www.whitefish-lodge.com

Victorian Oaks Bed and Breakfast

You can feel time slipping back to the 19th century when you stay with owners Louis and Barbara Foote at Victorian Oaks Bed and Breakfast. The renovated 1891 home in St. Cloud's historic district was placed on the National Register of Historic Places in 1978. Its floor plan remains unchanged, and its furnishings honor its graceful old age. Guests enjoy a candlelight breakfast served on china and crystal in a formal dining room. The three guest rooms share two full baths and one half bath. A claw-foot tub could be a destination for a relaxing soak. The Lake George Suite offers a queen-size brass bed and an adjoining private sitting room with a balcony

overlooking Lake George. A seven-foot headboard on a full-size bed is the centerpiece of the Blue Room, where light from a crystal chandelier and a wall sconce reflects off an embossed tin ceiling. Guests to the Garden Room enjoy a bay window view of a garden and fountain along with a king-size bed, flowered comforters and stained glass windows. Guests enjoy modern amenities, too, such as television with VCR, wireless Internet access and air conditioning. In 1998, the bed and breakfast became a quality assured member of the Minnesota B & B Guild. You can walk from here to St. Cloud State University, shops, restaurants and the attractions of Lake George recreation area. For old-style charm, stay at Victorian Oaks Bed and Breakfast.

404 9th Avenue S, St. Cloud MN
(320) 202-1404
www.vicoaks.com

Whiteley Creek Homestead Bed and Breakfast

A Minnesota Green Routes destination, Whiteley Creek Homestead Bed and Breakfast builds upon Brainerd's heritage as a community centered around farming, the railroad and mining. Guests are served an organic breakfast prepared with locally-grown ingredients in an 1890 railroad car tearoom. A signature entrée, Flossie's Eggs on the Rails, honors one of Whiteley Creek's most prolific laying hens. Vintage farm implements peek out from flower, vegetable and herb gardens that are planted to attract birds and other wildlife using sustainable growing practices. Vehicles from the 1930s to the 1940s are scattered about the grounds. Guests' freshly washed bedding from the three cottages and two inn rooms flaps in the breeze. An outdoor

fireplace on a screened porch takes the chill out of the evening. Close to the Paul Bunyan Trail and the Paul Bunyan Arboretum, the homestead's 35 acres offer walking trails and canoeing in a wetlands setting. Featured in *Country Home*, *Midwest Living* and many other publications, Whiteley Creek Homestead's slower, simpler pace is but a country road away.

12349 Whiteley Creek Trail, Brainerd MN
(218) 829-0654
www.whiteleycreek.com

Timberlane Lodge

You could think of Timberlane Lodge as a resort, or you could think of it as summer camp for the whole family. Long Lake is the main attraction, and whether you stay in a cabin or cabana, you'll be facing it. The units are spaced nicely apart to ensure privacy. Boats and motors for fishing, a pontoon craft for family cruises, paddleboats and fun bugs are available. The pleasure continues away from the lake with opportunities for games such as tennis or horseshoes. Your choices for recreation go on and on at Timberlane Lodge. Offering something for everyone, this vacation facility includes a playground for the little ones, a game room for teens and a heated indoor swimming pool for young and old. There is even a nine-hole golf course called the Bears Den. The lodge itself is a grand building overlooking the lake that features two large stone fireplaces. You can relax and read by the fire or gather for a card game with the whole family. The fire will feel especially cozy in the winter—unlike summer camp, Timberlane Lodge stays open for fun all year. Make Timberlane Lodge your winter headquarters for snowmobiling, cross-country skiing and ice fishing. Whatever the season, this resort has been a Minnesota choice for family recreation since 1948. Come see why.

18454 Dayspring Drive, Park Rapids MN
(218) 732-8489
www.timberlaneresort.com

Bay Window Quilt Shop

There is nothing as comforting, nostalgic or beautiful as a handcrafted quilt. Like fingerprints or snowflakes, every quilt is truly one of a kind. Bay Window Quilt Shop carries the supplies you'll need to create one of these treasures, including patterns, books, fabrics and notions. The shop offers 4,500 bolts of 100 percent cotton fabric, including more than 800 bolts of flannel. You'll find 1930s reproduction fabric here, along with batiks and retro prints from the 1940s and 1950s. Owner Sarah Hayden displays more than 400 model quilts in her 5,000-square-foot store. Bay Window has established a 17-year tradition of friendly service in a hometown atmosphere, thanks to in-house designer Katie Hennagir and to Jace Hennagir, who specializes in the use of long-arm quilting machines. The shop offers a newsletter, monthly clubs, guest speakers, bus tours and luncheons designed to foster the art form as well as its customers' creative expression. *Better Homes and Gardens Quilt Sampler* magazine chose Bay Window as one of the top 10 shops of 2007. Understandably proud of its website, which is continually updated, Bay Window ships its products around the world on a daily basis. Instead of just envying all the quilt owners you know, come to Bay Window Quilt Shop and begin the custom-made quilt of your dreams.

116 2nd Avenue SW, Perham MN
(218) 346-7272 or (888) 346-7275
www.baywindowquiltshop.com

Country Fabrics

Quilters in the Brainerd Lakes area know they are lucky to have owner Deb Burton looking out for them at Country Fabrics. Deb started out in 1970 working with her mother and knows all the latest quilting designs, materials and techniques. Country Fabrics, located in a 1890s mercantile, is a rich quilter's and knitter's resource. You'll find country and baby flannels, vibrant brights, soft florals, exquisite batiks and vintage reproduction fabrics at Country Fabrics. The second floor is filled with antiques and gifts. Country Fabrics also stocks quality yarn, knitting patterns, books and Addi Turbo Needles. Inspirational samples decorate the store and many of them are available as a kit. Today's quilters often rely on computerized sewing and embroidery machines, so Deb and her staff teach classes on operating them. Country Fabrics is an authorized dealer for Bernina, BabyLock, the Handi Quilter and sewing cabinets by Horn of America. Country Fabrics has a technician on staff who can service all brands of sewing machines and sergers. Deb and her staff want you to succeed with your projects. They are never too busy to help you find what you need. Bring your ideas and prepare to be inspired at Country Fabrics.

909 S 6th Street, Brainerd MN
(218) 829-7273

The Quilted Ladybug

Experienced quilters appreciate the large selection and well-organized bolts of fabrics and supplies at the Quilted Ladybug, while beginners find the inspiration to start on this rewarding hobby in a store that is both stimulating and laid out for efficiency and convenience. Since opening in 2003, owner and operator Cheri Steenbock has made incomparable customer service her focus. Cheri believes in helping every customer achieve maximum success, and her customers run the gamut from complete beginners to experienced pros. The layout of this Moorhead shop is a joy for any shopper. Sample quilts and kits are displayed throughout the store. Fabrics are easily accessible and neatly arranged by color. The Quilted Ladybug's classroom is equally neat and easy to use. Here, you can dip into quilting for the first time with such classes as Beginning Quilting 101 and Beginning Machine Quilting. The more advanced quilter can benefit from the T-Shirt Memory Quilting class, which focuses on turning your favorite old T-shirts into quilts, and the Photo Memory Wall Hanging class, which presents techniques for creating a wall hanging to display such cherished objects as photographs, fabric postcards and quilt show pins. For quilting ideas as well as patterns, fabrics and supplies, visit the Quilted Ladybug.

2921 S Frontage Road, Moorhead MN
(218) 284-LADY (5239) or (888) 892-5239
www.quiltedladybug.com

Red Horse Ranch Arena

Horses and the people who love them have something new to delight in. Tucked in the rolling hills of west central Minnesota, the Red Horse Ranch Arena opened in 2004, fulfilling the need for a state-of-the-art equine facility capable of hosting the finest equestrian events in the Midwest. Offering both indoor and outdoor arenas, Red Horse Ranch Arena covers a vast 220 acres which includes a main arena, training facility and boarding paddocks. Breed and competition shows mark the busy schedule of events along with trade shows, concerts and an annual Professional Rodeo Cowboys Association rodeo. Between events, the facility hosts open riding and lessons. The Red Horse Ranch Arena also holds classes in such topics as Horse Ownership 101. If you are thinking of owning a horse, this course will take you through the basics, from bits and tack to hoof care. Whether you come to the arena as a spectator or participant, you will be struck by its beautiful country setting with trails and hills along the Otter Tail River. Located six miles north of Fergus Falls, just eight miles off Interstate 94, this is one spot in the country that you won't have to drive obscure back roads to find. Just follow the line of horse trailers when you exit the Interstate. For the love of horses, check out what's happening at the Red Horse Ranch Arena.

22671 County Highway 10, Fergus Falls MN
(218) 736-3000
www.redhorserancharena.com

Little Falls

Little Falls is where the Mississippi pauses. The city takes its name from a distinctive waterfall that attracted explorers and later provided power for lumber and paper companies. Today's travelers can start their exploration of the city with a visit to the Little Falls Convention and Visitors Bureau. The Bureau, housed in a 1903 mansion, can direct you to the outdoor recreation of your choice and recommend historical sites, such as the boyhood home of famed aviator Charles A. Lindbergh. The Charles A. Weyerhaeuser Memorial Museum recounts local history and offers natural prairie gardens. The Pine Grove Zoo, located in the last standing grove of white pines, provides walking trails, picnic grounds and a petting stable, as well as exotic and native animals. For greater understanding of area plants and animals, groups can schedule tours of the Camp Ripley Environmental Education Center. The center's museum contains almost 200 mounted birds and animals. The Minnesota Fishing Museum contains over 6,000 fishing artifacts. Just south of Little Falls at Blanchard Dam, treasure hunters look for starlight crystals, called cross rocks. These rare cross-shaped rocks are prized as good luck charms. Get to know Little Falls, a place where you can make memories.

606 1st Street SE, Little Falls MN
(Little Falls Convention and Visitors Bureau)
(320) 616-4959 or (800) 325-5916
www.littlefallsmn.com

Otter Tail County Historical Society

With historical artifacts and documents, educational exhibits and outreach, the Otter Tail County Historical Society offers a glimpse back into the early days of Minnesota. The society was organized in 1927 and opened its current Fergus Falls museum in 1972. The museum features more than 100 permanent and changing displays. You'll see lifelike dioramas and authentically furnished period rooms, including a 19th century saloon, kitchen and one-room schoolhouse. Other exhibits feature authentic Ojibwa and Dakotah Indian artifacts and displays on local wildlife. Visitors can get a look at tools used in the region's agricultural development, and children enjoy engaging in such old-time activities as grinding corn or coffee. Customized guided tours are available; the most popular is an overview of the entire museum. The historical society's E.T. Barnard Library offers a large collection of historical and genealogical records to assist researchers. The society also extends its educational opportunities beyond its doors with tours of historic Fergus Falls and visits to classrooms with artifacts and activities. Among the popular special events sponsored by the society is the Brown Bag Local History Series, where participants enjoy discussions on local history over lunch. The Otter Tail County Historical Society invites you to get in touch with the past.

1110 W Lincoln Avenue, Fergus Falls MN
(218) 736-6038
www.otchs.org

Runestone Museum

Long before Columbus, Europeans came to North America and left traces of their time spent here. The 202-pound Kensington Runestone, the main attraction at the Runestone Museum in Alexandria, is believed to be an artifact from Viking exploration. It was discovered in 1898 clutched in the roots of an aspen tree on the Olaf Ohman farm near Kensington. The Runestone has led researchers from around the world on a century-long, exhaustive quest to explain how Vikings from medieval Europe could have carved the Runestone found in central North America. The stone, with its runic carvings dated 1362, remains a subject of controversy. Ongoing research into its authenticity continues to attract visitors and scholars from near and far. Opened in 1958, the Runestone Museum also includes an extensive Native American exhibit, the 1880s Pioneer Room, an exhibit of Minnesota wildlife and a hands-on children's exhibit. The expansive museum complex includes a replica of Fort Alexandria with five log buildings which have period displays, tools and agricultural equipment, along with a 40-foot Viking merchant ship and a one room school house. Visitors enjoy having their picture taken in front of Big Ole, a 28-foot statue of a Viking that represented the state at the 1965 Worlds Fair. Big Ole proudly stands guard across the street from the Runestone Museum. For an encounter with history that leaves no stone unturned, visit the Runestone Museum today.

206 Broadway Street, Alexandria MN
(320) 763-3160
www.runestonemuseum.org

Munsinger & Clemens Gardens and Gift Shop

The Munsinger & Clemens Gardens are two separate but adjacent public gardens that dazzle the eye from late spring into fall. Munsinger Gardens, which dates from the 1930s, still displays WPA-constructed beds and rock-lined paths. This informal 14-acre garden contains swaths of grass that flow between naturally shaped island beds, much like the Mississippi River adjoining it. Tall pines overlook a greenhouse, lily pond and fountain. Clemens Gardens, sited on a sunny hill above Munsinger, contains six formal gardens of European design that feature American plant material. Developed in the 1990s by Bill and Virginia Clemens and later donated to the City of St. Cloud, the gardens include the Virginia Clemens Rose Garden, home to more than 1,100 roses, including floribundas, tree roses, hybrid teas, shrub roses and grandifloras. The Treillage Garden shelters a fountain under the 24-foot high dome of a 104-foot long arbor trellis. Still other gardens include the Rest Area Garden, White Garden, Formal Garden and Perennial Garden. Each garden is embellished with decorative ironwork and fountains. The Munsinger Clemens Botanical Society sponsors educational and social events, such as a popular Music in the Garden series during the summer months. Whether you're a serious gardener, a nature lover or just appreciate beautiful things, be sure to put the Munsinger & Clemens Gardens on your must-see list and stop by the gift shop for a memento of your visit.

1399 Kilian Boulevard SE, St. Cloud MN
(320) 650-1050
www.ci.stcloud.mn.us

Pete & Joy's Bakery

You won't have any trouble spotting Pete & Joy's Bakery in Little Falls, because the outside of the bakery features a large mural depicting the downtown business district. The bakery, owned by Peter and Joyce Kamrowski, has been part of the fabric of the community since 1938. Everything about this bakery is welcoming, from the aroma of freshly baked breads, cookies and cakes to the gift assortment, which includes imported Polish pottery and limited-edition cookie jars. You might want to come with an appetite, because Pete & Joy's is a place to linger and enjoy a sandwich, salad or the house soup or chili. You could even be named customer of the month and win a gift certificate. Peter is a master baker who specializes in cakes. His poppy-seed coffee cake is well known in the neighborhood, and he also bakes an assortment of specialty cakes, including wedding cakes. Printing an edible photograph on

Great River Arts Association

Great River Arts Association (GRAA) celebrates art in ways that benefit everyone who visits or lives in Little Falls. This private, nonprofit organization began in 1992 and today manages three fine arts galleries, including the spacious exhibit space at the association's downtown Arts Center. Other galleries are located at the Morrison County Government Center and the Family Medical Center. GRAA's Arts Center

is flexible and spacious enough to hold several classes at once. If the fine art on display here or the consignment pieces in the gift shop inspire you, try a class in painting or drawing. A pottery class lets you sit at a potter's wheel to throw pots of your own. Artisans sell pottery, jewelry, wood carvings and blown glass at the Arts Center, which also offers custom framing. GRAA celebrates music with a year-round concert series. In winter, groove to the Unplugged Series indoors. In summer, the music moves to nearby Maple Island Park, just a few blocks south of the Arts Center. If you like art, you'll love a visit to GRAA. The staff can tell you about performing and visual arts events elsewhere in the area. Let the Great River Arts Association be your bridge to the arts.

122 SE 1st Street, Little Falls MN
(320) 632-0960

The Rourke Art Gallery and Museum

The Rourke Art Gallery and Museum are complementary institutions with deep roots in the Fargo-Moorhead community. Each season, the organization hosts some 20 exhibitions, giving visitors multiple reasons to return throughout the year. Every year on June 18 the organization celebrates its founding with the Midwestern Art Exhibition, an event that showcases the work of 100 artists. The gallery and museum have shown the work of many renowned local artists, including woodcuts and paintings by Charles Beck, the vivid reduction woodcuts of Gordon Mortensen and Midwest landscapes in oil and watercolor by George Pfeifer. Nationally known artists also exhibit here, such as pop artist James Rosenquist and the multi-talented sculptor, watercolorist and printmaker Leonard Baskin. Since 1961, the art gallery has occupied the

historic Martinson House, a restored Victorian home complete with prism-cut leaded glass windows. The art museum is in the former Moorhead Federal Post Office. Its permanent collections include more than 3,000 works of art, ranging from American contemporary pieces and pop art to African, Native American, Pre-Columbian and Hispanic artwork. The museum and gallery offer tours and classes, with discounts to members. Make art a part of your life with a visit to the Rourke Art Gallery and Museum.

521 Main Avenue, Moorhead MN (Museum)
523 S 4th Street, Moorhead MN (Gallery)
(218) 236-8861

Ripple River Gallery

When Bob Carls and Amy Sharpe opened Ripple River Gallery and Woodturning Studio in 2000, they couldn't be sure that folks would venture off the main highway to find their one-room gallery in Minnesota's lake country, two-and-a-half hours north of the Twin Cities. Art lovers came, however, enough of them to justify adding a second room during the gallery's first winter. Bob is the artist behind the woodturning studio, while Amy weaves and creates nature prints. They once sold their artwork at shows from Montana to Ohio. Now their gallery gives them the flexibility to show their own work close to home and represent some 50 regional artists as well. Bob's lathe-turned and carved bowls are one of the highlights of a trip to Ripple River. He crafts the bowls from some of the world's most beautiful woods. Other highlights are woodblock prints, paintings and carved birds by Charles Beck. Offerings change frequently and include pottery, paintings, drawings, jewelry, weavings and baskets. The gallery hosts receptions for rotating exhibits as well as special programs and classes. "Art connects us all," say Amy and Bob. Visitors appreciate the gallery's setting among seven acres of maples, pines, fruit trees and gardens, three miles east of Ruttger's Bay Lake Lodge. Journey to Ripple River Gallery for quality artwork with regional flavor.

27591 Partridge Avenue, Aitkin MN
(218) 678-2575
www.ripplerivergallery.com

Amish Oak and Americana Furnishings

Your source for Amish craftsmanship in downtown Park Rapids is Amish Oak and Americana Furnishings. Such hand tooled items as bedroom suites, dining sets and office furniture in oak, cherry, maple and hickory fill the 7,100-square-foot showroom. Owners Diane Smith and Denise Hafner purchase the solid wood merchandise directly from the Amish families who make the pieces in Ohio and Indiana. These families typically employ anywhere from one to 15 of their neighbors and friends, who take great pride in their work. Diane and Denise have enjoyed bringing a part of Amish culture to northern Minnesota since 1995. "We opened our doors as a privately owned family business with a goal to provide the finest quality items," they say. They carry Amish quilts and dish cloths in their store in addition to furniture, and they have been known to share Amish recipes with their customers, such as one for a delicious pineapple cake. Indeed, while a great selection of wood furniture is the main draw, Amish Oak is a fun place to shop for everything from home accessories and Life is Good T-shirts to such irresistible munchies as licorice and cashew crunch. If you can't make it to the store, be sure to browse its website. The shop ships nationwide and delivery is also available. For furniture crafted and sold with pride, stop by Amish Oak and Americana Furnishings.

403 S Main Street, Park Rapids MN
(218) 732-9544 or (800) 286-7625
www.amishfurnishings.com

Geneva Golf Club

The Geneva Golf Club can treat you to an afternoon of golf and instruction or an entire golf vacation. You can stay right on the property in a two-bedroom lodge overlooking the golf course or in a deluxe lodge with such amenities as a full kitchen, private patio, living room and dining room, and which can hold four adults with room to spare. Let the professionals help you plan a trip for business or pleasure. Of course, the real draw is the golf. You will be challenged by 27 holes of championship golf on three very different courses—the Ponds, Island and Marsh courses, designed by Joel Goldstrand and featuring bent grass greens and natural water hazards. With five sets of tees, the best golfer and the beginner both face challenging ground. You can also improve your swing at the Geneva Golf Academy, which offers two and three-day golf schools, clinics and player development programs, with a four to one student to teacher ratio that assures individual attention. LPGA instructor Lisa Grimes and her PGA staff can provide pointers to help you improve your game and maximize your potential whatever your skill level. The pro shop also offers clothing and equipment that's appreciated by golfers. Celebrate a day well spent with an after-game visit to the Geneva Grill, featuring drinks, light snacks or full meals. Challenge your golf skills with a visit to the Geneva Golf Club.

Anton's Restaurant

Anton's Restaurant, located right outside of St. Cloud on the banks of the Sauk River, is a remarkable establishment with a great view and many different rooms, each with its own character. In addition to top-quality steaks and outstanding seafood, Anton's features specialty dishes such as Chicken Boursin, made with parmesan-breaded chicken breasts and a garlic and herb cream sauce, or the barbecue ribs, which are done to perfection with a honey-based barbecue sauce. But the true signature items are the giant popovers. Baked fresh daily and served warm with honey butter, these popovers draw customers from all over the state. The authentic log cabin that houses the restaurant has a story of its own. Built in the 1920s, the building was originally a speak-easy operating under the name of Bricky's. Throughout the years there have been many different owners, but all of them kept the name and the spirit of the original Bricky's establishment. Tony (Anton) and Lorraine Gaetz purchased the building in 1973 and changed the name to Anton's. The menu and the building have been expanded to create the unique atmosphere that exists today. Most of the seats have a view of the Sauk River and window seats are in high demand. Another favorite are the covered wagon booths, complete with tops that look like old-time wagons. The staff members at Anton's Restaurant welcome you to join them for lunch or dinner and enjoy a full bar, extensive wine list, a spectacular menu and a charming atmosphere.

2001 Frontage Road N, Waite Park MN
(320) 253-3611
www.antonsrestaurant.com

Place in the Country/
The Gathering Grounds Coffee Shoppe

A visit to the Perham gift shop called Place in the Country invariably ends up including a meal or snack at the Gathering Grounds Coffee Shoppe located there. The fresh, healthy food choices are sure to entice, and the atmosphere invites lingering. Place in the Country occupies two levels in a 100-year-old building that features exposed brick walls, original distressed wide plank flooring and a lattice and vine motif on the ceiling. You will want to check out the antique cupboards overflowing with gifts and country charm before settling back for a sandwich on multi-grain bread, some fruit or fresh veggies. Over the past 10 years, owners Lynn Johnson and Kari Roberts have allowed their menu to evolve according to their customers' desires. You can build your own sandwich or try such signature sandwich delights as the Nutty Bird or Crabby at Noon. The shop also serves salads, vegetable quiche, chilled peach soup and items from a kid's menu. A new gelato bar lets you indulge in Italian ice cream, which has fewer calories than its American counterpart. Not everything here is slimming. The Gathering Grounds retained its slightly sinful chicken salad and such favorite desserts as cookies, muffins and caramel rolls at the request of customers. For an enjoyable shopping excursion full of gifts and healthy foods, visit Place in the Country and the Gathering Grounds Coffee Shoppe.

134 1st Avenue S, Perham MN
(218) 346-7969

Peppercorn Restaurant & Lounge

The Peppercorn Restaurant & Lounge is one of Northern Minnesota's best steak, rib and seafood restaurants. It was recently voted the most romantic restaurant in the Northland, and the reality exceeds the reputation. For two decades, the innovative dishes of Chef Mark Little have pleased every palate. Locals know the Peppercorn for its hand-cut steaks, in-house smoked ribs and distinctive entries such as the portobello mushroom ravioli. Delicious desserts such as Chocolate Beyond Reason provide the perfect complement to any meal. The Peppercorn boasts an extensive wine list and a full-service lounge. With more than 12 banquet menus and rooms that accommodate groups of 10 to 65 people, the Peppercorn is ideal for groom's dinners, pre-game meals, small parties and business meetings. The Peppercorn is owned and operated by Murray Williamson and his son, Kevin. Murray is a two-time U.S. Olympic hockey coach, and his interest in the Bemidji community began when he founded the world-renowned Bemidji Hockey Camp. An estimated 33,000 young people have benefited from this camp throughout its 35 years of existence. In 1986, Williamson turned his vision of fine dining into reality by establishing the Peppercorn Restaurant. For an elegant and sophisticated culinary journey, experience the Peppercorn for yourself. Discover why it has become a favorite of Bemidji locals and tourists.

1813 Paul Bunyan Drive NW, Bemidji MN
(218) 759-2794
www.peppercornrestaurant.com

A.T. The Black & White

A.T. The Black & White has evolved since it opened in 1931. It began as a small diner-style hamburger shop. Today, it seats 100 and sports wall-length murals by local artists. Owners Amanda and Tomas Zimmerman (the A and T) honor the restaurant's origins with such breakfast staples as biscuits and gravy, omelettes and pancakes. At lunch, enjoy innovative sandwiches such as the turkey artichoke, hand-patted hamburgers or house-made soups. Amanda and Tomas are both chefs trained at Le Cordon Bleu. At dinner, they put their expertise to work using fresh seasonal ingredients to prepare steaks, seafood, pasta and salads. Few can resist the desserts, which include the signature Black & White Express, a chocolate mousse dressed up with dark chocolate ganache, white chocolate, strawberry sauce and whipped cream. Coffee drinkers will appreciate the freshly ground Black & White blend. Wine and beer are also available. The atmosphere changes at night when the Black & White transforms into a club that would fit right into Chicago's Uptown. White tablecloths and black napkins match soft jazz music. Whether you're out on the town with your sweetie or crave a special sandwich, A.T. The Black & White will provide delicious surprises.

116 SE 1st Street, Little Falls MN
(320) 632-5374
www.attheblacknwhite.com

Bello Cucina

Everyone has a picture of Italy in their minds, whether from memory, movies or dreams: the sunlit vineyards, romantic architecture, and of course, the sumptuous cuisine. But can you get a taste of Italy in Morris, Minnesota? You certainly can, at Bello Cucina. Offering an authentic Italian experience without the trip to Italy, Bello Cucina is a refreshing option for restaurant-goers seeking a touch of European bounty and atmosphere. The pleasing Old-World décor includes wainscoted walls, hardwood floors and wrought-iron decorative pieces adorned with hanging vines. Small café-style tables can be moved and arranged to accommodate larger parties. Jason Mueller, the formally trained chef, provides a menu with dishes that have the colors and flavors of Italy, from artichoke dip and tomato bisque to the very popular Champagne chicken. The menu changes four times a year with the seasons and is accompanied by a great selection of wines. Come to Bello Cucina and experience dinner from a beautiful kitchen.

506 Atlantic Avenue, Morris MN
(320) 585-7000
www.bellocucina.com

The Jazzy Fox Bistro

As the name might imply, the Jazzy Fox Bistro has an ambience all its own. Over the last few years, Jan Kjellerup and Ted O'Connell have created a little spot in downtown Fergus Falls where fine dining goes hand in hand with the atmosphere of a small, 1940s style jazz club. You can listen to live piano music while enjoying international cuisine and a glass of wine from an extensive wine list. You might even find a singing server presenting the wild game specialties. The brick interior sets well with the jazz and offers an atmosphere conducive to fine dining. "Our goal is to be different and remain consistent," says O'Connell. Meals are presented with the kind of attention to detail you could expect from the most exclusive restaurants. You are sure to be delighted by Chef Scott Ellingson's duckling with raisin sauce or any of the perfectly prepared steak, seafood and pork dishes. On Sundays, the Jazzy Fox Bistro's champagne brunch is a popular place to stop with family and friends. The bistro makes a perfect addition to a day spent enjoying the sights of Fergus Falls. You can follow your dinner here with a visit to the Riverwalk and the opportunity to experience quaint shops and historic architecture. Relax with food, friends and live jazz music at the Jazzy Fox Bistro.

106 Lincoln Avenue W, Fergus Falls MN
(218) 998-JAZZ (5299)
www.jazzyfoxbistro.com

Gilly's Prime Time Bar & Grill

Prime rib reigns supreme at Gilly's Prime Time Bar & Grill, where every day of the week Chef Ric Saunders receives more orders for this than for any other dinner on the menu. He rubs the prime rib with a special blend of 13 herbs and spices, and then slow roasts it to ensure excellent taste and tenderness in every bite. Whether topped with barbecue sauce, sauerkraut or melted Swiss cheese, the prime rib sandwiches are popular here, too. Finger foods, salads and burgers are other highlights, along with walleye, rib eye or sautéed sea scallops. Rick Berg owns Gilly's, though you could say that it belongs to the community. It started under a different name in 1972 and has become such a fixture that downtown Elbow Lake wouldn't be the same without it. Its two dining rooms fill up with locals on the weekend. Open for lunch and dinner seven days a week, Gilly's also offers a Saturday breakfast and Sunday brunch. The lounge is definitely the place to be on Sundays, where patrons can watch the Vikings on a big screen television and enjoy happy hour pricing all day. You can play Texas Hold 'Em on Monday nights. Have yourself a prime experience at Gilly's Prime Time Bar & Grill.

12 Central Avenue N, Elbow Lake MN
(218) 685-4242
www.gillysprimetime.com

Tutto Bene Italian Restaurant

Tutto Bene Italian Restaurant offers fine Italian dining that not only tastes like Italy but feels like it, too. The décor in this Bemidji building will remind you of northern Italy—tapestries, tiles and artwork depict that region. Tutto Bene serves fine Italian cuisine and features house-made pastas, breads and desserts. Portions are generous, and even appetizers are sufficient for a light meal. Along with the extensive menu of pasta dishes, Tutto Bene serves steak, seafood and chicken. The menu has been expanded to include many American dishes as well. An extensive wine list is available, and a small espresso bar occupies a corner of the dining room. By achieving the flavor and feel of Italy, Thomas Allen, owner of Tutto Bene, offers his customers an escape from the usual with a laid-back and informal evening. The courtyard can seat up to 32 people and makes a pleasant outdoor dining experience during the summer months. The restaurant offers a convention room with a seating capacity of 66, and the dining room that can handle individual parties of up to 15 guests comfortably. Meals are moderately priced, and run from $8 to $16. The 11-year-old restaurant is conveniently located just one block from Highway 197. To immerse yourself in the pleasures of Italian casual dining, make reservations at Tutto Bene Italian Restaurant.

300 Beltrami Avenue NW, Bemidji MN
(218) 751-1100

Speak Easy Restaurant & Lounge

For an exciting taste of nostalgia, Speak Easy Restaurant & Lounge will take you roaring back to the days of Prohibition. In a world of flappers and gangsters, you will be served the finest Italian food, steaks, seafood and pizza. Your getaway car is a 1931 Model A Ford. It's showcased in Speak Easy's lounge, which offers a wide range of legal boot-leg. With spacious banquet facilities, Speak Easy offers catering for 10 to 320 partygoers, making it the ideal place for a groom's dinner, wedding dance, Christmas party or birthday celebration. A full bar and gaming extravaganza add to the fun. Speak Easy can also meet the needs for a professional business atmosphere, making this a suitable place for a corporate meeting or banquet. From Prohibited Pastas to Capone's Combos these gangsters are duly famous for their catering and take-out pans to go. Their lasagna, spaghetti, rigatoni, tortellini, carbonara, seafood, and fettuccine will each feed up to 10 mobsters, with bread included. The food is so good you'll wonder if it's even legal. Double Bubble hours keep the Feds busy every day between 11 am and 6 pm. Sunday Brunch starts at 10 am, and you are well advised to save room for the homemade caramel rolls. On Sunday through Thursday from 9 pm until 11 pm, you can get 2-4-1s (that's a two-for-the-price-of-one drink) with the rest of the mob in the bar. Make a clean getaway after you've had a blast at the Speak Easy Restaurant & Lounge.

100 N Shore Drive, Detroit Lakes MN
(218) 844-1326
www.speakeasydl.com

Bookin' It

Owner Laura Hansen and her Bookin' It team have the kind of enthusiasm for reading that is a magnet for anyone who loves books. You can spend hours in this restful cottage-style haven reading, flipping through the volumes and drawing up a mile-long wish list. The staff will help you narrow down that list to those choice few titles you just cannot go home without. At Bookin' It, the knowledgeable staff members are always happy to recommend a new author who will appeal to you. The shop's inventory of titles, cards and book-related gifts is exciting and eclectic. Everything about Bookin' It is designed to put you at ease, including the softly colored walls, an original tin ceiling and the barn-wood walls in the children's room. Across from the historic Morrison County Courthouse, Bookin' It invites lingering. Jack, the store dog, makes everyone feel welcome. Laura and her staff, which includes lead bookseller Maryjude Hoeffel, add energy to the store with author events throughout the year. The store sponsors three book clubs: The Good Living Cookbook Club, The Contemporary Fiction Book Club and The Spirituality Book Discussion Group. With the release of *Diving the Drop-off*, a volume of poetry, Laura is now a published author with a book on display in her own shop. Come to Bookin' It soon and experience the charm.

104B 2ⁿᵈ Street, Little Falls MN
(320) 632-1848 or (800) 809-1848
www.bookinitontheweb.com

Albany Antique Center

For many antique specialties under one roof, turn to Albany Antique Center, where several dealers combine to offer an old and unusual inventory. Terri and Bob Gertken own a neat and clean store that invites browsing. You'll find furniture, glassware, pottery and sporting collectibles sharing space with books, primitives and old advertisements. Each booth has a personality of its own, which adds to the adventure. In addition to a vast selection of older merchandise, the store features a small boutique area that includes new items. Terri and Bob, their daughter Mandy, and their good friend Sandie Salzl are all knowledgeable and happy to help you find that elusive piece that may be missing from your collection. Whether you enjoy the surprise around every corner, delight in an opportunity to step back in yesteryear or are on the prowl for something special to decorate your home, visit Albany Antique Center.

740 Railroad Avenue, Albany MN
(320) 845-6575

Ambiance @ Fifty-Three

Some gift stores just beg to be explored, and Ambiance @ Fifty-Three is one of these. This Little Falls shop sits at the southern end of the business district. Once upon a time, it was a gas station.

Owners Mary Uhlhorn and Susan Paulson had something more creative than fill 'er up in mind when they opened the shop in 2002. You'll want to take time to explore the treasures gathered at this shop. The items are the kind of finds that could change the feel of your home. Mary and Susan have gathered together an eclectic array of merchandise, including pictures, lamps, kitchen items, baby gifts and more. The clothing is also far from ordinary. Not only do Mary and Susan carry creative objects, they display them with creativity, too. A birch tree limb becomes an artful Northwoods-style display area. Word of mouth is out about Ambiance. Shoppers make special plans to visit this memorable store, where they'll meet upscale gifts and the bubbly personalities of the owners. Shake up your thinking about gifts and home décor by making Ambiance @ Fifty-Three part of your next shopping trip.

302 SE 1ˢᵗ Street, Little Falls MN
(320) 632-0484

Crooked Willow

Crooked Willow offers an inviting shopping experience filled with gifts, antiques and vintage home accessories. You'll find European antique furniture and Woodwick Candles. Crooked Willow sells personalized lake signs and lovely textiles from Heritage Lace and Northland Woolens. It's not surprising that customers find the shop an inspiring place to purchase a piece of the past, since it was inspiration that first gave owners Terri and Christopher Anderson the idea for the retail space. Only after they put up a storage building on an investment property and started renovating the 1930s house that they decided to move forward with a store. Terri says she has always wanted to own a shop, and she and Christopher had collected antiques for many years. The business name comes from the grand old tree in the yard and evokes the nostalgia customers feel when they enter one of several buildings on the property—a converted granary, a garage called the Hen House, or the home itself. Take a break in the midst of your shopping to relax in the beautiful gazebo and enjoy an old-fashioned soda. For fine furnishings and accessories in an idyllic country setting, visit Crooked Willow.

11181 Highway 27 E, Osakis MN
(320) 859-3624
www.crookedwillow.net

Moorhead Antique Mall and An Old Friends Cottage

Mark and Mary Ann Nelson know a good thing—and an old one—when they see it. They are the owners of the Moorhead Antique Mall, the largest and oldest antique mall in the Moorhead region. They also own An Old Friends Cottage, the newest antique mall in the region. The two businesses share one space and together offer one extravaganza of a shopping experience. The 8,000-square-foot Moorhead Antique Mall and the 3,000-square-foot Old Friends Cottage are located in a country-like setting that is only 45 minutes from the Minnesota Lakes Country and one of the most important attractions in the area, according to the *Moorhead Attractions* brochure. Mark and Mary Ann have been in business for 11 years and hold a reputation for quality merchandise in a neat and organized environment. Their original store offers selections from more than 70 vendors and specializes in North Dakota pottery plus shabby chic and Victorian style furnishings. An Old Friends Cottage adds all sorts of antiques, collectibles and home furnishings for a surprise in every booth. You will also find a section among the sea of antiques devoted to new gifts and home décor items. The two antique malls are open seven days a week. Plan on plenty of time for your excursion to Moorhead Antique Mall and An Old Friends Cottage, because there's no telling what you will find.

2811 SE Main Avenue, Moorhead MN
(Just off I 94, Exit #2)
(218) 287-1313

Victor Lundeen Company

Printing is an important specialty of the Victor Lundeen Company, the oldest retail establishment in Fergus Falls. The company's building is well-known to the community and features a sign dating back to the original store opening. Since its establishment in 1914, customers have been trusting Victor Lundeen Company with their printing needs and experiencing the kind of reliability and value that builds a lasting reputation. The company prints checks, business forms, letterheads and envelopes. It can place a client's logo and promotional message on a key chain, a pen or a calendar to help clients build company identity with specialty advertising. Lundeen's graphic arts department has gained a reputation for the kind of quality products that keep offices functioning profitably and efficiently. Lundeen's retail store, in the heart of downtown, is the oldest family-owned and operated store in Otter Tail County. It offers an interesting mix of products including collectibles, accessories for the lake, home and garden, a grand collection of greeting cards and stationery, Minnesota keepsakes and a full range of office products. The store's book department offers an exceptional selection of children's books, works by regional authors and national bestsellers. Victor Lundeen, Jr. upholds the same principals of reliability and value that have served customers for the better part of a century. Next time you need printing, office products, a gift, a book or a help with a promotional product, come to Victor Lundeen Company.

126 W Lincoln Avenue, Fergus Falls MN
(218) 736-5433
www.victorlundeens.com

Christmas Point Wild Rice Company

Twenty years ago, Christmas Point Wild Rice Company was a small, family-owned wild rice processing plant in Walker. It is now an amazing 26,000-square-foot three-story structure offering an ultimate Northwoods shopping experience. One thing hasn't changed: Christmas Point is still a family business. Owners Larry and Susan Olin, along with daughters Jody and Jennifer, son Joshua and son-in-law Scott, operate two retail stores, Christmas Point's manufacturing facility and a 400-acre wild rice farm and processing plant. The family is passionate about its products and the goals of the business, and it strives to be a front runner in Minnesota shopping destinations. The Christmas Point stores have a Northwoods feel with wood-plank floors, exposed beams and knotty pine walls. Instead of pickle and cracker barrels, these modern-day general stores are filled with gourmet foods, kitchen accessories, stoneware and glassware. You'll also find boutique clothing, shoes, jewelry and home décor items beyond your wildest dreams. Last but not least, wild rice and wild rice soup mixes are a staple in the Christmas Point stores. The Baxter location features an espresso bar and café serving a full lunch menu. The Christmas Point Family invites one and all to visit: "Shop with us; spend the day with us. It will be a memorable experience."

14803 Edgewood Drive, Baxter MN (218) 828-0603
523 Minnesota Avenue, Walker MN (218) 547-2170
www.christmaspoint.com

Nordic Galleri

Downtown Fergus Falls is home to a quaint gallery filled with Scandinavian gifts and products. For 21 years, the Nordic Galleri has been owner Arna Stedjan's way of sharing her heritage with the customers who come through her doors. Arna immigrated from Norway, and her presence alone imparts authentic Norwegian flavor to the gallery, which features gifts from Norway, Sweden, Denmark and Finland. Arna also carries a fine array of German products. Those planning a wedding often choose to add china by Porsgrund or crystal by Orrefors and Kosta Boda to the wedding registry. Scandinavian Christmas ornaments are prized throughout the world, and Arna offers a generous assortment in her shop. Gifts of pewter and jewelry are ideal in any season, and the chocolate from Norway may just win someone's heart. For the kitchen, you'll find *krumkake* and waffle irons, rolling pins for making lefse and lefse grills and sticks. Getting through a Minnesota winter becomes a warm and fashionable undertaking with one of Nordic Galleri's imported Norwegian sweaters. To find a little bit of Scandinavia in the Riverfront Square, come enjoy the collection of Scandinavian gifts at the Nordic Galleri.

221 W Lincoln Avenue, Fergus Falls MN
(218) 739-9665

Scandinavian Gift Shop

For Scandinavian treasures, ethnic foods and holiday ornamentation, you're *velkommen* at the Scandinavian Gift Shop. For 24 years, the shop has provided a place to discover Scandinavian heritage through gifts, books and cards. Many customers come in just to browse and end up becoming regulars after discovering the china, linens, jewelry and art prints. Look for T-shirts, Bastad and Dala clogs, sweaters by Dale of Norway, and Brio toys and trains. Owners Doris and Wally Miller can share the history on products from Norway, Sweden, Finland, Iceland and Denmark. Collectibles abound, including Royal Copenhagen, Bing and Grondahl, Porsgrund, Orefores and Kosta Boda. You will find trolls, plus carvings from Henning Studio in Norway. Such Scandinavian stitchery as hardanger, Swedish huck weaving and Danish cross-stitch abound. On-the-spot crash courses in needlework provide opportunities to try fabrics, books and patterns. The Scandinavian love of Christmas is evident in ornaments at the shop's year-round Christmas Corner, which includes collectible *tomte* or *nisse* (gnome) figures from all of the Scandinavian countries. In honor of Scandinavian cooking, look for imported foods, specialty cookware and recipe books, or try a sample at one of the store's popular events or demonstrations. Traditional music and window dressings find a home at the shop, too. Experience the culture and charm of the Nordic countries with a trip to the Scandinavian Gift Shop.

604 Broadway Street, Alexandria MN
(320) 763-6363
www.scandinaviangifts.com

The Pines Gift Shop Inc.

Owners Kimberly Winter and Stephanie Disse have outfitted a historic building in downtown Perham to create a warm welcome for shoppers at The Pines Gift Shop. Since the mid-1960s, The Pines has provided its customers with gifts for weddings, birthdays and other occasions. In the summer, you can beat the heat with a cool and tasty ice cream cone or satisfy your sweet tooth with chocolates and candies from Nelson Confections. If you're shopping for the person who has everything, or you need a thank-you gift for someone special, The Pines staff is ready to help you spot the perfect item. Once you find it, remember that The Pines will always gift-wrap your purchases for free. The shop stocks jewelry, candles and calendars and has a wide selection of furniture, collectibles and rugs. The Wooden Spoon, a separate business located inside The Pines, provides kitchen gadgets, cookware and accessories. You can find a wide variety of collectibles at The Pines, including items from Department 56 villages, Beanie

Babies and Willow Tree Angels. You can pick up Christmas decorations any time of the year. As a special touch, The Pines offers Taste of Perham baskets filled with Perham-made products. Whether you're looking for something sweet, a special gift or something for yourself, Kimberly and Stephanie invite you into The Pines Gift Shop Inc.

101 W Main Street, Perham MN
(218) 346-5435 or (877) 56-PINES (567-4637)
http://thepines.perham.biz

Gruber's Quilt Shop

You can fulfill many needs with a stop at Dan Tree Court in Waite Park. The shopping center is well-known to quilters who make a point of stopping at Gruber's Quilt Shop, named one of the top 10 quilt shops in the country in 2001 by *American Patchwork* and *Quilting* magazines. Gruber's features 10,000 bolts of fabric plus supplies and has hosted celebrities such as First Lady Laura Bush. From Gruber's, you can continue your shopping spree without getting back in your car. The Mad Scrapper shop helps you organize your memories with scrapbook, paper craft and rubber stamp supplies. LC Scrubs provides professional uniforms in a wide variety of styles, colors and sizes. Naturally Enchanting is a boutique that features handcrafted custom jewelry and jewelry repair, plus home accents and imported purses. Weddings and parties often begin with a visit to Blooming Creations Floral & Gifts for flowers, cakes and balloons to celebrate the occasions in your life. For antiques, collectibles and custom furniture, shoppers turn to Antiques and . . ., where 20 dealers bring together their goods under one roof. After a full day of shopping, a pampering visit to the Dan Tree Salon for a massage or new hairstyle is an added treat. Complete your excursion with a stop at the Urban Garden Café, where coffee, tea and such deli items as sandwiches, soups and salads promise refreshment. The café also provides catering services. Next time you need quilting supplies, or almost anything else, make a day of it at Dan Tree Court.

310 4th Avenue NE, Waite Park MN
(320) 259-4360
www.grubersquiltshop.com

The Red Willow Gift Shop

The Red Willow Gift Shop can satisfy any dedicated browser with gifts to suit many interests. Charmingly situated in a one-of-a-kind 13-bedroom home, the Red Willow organizes each room with a separate theme and offers a continually changing assortment of wares. You'll find gifts with garden, nautical and Northwoods themes, as well as rooms with merchandise for kids or wine aficionados. Christmas decorations, home décor and collectibles abound. Owners Barbara and Lane Engberg were born and raised in Detroit Lakes and continue to call the area home. They opened their treasure-chest rooms in 1984, delighting customers with their well-stocked pantry of tasteful gifts, where fascinating finds fill every corner and closet. A recent addition to the Red Willow is an extensive kitchenware and gourmet food department. The Engbergs provide a welcoming atmosphere in even the smallest and coziest of their rooms, so that you can feel at home inspecting the nooks and crannies of this pleasant emporium. If you are an imaginative and discerning gift giver who seeks more than run-of-the-mill fare, plan a visit to the Red Willow Gift Shop.

1160 S Washington Avenue, Detroit Lakes MN
(218) 847-6297

Sweet Seasons

Marlene Bettin, the owner of Sweet Seasons, wants you to have fun picking out gifts, whether you seek the newest look in home décor, gourmet foods, a collectible or an antique. The blend of old and new products at her shop lets you match the tastes of even the most challenging gift recipient on your list. The great displays in antique cupboards add charm to the space, where Marlene's selections mix beautifully with nostalgic merchandise. If you're buying for someone with a sense of humor, you will appreciate the whimsical figurines, vases and stationery. Kitchens can be dressed up with an array of items as diverse as funky chickens, classic stoneware and hand-painted dinnerware. Consider a Woodwick soy candle or an oil lamp from Lampe Berger that both purifies and scents the air. Sweet Seasons has Christmas-themed gifts that are artistic expressions of the season, such as snowmen and angels with folk art appeal, and Santas and nativity scenes from Williraye Studios. Remember to add some pampering gifts that include olive-oil-enriched Cali lotions and soaps, plus Caren skin care products. Who wouldn't love a basket filled with gourmet foods? Sweet Seasons offers such delicacies as aromatic coffees, teas, fruit dips, grilling sauces, hot mustards and decadent sipping chocolate. Turn gift shopping and home decorating into a fulfilling experience with a visit to Sweet Seasons.

507 Broadway, Alexandria MN
(320) 762-5534
www.sweetseasonsgifts.com

The Flower Dell

It's hard to walk by the Flower Dell, located inside the Old Historic Sands Café building, without feeling the urge to explore. Everything about this florist shop cries out for attention, from the inviting storefront to a central gazebo filled with gifts and home décor. Plants get the attention they deserve in attractive displays. Brian and Patty Mackinac bought this 25-year-old floral business three years ago. Once you have met them, you'll have another reason to visit the Flower Dell. You'll notice that Patty and her staff pay extraordinary attention to their customers, which allows them to create just the right fresh or permanent floral design for the clients' individual needs. A small balcony surrounded by decorative wrought iron is a stage for live musicians during the annual holiday open house, which is always held the first Sunday in November. At other times of the year, the balcony is a display space that adds to the store's charming character. For beautiful gifts and floral arrangements, let the Flower Dell tempt you inside.

119 SE 1st Street, Little Falls MN
(320) 632-8588 or (800) 645-2840
www.flowerdell.net

The Gumdrop Tree

Visit any of The Gumdrop Tree stores and you'll find a toy selection that puts a child's imagination to work. The first Gumdrop Tree opened in Aitkin in 2001. Since then, stores in Pequot Lakes, Nisswa, Baxter and Little Falls have opened. Each store is unique and individually owned. The Gumdrop Tree carries toys for kids of all ages and for the kid at heart. You'll find craft kits, bath toys, games and puzzles for the whole family, books, seasonal toys and timeless toys from the past. The Gumdrop Tree is a favorite place to buy nostalgic candies such as Chuckles, Candy Buttons, Razzles and Mallow Cups that have become hard to find. Customer service is number one at The Gumdrop Tree. The friendly staff will help select toys for a child of any given age and will even gift wrap it for free. Customers love coming in and finding a gift, having it wrapped and going straight to the birthday party from the shop. Have fun with your child. Come pick up and play with toys that are durable, fun and educational from The Gumdrop Tree.

(320) 631-0013 (Little Falls)
(218) 927-2253 (Aitkin)
(218) 967-0301 (Nisswa)
(218) 568-7791 (Pequot Lake)
(218) 822-3814 (Baxter)
www.thegumdroptree.com

Touch of Class

Touch of Class is a full-service bridal and floral salon offering exclusive designer collections, luxurious creations and elegant accessories for the bride and her entourage. Look for everything from bridal gowns and tuxedos to floral designs and invitations. You'll also discover a vast line of quality gifts, such as candles, gourmet coffees, porcelain dolls and more. Touch of Class opened in 1996 in Granite Falls and moved to the Lake Minnewaska area in 2001, where it is now located in downtown Starbuck. The 100-year-old building it is in features an original steel-engraved tile ceiling and old-fashioned pillars. Touch of Class has the gown to suit your ceremony and personality, and it provides expert fittings. The salon also has more than 400 one-of-a-kind prom gowns in styles ranging from traditional to trendy. Tuxedo choices include the European look as well as traditional tails. The priority and goal at Touch of Class is to make your wedding dreams come true. With more than two decades of floral decorating expertise, owner Lori Vaadeland will create an enchanting atmosphere for your special day. You can be certain that the bouquet, boutonnieres and corsages will be fresh and creative. For a wedding celebration filled with exquisite detail, make your plans with Touch of Class. Its staff will strive to make your day An Affair to Remember.

101 E 5th Street, Starbuck MN
(320) 239-3955
www.touchofclassstarbuck.com

A white-tailed fawn in the Big Stone Wildlife Refuge

Southwest Minnesota

Bingham Hall Bed & Breakfast

Shannon and Todd McKeeth spent seven years restoring an 1893 residence to its former grandeur and today welcome visitors to stay in their Victorian treasure. Bingham Hall Bed & Breakfast in New Ulm now combines a charming atmosphere with contemporary amenities and the McKeeth's hospitality. Each of the four guest rooms comes with a private bath, a 32-inch television and a DVD player, so you can enjoy a movie along with your complimentary microwave popcorn. Your queen-size bed comes with a down comforter, and such special touches as chenille bathrobes put you totally at ease. You can even choose a room with a fireplace or a whirlpool bath. The real treats here are the casual comfort and the friendly gathering with other guests for a gourmet breakfast or a visit in the parlor. The home-like atmosphere at Bingham Hall eases the business traveler's time away from home, while such amenities as complimentary high-speed wireless Internet get the job done, and the shiatsu massage chairs in some rooms offer ultimate relaxation at day's end. Bingham Hall is within walking distance of several restaurants and the downtown historic district. Shannon and Todd invite you to make Bingham Hall Bed & Breakfast your home base for exploration of a town that honors its German heritage.

500 S German Street, New Ulm MN
(507) 354-6766 or (800) 486-3514
www.bingham-hall.com

Dickerson's Lake Florida Resort

Window boxes overflowing with flowers and a plate of fresh-baked cookies on your table tell you that this resort specializes in hospitality. Fourth-generation owners Bob and Connie Dickerson want guests to "build sandcastles and memories." The 13 nicely decorated cocoa-brown cottages stand steps from the shore of shimmering Lake Florida. Each of the fully furnished cottages has a deck with a picnic table and chairs. The cottages range in size from one to five bedrooms, sleeping up to 10 people so a family can invite grandma and grandpa to join them. The resort is six miles west of the quiet resort town of Spicer in the Little Crow Lakes Area of west-central Minnesota, 95 miles west of Minneapolis/ St.Paul. Vacationers head straight for the beach to enjoy the free paddleboats, kayaks, hydro-bikes, sailboat, canoe and rowboats. There are also bikes, tricycles and wagons of all sizes. The bikes can be used to tour the new Glacial Lakes State Trail. Motors for the fishing boats that come free with the cabins and a 40-horsepower pontoon are available for rent. The Dickersons create much of the fun for guests by serving homemade doughnuts at Sunday morning mixers and hosting pizza parties, hayrides for the children and campfires for roasting marshmallows and making s'mores. When planning your next vacation, come to Dickerson's Lake Florida Resort, where Bob and Connie continue the tradition of gracious hospitality started over 80 years ago by Bob's great grandparents.

13194 2nd Street NE, Spicer MN
(320) 354-4272
www.dickersonsresort.com

Miller Armstrong Building

Built in 1900, the Miller Armstrong Building has long held a place in Waseca's history. Known originally as W.J. Armstrong Wholesale Grocers, the building continued to serve southern Minnesota as a grocery warehouse until the early 1980s. In 1981, it was placed on the National Register of Historic Places as a best-preserved building and for representing an important historic link to the railroad. The building was nearly torn down in 1999 but instead was purchased by Gene and Bonnie Miller. Today, the historic Miller Armstrong building is beautifully renovated. Columns, beams and 14,000 square feet of maple flooring provide unmatched atmosphere. On the top floor, Millers Bed and Breakfast offers four cozy suites, each with a fireplace and one with a whirlpool bathtub. (Millers also provides cedar-lined cabins at Veterans Landing on Clear Lake.) Bed and breakfast guests enjoy their free breakfast at Jonnie Beans Internet Coffee House and Wine Bar, which serves Fair Trade organic coffee and espresso drinks as well as pastries, plus breakfast, lunch, wine and imported beers. Four computers and wireless Internet access are on-site for your convenience. The building's main level hosts the 96-seat Armstrong Conference Center, where your events can be catered. Club 57 Sports Bar & Grill is also on the main level. A tasteful den with cedar walls and a stone top bar, Club 57 offers eight beers on tap and the widest assortment of appetizers in town. Whether you are looking for a relaxing getaway or planning a business event, the Miller Armstrong Building has all the amenities you need in an environment with character.

204 2nd Street SW, Waseca MN
(507) 835-1146
www.wasecamac.com

Spicer Castle Bed & Breakfast Inn

Murder reported at Spicer Castle Inn by state newspapers. Guests solve the crime during a banquet often interrupted by fits of laughter. The five-course murder mystery dinners and three-course dinner cruises bring people back to Spicer Castle time and again. Some couples come back more than a decade after being married here to celebrate their anniversaries each year. Others celebrate occasions that call for a special place—birthdays, retirement, promotions and other times to remember. The Spicer Castle, built by land baron John Spicer, overlooks spring-fed Green Lake. Guests enjoy swimming, boating, fishing and a delightful dinner cruise on the Spicer Castle Belle. It is a popular get-away for local and international guests. Originally known as Medayto Cottage, a tower crowns this landmark, which was called the Spicer Castle by fisherman who used it as a landmark to locate their favorite fishing holes. Green Lake is renowned for fishing and hosts fishing tournaments that have attracted people for many years. The property is still owned by Spicer descendants and is managed by Mary Latham Swanson, a great-granddaughter of John Spicer, who loves serving fabulous food in a gracious setting. There are 18 guestrooms including cottages on five wooded acres. With space for up to 300 guests, this is a favorite place for weddings, retreats and meetings. Guestrooms feature great beds, double whirlpool or claw foot tubs, romantic wood or gas fireplaces and wonderfully diverse décor with family furnishings. You'll love your Spicer Castle Bed & Breakfast Inn experience.

11600 Indian Beach Road, Spicer MN (320) 796-5870 or (800) 821-6675
www.spicercastle.com

Grand Cottages

A trip to the Willmar area becomes more attractive than ever when you choose your lodgings from Grand Cottages. Cecil and Sue Meyer will be your hosts at Corner Cottage Bed & Breakfast, a 1914 cottage-style inn near Willmar's historic downtown area. Guests enjoy the comforts of a living room with a fireplace, a billiard room and a formal dining room. You can read your morning paper or look out at the flowers while eating a leisurely breakfast on the sun porch. The inn's four guest rooms feature stunning wood furniture and warm accents. The Honeymoon Suite is the most spacious accommodation with its four-poster king-size bed and a private bath equipped with a whirlpool tub. This suite includes a kitchen, living room and dining area for the ultimate in privacy and convenience. All rooms offer cable television and wireless Internet access. A DVD/VCR unit is available on request. Those planning a business meeting can reserve the billiard room, which has its own kitchenette. You can walk through the tree-lined streets in this quiet neighborhood of well-kept homes or venture downtown for shopping and dining. Retreat to the comforts of Grand Cottages on your next trip to Willmar.

615 Becker Avenue SW, Willmar MN
(320) 235-8002
www.grandcottages.com

Okaman Elk Farms

The sons of about two dozen antler champions are included in the herd of bulls at Okaman Elk Farms. These healthy and majestic animals, the pride of their species, provide visitors to this working farm with prime viewing opportunities. Okaman is in the business of supplying breeders and hunting preserves with trophy bull elk. How many points will you count on the largest rack in the herd? Okaman Elk Farms also offers a petting zoo, playground and picnic area that make the farm a popular destination for family outings. Group tours are welcome. No admission fee is charged. After you have admired the herd, you will enjoy browsing the Wapiti Creations Gift Shop, which carries lamps, jewelry and a wide range of other products made from elk antlers and ivory teeth. You will find elk steaks, burgers and roasts for sale as well as elk sausage and jerky. Owners Don and Joyce Kaplan invite you to drop by and enjoy your experience at Okaman Elk Farms.

43978 Reeds Lake Road (Junction Waseca City 3 and 5), Janesville MN (507) 267-4054 *www.okamanonline.com*

Photos by Evenson Portrait Design

Main Street Cotton Shop

A passion for quilting drives Main Street Cotton Shop. When you enter, you'll be greeted by an enjoyable splash of color and design, with thousands of fabric bolts and a mini-quilt show on the walls. Quilters flock to the shop not only for the fabric, but for the books, patterns, kits and accessories. Owner Jean Lepper is an accomplished quilter and understands first-hand the needs of her clientele. The Cotton Shop specializes in Thimbleberries products. In fact, it is housed in the same building as the Thimbleberries design studio—the base of internationally known author and fabric designer Lynnette Jensen. The building has character. The original hardwood floors and a tin ceiling provide a complementary setting for the wares displayed within. Main Street Cotton Shop started out in Redwood Falls and the catalog division still operates there. In the premier issue of *American Patchwork and Quilting Sampler* magazine, Main Street Cotton Shop was selected as one of the top 10 shops in North America. The shop also has a well-developed website that serves as an additional showroom you can view from your home. The most satisfying way to see the full panorama of color and texture, however, is to visit Main Street Cotton Shop in person. It may give you the inspiration you need for your next project.

7 N Main Street, Hutchinson MN
(320) 234-7298
141 E Second Street, Redwood Falls MN
(catalog division)
(507) 637-5221 or (800) 624-4001
www.mainstreetcottonshop.com

Shades of the Past

The spirit of creativity, fellowship and charity that has brought quilters together for centuries lives on at Shades of the Past. Darci Schipnewski, who opened her quilt shop four years ago, specializes in hand-dyed and felted wool. Quilters love Darci's selections as well as the primitive charm of the shop, a former motel that now features wide plank flooring and quilts displayed from exposed rafters. Shades of the Past is an exciting place where the employees share the customers' enthusiasm. Quilters are always glad to visit with Darci, her daughter Lacey and her mother, Phyllis. In addition to fabrics and specialty products for quilting projects, the shop carries supplies and patterns for punch needle, rug hooking and needle felting. If you're searching for quilting patterns featuring appliqué, you'll be thrilled by PastThyme Patterns, created right in the shop. Shades of the Past offers a variety of quilting classes. The store and the dedicated quilters who shop here also create quilts for charity. In 2006, as part of a national effort to fight breast cancer, Quilt Pink Day brought in enough handmade quilt blocks to make three quilts. Put your old-fashioned passion to work with a visit to Shades of the Past.

211 SE 1st Avenue (Hwy 23), Clara City MN
(320) 847-4040

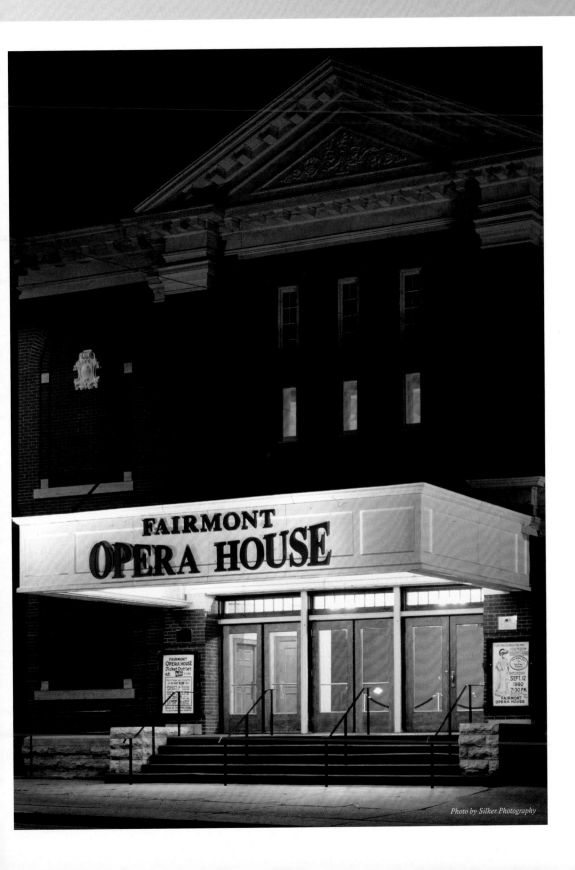

Photo by Silker Photography

Fairmont Opera House

After 100 years, the Fairmont Opera House continues to live up to its nickname, Jewel of the Prairie. This Victorian charmer rarely hosts an opera. What you will find is a delightful mix of entertainment genres, including music and comedy. Richie Havens, Arlo Guthrie and Ricky Skaggs have all performed here. Children are also an important part of this performing arts space—the theater puts on student productions and brings in professional children's theater. Fairmont Opera House is owned by its members; Managing Director Michael Burgraff and a board of directors oversee the theater's daily operations. The opera house first opened in 1902. Within a decade, its focus had shifted from plays to movies. It would alternate between performance hall and movie house until 1980, when it closed its doors. That was when the community took action to save a precious resource. The refurbished theater is on the National Register of Historic Places and operates as a center of entertainment and culture in Fairmont. "The Fairmont Opera House speaks to this region's quality of life," says Burgraff. Come experience the arts at Fairmont Opera House, a building at the heart of its community.

45 Downtown Plaza, Fairmont MN
(507) 238-4900
www.fairmontoperahouse.com

BitterSweet Coffee and Gifts

BitterSweet Coffee and Gifts offers a wide variety of coffee and espresso drinks, homemade soups, fresh salads and sandwiches in a quaint historic building. Lunches feature incredible soups such as Vomacka, loaded baked potatoes and chicken tortellini. Early morning customers can order fresh-baked goods or a breakfast sandwich made with farm-fresh eggs, cheese and pulled smoked ham. BitterSweet holds many events such as wedding showers, spa nights, murder mystery dinners, rug hooking retreats and classes. The upstairs gift shop contains everything from antiques to artwork and is sure to have something special for everyone. You'll find watercolor prints and originals, furniture and jewelry. The Room of Wool Repute is an area dedicated to wool and rug hooking. BitterSweet has hand-dyed wool, patterns, frames and hooks. Owners Laurel Brummund and Lisa Steinborn have created a fun, relaxing atmosphere in a completely renovated 1870s brick building in historic Henderson. They invite you to BitterSweet Coffee and Gifts for a fabulous cup of coffee, a sweet, soup and sandwich and a bit of shopping.

522 Main Street, Henderson MN
(507) 248-3850
www.hendersonmn.com/bittersweet

Deidra's Espresso Café & Bakery

The lunch hours hum with happy chatter while the community enjoys the good coffee, popular meals and tasty goodies at Deidra's Espresso Café & Bakery. Quilts made by owner Deidra Anderson's mother decorate the cozy setting. Flavorful sandwiches and crisp, cool salads draw a constant clientele. If sweet treats are what you're craving, a variety of luscious candies are on hand. In the summer, go for the hard-scoop ice cream. Scones, rolls and pastries are baked on-site. Customers can settle into comfortable wicker chairs by the light of a warming fireplace in the winter, surrounded by a pleasantly muted red and tan decor. Deidra's adjoins the Heritage Bank, and a door between the two enterprises is open during banking hours. The bank's boardroom can be reserved for meetings, book studies or other gatherings. The café and

bakery has been so successful that Deidra has opened a second branch in nearby Willmar, complete with its own wicker chairs and fireplace. At both locations, after you have enjoyed a dozen brewed coffees, your next 16-ounce espresso drink is free. When you feel the need to re-energize, come to Deidra's Espresso Café & Bakery for a warm and friendly respite from the cares of the day.

120 South Street W, Spicer MN
(320) 796-6765
309 Lakewood Drive, Willmar MN
(320) 214-7007

The Daily Grind Espresso Shop

Eight years ago, two enterprising friends, Randy Abay-Abay and Tracy Jevning, decided to take over a local coffee shop and put their creativity to the test. Their first innovation was to expand the shop to include soups, salads and sandwiches along with the gourmet coffee that had already made the Daily Grind Espresso Shop a fixture in Waseca. Lunch was only the beginning, however. Two years later, the historic First National Bank Building went up for sale. Tracy persuaded her husband, Mike, another creative innovator, to purchase and remodel the building as the new home of the Daily Grind. Mike restored the building's historic exterior, renovated its interior, and as a result, created a

contemporary community gathering place. Occupying the main floor of the old bank building, the Daily Grind now has more than enough room to expand its lunch menu and venture into breakfast. The café's prominent new downtown location makes it a perfect venue for local artists, musicians and authors to display their works. Art lines the walls of the café, while frequent readings and performances are free to the public. Start at the heart of Waseca with a hearty cup or tasty meal from the Daily Grind Espresso Shop.

100 N State Street, Waseca MN
(507) 835-9186

Clay Coyote Gallery

Overlooking the waving grasses of a 30-acre restored prairie is the Clay Coyote Gallery, an amazing find in such a rural spot. An outgrowth of Tom Wirt and Betsy Price's Clay Coyote Pottery showroom, the gallery showcases one-of-a-kind handcrafted works from more than 150 North American artists. You'll see functional and art pottery, decorative and functional wood, contemporary art glass, fabric and leather accessories. Tom and Betsy personally visit national studios, galleries and shows to search out high-quality work for the gallery. The focus is on functionality and fair prices, and Tom and Betsy encourage hands-on browsing. You're sure to establish a lifelong love for the pieces you bring home. "We want you to know the processes and skills that go into making these pieces. Pick them up, feel the balance and experience the difference that handcrafted work makes," Betsy says. Tom and Betsy have been creating their own functional pottery for more than 10 years. Hand-thrown by Tom and hand-fired and glazed by Betsy, each unique piece is safe for oven, microwave and dishwasher use and guaranteed to perform for generations. The Clay Coyote Gallery reflects Tom and Betsy's belief that art belongs in everyday life, not merely glass cases. The prairie setting adds to the appeal of the gallery, and visitors enjoy strolling the trails by the duck ponds or picnicking at Todd Lake. Visit the Clay Coyote Gallery and discover a hidden prairie treasure.

17614 240th Street, Hutchinson MN
(320) 587-2599
www.claycoyote.com

Interior Motives

According to the experts at Interior Motives, there's a step in the design process that comes even before the color samples and sketches. That crucial first step is listening. A staple of downtown New Ulm, Interior Motives offers more than just the latest in premiere home furnishings, lamps and accessories. It offers the ears and 40 years of collective experience of its design team, professionals who pride themselves on helping customers create beautiful spaces to fit their lifestyles. You'll never be pulled in the direction that a salesperson wants you to go. Instead, your ideas set the agenda for the designers, who will guide you through the process of space planning, color coordination and material selection while striving to fall within your budget. The goal is to translate artfully your personal style into a room design that lives for you. Three fine cabinetry lines allow you to create the kitchen of your dreams. Interior Motives also sells C.R. Laine and Sam Moore in its upholstered lines. Both offer a vast assortment of fabric choices. The floor-covering department carries carpets representing all the major mills in addition to many lines of laminates, woods, vinyl and ceramic tile. Find the expertise, resources and creativity you need to create beautiful spaces in your home at Interior Motives.

The Landmark Bistro

The Landmark Bistro is indeed a culinary landmark in the Midwest, offering upscale cuisine in an elegant building. This downtown Marshall restaurant is on the bottom floor of the historic New Atlantic Hotel, built in 1926. Since that time, the building has been a social and cultural center for the city, a position the Landmark has continued to support. That old-time ballroom feel is enhanced by the décor, which includes classic high ceilings, wood floors and brushed-nickel fixtures. Warm colors, specialty linens and table décor help to create a cozy atmosphere. You can watch as your dinner is made in the restaurant's display kitchen. Executive Chef Sarah Longley prides herself on offering an eclectic menu that changes throughout the year, allowing for the finest, freshest seasonal ingredients. You'll find everything from pizza, cooked in the impressive wood stone oven, to an array of thoughtfully balanced and creative entrées. The Landmark maintains an extensive wine list and can help you find the perfect vintage to enjoy with your meal. Make sure to save room for cheesecake and other special dessert offerings from pastry chef Amy Ross. General Manager Cynthia Booke welcomes guests with her warm smile and genuine hospitality, a tell-tale sign of her Southern roots. Relax by the fireplace in the restaurant's lounge as you enjoy one of a variety of martinis or other drinks, as well as a selection of tapas and pizzas from the main menu. For a landmark dining experience, come to the Landmark Bistro.

100 W College Drive, Marshall MN
(507) 337-6600
www.landmarkbistro.com

Veigel's Kaiserhoff Restaurant

Word is out—about the ribs and the authentic German food at Veigel's Kaiserhoff Restaurant. Barbecued ribs, chicken and hamburger steak were the three items on the menu back in 1938 when Don Veigel's parents established the restaurant. Ribs cost 45 cents then, and beer cost a dime. Don started working in the family restaurant at the age of 15 and took over the establishment in 1946, moving it to a dilapidated building that he rebuilt over subsequent years. In 1963, Don expanded the restaurant; two years later he added the bar. The ribs still attract customers to Veigel's, along with good food and great prices. But these days, a visitor is as likely to come for the authentic German dishes as for the ribs. It wasn't until 1991 that Don's wife, Jan, added the German menu that has increased Veigel's popularity and earned *Minnesota Monthly* magazine's recognition as Best German Restaurant. In 2006, Veigel's was honored as New Ulm's business of the year, partly due to the number of visitors it brings to town. Word of mouth continues to be Veigel's strongest advertisement, and after more than 60 years of operation, word is Don plans to keep the restaurant going just as long as possible. Much has changed in New Ulm, but like this City of Charm and Tradition, the Veigel family has held onto its German beginnings. Come to Veigel's Kaiserhoff Restaurant, where family tradition is alive and well.

221 N Minnesota Street, New Ulm MN
(507) 359-2071

The Country Loft

As much as the dolls at the Country Loft enjoy life at this cheery store in downtown New Ulm, they know that they are destined to bring joy to somebody's home. They would love to be cuddled ever-so-gently or be put on a special shelf to be admired. The inventory of collectible cuties at the Country Loft includes heart warmers from Lee Middleton, Betsy McCall and the Ideal Patty Playpal Family of dolls. Family-owned and in business since 1983, The Country Loft offers not only dolls for kids and kids-at-heart but also stocks home décor, fragrances and linens for their mothers. The store is arranged like a home, with different departments representing different rooms, inviting you to wander from one pretty display to the next. You can even dress yourself up with fashionable purses inspired by Fendi, Gucci, Prada and Dior for a fraction of what the originals cost. Don't forget to sample the featured handmade fudge-of-the-month at the candy counter. For every reason and every season, visit the Country Loft.

204 N Minnesota Street, New Ulm MN
(507) 354-8493
www.countryloftdolls.com

Lambrecht's Gifts & Floral Studio

Lambrecht's Gifts & Floral Studio combines gifts, clothing and jewelry as well as collectibles, home accents, seasonal décor and a floral studio in a restored downtown building with 8,000 square feet of display space on two floors. Curt and Donna bought the business in 1983 when it was only 2,500 square feet on one level and they used the upper level as their home. Five years and four kids later, they moved to a real house, acquired the adjoining retail store and created a major shopping destination. At Lambrecht's you will find home accents including lamps, framed prints, clocks, candles and constantly changing seasonal décor. Another 2,000 square feet is dedicated to a clothing boutique filled with affordable fashions, jewelry and accessories. The shop also has 30 running feet of alternative greeting cards, a room full of baby and children's gifts, a Dept 56 village and Snowbabies boutique and four floral designers who are always on-hand to help you with floral and decorating needs. Lambrecht's Gifts & Floral Studio in downtown New Ulm truly has it all.

119 N Minnesota Street, New Ulm MN (507) 233-4350 or (866) 257-2993
www.lambrechtsgifts.net

Mill Pond Mercantile

Mill Pond Mercantile was an artists' co-op in the 1980s. In the mid-1990s, Anita Stulen and Ginny Knaap purchased the business, changed its focus and expanded its product lines. They have outgrown several locations since their first 900-square-foot shop, and in 2003, they built a 5,000 square foot store in downtown New London. You will find such home décor as dishes, rugs, curtains and kitchenware here. The gift possibilities continue with framed prints, candles and greeting cards, plus personal care products and clothing. After 10 years, Anita and Ginny still find new things to talk about every day. Graduations, weddings and grandbabies enrich their lives along with the customers that have become friends over the years. Many of those customers contributed personal recipes to the cookbook published to celebrate Mill Pond Mercantile's 10th anniversary. Some of the recipes highlight the gourmet food products you can find in the store. Come get to know Mill Pond Mercantile's owners and staff and find out for yourself why so many customers become loyal friends.

24 Main Street, New London MN
(320) 354-5557
www.millpondmercantile.com

Heritage Falls Market

Heritage Falls Market owner Becky Carlson grew up in a family with a rich appreciation for Scandinavian arts, crafts and foods. Naturally, many of the gifts at Heritage Falls Market come from Scandinavian countries. Still, Becky and her husband, Todd, are more interested in expressing heritage broadly than in connecting with any one nation. "We try to cross many cultures," says Becky. Todd appreciates German cuckoo clocks, and the assortment found here put on quite a show at the top of the hour. Look for Norwegian sweaters, toys and handmade truffles as well as candles by Colonial and lotions by Thymes. Becky's sister, Naomi Noeldner, has designed a creative line of toddler T-shirts, infant onesies, picture frames and baby gifts for the shop. Swedish cookies, hearty soups and bread mixes are part of the gourmet foods in stock. Russian items honor the child Becky and Todd adopted. You can appeal to just about any gift recipient with a Heritage Falls gift basket, whether it's ready-made or a custom creation. The Carlsons opened their New London shop in 2006. They chose Karen Lindquist as store manager and designer so that they could continue to work in their professions. Becky is a schoolteacher, and Todd is a deputy sheriff. For truly unexpected sundries, come to Heritage Falls Market.

19655 71st Street, New London MN
(320) 354-3291

Weeds & Reeds

Kappy and John Schladweiler bring an interest in recycling vintage items to their New Ulm gift shop Weeds & Reeds. Even their location in a quaint corner building speaks to their interest in borrowing from the past. The building, built as a gasoline station in 1926, is a replica of a Dutch windmill and one of only two remaining buildings in a set of 10 special buildings designed by the American Artstone Company and made of rainbow Artstone cast block. The building is on the National and New Ulm Register of Historic Places. On its way to becoming Weeds & Reeds, the building saw several changes in ownership and use. It went from a Pure to a Wood River brand gasoline station, then back to Pure before it stopped selling gas in 1963. The building was given over to personal use by subsequent owners and then sat empty for a number of years until Kappy and John purchased it 1995. They undertook a full restoration of the building and soon opened Weeds & Reeds, an eclectic gift shop with an espresso bar. The store carries children's books and toys as well as a charming blend of new, vintage and antique gifts. In the spirit of borrowing from the past, Kappy has found uses for 300 pounds of vintage buttons that John brought home from an auction. *Country Living* magazine featured her buttons, which she fashions into magnets, cards and other gifts. If an old quilt has a hole in it, she'll find another way to recycle its remains. It's just in her nature. Stop by Weeds & Reeds and see what comes of honoring old things.

500 N Broadway, New Ulm MN
(507) 359-1147

Arneson Snyder Drug

Arneson Snyder Drug has been serving the prescription and healthcare needs of the community since 1905. Celebrating its 100th anniversary in 2005, it is the oldest drugstore in Montevideo and the oldest business continuously owned by one family in the city. Dave Arneson represents the third generation of pharmacists and owners of Arneson's to operate the store. Dave and his wife, Pam, not only work together in the pharmacy but also work together to seek unusual pieces for the giftware department. Along with their talented and dedicated staff, they help create a warm and welcoming place for everyday, every season and every occasion. The Arnesons invite you to come and stroll through the intriguing giftware area, which features Terry Redlin, Department 56, Precious Moments, Hallmark, various collectibles and many other gift lines. If you have a passion for fragrance, let the candle department capture you with its true-to-life fragrances. Select from Yankee Candle, Root or Beanpod candles made from soybeans grown by American farmers. Whether you're out and about for a special occasion, a lazy afternoon or a weekend shopping trip with the girls, let Arneson Snyder Drug be your destination. David, Pamela and the entire staff welcome you to Montevideo and invite you to visit the store.

1234 E Highway 7, Montevideo MN
(320) 269-6412

Clara City Drug & Gift

The peaceful town of Clara City has two parks, a glowing reputation and a wonderful pharmacy and gift store. The soothing music and solid oak antique pharmacy display cabinets and shelves at Clara City Drug & Gift create a serene atmosphere. It's easy to linger as you browse through the fascinating assortment of decorative and useful gifts. The shop has an impressive selection of Terry Redlin's tender portraits of the heartland. Woodwick candles have wooden wicks that produce a clean, long-lasting burn and the romantic sound of a crackling fire, combined with premium fragrances. Collectors of Christmas Village items will find them here, and there is a large assemblage of crystal and decorative pottery. For those cold Midwest winters, stock up on some cheerful afghans. If you're looking for jewelry, you'll find pieces fashioned from genuine Black Hills Gold. Wrought iron frames and other home accessories make it easy to spruce up your dwelling. You can fill your prescriptions in the pharmacy, so sink into one of the two stuffed chairs while you wait. Mike and Nancy Fritz opened the shop in 1999 to provide the community with pharmacy services, a full line of gift items and an expert picture-framing service. For matters practical and whimsical, visit Clara City Drug & Gift.

110 N Main Street, Clara City MN
(320) 847-2419

Louie's Toy Box

Scale models can become a lifelong hobby or the beginning of a child's future career. At Louie's Toy Box in Mankato, owners Louis Goettl and his wife, Donna, try to keep collectors up to date with their collections, but they especially love using scale models of farm equipment to interest farm children in the farming business. Louie's carries equipment miniatures from such manufacturers as Ertl, Scale Models and Spec Cast. Adult collectors and children take pleasure in these tiny replicas. Many little farmers, as well as their dads, have used 1/64-scale Standi toys to recreate scenes from their own farms. Louie's stocks the precision series, shelf models and vintage pieces, including many hard-to-find items. Need a John Deere hay wagon or corn planter with realistic moving parts? Does an International utility trailer sound appealing? If your preference is race cars, Louie's standing as a certified dealer for NASCAR scale models opens possibilities for all sorts of special finds. Louie's also carries Duck House dolls. Louis enjoys restoring pedal tractors, which could inspire fond memories of riding around in these miniature versions of dad's tractor. Those who can't visit Louis in person can get a feel for his collection at Louie's Toy Box store on eBay. For models that inspire dreams in the young and the old, visit Louie's Toy Box.

1400 Madison East Center, Suite 312, Mankato MN
(507) 340-5747 or (507) 257-3149
http://stores.ebay.com/louies-toy-box

The Valley Troll

The Valley Troll is an attractive Scandinavian gift shop set in a charming red house. Norwegian, Swedish, Danish, Icelandic and Finnish flags wave festively from the eaves. It's a great place to browse, soak up the rich heritage and enjoy a cup of Scandinavian coffee on the front deck. Owned by Norwegian Ann Stensrud, the store offers a large selection of authentic Nordic gifts, including coveted brand-name products such as Dale of Norway and Oda sweaters, Carl Larsson prints, Porsgrund dinnerware and flatware by Fjord Design. Its centerpiece is an enchanting collection of troll dolls, popular with young and old alike. Trolls, which originated in Scandinavian mythology, are a staple of Scandinavian popular culture. The Valley Troll also features Trollbeads, hand-modeled charm beads in shapes referring to mythology, history and local flora and fauna. Trollbeads are Danish collectibles in a tradition much like French charm bracelets, and are sure to ignite a long-lasting enthusiasm. The Valley Troll celebrates Norwegian Independence Day, *Syttende Mai,* in May, with traditional goodies such as lefse, *rommegrot*, and sweet soup for the tasting. Visit The Valley Troll to discover what the Nordic lands have to offer.

1222 Granite Street, Granite Falls MN
(320) 564-4041
www.valleytroll.com

Past & Present Antiques and Gifts

On North State Street in Waseca, the cheerful red-and-brick face of Past & Present Antiques and Gifts beckons to strollers-by with its spread of potted flowers, string lights and wicker furniture. Over the past 10 years, Past & Present has become a destination for gift and home accent shoppers in southeastern Minnesota. Past & Present's large variety of gifts and seasonal items is continually changing. With home accents that include furniture and glassware, linens and lampshades, you'll find plenty of unusual items to give your home that special touch. Indulge yourself in accessories such as candles, silk florals and garden décor to bring beauty into every corner. Once an old gasoline station, the shop has been attractively renovated and expanded to nearly 5,000 square feet while maintaining its quaint historic flavor. As you wander through the many rooms filled with old and new treasures, you may spot the original gas pump in the corner, or an old-fashioned 1948 Plymouth raised up on its original hoist and surrounded by gifts. Owners Sandi and Randi Prange take pleasure in what they do, and it shows in the tasteful arrangement of their space and their assortment of merchandise. Stroll through Past & Present Antiques and Gifts and find something delightful in every season.

1101 N State Street, Waseca MN
(507) 835-4000

Edelweiss Flower Haus

Edelweiss Flower Haus has the perfect way to bring cheer to anyone's day. From anniversary to new baby, this full-service florist in New Ulm will create a fresh arrangement to mark any occasion. Weddings are a specialty at Edelweiss, which offers an entire gallery of wedding flowers and bouquets for your consideration. The staff enjoys working one-on-one with brides-to-be and incorporating personal concepts into the designs. Bring color samples of your attendant's dresses to your consultation and let the staff's expertise go to work for you. In addition to its large inventory of fresh flowers, tropicals and plants, Edelweiss offers dish gardens and silk arrangements. Order a balloon bouquet to make someone smile. This is not only a flower shop. Edelweiss also carries a gift line of home accessories such as candles, lamps and wall art. The courtyard, which is brimming with flowers and shrubs, opens the first weekend in May with a large variety of accessories out of the past. Come see the antique furniture and restored shabby chic items made by local craftsmen. A visit to Edelweiss is a one-of-a-kind experience.

304 N Minnesota Street, New Ulm MN
(507) 354-2222
www.edelweissflowerhaus.com

The Village Shop

The minute you step in the door of the Village Shop in downtown Hutchinson, a complete sensory experience washes over you. The shop is decked floor to ceiling with home décor and gift items ranging from books to toys, linens to lamps. The floors are strewn with decorative rugs and the beams of the ceiling are loaded with dried flowers and other hanging treasures. Wedding invitations and supplies are an important part of the inventory. An appealing selection of kitchen items is a particular draw for local customers. With something new to look at every turn, you're guaranteed to linger in the Village Shop. Owner Joanne Willmert creates a soothing, atmospheric shopping experience in her store with aromatic candles and soft music—CDs are on sale, too. A mural of moon and stars on the back wall adds space to the crowded room. The Village Shop has been a favorite shopping spot in Hutchinson for more than 35 years. Visit yourself to find out why.

114 Main Street, Hutchinson MN
(320) 587-2727

Wit's End Antiques

In the classic river town of Henderson you can catch a glimpse of the 1870s while browsing the completely restored historic district. In keeping with the era, Wit's End Antiques is comfortably set in the beautiful Opera House Saloon building on Main Street. Here, you will find a charming shopping experience with period furniture in living room arrangements. The scene is completed with fine linens and tableware on display. Country chic and primitives mingle in other rooms, showcasing the charm of rural homes and farms of the past. Owner Patty Lathrop takes pride in presenting quality antiques from a select group of dealers in attractive home-like settings. "It does not look like most antique stores. We like nice things and show them in an organized manner pleasing to the customer who wants to browse and enjoy themselves." Whether your passion is antique furniture, vintage pottery, woodenware, linens or stained glass, you'll find much to admire at Wit's End Antiques. It's open Wednesday through Sunday year-round; be sure to call for regular and winter hours or to make an appointment.

503 Main Street, Henderson MN
(507) 248-9696

Morgan Creek Vineyards

Morgan Creek Vineyards is the result of a century-long family tradition, and produces wines grown with the love and care that only the Marti family can provide. The winery is set on a sunny south-facing hillside overlooking 10 acres. A babbling tributary of the Minnesota River winds its way along the property. Morgan Creek features the state's only underground winery and is proud to provide its patrons with a one-of-a-kind tasting room. Patrons can sample the superb selection of wines in a genuine earth cellar with an average year-round temperature of 51 degrees Fahrenheit. The Marti family focuses on German, French and Minnesota cold-hardy varietals, allowing them to address each wine's unique attributes and quality. One wine they're known for is Bacchanal, a red blend made from Minnesota-grown St. Croix and Marechal Foch grapes. Connoisseurs can sample Bacchanal and other seasonal favorites at one of the winery's several special events, which include the Spring Bacchus Festival, Summer German Winefest and the popular Christmas Candlelight Winetasting. Visitors can book a stay at one of the charming nearby bed and breakfasts to stretch a wine-tasting adventure over several days. Wine enthusiasts are certain to enjoy the Marti family's wine when they visit Morgan Creek Vineyards.

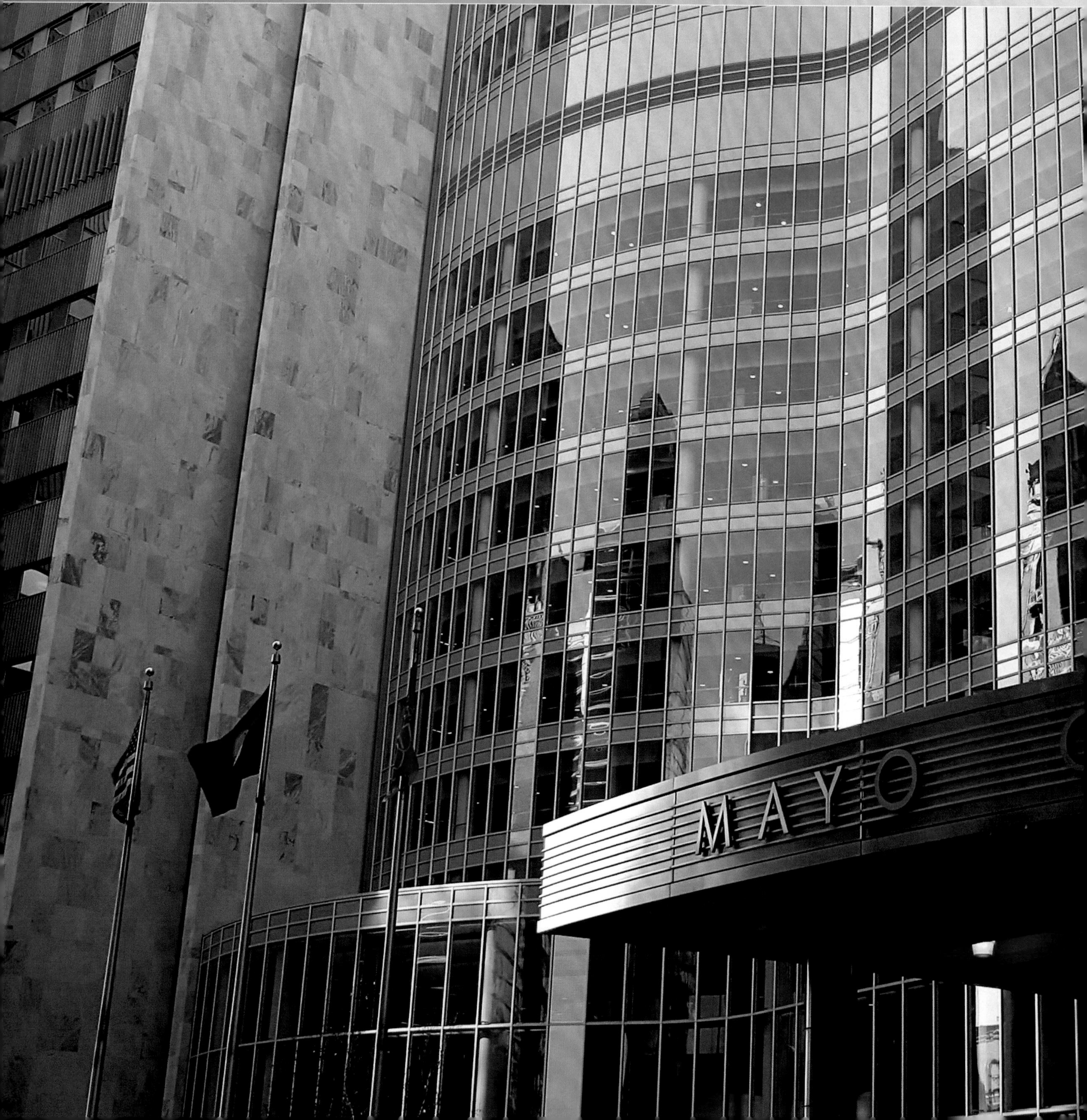
MAYO

The Rochester Skyline reflected in the
windows of the Mayo Clinic's Gonda building
Photo by Michael Hicks

Southeast Minneosta

Berwood Hill Inn

High on a bluff overlooking the Root River Valley sits the Berwood Hill Inn, a magnificent refurbished 1873 Victorian country home. This multiple-award-winning bed-and-breakfast has earned mentions in countless travel and living magazines for its artful decor, fabulous flower gardens and world-class service. Owner Fran Scibora grew up in the house, which her grandparents purchased in 1936, and opened it to the public in 1998. Her artistic hand is in every aspect of the business, from the refurbishing of the inn's five bedrooms, each with its own character, to the turndown service, which leaves homemade chocolates on the pillows. Fran takes obvious pleasure in rolling out the red carpet for her guests and sharing all that Berwood Hill has to offer. A first-rate culinary staff serves Berwood Hill Inn's famous five-course breakfast, in addition to candlelight dinners, afternoon teas and gourmet chocolate tastings by request. A licensed massage therapist and a licensed esthetician, available through the inn, offer personalized spa services and therapies. The 200-acre property at Berwood Hill includes acres of flower gardens and a web of woodland footpaths. From the wraparound porch, guests can look down on breathtaking views of the valley, including farmland and wildlife. *Better Homes and Gardens* actually filmed an episode on the front lawn. *Arrington's Bed & Breakfast Journal* named the inn Best Bed and Breakfast in the Midwest. *Inn Traveler* named it a Best Holiday Getaway. Let Berwood Hill Inn welcome you to an unforgettable retreat.

State Route 16, Lanesboro MN
(800) 803-6748
www.berwood.com

The Kahler Grand Hotel and the International Hotel

It all began in the early 1900s with the vision of two men, Dr. William Worrall Mayo and John Henry Kahler. Dr. Mayo and the congregation of the Sisters of St. Francis recognized a need for medical services after a tornado destroyed much of Rochester, and so they opened St. Mary's Hospital. Not long after, Kahler arrived and opened his first hotel, the Cook House, to accommodate the growing needs of patients and guests. With word spreading that St. Mary's Hospital and Mayo Clinic were one of the world's elite medical facilities, Kahler built the Kahler Grand Hotel in 1921. Today, the Kahler Grand welcomes guests from around the world, while providing specialty rates and Mayo-centric amenities. A Right Choice menu is created by Mayo dietitians and Kahler chefs. A pharmacy delivers prescriptions to rooms, and a full-service spa and salon is available. The Kahler Grand features 708 guest rooms, a historic Victorian design and wireless Internet access throughout. It is an all-in-one building with an underground shopping complex offering access to everything a guest needs, including many dining options, specialty shops, clothing and accessory stores, boutiques and services. Since opening as the penthouse of the Kahler Grand in 2006, the International Hotel has hosted large entourages from the Middle East, not to mention CEOs and rock stars. The 25-room VIP floor features upscale suites, in-room executive desks and office equipment, personal escort check-in, international cuisine and Ask Mayo buttons on in-room phones for direct access to Mayo. For more information about the Kahler Grand and International Hotel, visit the website.

20 SW 2nd Avenue, Rochester MN
(507) 280-6200 or (800) 533-1655
www.kahler.com

Treasure Island Resort & Casino

Nestled among the scenic bluffs of the Mississippi River Valley, Treasure Island Resort & Casino is the Midwest's tropical getaway. Treasure Island offers guests award-winning gaming, top-notch accommodations, distinct dining experiences and nationally acclaimed entertainment in a variety of venues. The casino features 2,500 slots, 44 table games, a 10-table poker room and a 550-seat high-stakes bingo hall. The luxurious poker room, dressed in rich woods and custom copper ceiling tiles, offers Texas Hold 'Em, 7-Card Stud and Omaha Hi-Lo. After gaming, guests can relax in Treasure Island's 250-room hotel that has a variety of standard, extended-stay and whirlpool suites. The hotel's year-round swimming pool is set in a lush rain forest environment with exotic flowers and a beautiful cascading waterfall. For the more adventurous visitors, Treasure Island also features a well-equipped, 95-site RV park and a 137-slip marina. In addition, the casino offers a variety of restaurant options, from the hearty home-style entrées of Java's Restaurant to the international selections at Tradewinds Buffet, which are reminiscent of a Caribbean marketplace. For an exceptional dining or sightseeing experience, guests can board *Spirit of the Water*, the resort's elegant 125-passenger cruise yacht that reveals the true beauty and allure of the mighty Mississippi. Treasure Island boasts a variety of entertainment venues with international and national acts. Indigo Bay Showroom features headlining entertainment while Emerald Bay and the posh, upscale Parlay Lounge host free live bands that guests can enjoy while sipping on a signature cocktail or playing their favorite slot machine. There is something for everyone at the tropical paradise set in the middle of Minnesota—Treasure Island Resort & Casino.

5734 Sturgeon Lake Road, Welch MN
(800) 222-7077
www.treasureislandcasino.com

Cedar Valley Resort

Located on 30 acres in the lush Root River Valley, Cedar Valley Resort is a luxurious destination for those looking for outdoor fun and spacious, private accommodations. Families enjoy coming together here, and group retreats are popular. Located near Lanesboro, the resort's large cabins, built since 2001, are designed to deliver rustic charm and modern convenience. Guests enjoy a choice of seven deluxe cabins in varying sizes, ranging from a three-bedroom, 1,400-square-foot model to one with eight bedrooms that can hold 40 guests. Each cabin is completely outfitted with a fully equipped kitchen, including all the cooking utensils you could need. There's plenty to do, with facilities for basketball, volleyball and croquet, plus many green places for kids to romp. If you're looking for an outdoor adventure, Cedar Valley Resort is ideally situated along the Root River. The outfitters at the resort can equip you with bicycles, canoes or kayaks for exploring the river and its surroundings. If you're looking to hook the big one, day floats and fly fishing guides are available to assist you. Those looking for an on-land outing can hike, bike or rollerblade on the Root River Trail, rated the number one trail in Minnesota. You'll find the gifts and groceries you need at the resort's retail store. Plan a getaway for a family, reunion or retreat at Cedar Valley Resort.

905 Bench Street, Whalan MN
(507) 467-9000
www.cedarvalleyresort.com

Golden Lantern Inn

If lounging on the back porch surrounded by a luscious garden and the warmth of an outdoor fireplace sounds like a dream, then wake up and enjoy the reality. The Golden Lantern Inn, filled with 7,000 square feet of master craftsmanship, is customized with walnut, birch, maple and oak. Originally built by J.R. Sweazy, the president of Red Wing Shoes, this 1934 home was transformed in 2004 by new owners Gary and Pat McKenna. Gary is the master gardener and chef—the sprawling gardens and home cooking are major attractions for the guests. The inn's rooms are all unique. Most are suites. All have private baths, fireplaces and/or whirlpools or a porch. Morning coffee or tea is served early, followed by a full breakfast in the dining room, your room or in the garden area. There are even nightly bonfires complete with s'mores. With three patios, many sitting areas, a library and a stone porch facing the gardens, amenities are aplenty. For business retreats, weddings, family getaways or second honeymoons, the Golden Lantern Inn is the perfect place to relax. Only a few blocks away you'll find more dining options, plus shopping and live entertainment. Activities nearby include the Cannon Valley Trail, Mississippi river parks, skiing and four championship golf courses. From the chocolate cookies fresh from the oven as you arrive, to the carefully maintained gardens, the Golden Lantern Inn is the ultimate bed and breakfast experience.

721 East Avenue, Red Wing MN
(651) 388-3315 or (888) 288-3315
www.goldenlantern.com

Historic Scanlan House Bed & Breakfast

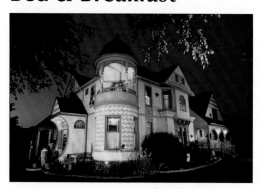

The Historic Scanlan House Bed & Breakfast was recently recognized again as one of the Top 10 Places to Wake Up in the State of Minnesota. For 21 years, the Mensing family has hired friendly staff members who ensure the Queen Anne Victorian-era mansion remains both homey and luxurious. The house was built in 1889 by Michael Scanlan, a founder of Lanesboro and a local banker. It was the first in town to boast indoor plumbing and electricity. It has now been completely renovated. No detail was overlooked, including all the original woodwork, stained glass windows and a rare stamped leather paneling in the main dining room. Period antiques and fine linens fill every romantic room or suite. Each has a fireplace, a whirlpool tub for two or both. Guests can relax and enjoy the sitting parlor, library or one of the outside patios. An array of refreshments is available 24 hours a day. Wireless Internet is also available. You'll wake to a nationally recognized gourmet multi-course breakfast, which even includes dessert. Stroll through Victorian flower gardens or play croquet on the front lawn. For the outdoor enthusiast, biking, golfing, canoeing, kayaking or tubing are popular. Explore historic downtown Lanesboro. Attend live theater or perhaps take a horse-drawn carriage ride. The local winery is outstanding and the Amish tours are fun and educational. Also, inquire about the new gift certificate program. For unsurpassed hospitality in an authentic, old-fashioned setting, visit the Historic Scanlan House Bed & Breakfast.

708 Parkway Avenue S, Lanesboro MN
(507) 467-2158 or (800) 944-2158
www.scanlanhouse.com

The Inn at Sacred Clay Farm Bed & Breakfast

A retreat from the hectic pace of everyday life is what you'll find at the Inn at Sacred Clay Farm Bed & Breakfast. Sandy and Fred Kiel afford their guests both comfortable and memorable accommodations and services. Situated on 100 acres of pastoral land, the inn offers breathtaking views of the local countryside and the gorgeous adjoining gardens. For active naturalists, the property includes groomed walking trails and a cold trout stream. The inn itself has an extraordinary post-and-beam structure. Exquisite artwork, rugs and accessories adorn the lush interior. Arts and crafts provide an earthy international ambience. Indoor types will delight in a turret room for reading and games, a mediation room and a workout room. Pleasant sitting areas overlook the Great Room. Each of the five guest rooms holds a queen-size bed, and some feature old-fashioned gas stoves and whirlpool tubs. Perhaps the greatest benefit for those truly trying to get away is what's missing—you won't find televisions, computer hookups or telephones. You can't get further away than that, no matter how far you travel. The organic, locally grown foods and Fair Trade teas and coffees offered by the Kiels accentuate their desire for good health as well as luxury. Historic Lanesboro, known as one of the best small towns in the country for art, lies just two miles away. When you are ready to retreat from everyday cares, pay a visit to the Inn at Sacred Clay Farm.

23234 Grosbeak Road, Lanesboro MN
(507) 467-9600 or (866) 326-8618
www.sacredclayfarmbandb.com

Moondance Inn Bed & Breakfast

From the grand staircase and gilded ceiling of the lobby to the 1905 light fixtures and Steuben chandeliers, the Moondance Inn Bed & Breakfast is a unique venue for weddings and receptions or a romantic vacation getaway. Owners Chris Brown Mahoney and Mike Waulk looked at property for two years before they found the A. B. Hawley House in Red Wing and knew they'd discovered a treasure. Built in 1874 by a local physician, the Moondance Inn is on the National Register of Historic Places and exudes the elegance of an earlier era. Spend a night in one of the five beautifully appointed bedrooms and in the morning you can choose to enjoy a continental breakfast with a home baked goody in your room, or a sumptuous full breakfast in the dining room. The Moondance Inn provides a beautiful setting for a company retreat or business seminar. The entire third floor is a rustic meeting room, full of charm and character. Limestone block walls 18 inches thick guarantee an event free from outside distractions. The Moondance Inn is surrounded by gardens complete with fountains and paths for walking, or take a stroll through the historic district of Red Wing to the downtown shops and the parks along the Mississippi River. An hour's drive from the Twin Cities, the Moondance Inn Bed & Breakfast is an experience that shouldn't be missed.

1105 W 4th Street, Red Wing MN
(651) 388-8145 or (866) 388-8145
info@moondanceinn.com
www.moondanceinn.com

St. James Hotel

Experience Victorian warmth and charm coupled with modern-day conveniences at the classic St. James Hotel. A member of Historic Hotels of America, this 1875 Minnesota landmark is nestled along the banks of the Mississippi River in the heart of downtown Red Wing. Each of its 61 rooms is uniquely decorated with period furnishings and named for an historic riverboat. The hotel has kept pace with contemporary amenities, but offers a chance to rejuvenate and enjoy a slower pace. A complete restoration of the Italianate structure in 1977 and succeeding renovations have continued to provide the highest standards of comfort and convenience. Designed for a wide range of formal, business and casual uses, the St. James Hotel offers five dining options ranging from the light and airy Veranda Café, through the elegant Port Restaurant, to the top-level Summit, which accommodates groups up to 300 and offers spectacular views of the Mississippi River. The staff prides itself on its friendliness and commitment to personalized service and is dedicated to guaranteeing each guest a memorable experience. Red Wing is famous for Red Wing Shoes and Red Wing Pottery and Stoneware, but offers much more to visitors. The vibrant downtown business district features shops, restaurants and recreational opportunities such as the renowned Cannon Valley Trail. Two wineries and several fine golf courses are nearby. Couples and individuals of all ages will enjoy the comfortable accommodations, charming amenities, and retreat experience of the elegant St. James Hotel.

406 Main Street, Red Wing MN (800) 252-1875
www.st-james-hotel.com

Stone Mill Suites

Stone Mill Suites features 10 plush and imaginatively themed rooms in a captivating 19th century stone building set in the heart of legendary Lanesboro, a quaint village in the scenic Bluff Country of southeastern Minnesota. The building, constructed from limestone taken from the area's bluffs, once served as a feed mill. In 1999, owners Randy and Colleen Mortimer opened it as a historic inn with rooms that reflect the building's history and the undeniable charm of the area. Today, the Stone Mill pampers guests with an attractive blend of homespun charm and modern day convenience. Children are welcome. The Mortimers' renovation retained the wood ceilings and pipe stair railings while adding such modern amenities as Internet access, televisions, microwaves and refrigerators. Some rooms feature iron-claw fireplaces, double whirlpool baths and lofts. The Mortimers' delectable Continental breakfast may include English muffins, baked goods from Lanesboro Pastries or French toast topped with strawberries, blueberries and whipped cream. With an event center that can accommodate weddings, rehearsal dinners, family reunions and meetings, the Mortimers are well prepared to make your experience fun and memorable. You can count on the service and attention to detail at Stone Mill Suites, an inn that has earned a select status as a member of Better Bed and Breakfast Inns. Come create a new tradition for yourself and your loved ones with a visit to Stone Mill Suites.

100 Beacon Street E, Lanesboro MN
(866) 897-8663 or (507) 46-STONE (467-8663)
www.stonemillsuites.com

Windom Park
Bed & Breakfast

Windom Park Bed & Breakfast is a handsome Colonial Revival structure built in 1900 and located in an area of historic homes surrounding Windom Park, a Victorian-style village green. When you enter, the resident pups, Catalina, Spirit and Alouette, will greet you. Windom Park Bed & Breakfast offers a choice of six accommodations, all with private baths. You'll find three rooms, two deluxe lofts and a luxurious suite. The rooms include Ligia's Nook, furnished with two comfortable twin-sized beds, and Kira's Corner, which features a four-poster. Brett's English Garden Room provides a king-sized bed and has views of the side garden and the park. Jack and Michael's Coach House Lofts offer the ultimate in privacy and amenities, including fireplaces and two-person Jacuzzis. Jamie's Library Suite is reminiscent of a vintage library with its Oriental rug, four-poster bed, wicker chairs and adjoining sitting room. In the morning, sit down to a delicious, five-course breakfast served in the dining room. You can relax in the Benjamin Arthur Great Room or in Ilse's parlor. The inn also offers wireless Internet and access to a fax machine, copier and printer. Your hosts are Karen and Craig Groth. Their dream of owning a bed-and-breakfast began on their 1972 honeymoon when they stayed at a bed-and-breakfast in London. Craig is a retired Chicago police detective and Karen is a flight attendant. Share Craig and Karen's home and their dream while you unwind at Windom Park Bed & Breakfast.

369 W Broadway, Winona MN
(507) 457-9515 or (866) 737-1719
www.windompark.com

Meadows Inn Bed & Breakfast

A warm and inviting welcome awaits you at the Meadows Inn Bed & Breakfast. Your gracious hosts, Marie and Doug, provide you with a quiet, peaceful opportunity to relax and renew. This bed-and-breakfast feels like a European manor house and makes an ideal home base for a stay in the historic bluff country of southeastern Minnesota. Before the couple owned Meadows Inn, Marie once visited it and fell in love with the beautiful house and location. When the inn became available in 1999, she and Doug, who are natives of the area, purchased it. The inn offers five upstairs guest rooms, each with its own luxurious style. Regardless of which room you pick, you're certain to enjoy the comfortable beds and fine linens. Each morning, Marie and Doug deliver freshly ground coffee and snacks to the upstairs parlor, so early birds can relax in comfort while awaiting the highly acclaimed multi-course breakfast, which may be either inside our outside depending on the weather. Snacks and beverages await guests in the late afternoon. The brick patio is a favorite dining spot during the virtually mosquito-free summer months. Meadows Inn is a birdwatcher's paradise, so birding books and binoculars are provided for guests. *Travel + Leisure Magazine* praised this inn, saying, "Just outside town, the Meadows Inn is a little far from the trail for cyclists, but worth the extra mileage." For elegance surrounded by natural beauty, visit the Meadows Inn Bed & Breakfast.

900 Pine Meadows Lane, Rushford MN
(507) 864-2378
www.meadowsinn.com

Hillcrest Hide-Away

Guests at the Hillcrest Hide-Away wake up in the morning to the smell of fresh-baked bread delivered to their door. It's that kind of personal attention that makes this Lanesboro bed-and-breakfast an ideal destination. Owners Marv and Carol Eggert had dreamed of owning a bed-and-breakfast for years. That dream came true in 2004 with the discovery of this beautiful Craftsman-style home. Hillcrest Hide-Away offers two rooms and two suites, each with its own bathroom. The Joy Suite, with its queen-size bed and double-sized futon, is ideal for guests with limited mobility. The Harmony Suite offers beds in two separate areas, which appeals to small groups. The spacious, pink Peace Room is an ideal accommodation for sitting back and enjoying a good book from the Eggerts' library. The Hope Room, with a king-size bed and queen-size sofa bed, features a private patio. In addition to fresh-baked bread in the morning, guests receive a hearty breakfast with fresh fruit (in season) and a main entrée. Hillcrest Hide-Away is just four blocks from the Root River State Trail and Lanesboro's main street. Guests appreciate the views of the green Root River Valley and the quiet neighborhood. Hillcrest Hide-Away offers discounts for those who recommend the bed and breakfast to others as well as a discount for members of the clergy. For tasteful surroundings with a personal touch, come to Hillcrest Hide-Away.

404 Hillcrest Street E, Lanesboro MN
(507) 467-3079 or (800) 697-9902
www.hillcresthideaway.com

The Barteau House Bed & Breakfast

When guests call the Barteau House Bed & Breakfast a "happy house," owners Scott and Kim Jensen couldn't be more pleas picturesque Zumbrota estate has been restored and filled with pleasures from another, less-hurried era. The 1895 home featu: Anne styling in such architectural details as a wraparound porch, tile fireplaces and leaded glass windows. The restoration h an award from the Preservation Alliance of Minnesota, and the inn as a whole has received multiple recognitions from *Arring Traveler.* The four guest rooms feature whirlpool tubs, antique furnishings and Victorian parlor stoves. Modern delights inclu conditioning, wireless Internet access, and CD players with CDs. Guests enjoy a hearty candlelight breakfast, a bottomless s cookies in the treats cupboard and opportunities for relaxed conversation. The four-acre property includes walking paths, a f gardens. Recently, the Jensens opened the Gathering Place Retreat Center on their property. The updated masonry barn, ou tables and chairs, is a great spot for family gatherings, retreats and group get-togethers for scrapbooking or crafting. Relaxati the moment you glimpse the house from the long driveway. Discover happiness with a visit to the Barteau House Bed & Brea

Minnesota Equestrian Center

Offering breeding services, champion-bred horses and some of the most advanced riding facilities in the Midwest, Minnesota Equestrian Center is a horse fancier's delight. After years of showing, training and breeding paint horses, owners Jason and Jessie Stender opened the center in 2003. Located on three acres, the center offers an impressive array of facilities under one roof, including more than 300 stalls and a fully heated show facility with electrical hookups. A large indoor show ring and warm up area complete the facilities, which are used for many equine events throughout the year. These include Arabian, Pinto and Quarter horse shows and dressage events. Most of these events are free of charge, with concessions available. The center is open to the general public during these special events. Jason and Jessie also offer breeding services. Three of the center's champion stallions have sired offspring that have scored high in show events. Broodmares and foals are also for sale. Whether you're looking for a show horse or just the riding-around kind, you'll find it here. For advanced riding facilities or a new horse, trot on down to Minnesota Equestrian Center.

24621 Gilmore Valley Road, Winona MN
(507) 452-5600
www.minnesotaequestrian.com

Rockie Hill Bison

On the bluffs overlooking Winona, the buffalo roam on the Rockie Hill Bison farm. You can take a wagon ride through the sprawling herd of 100 wooly giants that grazes on the 80 acres. You'll want to have your camera ready when these mighty creatures look up to see who's coming. Your vantage point on the farm also affords fantastic views of Winona, with the Mississippi River and Wisconsin as backdrop. The herd evokes strong emotions in all who come to see it, because the buffalo, or bison, symbolize both majesty and tragedy. A fascination with the animal's role in American history was a major factor in Dave and Gail Griffin's decision to start a herd in 1992. They also realized that the terrain of the farm was better suited to raising livestock than harvesting crops, and they liked the self-care nature of the buffalo. Beyond great flavor, buffalo meat contains more protein and nutrients with less fat than traditional meats. Rockie Hill sells buffalo steaks, roasts, burger and sausages. Dave and Gail follow the code of ethics of the National and Minnesota Buffalo Associations, which dictates that the animals never receive growth hormones or consume animal by-products. Offspring from the herd have won recognition at shows in Iowa, Minnesota and Wisconsin. Climb aboard the wagon and ride out to see the herd at Rockie Hill Bison.

22627 Buffalo Ridge Road, Winona MN
(507) 452-8951

Winona County Historical Society

The history of life in Winona County is in good hands at the Winona County Historical Society, which owns three thriving properties—the Armory Museum, the Bunnell House and the Arches Museum of Pioneer Life. At the Armory Museum, visitors experience the award-winning children's exhibit, *Walking through Time*, plus many other interpretive exhibits. The museum's other highlights include a large Native American collection, a timeline of Winona County history from the prehistoric era to the present and a large collection of vehicles. The Bunnell House, built by Winona's first non-native inhabitant, Willard Bunnell, is a remarkably well-preserved 1850s Gothic-style home. It offers seasonal guided tours during the summer months and is located on Highway 61 in Homer. The Arches Museum of Pioneer Life offers visitors a glimpse into what life was like for the early pioneers of Winona County. Located between Stockton and Lewiston on Highway 14, the museum features a schoolhouse, barn, log cabin and antique farm machinery in stunning surroundings. It is open during the summer months. The Winona County Historical Society holds many special events throughout the year, such as the Chocolate, Shakespeare & Champagne event in June, the Heritage Fair in September, Voices From the Past: Woodlawn Cemetery Discovery Walk in October, and the Christmas Candlelight House Tour in December.

160 Johnson Street, Winona MN
(507) 454-2723
www.winonahistory.org

Crossings at Carnegie

"If your definition of recreation includes freeing the spirit, energizing your body and stretching your mind, then Crossings is the place for you," says owner Marie Marvin, who opened Crossings in Zumbrota's former Carnegie Library building five years ago. The gallery space is home to 12 annual art exhibits. For further inspiration, you can try one of Crossings' many classes and workshops, which range from painting, sculpture and pottery to writing, Spanish and yoga. Kids enjoy special classes and art camps just for them. Folks who have discovered the musical concert series appreciate the excellent acoustics and intimate venue showcasing local and international talent. Styles are as diverse as classical, folk and jazz. Plays and lectures also take place on this stage. The gift shop is a creative outpouring of one-of-a-kind crafts. Visitors delight in sarongs, glass garden balls and music from around the world. Handmade soaps,

wooden boxes and glass beads join mirrors, candles and tiles. Just about everybody who visits Crossings meets the official greeter, Marie's dog Biscuit. Together, they set about "enriching the lives of all who enter our doors," says Marie, who seeks as many ways as possible of "connecting people with the process of creating." Celebrate creativity with a visit to Crossings at Carnegie.

320 East Avenue, Zumbrota MN
(507) 732-7616
www.crossingsatcarnegie.com

Commonweal Theatre Company

The Commonweal Theatre Company in Lanesboro is a nonprofit theater group that has been dedicated to delighting and challenging the people of Minnesota's Bluff Country since 1989. Executive Director Hal Cropp is proud to be a part of the only theater company in North America that makes an annual commitment to producing the plays of Norway's greatest playwright, Henrik Ibsen. You'll also see contemporary and world premiere performances as well as classics by George Bernard Shaw, Charles Dickens and Shakespeare. Commonweal wants to make theater accessible to everyone by offering plays at reasonable prices. It provides specially priced matinees, half-price previews and discounts for students and groups. Season

ticket holders save more than half of the regular ticket price. Commonweal's theatrical company is a community of highly trained artists who work together to hone their craft, celebrate diversity and promote artistic integrity through collaboration. The company seeks to make the world more compassionate by sharing soulful stories with the audience. It invites you to share in the memories only live theater can offer by visiting the Commonweal Theatre.

208 Parkway Avenue N, Lanesboro MN
(507) 467-2525 or (800) 657-7025
www.commonwealtheatre.org

Theatre du Mississippi

Music fans in and around Winona can't wait to find out who is coming each year to Theatre du Mississippi. The venue is a favorite stop for some of the hottest acts on the contemporary blues and folk scene. The setting is more intimate than at the big arenas, and the acoustics inside this historic 1907 Masonic theater are sparkling. Theatre du Mississippi is also the place to catch an occasional play. During summer months, it opens its collection of antique scenic drops to the public. One of the largest collections of its kind in the Midwest, the 98 backdrops, leg drops and cut drops are made of sheets of cotton muslin and linen and painted with dry pigments mixed with animal glue. They were painted by Thomas G. Moses, a senior artist for Sosman and Landis of Chicago, a company that created drops for commercial and fraternal theaters across the Midwest. The local Mason lodge has been using the drops in rituals since 1909. When January rolls in, Theatre du Mississippi offers relief from the winter chill with the four-day Frozen River Film Festival, which features intellectually stimulating films focusing on environmental issues plus adrenalin-pumping documentaries on extreme sports and adventure travel. Make the Theatre du Mississippi your arts and entertainment destination in Winona.

902 E Second Street, Winona MN
(507) 459-8090
www.tdmwinona.org

Watkins Museum

The story of the oldest direct-selling company in the world is told vividly through photos, product samples and old advertisements at the Watkins Museum. The Winona facility offers a glimpse into the formative years of direct selling in this country, focusing on the accomplishments of J.R. Watkins, who began selling liniment in 1868. The company grew quickly, and soon the Watkins trademark became a symbol of quality in everything from vanilla and spices to salve and cathartic pills. Did you know that Watkins was the first American company to offer a money-back guarantee? From peddling products directly to the customer through horse and wagon to mainstream mass retail, the company has never stopped marketing its products. The store at the museum neatly displays 350 apothecary, gourmet and personal care products, all bearing the old-fashioned Watkins label. It's worth visiting the museum just for the chance to step inside the Watkins Administration Building, a Winona landmark listed on the National Register of Historic Places. Completed in 1912 at a cost of more than a million dollars, it is a statement of elegance and opulence with Italian tile and marble, stained glass and gold leaf. Learn how one man achieved the American dream with a visit to the Watkins Museum.

150 Liberty Street, Winona MN
(507) 457-6095
www.jrwatkins.com

Tours and Treasures

In historic Lanesboro, a town with a main street that is almost entirely listed on the National Register of Historic Places, the first-stop destination for both tourists and shoppers is a converted 1800s feed mill. Lovingly restored by Rick and Cheryl Lamon, the feed mill is home to four separate businesses: Tours and Treasures, Cheryl's Apparel, Molly the Trolley and R & M Amish Tours. At Tours and Treasures you can browse a wide range of merchandise cleverly arranged around the feed mixers, augers, lags and pulleys of the mill. Cheryl's Apparel offers Lanesboro's largest selection of fine women's clothing and accessories, including jewelry, the Tribal line and Picadilly Fashions. Men and children can browse the book collection or kick back in one of the Amish gliders to watch the traffic.

102 E Beacon Street, Lanesboro MN
(507) 467-4466 or (866) 349-4466
www.tourstreasures.com
www.funfashionstt.com

Molly the Trolley

Molly the Trolley departs daily at 1 pm. The one-hour tour passes through Lanesboro's historic residential district, business community, agricultural community and past the fish hatchery. The trolley also visits some scenic vistas in town, so bring your camera along. Molly will give you a great overview of Lanesboro, so don't miss it.

102 E Beacon Street, Lanesboro MN
(507) 467-4466 or (866) 349-4466
www.tourstreasures.com

R & M Amish Tours

The R & M Amish Tours last about two hours and will take you into the heart of the Amish Community. Your guide will discuss Amish society as you travel between the farms in an air-conditioned van. At the farms you will have the opportunity to get out and talk to the families or purchase produce, furniture, baskets or quilts. This is an insightful tour you won't want to miss.

102 E Beacon Street, Lanesboro MN
(507) 467-4466 or (866) 349-4466
www.tourstreasures.com

Great River Shakespeare Festival

His touch for comedy has never been rivaled, and his tragedies leave audiences pondering the very meaning of life. We're talking about William Shakespeare, of course. No matter which two plays are performed this season at the Great River Shakespeare Festival (GRSF), you can expect them to be highly entertaining illustrations of Shakespeare's deft command of language and human emotions. GRSF, comprised of professionals from the region and from across the country, has taken the Upper Midwest by storm in its three short years of existence. The plays perform in repertory, Tuesday or Wednesday through Sunday, from June 27 to July 29, on campus in the Performing Arts Center at Winona State University. Besides the plays, GRSF offers live concerts before the weekend performances; a series of guest conversations with visiting scholars, authors, and artists; and workshops for educators who want to enhance their teaching of Shakespeare. GRSF also provides opportunities to meet the actors, directors, designers and other company members at a local coffeehouse on Saturday mornings or following Thursday evening performances. Be refreshed and renewed with a visit to the Great River Shakespeare Festival.

79 E 3rd Street, Winona MN
(507) 474-7900
www.grsf.org

Houston Nature Center

The Houston Nature Center has been teaching adults and children about local plants, animals and art since 2001. Director and Naturalist Karla Kinstler oversees the nature center, which doubles as a tourism information center for folks just passing through. Karla's personal and professional interest in owls can be appreciated during the annual Festival of Owls in March, and Alice, the resident great horned owl, is one of the biggest draws here. The communication between Alice and Karla, who handles the owl, is remarkable and may lead to a desire to purchase a T-shirt featuring You Know Hooooooo. Still other programs concentrate on wolves, invasive plants and fossil collecting. School programs include a host of owl activities suited to every age level, frog ear training, and experiential prairie walks to stimulate the sense of smell.

The center's 18-acre park features hundreds of native plants. It's also home to unusual artwork, including an impressive selection of recycled bicycle art. Hands-on nature displays are so much fun that children effortlessly absorb lessons on conserving the local plants and wildlife. Karla hopes the lessons they learn will carry them into their adulthood and make the world a better place in the future. Plan a family trip to the Houston Nature Center for fun, adventure and learning.

215 W Plum Street, Houston MN
(507) 896-HOOT (4668)
www.houstonmn.com/nature/nature2.htm

Minnesota Marine Art Museum

A handsome example of waterfront architecture, the Minnesota Marine Art Museum opened its doors in 2006 on the banks of the Mississippi River. Long before interstate highways, the Mississippi was one of America's most important conduits of commerce and travel. A collection of rare, historic photographs by Henry Peter Bosse of the Army Corps of Engineers captures river life during its heyday in the 19th century. The Burrichter-Kierlin Marine Art Collection fills another gallery with canvases of majestic sea-going ships and the sailors and fishermen who populated them. You can almost feel the roll of the waves as you view what is regarded

as one of the finest private collections of marine paintings in America. The Leo and Marilyn Smith Folk Art Collection includes more than 400 original wood and bronze sculptures of regional people, flora and fauna. In 2008, visitors will walk the decks of the dredge boat, *William A. Thompson*, a vessel that began clearing the Mississippi's channels in 1937. Be sure to stop by the café and gift shop. May the winds be at your back as you navigate your way to the front door of the Minnesota Marine Art Museum.

800 Riverview Drive, Winona MN
(507) 474-6626
www.minnesotamarineart.org

Blooming Grounds Coffee House

In four years, Blooming Grounds Coffee House has become an integral part of downtown Winona. This bustling shop sells coffees and smoothies along with a pleasing lunchtime assortment of soups, sandwiches and salads. Visitors to Blooming Grounds often find themselves buying a house-made cake, pie or other dessert treat. The signature line of truffles gets the attention of every chocolate lover. Your sweetie will think you've gone out of your way to purchase these, even though you were just frequenting your favorite haunt. In still one more departure from standard coffee house fare, owner Amy Jo Marks offers wedding cakes—you might need one after your sweetheart tastes those truffles. Perhaps the atmosphere at Blooming Grounds inspires creativity. For certain, it's the favorite hangout of the directors of the Great River Shakespeare Festival. Just down the street is Amy's second enterprise, Pretty Things on Third. She collaborates with her mother-in-law on this gift store and somehow finds time to work there as well as in the coffee house, another endorsement for the inspirational power of Blooming Grounds. Add some stimulation to your day with a visit to Blooming Grounds Coffee House.

50 E 3rd Street, Winona MN
(507) 474-6551
www.bloominggrounds.net

Aromas Coffee House

What happens when a chef who served his apprenticeship at a four-star restaurant in St. Paul takes over the ownership of a coffee shop? Suddenly Italian wedding soup starts showing up on the menu along with such dishes as beef roulade, beef wrapped in a pastry with Burgundy mushroom sauce. The shop offers soups, salads and panini sandwiches at lunchtime and tapas-style dining at night. Aromas Coffee House has always served delicious pastries and sandwiches to complement its robust gourmet coffees. Since Chef Paul Paladie appeared in January 2007, customers have been raving about the broadened menu selection. "People want to try new things," says Paul, dismissing the risk in pushing the envelope in small-town America. (Zumbrota is 20 minutes north of Rochester.) "My approach has been very well received," he adds. In addition to coffee, Aromas offers fine wines and beers. The establishment is a WiFi site, so you can linger with your laptop. Continued creativity is Paul's main goal for the future. Expanding the entertainment beyond the monthly musical performances that Aromas currently features is another priority. Discover sophisticated treats for the palate while mingling with local java fans at Aromas Coffee House.

365 Main Street, Zumbrota MN
(507) 732-7600
www.aromasbistro.com

Lily's Coffee House

In historic downtown Red Wing, just two blocks from the banks of the Mississippi River, you'll find Lily's Coffee House, where owners Brian Schneider and Tom Quanrud offer award-winning espresso drinks, a popular lunch menu and an assortment of homemade baked goods. Lily's opened its doors in 1998. The friendly staff and warm atmosphere, decorated with bold and inspiring colors reminiscent of Italy, soon made Lily's a Red Wing icon for locals and tourists alike. The outdoor courtyard, canopied by blossoming trees in the spring, provides a beautiful setting for dining and a comfortable place to socialize. Brian and Tom are very proud of the sense of community that their customers have come to associate with Lily's. Lily's has received many awards and recognition, most notably the 2002 Small Business of the Year award by the Red Wing Area Chamber of Commerce. The *Minneapolis Star Tribune* declared Lily's to be "the city's most appealing java joint." In July 2007, *Minnesota Monthly Magazine* named Lily's one of 105 Restaurants Worth the Drive. In the spring of 2007 Brian and Tom's new shop, Inspired Home & Flower Studio, opened right next door to Lily's, offering customers creative and unique fresh flower arrangements and interior design services. Visit Lily's Coffee House for a warm welcome and a little indulgence. Relax and enjoy.

419 W 3rd Street, Red Wing MN
(651) 388-8797
www.lilyscoffeehouse.com
www.inspiredredwing.com

Tale of Two Sisters Tearoom & Gift Shoppe

When you walk into Tale of Two Sisters Tearoom & Gift Shoppe, you walk into a dream. Bonnie Kiefer Tracy opened the doors to her dream in 1998. The tearoom was the brainchild of Bonnie and her sister Susan Kiefer McLeran. When you enter the etched front doors of this haven, you step back into a more genteel era. Enjoy a peaceful Morning Repast with friends, an uninterrupted Cottage Tea, or the Traditional English Afternoon Tea in a beautifully decorated parlor, regal dining room, or sunny garden room in a historically significant 1880s Victorian home. Plan to come to one of the six-course theme teas held on selected Saturdays throughout the year. As you enter the tearoom, the aroma of freshly baked scones, cinnamon bread, and Grandmother's Old Fashioned Bread Pudding remind you of a visit to grandma's house. Patrons return again and again to drink in the ambience, savor a delicious meal and enjoy a pleasant conversation. A screened porch overlooks a delightful English garden, and during nice weather you can dine al fresco or enjoy a cuppa in the garden's colorful setting amid fragrant aromas. Gifts are tastefully displayed throughout the home. An extraordinary staircase leads to four upstairs rooms brimming with gifts for everyone—a gardener, a collector, a special child, a cook, the tea novice or the tea connoisseur. Tale of Two Sisters is open Tuesday through Saturday from 9 am to 4 pm. Traditional English Afternoon Tea is served by reservation Tuesday through Friday at 2 pm and on Saturdays at 11 am and 2 pm.

204 W 7th Street, Red Wing MN
(651) 388-2250 or (866) 328-2300

Cornucopia Art Center

Cornucopia Art Center in Lanesboro is an artistic center in a town that's been named as one of the 100 Best Small Art Towns in America. You can take a class at Cornucopia or buy art from one of the 70 represented artists. Some 25,000 people attend exhibits, workshops, demonstrations and other events each year, and hundreds of area children get their first taste of art at Cornucopia's art appreciation program, Picture Parade. Cornucopia's Exhibition Gallery offers visitors the opportunity to see varied artwork from the Root River Valley and around the world. A Juried Sales Gallery represents the endeavors of a select artist membership. The public can purchase a variety of artwork, including paintings, photographs, ceramics, fiber art and jewelry as well as literary work and music. Schools and other groups can take free guided tours by appointment. Cornucopia Art Center offers two and four-week artist residencies. These residencies, which include a place to live and a small stipend, are available to a select number of emerging sculptors, painters, poets and writers. Resident artists engage in workshops, lectures and public art activities during their tenure. When you visit Lanesboro, stay in one of the spacious Art Lofts above Cornicopia Art Center, which feature spectacular views of the historic downtown district. If you're an artist or an art lover, Cornucopia Art Center is for you.

103 Parkway Avenue N, Lanesboro MN
(507) 467-2446
www.lanesboroarts.org

Optical Vision with Flair

You've just tried on a Maui Jim eyeglass frame with wrap styling and large lenses, but Linda Smith is shaking her head. She thinks your face would be better set off by a rectangular Etnia Barcelona frame in a peppy blue. Linda's customers appreciate the refreshing honesty that accompanies eyeglass shopping at Optical Vision with Flair. Eyeglasses make a strong, personal statement, and Linda wants you to benefit in every way possible from the designer frames she has assembled at her four-year-old Rochester shop. She is committed to carrying trendy frame styles by such designers as Georgio Armani and EyeEye Denmark. Linda also likes to get to know her customers, and she considers your career and lifestyle as well as your style of dress, coloring and, of course, the look you want to put forward. Her personal interest in a successful match between frame and face has earned loyal customers and doubled the size of her operation in its first two years. Linda has been an optician since 1977. She got into the profession by chance after high school when a local optometrist offered to train her on the job. The combination of working with frames, fashion and people every day proved to be an ideal career and after many years working in eyeglass shops, Linda was ready to put her ideas to work in her own business. Linda stays on top of cutting-edge styles by traveling to frame shows in New York, Las Vegas and Paris. Update your look and make a friend in the bargain with a visit to Optical Vision with Flair.

15 1st Avenue SW, Rochester MN
(507) 287-8444
www.opticalvisionflair.com

Pieces of the Past

Beautiful handcrafted wood furniture built from reclaimed barns is the family business at Pieces of the Past. Old World craftsmanship gives these sturdy pieces their beauty and sense of history. From sleigh beds and armoires to harvest tables and hutches, the high-quality family heirlooms carried by this shop will make every room in your home cozy. In addition to furniture, Pieces of the Past carries a large variety of accents to spice up your home décor, including lamps and lampshades, baskets, braided rugs in a wide variety of colors and sizes, quilts, linens including table and window accessories, garlands, wreaths and aromatic candles. Finding something for everyone on your gift-giving list has never been more fun. Owners Cheri and Duane Peterson opened the store in 1991, but their history with fine furnishings goes back much further. Cheri's parents, John and Pat Schuler, had been building beautiful furniture out of their home since 1974. John and Pat have since gone into semi-retirement, but the family tradition lives on. Stop in and enjoy this wonderful shop located in historic downtown Winona.

79 E 2nd Street, Winona MN
(507) 452-3722
www.piecesofthepast-winona.com

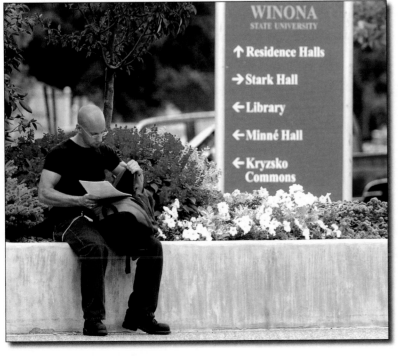

Winona State University

Winona State University (WSU) is known for the quality of its education and the beauty of its campuses. WSU, which is celebrating its 150th anniversary in 2007 to 2008, was founded in 1858 as a normal school to educate teachers. Fast forward to the 21st century and discover a school that offers 80 academic majors, 10 pre-professional programs and 18 graduate programs to 8,000 students on three campuses. *America's Best College Buys* has featured WSU for 11 years in a row, and the school was recently selected by the Carnegie Foundation for its new Community Engagement classification. WSU's pre-medical program operates in cooperation with Mayo Medical School, which is affiliated with the Mayo Clinic in Rochester. The university's student-to-faculty ratio is low—21 to one. WSU was one of the first Laptop Universities in the country, and its laptop program, in which each student leases a laptop computer from the university, has been a model for many like it nation-wide. The university is home to many cultural events, including the Great River Shakespeare Festival, the Frozen River Film Festival and the Lyceum Series. WSU is in the beautiful bluff country of the Mississippi River Valley. If you're looking for first-class educational value, check out Winona State University.

8th and Johnson Street, Winona MN
(507) 457-5000 or (800) 342-5978
www.winona.edu

Das Wurst Haus

Owners Rick and Vicki Darling and the Das Wurst Haus Band keep the polka music going every day from April to November at Laneboro's Das Wurst Haus, a marketplace that has been celebrating the tastes of Germany for 21 years. Beyond the oom-pa, Rick and Vicki have provided four shops in one: a deli haus, a sausage haus, an ice cream haus and a Bavarian fudge haus, known collectively as R & V's Specialty Meats & Homemade Sweets. A visit to the sausage haus, Rick's Meat Counter, is your opportunity to pick up brats made in-house, plus hot dogs, summer sausage and jerky. Add some flair to sandwiches you make at home with turkey pastrami, cheese curds and string cheese along with homemade mustards. If you would rather have something made for you, the deli awaits with specialty sandwiches served on homemade German rye and featuring such side dishes as house-made sauerkraut, German potato salad and soups. Beer and wine are also available. Every good German appreciates a good dessert, especially an ice cream dessert. At the Ice Cream Shoppe, your root beer float features root beer made on the premises. V's Fudge & Sweet Shoppe can treat you to handmade truffles, candy and fudge made right here with real cream and butter. Das Wurst Haus can be rented for private functions, complete with the polka band. Make a visit to Das Wurst Haus part of your visit to historic downtown Lanesboro.

117 Parkway Avenue N, Lanesboro MN
(507) 467-2902

Little River General Store

Before heading out on the Root River or the Root River State Bike Trail, outdoor enthusiasts turn to one of the area's most popular outfitters, the Little River General Store. Owner Kirsten Mensing has been putting the customer's safety first for 16 years with new, updated and fully maintained equipment for sale or rent. Need a bicycle, canoe or kayak for a day? You can rent recumbent, hybrid, tandem or mountain bikes as well as four-person surreys and Kiddie Karts. Helmets are supplied with your rental. Come in at the end of the season to purchase this year's rentals at the year's biggest discount or choose from a selection of new bikes and watercraft. You'll find such bike brands as Fuji and Cycle Genius, in addition to canoes by Wenonah and kayaks by Current Design. A full-service bike repair shop is also available to keep your own two wheels on the ground, and you can shop for bike accessories and clothing in all sizes. The General Store has a new addition, the Woodland Country Store, which includes country gifts, furniture, lamps and jewelry. Whether you are a full-fledged adrenalin junkie or just spending the afternoon with your family, stop by the Little River General Store, and you're sure to find something that meets your needs.

105 Coffee Street, Lanesboro MN
(507) 467-2943 or (800) 994-2943
www.lrgeneralstore.com

Tyrol Ski & Sports

Robb and Kristin Welch, the owners of Tyrol Ski & Sports, know it's not just what sporting equipment you carry that counts but what you know about sports. They are the second generation to own the store, which was founded in 1965 by Kristin's parents Jerry and Barbara Schliep. At Tyrol, all the employees have first-hand experience of the sports equipment in stock. The folks who mount, tune and repair your skis and snowboards are out on the slopes when they're not in the shop. The snowboards, snowshoes, downhill and cross-country ski equipment at Tyrol don't just have good industry ratings; they've been tested by the people who are fitting you. The same goes for camping and backpacking gear, kayaks and canoes. Tyrol rents winter gear as well as kayaks and canoes, giving you the option of trying out winter sports before buying the gear. Robb and Kristin stock a large selection of sportswear, hiking footwear and casual shoes year-round. Other areas of specialty include porch and patio furniture as well as travel luggage and clothing. The day we visited, we watched seasoned staff members apply their knowledge by matching product selection to customer needs, producing one satisfied customer after another. Get the inside story from people who work hard and play harder at Tyrol Ski & Sports.

1923 2nd Street SW, Rochester MN
(507) 288-1683
www.tyrolskishop.com

Mississippi National Golf Links

No golfing enthusiast should pass up an opportunity to enjoy a round at Mississippi National Golf Links, where you can choose between two championship 18-hole public golf courses. Enjoy the spacious greens and rolling fairways of the more traditional Lowlands 18 course, or the spectacular scenery and challenge of the Highlands 18. The signature Highlands hole #17 features a 150-foot drop from the tee to the green. Owned by Wendell Pittenger, Mississippi National Golf Links has received a four-star rating from *Golf Digest* and has been voted the Best Public Golf Course in southern Minnesota. Larry Norland is both the general manager and the head golf professional at Mississippi National Golf Links. With 14 years as a PGA professional under his belt, Larry oversees a wide range of instructional opportunities, from private lessons to golf clinics. If your game is a bit rusty or if you simply want to perfect your skills, take advantage of the fully equipped practice facility with a 300-yard driving range. A short game area and a bunker are among the many offerings. After a stimulating afternoon of golf, stop in the Pavilion and refresh yourself with a drink or meal and a view of the ninth green. Two miles south of Red Wing in the beautiful Hiawatha Valley bluff lands, Mississippi National Golf Links provides a golfing experience you will treasure.

409 Golf Links Drive, Red Wing MN
(651) 388-1874
www.wpgolf.com

Signatures Restaurant & Event Center
The Bridges Golf Club

Dine, party and golf—you can do it all at Signatures Restaurant & Event Center and the Bridges Golf Club. Signatures' gourmet menu changes frequently. Choose from tantalizing appetizers, salads, soups, entrées and desserts. A full bar includes one of southeastern Minnesota's most diverse wine lists. Signatures celebrates Winona's rich history with vintage photos, postcards and art displays, many on loan from the Minnesota Marine Art Museum, the city's newest star attraction. Signatures also caters for the Visions Event Center, your destination for the perfect wedding reception, reunion, retirement party or conference. The center can hold up to 350 guests comfortably. Its high ceiling and tall windows provide stunning views. For a more intimate gathering, such as a rehearsal dinner, anniversary or business meeting, the Captain's Quarters room is perfect. Stretch your legs on the private patio amid lush greens or take a stroll in one of the fabulous gardens. Experience golf at its finest when you tee off at the Bridges. This Minnesota masterpiece, a par-71 championship 18-hole course, has been rated one of the state's best and has hosted several of the state's amateur events. With four tees and a layout that incorporates hilly terrain, ancient oaks and a meandering stream, this course appeals to players at all levels. Visit Signature Restaurant & Event Center for good friends and fine dining, and enjoy the best of golf at Bridges Golf Club.

22852 County Road 17, Winona MN (507) 454-3767
www.signatureswinona.com www.winonagolf.com

Bilotti's Italian Village

Bilotti's Italian Village has perfected pizza and many other Italian and American dishes over its long history. The Rochester restaurant, in business for 52 years, serves many fourth-generation local customers. Visitors appreciate Bilotti's, too, and repeat visitors to the Mayo Clinic often make Bilotti's a first stop. For 32 years, Ron and Lois Kazos managed Bilotti's, and all who frequented the eatery knew them as the heart and soul of the place. Lois passed on in 1999, and Ron has since retired. For the last 12 years, Karla Sperry has owned Bilotti's and makes sure that the first pizza restaurant in Rochester remains as beloved as always. *Rochester Magazine* has voted Bilotti's Best Pizza four times, most recently in 2007. The magazine called the flaky crust, mild tomato sauce and meat and vegetable toppings tantalizing, but noted "it's the one quarter inch of mozzarella cheese and rectangular-cut slices that set Bilotti's apart from the rest." The homemade soups and daily lunch specials, along with pasta, salads, steaks and sandwiches, assure still more happy customers. It's fitting that a landmark restaurant should sit on a landmark corner in a red brick building filled with historic charm. Those in a hurry will appreciate Bilotti's take-out location. Find out what it takes to become a classic with a visit to Bilotti's Italian Village.

304 1st Avenue SW, Rochester MN (restaurant) (507) 282-8669
24 6th Street SW, Rochester MN (take out) (507) 282-8668
www.bilottispizza.com

Prescotts

Christopher Rohe has wanted to be a chef from the age of six. In 2006, he and his wife, Jenna, opened Prescotts, where diners experience Chris' passion in each savory bite. Chefs are different than cooks, says Chris. "Chefs always want to learn more, improve themselves and improve their craft." That creative edge shows up in every soup, salad and entrée Chris creates. His tomato basil soup is nearly legendary after 15 years of variations at three successive restaurants. The most popular entrées at Prescotts are the seafood-stuffed prawns, the crab-stuffed chicken and the stuffed pork chop, which won an award for best single food item from *Rochester Magazine*. The readers of the magazine have also honored Chris as Best Chef in Rochester. Meals come with crusty European-style bread. The décor and relaxed atmosphere enhance the dining experience. Jenna is a trained wine sommelier who handpicks artisan wines to complement Chris' menu items. Chris, a Rochester native, began working in area restaurants at the age of 13. He attended culinary school, served as executive chef at several local restaurants and has been certified by the American Culinary Federation. During Chris and Jenna's honeymoon in 1998, the pair began discussing their restaurant dream over appetizers at a beachfront café. Today, they are well on their way to becoming the number one restaurant in Rochester. Find out how good a dream can taste with a visit to Prescotts.

1201 S Broadway, Rochester MN
(507) 536-7775
www.prescottsgrill.com

Whistle Binkies

Rochester has two British pubs—Whistle Binkies on the Lake and Whistle Binkies Olde World Pub. These hot spots, which are also known as Whistle Binkies North and South, are locally celebrated for some of the town's happiest happy hours. The English-style fare is a cut above the norm, too, thanks to an executive chef on staff. Randy Lehman opened the award-winning north location in 2002 and followed with the south pub in 2006, immediately capturing a *Rochester Magazine* vote for Best Outdoor Dining. The pubs feature 200 brands of beer with 16 on tap in the north and 31 in the south. The cocktail choices get downright creative, with names such as Blue Bombsicle and Jamaica Me Crazy. Daily drink specials tempt regulars to reach beyond their usual favorites. When it comes to food, expect a long and intriguing selection that ranges from typical English pub fare, such as fish and chips or bangers and mash, to flavors from around the globe. The appetizer list is a cultural feast that includes Scotch eggs, Cajun swordfish, steak quesadillas, egg rolls and a full pound of French fries. Expect similar variety in salads, burgers, pastas, seafood and steaks. You will find a kids' menu and lively sandwich choices. The pub mixes it up with such annual celebrations as Oktoberfest, Mardi Gras and the Caribbean Beach Bash, each an excuse to try appropriate food and drink specials. Make any day a party with a visit to Whistle Binkies.

247 Woodlake Drive SE, Rochester MN (on the Lake) (507) 424-1227
3120 Wellner Drive NE, Rochester MN (Olde World Pub) (507) 289-9200
www.whistlebinkiespub.com

Canadian Honker Restaurant

Joe Powers was just 21 years old in 1984 when he opened Canadian Honker Restaurant. The restaurant was a rousing success and Joe and his brother Cris had to move twice to larger quarters near St. Mary's Hospital. In 1998, they built a brand-new 8,000-square-foot facility to comfortably fit up to 165 guests. At the heart of the Powers' popularity is their focus on the customer. Everything at the Canadian Honker is homemade on the premises to ensure consistent quality. The restaurant is open for breakfast, lunch and dinner. The Breakfast Feast is popular and reasonably priced. The lunch menu features the Honker of a Burger, fresh salads, loaded wraps and many signature sandwiches. The dinner menu has something for everyone, from steaks, chops and ribs to perfect pastas. Finish your meal with the award-winning Bunnie's Coconut Cake. Appetizers are also a must, including onion rings dipped in a homemade batter and dairy fresh cheese curds. Canadian Honker also offers plenty of healthy menu selections as well as senior citizen and children's menus. Canadian Honker is also known as southeast Minnesota's largest caterer. It can handle groups of any size and complexity, for any occasion, and serves box lunches, elegant buffets or full service sit-down meals. Friday and Saturday nights bring live music, including jazz, blues, classic rock and a little country. The full bar offers a fascinating selection of martinis. Joe and Cris named the restaurant after the 44,000 Canadian geese that flock to Rochester during the winter months. Just as Rochester welcomes the geese, the Canadian Honker will have a warm welcome for you.

1203 2nd Street SW, Rochester MN
(507) 282-6572
www.canadianhonker.com

The Big River Room

The menu at the Big River Room frees your appetite to lead you in any direction. Excellent choices abound in every category. You can try pasta, chicken or fish as well as steaks, burgers, soups and salads. You could eat at the Big River Room once a week for the next year and not order the same thing twice. Why not jump right into the Minnesota mood and order the walleye pike? Lightly breaded and pan fried, it comes in a white wine lemon caper sauce. Live jazz provides the background music for a dining experience that you will want to share with good company. "The food we serve takes time to prepare, especially on an individual basis," say the owners, who invite you to sit back, relax and enjoy the ambience. Even such stock items as French fries, cheese curds and the colossal onion rings are prepared daily from fresh ingredients, never from processed ones. Join the locals for Sunday brunch—another chance to sample the vast menu selection. The staff at the Big River Room takes pride in its smooth handling of weddings and corporate events. The River Rocks, adjoining the dining area, is an entertainment space that offers comedy on Friday nights and live dance music on Saturday evenings. Exercise your freedom to eat well at the Big River Room.

34648 Homer Road, Winona MN
(507) 452-8277
www.bigriverroom.com

Lakeview Drive Inn

"It's a Winona tradition," say the owners of the Lakeview Drive Inn, noting the local habit of dipping French fries into their homemade tartar sauce. Lakeview has been tickling the taste buds of folks in this town since 1938. It blends nostalgia with an all-American menu of burgers, fries, fish, fried chicken and premium ice cream. Lakeview Drive Inn made Travelocity's Top 10 list of Local Secrets, Big Finds in Minnesota. To experience the popularity of this original drive-in, catch the turn-out on a Cruise Night. About 150 classic cars and motorcycles roll into the parking lot each Wednesday evening in the summer to take part in Cruise Night. Sipping a root beer at Lakeview is another Winona tradition that goes back to the restaurant's conception in 1938. The Glowczewski family makes their root beer from scratch using a closely guarded secret recipe. A carhop will attach a tray of frosty root beers to your car or bring them to a picnic table. The drive-in is open from March through September and is proud to be Winona's oldest restaurant. Lakeview, located on the shores of Lake Winona, is a taste of days gone by.

610 E Sarnia Street, Winona MN
(507) 454-3723
www.lakeviewdriveinn.com

Pedal Pushers Café

If you still have visions of poodle skirts and Elvis, step back to the 1950s at the Pedal Pushers Café in downtown Lanesboro. You can still get an old-fashioned banana split, root beer float or cream soda from the Soda Fountain Classics menu, and while prices have changed some, the price of a slice of pie and a cup of coffee here is a nostalgic $1, all day every day. The restaurant specializes in classic 1950s fare, but owners Scott and Angie Taylor have thrown in some gourmet twists to keep Pedal Pushers interesting. Breakfast specialties include oatmeal buttermilk pancakes and several variations on classic eggs Benedict. The gourmet burgers, popular at lunch and dinner, come with such toppings as sautéed mushrooms, Brie cheese and caramelized onions. A kids' menu promises to make dinner selection a snap with choices like the Cosmic Spuds and a grilled cheese sandwich that features a divine combination of cheddar, Swiss and Muenster cheeses. Light eaters will appreciate health-conscious extras such as raw vegetables and dip or the fresh fruit. Beer and wine are available. The Taylors opened their diner in 2005. In addition to their daily fare and back-in-time atmosphere, they offer off-site catering. Take a trip down memory lane with a visit to the Pedal Pushers Café.

121 Parkway Avenue N, Lanesboro MN
(507) 467-1050
www.pedalpusherscafe.com

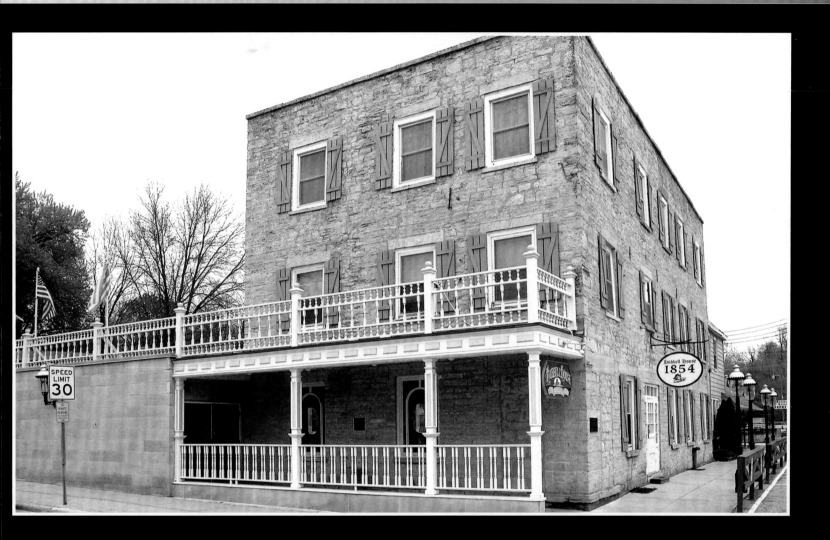

Hubbell House

"When you are involved in a place that's been around for more than 150 years, you get a special feeling for it," says Don Pappas, co-owner and operator of the Hubbell House. In 1854, John Hubbell opened a log cabin stagecoach stop in the new town of Mantorville. Two years later, Hubbell expanded into the three-story limestone structure that still stands. The restaurant honors its origins with a Civil War era interior with period paintings and artifacts. You can view the signature of Ulysses S. Grant in the lobby. Meals feature steaks, chops and seafood along with vegetarian offerings. Don's father, Paul, grew up in the restaurant business. Along with his wife, Irene, he purchased the historic structure from Irene's father. It had been in use as a boarding house. Getting a loan was tricky—others did not see the same potential in the building that he did, but in 1946, Paul and Irene opened the Hubbell House. Don remembers living above the restaurant with his parents and four brothers. The boys helped out in the restaurant, relishing such occasions as meeting Roy Rogers and Mickey Mantle. Don took charge of the restaurant in 1996 after his father's death. He credits his employees with his success and looks for workers who care about customers. Some of Don's

Signatures Restaurant & Event Center
The Bridges Golf Club

Dine, party and golf—you can do it all at Signatures Restaurant & Event Center and the Bridges Golf Club. Signatures' gourmet menu changes frequently. Choose from tantalizing appetizers, salads, soups, entrées and desserts. A full bar includes one of southeastern Minnesota's most diverse wine lists. Signatures celebrates Winona's rich history with vintage photos, postcards and art displays, many on loan from the Minnesota Marine Art Museum, the city's newest star attraction. Signatures also caters for the Visions Event Center, your destination for the perfect wedding reception, reunion, retirement party or conference. The center can hold up to 350 guests comfortably. Its high ceiling and tall windows provide stunning views. For a more intimate gathering, such as a rehearsal dinner, anniversary or business meeting, the Captain's Quarters room is perfect. Stretch your legs on the private patio amid lush greens or take a stroll in one of the fabulous gardens. Experience golf at its finest when you tee off at the Bridges. This Minnesota masterpiece, a par-71 championship 18-hole course, has been rated one of the state's best and has hosted several of the state's amateur events. With four tees and a layout that incorporates hilly terrain, ancient oaks and a meandering stream, this course appeals to players at all levels. Visit Signature Restaurant & Event Center for good friends and fine dining, and enjoy the best of golf at Bridges Golf Club.

22852 County Road 17, Winona MN (507) 454-3767
www.signatureswinona.com www.winonagolf.com

Photos by Wayne Christenson

Söntés—
A wine bar and tapas

Tessa and Nelson Leung fired up the city's imagination in 2006 when they opened Söntés —A wine bar and tapas. The downtown Rochester restaurant features tapas, small dishes that are as varied as the chefs who create them. These informal, innovative servings allow diners to share with others in their group or to combine dishes for a full meal. The Spanish tapas concept lets you explore new flavors of food and wine. "To eat tapas-style is to eat whimsically, liberated from time and rule," say the Leungs, who hope to impart a big-city feeling at Söntés. Tessa recently attended culinary school and has hired a classically trained French chef and a pastry chef to create the delicious morsels. A lounge with a full bar, a dining room and a private events room are part of the Söntés equation, along with 50 wines by the glass and 110 wines by the bottle. The restaurant is located in a building that served as Rochester's first bank in 1867 and for the last 50 years was Wong's, a Chinese restaurant. The Leungs flew in the face of advice when they decided to refurbish the building rather than demolish it. The results were magnificent. The couple preserved some of the past, such as Wong's distinctive front doors and a bank vault that now serves as a wine cellar. At the same time, they created a modern space with fireplaces and conversation areas. Removing the suspended ceiling revealed a bank of windows that floods the restaurant with light. Shake up your ideas about dining with a visit to Söntés.

4-3rd Street SW, Rochester MN
(507) 292-1628
www.sontes.com

Uff Da Shop

Since 1977, the Uff Da Shop has furnished Red Wing with Scandinavian imports, year-round gifts and other delights. Uff Da is Scandinavian slang for wow, whoops or good grief. The name reflects the playfulness customers find at this gift store. The Uff Da Shop is a destination for both tourists and locals. It supplies patrons with gifts for all occasions, decorative items for the home, ethnic foods, cards, flags, books, jewelry and apparel. Hand-blown crystal, Norwegian porcelain and Marimekko linens from Finland provide lovely accents in any home. Traditional Norwegian sweaters provide warmth and beauty. A full line of Swedish artist Carl Larsson's trays, figurines, books and prints are on hand for the art lover. The store stocks a wide selection of kitchenware and foods such as ginger cookies, Swedish coffee, Norwegian chocolates and other ethnic items. For holiday gifts and in every other season, the Uff Da Shop has something for you.

202 Bush Street, Red Wing MN
(651) 388-8436

The Blomma Stores

The Blomma Stores are two sister stores with different personalities. Skandinavien Blomma in Harmony and Liv Blomma in Lanesboro are owned and operated by Carol and Ralph Beastrom and their daughter Sharyl Bergen. Both stores take pride in offering giftware to meet many tastes. Skandinavien Blomma offers traditional and contemporary Nordic designs in a beautiful location. The renovated historic City Hall building is the backdrop for Norwegian sweaters, Finnish Iittala glassware and Hadeland crystal. You'll find Scandinavian linens, Danish iron candleholders and Sølje jewelry. The store also offers an art gallery with paintings, pottery and glass art by local and regional artists. Liv Blomma takes the visitor on a trip around the

world with fresh, colorful designs in clothing and jewelry as well as crystal and dinnerware, all with modern appeal. The Lanesboro shop also offers artwork from nationally recognized artists. For gifts and housewares that are both beautiful and practical, come see what the Blomma Stores have in store for you.

25 Center Street E, Harmony MN
(507) 886-2201 or (888) 525-6662
115 Parkway N, Lanesboro MN
(507) 467-3201
www.skanblomma.com

Gregory's Gifts & Greetings

The big windows on a busy street corner in downtown Winona have been enticing folks into Gregory's Gifts & Greetings since Gregory Ratajczyk opened the shop in 1988. Gregory's Gifts offers hundreds of ways to solve your gift giving dilemmas. Repeat visitors to Winona make a point of stopping at the shop to pick up cards and see what new items Greg has in his inventory.

Greg's Polish heritage and the strong Polish influence in Winona account for many of the Polish merchandise choices at the store. You will also find gifts for babies and Minnesota-themed souvenirs. The greeting card collection alone makes regular visitors out of many Winona residents. Greg has become well known in Winona for his friendly manner and affordable gift selection. Next time you need to express a sentiment or give a gift, stop in at Gregory's Gifts & Greetings.

101 E 3rd Street, Winona MN
(507) 454-3160

Artistic Framers

Owner Susan Schreiber, her husband and her children all take part in making Artistic Framers a fun place to come for a specialty frame or unusual gift. Susan is a certified framer who has been serving Rochester for 18 years. Among her specialties are mats that are as individual as the paintings they frame. Susan has a talent for original hand-cut matting designs that complement the artwork. The shop is prepared to meet your framing needs, whether you are framing a sentimental print or a fine art treasure. You can buy a ready-made frame or a 22-karat gold custom frame and everything in between. The shop carries cut-to-order products from eight frame companies and five glass companies. Beyond custom framing, the shop functions as both a gallery and gift store with one of the best selections of original fine art and crafts in the state. Bronze sculptures, lamps and wrought iron are showcased along with bath and body products and seasonal décor. Susan has a good time working with her customers, but gets serious about her commitment to standing apart from other shops. When you buy an item from Artistic Framing, you can be quite sure you won't find another item just like it down the street. If Susan finds an item she carries in another store, she will discontinue it in hers. For frames and gifts chosen for artistic integrity and good taste, visit the Schreiber family at Artistic Framers.

16 3rd Street SW, Rochester MN
(507) 281-4890

Flowers on Broadway and Pretty Things on Third

Businesswomen Sherry Russeau and Amy Jo Marks, Sherry's daughter-in-law, know a lot about starting and running businesses. Between them, they own three downtown Winona shops, which makes them major contributors to downtown Winona's revitalization efforts. Sherry has owned Flowers on Broadway for 14 years. Together, she and Amy started Pretty Things on Third two years ago. This shop is located just down the street from Amy's other business, Blooming Grounds Coffee House. Somehow the women juggle the responsibilities that come with each business. Sherry's floral shop offers an imaginative approach to flower design and handles everything from intimate events to corporate events, weddings and personal tributes. Blooming Grounds Coffee House serves excellent lunches and gourmet cakes. Both Sherry and Amy find time to manage their separate businesses and work at their new joint enterprise, Pretty Things on Third. The new shop is a natural extension of their talents. It's a hip, girly store that offers an eclectic mix of trendy gifts and accessories. The beauty and spa items here include the Pretty Things private label line of bath products. Both women enjoy traveling to markets throughout the country in search of engaging specialty items for the shop. Need flowers, presents or pretty things? You'll find what you need at Flowers on Broadway or Pretty Things on Third.

476 E Broadway, Winona MN
(Flowers on Broadway) (507) 453-9711
66 E 3rd Street, Winona MN
(Pretty Things on Third) (507) 474-4545

Austin's Mohair Gift Shop

Austin's Mohair Gift Shop is the place to get your goat, whether it's in the form of mohair yarn, socks, sausage or cheese. For 11 years, owners Jim and Ada Austin, aided by their adult children, Mike and Scott Austin, Konya Bloomquist and Tori Kenney, have been providing mohair products from their Harmony ranch. The hair of Ada's prized Angora goats goes into the lovely products sold at the shop. These products are fashioned mainly by stay-at-home moms, who wish to use their skills while staying home with their children. Ada is quick to point out that these moms aren't charity cases; they're skilled artisans. One look at her treasures and you'll agree. The beautifully designed mohair socks sold at Austin's keep your feet warm in winter and cool in the summer. The yarns also are used for Christmas angels and children's toys. Knitters and weavers can create their own mohair products with the mohair yarn sold here as well as the raw mohair waiting to be spun. No part of a goat is wasted at Austin's. You can even take home a goat skull to add a lodge feel to your home. For sweaters, socks and gifts from some very precious goats, come to Austin's Mohair Gift Shop.

14484 331ˢᵗ Avenue, Harmony MN
(507) 886-6731
www.austinsmohair.com

Moments on Main

Looking for that special present in Red Wing is a snap when you can turn to Moments on Main. Shannan Harris has been perfecting Moments on Main for some time as the answer to your home decorating and gift giving needs. You'll find outstanding gifts and accessories for you and your home. This shop is fresh, feminine and fun. Gifts and décor change with the seasons, so stop by often. You never know what new delight you will discover. Tyler candles are appropriate at any time of year. Shannan has chosen some exclusive lines that can't be found anywhere else in the area. If you need assistance, her design service is available. Be sure to fill out your very own wish list. You'll be sure to discover a new treasure every time you visit Moments on Main.

329 Main Street, Red Wing MN
(651) 388-2343

Ruth's German Haus

Ruth Lee Bertrand, owner of Ruth's German Haus, grew up in the German community of Sleepy Eye near New Ulm. When she moved to Red Wing she missed the German way of life she experienced in her youth, so she decided to open a German gift and grocery store of her own. Red Wing is an ideal location, Ruth explains. "If you look at the history of the area you find that Red Wing was also home to many German immigrants. Many of my customers immigrated after World War II and they miss the foods and friendships from the old country." This is one of the many reasons why her business is such a success. One of Ruth's main goals is to educate people about German customs and traditions. As such, Ruth's German Haus celebrates major German holidays throughout the year such as Karneval, Maifest, Oktoberfest and St. Nicholas Day. Ruth and her crew also like to travel to surrounding communities to give presentations to schools and other groups. Ruth's German Haus carries a wide assortment of European gift and grocery items. There are many reasons to visit, whether you are searching for that unique gift, just the right foods for your next German feast, or simply interested in talking about German culture. Set in the historic Pottery District of Old West Main Street in a 100-year-old icehouse, Ruth's German Haus has been in business for more than six years. Experience what the Germans call *Gemütlichkeit*, a real taste of the Old World, at Ruth's German Haus.

1811 Old W Main Street, Red Wing MN
(651) 388-0516
www.ruthsgermanhaus.com

The Nordic Shop

Scandinavians have turned staying warm into an art, as you will clearly see when you examine the large selection of beautiful sweaters at The Nordic Shop. This small, family-owned business, established in 1974, is among the largest Scandinavian sweater retailers in the world. Owners Walter and Louise Hanson carry all of the traditional designers in their store, including Dale of Norway, Skjaeveland, Vrikke and Devold. The Nordic Shop also features the entire fashion line of Oleana sweaters, knitwear and home accessories in its own special store-within-a-store area. In addition to sweaters, The Nordic Shop is a miniature department store of Nordic design, from the fine porcelains of Royal Copenhagen, Bing & Grondahl and Porsgrund, to the fine crystals of Orrefors, Kosta Boda and Iittala of Finland. The Nordic Shop carries it all. The Hansons and their staff have the knowledge to assist you with your purchase or help you create a gift registry for that special event. With customers from all over the world, The Nordic Shop specializes in special orders ranging from Flora Danica dinnerware at more than $5,200 a place setting to a matching ski hat for your Norwegian sweater. Nothing is too big or small for the staff to accommodate.

Skyway Level, the Shops at University Square, Rochester MN
(800) 282-6673
www.thenordicshop.net

Red Wing Pottery

Red Wing Pottery began over 140 years ago and is still in operation today. Visit this third-generation family business on Main Street and watch the potters at work. The studio is open seven days a week. Visitors can talk with the potters as they wheel-throw and decorate their pottery. All of the wares are hand-turned by skilled production potters, giving visitors an opportunity to experience how pottery was made before the mass-production methods of the 20th century. Today, Red Wing makes two styles of pottery. The first style is salt-glazed stoneware. These pots have a grey or tan clay body with a cobalt blue decoration. In the late 1800s, Red Wing's first potters produced only salt-glaze pots, and they are the most valued today by Red Wing Pottery collectors. The second style is Bristol glaze ware. The glaze is a more uniform smooth finish and replicates the pots made in the early 1900s. All pots are stamped with the Red Wing logo, the date and the potter's mark. The stamps add to the collectible value. Red Wing's pottery is historic, esthetic and functional, and also diverse, fascinating and fun. Not only does the company produce pottery, it also has the Red Wing Pottery Salesroom, a large pottery, dinnerware and gift store on the banks of the scenic Mississippi River. For additional fascinating shopping, visit Fiacre's Garden Shop, Loons and Ladyslippers and the Smokey Row Café, home to the Jenny Lind Bakery.

1920 W Main Street, Red Wing MN
(651) 388-3562 or (800) 228-0174
www.redwingpottery.com

Sopra Sotto—The Italian Living Store

Maureen McNally and her partner, Charles Wright, evoke Italy in a store devoted to Italian imports. Sopra Sotto—The Italian Living Store is located in downtown Rochester. Every item in the store is Italian, from housewares and bath products to hand-painted volcanic stone tables and leather accessories. Among the art and photography you'll find Fratelli Alinari photos. Look for dinnerware, tablecloths and handmade Italian terra cotta sculpture. Food products, such as pastas and sauces, join exceptional olive oils from small producers in four regions of Italy. Italian cooking is important to Italian culture, and the store offers cooking classes. One of the oh-so-Italian pleasures of Sopra Sotto is the chance to sit down and enjoy a relaxing visit over a cup of real Italian espresso. This is not the take-out version of the drink in a paper cup, but rather the Italian version, created with a replicated century-old espresso machine. A year and a half after leaving a longtime position in the corporate world, Maureen was diagnosed with breast cancer. She stayed with friends while receiving treatment for breast cancer at the Mayo Clinic and welcomed the diversion of planning Sopra Sotto. A percentage of the store's daily proceeds go to breast cancer research at the Mayo Clinic. Discover the many charms of Italy at Sopra Sotto—The Italian Living Store.

111 S Broadway, Rochester MN
(507) 252-5522
www.sopra-sotto.com

Garvin Heights Vineyards

Marvin and Linda Seppanen have long enjoyed traveling and visiting small family wineries, and they opened the tasting room at their own Garvin Heights Vineyards in 2007. The Seppanens became seriously interested in opening a small winery after harvesting 3,000 pounds of grapes in 2005 and making nearly the legal limit of 200 gallons of wine that a family can bottle without certification. Cold-climate grapes developed by Elmer Swenson and the University of Minnesota are the Garvin Heights specialty. The semi-sweet St. Urho White, ideal for pairing with light foods, is a blend of three Elmer Swenson varieties: Edelweiss, Lacrosse and St. Pepin. St. Urho, by the way, was a young man who, according to legend, drove the grasshoppers away from Finland's vineyards. A red wine, the GHV Frontenac, is a credit to the University of Minnesota grape-breeding program. It has a pleasant cherry aroma, with berry and plum also evident. The winery is located atop the bluffs overlooking Winona. A tasting room and event center can accommodate 60 people. Local art adorns the walls, and a deck affords prime views of the countryside. Marvin and Linda plan to celebrate the joys of wine and share their winemaking secrets with guests for many years to come. Drop by and see how they are doing at Garvin Heights Vineyards.

2255 Garvin Heights Road, Winona MN
(507) 454-7179
www.ghvwine.com

I Love Antiques

Customers looking for antiques, collectibles and home décor in Harmony trust Marcia Love at I Love Antiques. Marcia and her family have been part of the Harmony community for many generations. Formerly a school administrator, Marcia opened her shop in 2004 and runs it with the assistance of her mother. The antiques shop is located in an 1892 building that was home to the local daily newspaper, the *Harmony News*, from 1896 until the mid-1980s. Marcia has left many of the building's charming, old-fashioned details intact, including a rare tin ceiling and original wood floors. An antique cash register serves both as part of the décor and as a way to ring up customer sales. This register was originally used by Marcia's parents and grandparents at a clothing store they operated in Harmony back in the 1900s. Rare pieces and what Marcia describes as "funky stuff" fill the shop. Marcia and her husband also operate a 150-year-old family farm just outside of town. The Loves are an important presence in their community and a proud part of local history. They just might share a story or two concerning some of the merchandise at the shop. If you love antiques, it's time you met Marcia Love and browsed through the selections at I Love Antiques.

**15 W Center Street, Harmony MN
(507) 886-4321**

Falconer Vineyards

The thriving town of Red Wing isn't just known for boots anymore. This popular destination community is now the home to many art galleries and fine dining establishments, to fantastic shopping and a plethora of outdoor recreational opportunities. Red Wing is also the home of Falconer Vineyards. Established in 2000 by John Falconer and Ann Lowe, this family-run vineyard was honored with two bronze medals in 2004 at the Indy International Wine Competition in Indiana. The two winning wines were the Marechal Foch Reserve and the Frontenac. Falconer Vineyards specializes in Northern winter-hearty grapes. Using Frontenac grapes, they make five styles of wine annually. In addition to the vineyards, the facility includes the winery, the nursery and The Cellar. The Cellar is open on weekends from Memorial Day through Thanksgiving for tours and tasting and can be available to private groups, by appointment only, on weekdays. Through the nursery you can purchase your own grape vine and learn about the care and management of your vine from John or one of the other friendly family staff members, Allison, Alexander or Erica Falconer. Falconer Vineyards is located on a picturesque farm just outside of Red Wing proper, on Old Tyler Road. Falconer Vineyards offers crisp, flavorful wines in a stunning setting filled with wonderful people, so be sure to add it to your list of places to visit during your next trip to the area.

3572 Old Tyler Road, Red Wing MN   (651) 388-8849
www.falconervineyards.com

Index by Treasure

Index by City